# ON THE PRESS

*Many men held the post but Vivian Ridler was the Printer to the University*

# ON THE PRESS

*Through the Eyes of the Craftsmen
of Oxford University Press*

MICK BELSON

*Published by*
*Robert Boyd Publications*
*260 Colwell Drive*
*Witney, Oxfordshire OX28 5LW*

*First published 2003*

© *Michael Belson 2003*

*ISBN 1-899536-69-8*

http://www.onthepress.co.uk

*Designed by Nick Clarke*

*Typeset and Printed in Great Britain*
*by Oxuniprint*
*Oxford University Press*

*Bound at Green Street Bindery*

# PUBLISHER'S NOTE

THIS is probably the most important book that I will ever publish. It is a book *about* the craftsmen of Oxford University Press and was written, designed, typeset, and printed *by* the craftsmen of Oxford University Press.

As publisher of this unique social history I too had the privilege of being apprenticed at the Press and would, almost certainly, have been there at the end had it not been for a strange quirk of fate on 27 October 1969. It was customary for craftsmen to be moved around to various departments within their discipline and my manager at the time decided to move me to the Monotype Casting Department where they were short-handed. The Monotype Casters was a hot, noisy, and smelly environment. Although it was just about bearable to work there for short spells during my apprenticeship is was not a place that I wanted to be for the rest of my life. The fact that I was offered no end date—'it could be a week . . . it could be a month . . . it could be years'—I decided that I would leave and seek my fortune in the outside world of printing. My decision was tinged with sadness because it meant that I would no longer be able to share the company of all the wonderful characters that made up the staff of the Press. I moved to Alden Press and went on to gain new skills, where I eventually became Composing Room Manager, run my own independent publishing company, and became a director of another.

Apprentices at OUP led a nomadic existence and every 6 months were moved on to a new department to learn yet another trade skill. It was one such move that brought Mick Belson and myself together for a 6-month spell in the Monotype Keyboards Department. Although 'Noddy' was the senior apprentice I do not remember him teaching me anything about print. He did, however, do something far more profound by inviting me to take up Saturday employment as his 'drivers mate' for Webbers, the Oxford High Street department store. We were both very grateful for the 25 shillings that this Saturday employment generated to supplement our miserable apprentices' wages. We had a lot of fun together, the highlight probably being the day that we carried a complete set of bedroom furniture to the top floor of a multi-storey block of flats in Blackbird Leys because the lift was out of order. After assembling the furniture the customer decided that he did not like it after all and asked us to take it away. Noddy, drawing on his vast repertoire of Anglo-Saxon, asked him to re-arrange a well-known phrase or saying and we both left—without the furniture.

Working with Noddy was always entertaining; he was a bit of a lad, a joker with a sharp wit, and he missed nothing. Most of all I remember his determination when he was saving for a deposit on a house. It was a very hard thing to do on apprentice wage, but he doggedly stuck to his plan.

It is, of course, that same dogged determination and a deep need to record events in his beloved Printing House that has produced this book. I am not sure, even as we go to press, if he understands the importance of what he has achieved, and the enormous pleasure that this book will bring to so many others. The book has taken him many years to put together and it contains hundreds of stories and reminiscences from many sources. For those of us who care about the people who worked at this wonderful press 'Noddy' has done us proud. I congratulate him and thank him for allowing me the privilege to publish his book. I would also like to thank the management of Oxford University Press for generously supporting this project by funding the production costs.

Robert Boyd

# FOREWORD BY THE ARCHIVIST AT OUP

WRITING about your own life and times is a daunting prospect. Many of us might daydream about such a project, but it's a very different matter to actually put pen to paper and make the idea a reality. To shape an account of your career and an explanation of the skills you learnt, together with stories about the people you encountered on the way is also daunting. If your tale turned out to be both readable and amusing it would be a bonus. To make it historic into the bargain would be quite remarkable. Yet, as you will soon realize, when you start to read this book, Mick Belson has achieved all these things with ease.

Printing in Oxford has had a venerable tradition. The first book was printed in the city in 1478 by the splendidly named Theodoric Rood—a colleague of William Caxton's. Since then, the University has moved its press through a succession of grand premises, and printing has drawn in some of the most august figures in Oxford's history: archbishops, professors, fearsomely learned dictionary makers, and all manner of individuals boasting astonishing academic gifts. All too often, though, historians have focused on those individuals alone. Writers have concentrated on the executives and scholars connected with the Press: perhaps not surprisingly, since those people are most likely to leave stacks of letters or published memoirs behind them. Yet incredible as it may seem, there has never been a book written from inside the Press, describing it as a workplace. No author has emerged from the print shop and devoted a volume to the men and women who actually set all that scholarly effort on paper, and who laboured throughout their working life to translate mere notions into hot metal and cold print. You could trawl through your public library in vain for a volume given over to OUP's compositors, bindery staff, or expert readers. Your queries at the bookshop would produce nothing but blank stares and exasperation. What you wanted did not exist.

Until now. With this book Mick Belson tells his own story, but he has also rescued a vast body of experience that was otherwise lost to history. The anecdotes and slang he records from Oxford's print shop will fascinate scholars and general readers alike for years to come. Some of it is earthy. Some of it has its own poetry. Some of it, such as the linguistic skills of OUP's readers, is simply amazing. Little or any of it, though, has been written down, and none of it has appeared in such a readily available form as this.

The book is more a chronicle. It is also a memorial. Mick Belson saw the last days of hot metal at OUP. He witnessed the end of book printing at the Press in Oxford, and the introduction of computers—a revolution that continues to this day. It is the greatest change in printing since the time of Caxton and Rood, and it has turned the old ways of business upside down. Work that used to be handled at Oxford now takes place around the world. Processes once controlled by a craftsman with a seven-year apprenticeship behind him, are now governed by a single silicon chip. The business Mick describes in such loving detail has changed almost beyond recognition. This book, though, is a worthy commemoration of those older skills. Reading it brings home to you the precision, the dedication, and the sheer artistry that established Oxford as the world's greatest academic publisher— as well as the sense of fun that often pervaded the print shop itself. Readers and former colleagues alike have good reason to thank Mick Belson for his efforts in capturing all of this. In telling his own story, he has told us hundreds of others, and thrown new light on that most extraordinary of institutions: Oxford University Press.

*Oxford University Press*                          Dr Martin Maw, Archivist
*June 2003*

# PREFACE AND ACKNOWLEDGEMENTS

FOR MAISIE, LOUIS, AND NATHAN
SO THEY WILL KNOW WHAT GRANDPA DID

THERE is nothing special about the author of this book but there is something very special about the place where I spent most of my working life. What I have seen, heard, and done has been seen, heard, and done by thousands before me. It is just that, following the closure of the Printing Division of Oxford University Press in 1989, I felt that I would probably be the only one left to switch off the lights and put out the cat. I thought that I owed it to those thousands of craftsmen and craftswomen to put inkjet to paper. If you have not got the time or the inclination to read the entire book then you can simply read one man's recollection printed below because it sums up beautifully what life was like for a printer at Oxford University Press. It was penned by a Mr E. L. Gass who started work at the Press in October 1883 and retired on 28 September 1935. He, like me, came to the Press as an errand boy, worked in the composing rooms, joined the Reading Department, and ended his career in the Printing Division as Head Reader. He, again like me, knew all the hidey-holes, all the fiddles, and in the end blew the gaff on some of the sharp practices. This book is dedicated to him and to everyone like him who has had the fortune or misfortune to walk through the arch into the Garden Quad and hear the cry 'on the press!' and to know what it meant.

I first became acquainted with the inside of the Clarendon Press at the early age of twelve. A neighbour of my parents was the compositor who was responsible for setting up and preparing the *University Gazette* for press, and on the Tuesday evening of each week was too busy to go home to tea, so I was called on to take it to the Press. I well remember the climb up to the top of the dark staircase on the Learned Side, lit by two feeble gas-jets of the old flare pattern, one on each landing.

I began work at the Press in October 1883. The old order was changing. No more would the Printer to the University accompany the brass band on its annual excursion by boats to Godstow, where they held high festival. No more would he parade his company of volunteers in the quad and march them to the Parks for their weekly drill. Mr Horace Hart had arrived to take over the management as Controller, and the intimate association of master and man along with his family became a thing of the past. But at the date when I started work, Mr Pickard Hall had not entirely severed his connexion with the Press. He still roamed about the buildings and gardens for several more months, often accompanied by two snapping little Charles the First spaniels.

I wonder what the present-day apprentice would say if he had to start his day's work at 6 o'clock in the morning? Yet that was the rule of the Bible Side in 1883 and for a number of years later. Three-quarters of an hour were allowed for breakfast, from 8.15 until 9, one hour for dinner, 1–2 p.m., and work finished at 6 o'clock in the evening. On Saturdays during the winter months we worked until 2 o'clock, in consideration of which we received an extra day's holiday at Whitsuntide and the August Bank Holiday week; but there were other holidays which were given free. For instance, on each of the Fair days we closed down at 4 o'clock, all apprentices receiving 1s. to spend each day and each boy 6d. Shortly before my arrival at the Press the whole place was closed for two half-days during the Oxford Races, held on Port Meadow. On the August Bank Holiday took place the annual Wayzgoose, each adult employee receiving 15s. and each apprentice 5s.; a railway excursion was arranged, and everyone was expected to purchase a ticket.

My father always made a point of arriving at his work a few minutes before time, and as I had to accompany him on the early morning journey, we usually found in winter that the gas-jets had not been lit when we arrived. To reach the Bible Side composing-room on the middle floor of the south wing, where I had been introduced as the 'printer's devil', we had to walk through the machine-room and climb the back stairs, the composing-room staff not being allowed to walk through the stitchery, which was the nearest way, on account of the girls employed there. On those dark winter mornings we had to grope our way along the rooms, often running into obstructions which had been left projecting into the gangways overnight, and sometimes barking our shins as a result.

On taking up my duties I found myself in the company, among others, of a number of old-fashioned compositors who still retained the dress of their youthful days and came to work regularly in tall hats and frock coats. There were many so garbed working at the Press in those days—in the machine-room, on the Learned Side, and elsewhere, as I discovered later.

For a short time after my arrival the old composing room ran a very humdrum course: the new Controller had not yet completed his reorganization. My duties as errand-boy took me to all parts of the Bible Side buildings, but very rarely to the Learned Side, which was still a thing apart and rather sparsely inhabited. My journeys to the machine-room with proofs led to my discovery of the roller-making room, where it was possible by making a polite request to receive a piece of the trimmings of a new roller. This was made chiefly, I believe, of treacle and glue, and was considered quite good enough to eat when other sweetmeats failed.

As errand-boy I received 4s. 6d. per week, and among other jobs it was my duty to pull proofs on the old Stanhope hand-press, which came originally from the printing-room of the Old Clarendon [Building] and now has been presented to the South Kensington Museum. Another job I was put to was to paper-up the pages of type which had been used to produce the Revised Bible which had just been given to the world. But I often had time on my hands, and sometimes on the hot summer afternoons, along with the junior apprentice, I would climb through the trap-door in the room next to the top of the back staircase and wade in the tank of water which was fixed over the staircase-well. Sometimes we would get through a skylight which was over the tank and sit out on the roof. A favourite prank of ours was to remove a nipple from the old flare gas-fittings, and, taking a deep breath, blow down the pipe, which had the effect of dimming all the lights within a radius of many yards.

After a term of about six months I became apprenticed, my indentures being the first which bore the signature of the new Controller, Horace Hart. The system in use on the Bible Side in those days was for the apprentice to be handed over to some competent workman who was responsible for teaching him all the tricks of the trade. A double frame was provided, and apprentice and teacher worked together. For his trouble the compositor received one shilling per week. The apprentice received each week one-third of the first 15*s.* he earned (according to the compositors' scale) and half of all over that sum, and every time he earned 30*s.* a bonus of 1*s.* 6*d.* was put to his credit and paid out at the holiday periods.

When the apprentice had completed his indentures he invariably entertained the whole of the composing-room to a feast. The more opulent would hire a room at Jericho House and put on a superior spread, but generally the feast would be laid out under the frames of the composing-room and would consist of bread and cheese with plenty of beer. I remember being present at two of the Jericho House feasts; these always finished up with punch served in a loving-cup, which was passed round the company, each one before drinking having to repeat the toast:

> Here's to him who now is free,
> Who once was apprentice bound:
> We'll drink his health and merry, merry be,
> We'll drink his health all round.

It was while I was a compositor apprentice that I saw the beginnings of what afterwards became the Lithographic Department. A hand-press and its various appurtenances were set up in the Bible Side type-store, and here began the reproduction of old manuscripts for which we soon became so famous.

A considerable quantity of beer was consumed on the premises in those early days. It was, of course, forbidden to go out during working hours and fetch it into the Press. But the porter was old and not very alert, and there was the back gate behind the 'Clarendon Arms' open most of the day. Boys were encouraged to fetch it in, and one particularly artful card had a coat made specially for the job with a pocket running all round the skirt from one side to the other; here he could conceal as many as 6 or 8 half-pint bottles, which he retailed at a profit of a halfpenny on each bottle. Of one of his customers, who was always in a semi-fuddled condition, it was said that he frequently sold him a half-pint twice over. Having delivered one half-pint to his client, who would stand it down under his frame, the young rascal would steal up shortly afterwards round the back and take it away again, replacing it by an empty bottle. The old fellow could never remember whether he had drunk it.

After about two years as a compositor apprentice I was transferred to a reading-desk, and thenceforth, for the whole of the remainder of my service with the great Clarendon Press, I was connected with the Reading Staff.

After five years on the Bible Side I was transferred to the Learned Side, and I entered a different world. Instead of working in the composing-room with the noise and bustle all round and the roar of the machines underneath, I was given a desk in a glass-house just inside the middle composing-room door. This I shared with another reader. The reading staff, as also the clerical staff, of those days was a very small body. I can recall the names of only seven readers and four clerks.

During the course of my fifty-two years' service many famous persons visited the Press. I specially remember the great W. E. Gladstone coming here. He was editing a new edition of Butler's *Analogy* and came to see the Press during the course of production. Someone suggested to the Controller, who was escorting the Grand Old Man, that the workmen would like to hear him speak. Mr Gladstone consented to do so; a platform of planks supported on bales of printed paper was hastily erected under the archway looking into the quad, and standing on this he gave us a wonderful address on one of the early Dutch printers.

Such occasions furnish memories that are good to linger over when leisure is ours again.

After reading Peter Sutcliffe's *The Oxford University Press: An Informal History*, published in 1978 to coincide with the Quincentenary of OUP, I was a little sad to see that he had hardly had time to mention the people that worked 'on the shop floor' in the Printing House. The book concentrated on Archbishop Laud and his chums and the publishing business as a whole. I put this point to Peter while watching cricket and sipping some refreshment in the University Parks Pavilion one summer's day. He said that he was not qualified to write about the craftsmen that made the Press the finest and most respected publishing and printing business in the world but he said that he knew a man who could write the sister volume. He looked over the top of his spectacles and smiled at me. If it was not me he was thinking of then I have wasted more hours than I care to admit.

What follows is not just my story and the minor part that I played in OUP's printing history. It is the story of a great University Press over the last 100 years as seen through the eyes of many compositors, machine minders and their assistants, binders, staff, and maintenance engineers—the 'Clarendonians'. It was not my intention to write a monograph with countless footnotes and cross-references but a simple narrative on Press life. It is not a history of the Printing House but a social history that is held together by the addition of my experiences on a roller-coaster of a wonderful journey; one that lasted more than 43 years. My research has used no 'official' records and there are bound to be errors and omissions. The book casts no judgements and does not try to make a fool out of anyone. To tell the story as I have will probably only make a fool out of me! I cannot pretend that everything has been a bed of roses. Everyone has had their share of happiness and sorrow. The Press was filled to the cloisters with wonderful people and there has been, as in life, great joy and great sadness. It has been a privilege to work for Oxford University Press as a printer and a publisher and one that I would not have swapped for the world!

The period covered goes back much further than one hundred years because, as with Alex Hayley's *Roots*, the stories just kept on being handed down from generation to generation. When I read reminiscences of craftsmen who were working at the Press 50 years before I was born I feel that I really know them. I know about their working conditions, I know what made them laugh and what made them cry. I understand what they have been through because I have been on the same journey and so has everyone I have ever worked with. The reason for this is simple. Printing technology hardly changed from the day old Billy Caxton brought some of Johnny Gutenberg's recently invented movable type to this country in the 1400s. When I started in the Type Store on 10 November 1958 it was as if time had stood still.

I have gathered information from the *The Clarendonian: Issued by the Craftsmen of the Clarendon Press* (first published by the Council of the now defunct Clarendon Press Institute in 1919), from wonderful records passed on to me by George Perry when he handed over the baton as Editor of *The Clarendonian*, from personal interviews with pensioners and workmates, and from my own (now failing) memory. The views expressed are mine and the people that have helped me and they are not necessarily the views of Oxford University Press. I cannot mention everyone who has helped me but Cyril Cox, John Bowley, Brian Holloway, Colin Baldwin, Harvie Willshire (though *never* a Press man), Tony Bennell, Robbie Boyd, David Brown, Jim Chatting, Nick Clarke, Stephen Cook, Jean Crawford, Robin Denniston, David Duffy of the *Oxford Times*, Pat Duffy, David A. Evans, Canon Derek Fathers, Ted Heath, Leofranc Holford Strevens, Matthew Hollis, Derek Honey, Ken Hudson, Genevieve Hawkins, Letta Hilsdon, David Langford, Reg Little of the *Oxford Times*, Martin Maw, Doreen Millin, Isobel O'Leary, Mary Owen, Alan (Inky) Parsons, the late Anne Ridler (for an unforgettable lasagne and a plea for forgiveness for breaking my promise), Vivian Ridler (for the brief glimpse of the Perpetua Press), Robert Ritter, Richard Russell, Linda Wharton, Norman White, and Viv Williams have been inspirational and deserve special mention.

Every effort has been made to trace the owners of the photographs used in this book. Most of them were either taken by me or friends of mine. The copyright of these pictures remain with the owners and these include Geoff Elam, Charles Morgan, David Brown, and Stephen Cook. The copyright of the pictures on pp. 21, 47, 49, 57, 58, 64, 70, 85, 107, 136, and 213 belongs to Thomas-Photos Oxford.

I am grateful to Roger Boning, Ivon Asquith, Peter Mothersole, and Martin Slade for keeping the faith and, through them, Oxford University Press for unconditionally funding the project.

http://www.onthepress.co.uk                                               M.B.

*The Quincentenary flag celebrating 500 years of printing at Oxford*

*The famous OUP ducks*

# CONTENTS

# INTRODUCTION

THE Dictionary is not finished; it will never be finished. While the Thames flows under Folly Bridge our language flows past the Present; its particles are swirled in the stream, new organisms are taken into it, decaying matter is left on the banks. And when *Wise-Wyzen* is given to the world on 19 April Collins's 'ship will no doubt be recording a new-born significance of *Set*. Probably there are few words, other than pronouns, prepositions, and passionate expressions, more generally heard in printing houses than the word *Set*. In 1881 Dr Murray wrote that he supposed that this little word, so complex were its applications, would occupy three full pages of the *Oxford English Dictionary;* when *Set* finally was done thirty years later it surrendered only when eighteen pages had pursued it through our language.

This little comparison may suggest the magnitude of this work; may suggest also the almost alarming influence on the world's thought and activity exerted by all associated in its achievement. Printers and printing make possible the definition and disciplining of a language; and in making possible the publication of the *OED* we of the Clarendon Press have done something whose extent and permanence are beyond estimation. But the *OED* is only one of our responsibilities. The Clarendon Press imprint is the stamp of authority; and it may be said truly that we are the policemen of the English language; ours is the responsibility for a slipshod or distorted sentence, for a redundant or illogical comma; we guard the dignity of our written tongue, and so, indirectly, of our spoken . . .

Oxford books are significant books: they are contributions to the world's thought and add to the world's wisdom; most copies of them find some time or other a reader in some part or other of the world. In an average year two and a half million volumes are put into circulation from the Press; so in twenty years (a short time in the Press lives of many of us) the part played by each of us in the production of these books will have touched the minds of fifty million people; will have influenced, for good or ill, more than the population of the British Isles. Such reflections as these, like trying to look beyond the stars, are disconcerting; but, unlike looking at the stars, they make us feel very important people. And we are.

Anon 1927

'He will never make a printer as long as he's got a hole in his arse!' said the bald-headed old sod of a composing room manager to the personnel manager as I stood outside the composing room office of Mowbrays in 1957 waiting to hear if I had got the job as an apprentice to a compositor.

I wanted to be a printer from the age of 6 because my best friend, John Reid, who lived at the bottom of Newman Road in Littlemore on the outskirts of Oxford, always had stacks of coloured paper to scribble on. In the years following the Second World War paper was in very short supply and my mother always insisted that I used every available area of space before being allowed another sheet. But these rules did not apply to John Reid! He would sit at his dining-room table scribbling away to his heart's content, never considering to use the other side of the paper—coloured paper! What riches! How could any one kid have so much when I had so little?

His father, Lionel Reid, was a compositor at Holywell Press in Oxford. Holywell Press was a thriving jobbing printer set in the heart of Oxford and they produced a fine-quality letterpress printing service for both Town and Gown. All this meant nothing to me then. I just knew that if you were a printer you would get as much coloured paper and card as you wanted—and I wanted to be a printer.

When the time came for the Class of 1957 to leave Northfield Secondary Modern in Littlemore and think about the future, I was at the front of the queue when the careers adviser visited the school. I told him that I wanted to join the printing industry. I did not explain my reasons! The careers adviser was, of course, interested in my academic qualifications and asked me to highlight the parts that I thought would make me a suitable candidate for a career in the printing industry.

I decided to play down the fact that in 1953, although a 'borderline', I had failed the 11-plus at Lawn Upton Junior School in Littlemore and so never made it to a grammar school to sit any O-Levels or A-Levels. I had missed a lot of schooling prior to the 11-plus because I had contracted the highly contagious poliomyelitis and had spent some time paralysed in an isolation ward and almost 6 months in a wheelchair. I offered no excuses but had to try and make something of my 'Tests of Achievement' certificates. These tests were the prototypes of the CSE examinations that were introduced in Secondary Modern schools a few years later.

The careers man told me that there was a lot of competition for jobs in the printing industry but because I had shown so much enthusiasm he would arrange for me to attend a selection test which would be held at the Clarendon Press Institute, a very distinctive Victorian building in Walton Street, Oxford.

In the 1950s the printing industry was the second largest employer in Oxford; the British Leyland car works being the largest. The Joint Industrial Council under the leadership of John Hall, who was also the Personnel Manager of Oxford University Press, ran the industry. John Hall had started work at the Church Army Press in Cowley as a clerk before joining OUP after the Second World War during which he served in the RAF. It was the Joint Industrial Council (an organization that was made up of both local management and the local trade unions) that took responsibility for all apprenticeships in Oxford.

The Joint Industrial Council (JIC) was composed of sixty members divided equally between management and workers who were mostly Trades Union offi-

cials. There was a Health Committee, an Unemployment Committee, a Conciliation Committee, and an Apprentice Committee.

The Health Committee ensured that the workers had the benefit of good surroundings and conditions in their place of work. This was seen, very much, as an
advantage to both employers and employees. The Unemployment Committee
were less than successful during the War years but as prosperity returned to the
country more and more jobs became available. The Conciliatory Committee
dealt with the more explosive situations particularly in cases when workers had
been sacked or suspended. The hours worked each week were always negotiated
by the JIC until the trades unions used their national power to push for higher
wages and the lowering of those working hours. The Apprentice Committee had
been set up to 'eliminate wastage of human effort and morale by exerting guidance
as to the proper kind of candidate for employment and to the course of apprenticeship most likely to bring out his capabilities'. The Council as a whole was dedicated to the quality of work and the employment and remuneration that was fair
to both workers and employers.

The selection process began with a visit to the JIC's doctor in Beaumont Street
in the centre of Oxford. The tests were simple: stethoscope, 'tongue-out-say-arr',
'pee-in-a-bottle', and a colour blindness test. I passed the first three but was found
to be colour-blind. This explained why people always laughed at my drawings
when I was at school. As soon as the medical tests had been completed, I walked
along to the Clarendon Press Institute (or Stute as I was later to come to know it)
for the 'intelligence tests'. I remember hoping that I would do better at these tests
than I had done a few weeks earlier when I attended the intelligence tests at AERE
Harwell. The Atomic Energy establishment had been advertising for electronic engineering apprentices and for some inexplicable reason my mother thought that if
her baby boy did not make it into printing perhaps he could be a nuclear scientist!

I had sat down with forty other young hopefuls and a questionnaire was placed
in front of me. 'You have got 60 minutes to answer one hundred questions,' said
the invigilator, 'starting now!' I turned the paper over and could not believe my
luck. Question 1 was 'TWO PLUS TWO EQUALS ......'.' Question 2 was 'FOUR MUL-
TIPLIED BY THREE EQUALS .......'

Everyone else had their heads down with beads of perspiration dripping from
their furrowed brows. Why were they all rushing when we all had an hour to perform such a simple task? I had just completed my name and address on the top of
the sheet when the invigilator shouted 'pens down everyone, your sixty SECONDS
are up'.

The papers were collected up and mine was blank except for my name and
address. I knew that this was not a good start but I was confident that I could catch
up in the practical test. The practical test comprised a blueprint plan of a piece of
wire bent to a strange contorted design, a straight piece of wire about 2 ft long, and

a pair of pliers. We were told that we had 30 minutes to bend the piece of wire with the pliers to match the blueprint exactly. After 25 minutes I could see that my wire just needed the finest of tweaks with the pliers and I would have achieved perfection. This masterpiece would more than cancel out the earlier disaster on the intelligence test. I gingerly held the wire up and made my tweak. Snap! I had cut the wire in half. There was less than 2 minutes to go. I picked up another 2-ft length of wire just as the invigilator said 'pliers down'. I handed in a straight piece of wire! The world of electrical engineering and nuclear science was going to have to manage without me!

With not a little fear and trepidation I arrived at the Stute to be greeted by an incredibly tall, thin, sandy-headed man. He was John Hall and was officially entitled 'Personnel Manager' at Oxford University Press. But he was more than that. He was a somewhat dour and formidable High Churchman who was responsible for hiring, firing, settling disputes, negotiating with trade unions, organizing mortgages, visiting the sick, delivering the sick-pay, and attending funerals.

John Hall took me to the 'Council Room' and I was given another 'intelligence' test paper and was told that I had 60 minutes to complete it and then write an essay entitled 'Why I Want to be a Printer'. Having established that when he said '60 minutes' he meant 60 minutes I went to work.

The test was easy but when it came to the essay I decided not to mention the 'coloured paper' but simply wrote what I thought John Hall would want to read. I told of my lifelong love of books and how keen I was to discover how they were made but above all I said that I wanted to be an apprentice at Oxford University Press.

My paper and essay were checked on the spot and John Hall's face broke into what was as near a smile as I would ever see again. He told me that I had passed and that he would be recommending me for an apprenticeship in printing. I was overjoyed but this happiness was short-lived. He said that the next vacancy was at Mowbrays in St Ebbe's. Mowbrays was a Christian bookshop, a publishing business, and a printing business all rolled into one.

My interview at Mowbrays did not go well for two reasons. First, I did not want to work at Mowbrays; I wanted to work at Oxford University Press. Secondly, I was very nervous and the composing room manager who interviewed me in what I thought were scruffy surroundings kept eyeing his fob watch. I had the distinct feeling that I was not getting a fair crack of the whip at the interview owing to the fact that I was probably keeping him from his impending lunch break.

'Wait outside my office, boy', he growled as he picked up the telephone to indicate that my interview was over. A few minutes later the Personnel Manager arrived in the office and I overheard the verdict, with its anal reference mentioned above, that was to condemn me. I walked home to Littlemore because I did not want to make a fool of myself by crying on the number 3 bus. My dream had been shattered and I still had to explain everything to my parents. The depression hung

*John Hall —a major player*

over me for more than a week until I received a letter from OUP. It was from John Hall and he wanted to see me.

I arrived at the Walton Street Lodge and presented my letter to the uniformed Lodge Porter. He picked up the telephone and 5 minutes later I was collected by John Hall and taken through the archway and saw the Quadrangle in all its magnificence for the first time. We walked round the Quad without speaking until we reached the steps of the North House. Within seconds I was in the Personnel Office and sitting down in front of John Hall's antique desk and chair. At the time I had not realized what a major player he was in OUP's history.

The sudden death of John Hall shortly after he had arrived for work on the morning of 21 November [1974] came as a great shock to all his colleagues. Throughout the year he had as usual been working himself hard, and occasionally shown signs of strain, but his collapse was completely unexpected.

The large number of friends and representatives of the industry who attended the service of thanksgiving in St Mary's on Saturday, 14 December, was a sign of the high esteem in which he was held. The vicar, the Revd Ronald Gordon, conducted the service and John Alden, President of the South Western Printers' Alliance, read one of the lessons. The Address was given by the Printer. At the close of the service the church bells were rung by members of the Oxford Diocesan Guild of Church Bell Ringers; several of the ringers are employed at the Press:

'We have come here today to honour the memory of John Hall, who until his death some three weeks ago had served the Press of this University for over twenty-seven years with rare and single-minded devotion.

'Actions speak louder than words. This well-worn proverb, in some contexts so trite, sums up the man. He was not particularly at ease with words, whether in speech or on paper. But when it came to doing something, to solving a problem, breaking a deadlock, helping the sick, rebuking the transgressor, John would be there, and he would act. To be at hand when he was needed, that is how he saw himself: he would never turn away from any problem, however daunting, or refuse an appeal for help, however trivial; and his help would always be given without ostentation or self-advertisement.

'Before the war, John had learned his trade in Oxford with the Church Army Press. After distinguished wartime service with the Royal Air Force he joined another printing house in Wales, but wishing to enlarge his experience he eventually wrote to my predecessor, Charles Batey, who had not long taken office and was then building up his staff. Batey, sensing his quality, made him his personal assistant, and it was in that role that I first knew him when I joined the Press some twelve months later, in the spring of 1948.

'The intense concern shown by this rather shy, reserved man for the well-being of others made an immediate and deep impression on me, and I was not surprised when, in the autumn of 1948, he was appointed to a post new to the University Press, that of Personnel Manager.

'John may not have been aware at the time of his appointment that the care and training of apprentices and other young people was to become one of his most rewarding interests. It was, I think, through Charles Batey's own involvement in establishing a national apprenticeship authority that this came about. At any rate John threw himself into this work with his characteristic tenacity, and very many young people must have passed through his hands during the seventeen years in which he served as secretary to our own local apprenticeship committee. His influence of course was far more than local: his advice was sought by our national Federation, by the Institute of Printing, and by technical colleges; and when the Training Board for the industry was formed in 1968 it seemed inevitable that he should serve upon it.

'Perhaps I can best convey to you the impression he made in the educational world by quoting from a letter I received last week from the head of a college printing department. He wrote "In all my contacts with training and personnel managers I have never known anyone who took such a deep personal interest in the development of young people undergoing their education in college and industry. John Hall was outstanding in his integrity and dedication, qualities which have been an inspiration to me."

'This tribute was well deserved, although I suspect John would have been embarrassed to read it. This brings me to another aspect of his character. With all his compassion and concern for others, there was no trace of sentimentality in his make-up. It is fair to say that John's essential kindliness persuaded him to suffer fools quietly, if not gladly; but he was a man of strong will, with a strong sense of what used to be called right and wrong; and if he was as harmless as the dove—as indeed he was— neither did he lack, if I may slightly misquote the scriptures in this place, the shrewdness of the serpent. It does so happen, however regrettably, that in the field of industrial relations voices are sometimes raised and tempers sometimes lost; and

John, in his determination to be both firm and fair, could lose his temper with the best.

'He was not given to the easy concession for the sake of peace and quiet. I well recall a doughty and disgruntled member of the Press, having as he said "got nowhere with Mr Hall", coming to me no doubt on the sound trade-union principle of the higher the softer, and prefacing his case with the observation that "the trouble with Mr Hall is that even when he opens his hand there's nothing but moss in it". John enjoyed dining out on that story.

'To his other duties as personnel manager, and later as personnel director, he brought the same seriousness of purpose and unceasing vigilance, whether it was to do with the Housing Association, the Athletics Clubs, or visiting the sick and the pensioners or their dependants. His inability to refuse any call for help, however remote, gave him little time for his own pursuits, particularly in later years. He enjoyed cricket and was sufficiently enthusiastic to become a member of the MCC. But perhaps his greatest love was choral music. As a boy he had been a diligent member of the choir of St Michael at the Northgate and throughout his life he seized the opportunity whenever he could of singing with a number of college choirs. He was, as many of you will know, a staunch member of this University Church, both as chorister and sidesman, and in this service of thanksgiving we are singing some of the music that he loved so much.

'With the death of John Hall we have to reconcile ourselves to the loss of a fine man and a steadfast friend. He was proud to be in the service of the University Press, and we are proud of him and of the memory he leaves.'

He seemed so dour at our last meeting but this time he was different—almost like a father figure. He said that he could sense my disappointment following the Mowbrays affair but that I was not to worry because he had decided to offer me an apprenticeship at OUP. I was overjoyed at this wonderful news but soon brought down to earth when I discovered that there was a waiting list of one year. John Hall said that I had two choices. I could either work for the Press as a feeder in the Croppers for a year while waiting for an apprenticeship or I could look for a job elsewhere in the city and he would send for me when a vacancy arose.

The Croppers was a slang name given to the Platen Machine Room under the fatherly 'clickership' of George Hope. It was a glass-roofed shed (now demolished) which joined the North House to the North Wing and it housed the small letterpress platen machines that produced all the letterheadings, business cards, pamphlets, University Hebdomadal Council and General Board of Faculty Papers, and 4- and 8-page examination papers. The 'feeder' was the boy labourer who inked up the platen each morning, washed the machine up at night, and all day long fed every sheet individually into the machine risking the tips of his fingers being crushed on every impression.

I did not like the sound of this option and suspected that this was a trick on John Hall's part to get me to accept a dirty unskilled labourer's job. I was wrong on both counts. First, John Hall would never have behaved in such an underhand way and secondly, the job of a feeder was definitely not unskilled, as I was to learn to my embarrassment many years later when working at my desk in the Machine Revise Department of the Letterpress Machine Room. I was being particularly cruel to a Feeder (Machine Assistant), berating him that I was a skilled man and that he was 'just an oil-rag' with no skills. His Machine Minder boss, Gerry Fulton, appeared at the door having overheard our conversation: 'So you think that the feeder's job is easy, do you?' He grabbed my ear and led me to the mighty Miehle letterpress machine followed by a stream of 'unskilled' labourers. 'Let's see how you get on feeding sheets of double-demy through the machine', said Gerry. I clambered on to the feeding board and tried to feed the paper into the grippers. It was a disaster. The paper was going into the machine at all angles and the machine ground to a halt. With my tail very much between my legs I ran off back to my office to the sound of derisory laughter from the 'oil-rags'. It was another great lesson in life and taught me to respect others however lowly their job might appear.

I decided to go out into the world and seek my fortune for a year and turn my back on the £5 per week that John Hall offered me to take the feeder's job. He wished me luck and said he would contact me in one year's time. I left school in the summer of 1957 shortly after my 15th birthday and started work on the following Monday at Parker's Bookshop on the corner of Broad Street and Turl Street in Oxford.

The shop was a part of the Basil Blackwell empire and was run by the Managing Director 'Old' Mr Thomas, his son Tony, and the Bookshop manager, Mr Powell. Old Mr Thomas had interviewed me and offered me the job of Unpacker of Books and Invoice Clerk for the princely sum of £4 per week with another £1 per week if I 'fitted in' with the team. I remember thinking that for £5 a week I would make damned sure I fitted in! I had not realized that the £4 was not all that it seemed. Old Mr Thomas said that out of my £4 I would have to pay £1 per week for Income Tax and National Insurance. Still, £3 per week was still good compared with my weekly paper round that paid 10 shillings (50 pence) per week and my pocket money from my father, mother, and brother, which amounted to 6 shillings (30 pence) per week.

I cheerfully went home to my parents to tell them about the new job and its related riches only to discover that they thought £2 per week would be an appropriate amount of money to pay my mother for my keep. This would leave me just £1 a week to spend in any way that I wanted to . . . or so I thought. How was I going to get to work? Sixpence a day return on the number 3 bus from Littlemore to Oxford would eat into my exchequer at an alarming rate. I would have to buy a bicycle. Broadribs in New Inn Hall Street supplied me with a spanking brand new Raleigh and allowed me to pay for it at the rate of 10 shillings (50 pence) per week.

*Parker & Son on the corner of Broad Street and Turl Street was wrapped round Exeter College*

I was going to be left with 7s. 6d. a week to live on—less than I had when I was at school!

Parkers was a lovely place to work and all the people employed there were friendly to the new kid in the cellar. I still remember the wonderful smell of the newly printed books as I prised open the cartons that had been delivered fresh from the publishers. Every few hours a lorry would arrive at the unloading bay with tons of new books in cartons. Each carton had to be opened, the books checked against the invoice and delivery note, and then placed on the bookshelves in the relevant department in strict alphabetical order by author. Every time I opened an OUP box I would dream of one day helping to make those wonderful books. I could never have dreamed that one day I would not only help make the books but would meet and socialize at book launches with some of the most famous academic authors in the world at such wonderful venues as the Groucho Club in Soho, embassies in Belgravia, and both Houses of Parliament.

The distribution of the books in the shop upstairs meant that I could pretend that I was a sales assistant. If I had been an assistant I would have been about number 10. There was a strict code regarding the way sales were conducted. All the assistants had a number based on their seniority of service. When a prospective customer entered the shop it was always the Number One assistant that would go forward to make the sale. Number Two assistant did not get a chance to step forward until a second customer came into the shop. If a third customer entered the shop and the Number One assistant had just finished with the first customer he would automatically take over the sale before Number Three assistant could make a sale himself. I later learned that all the assistants were paid a small commission on their sales by way of a bonus in their pay packets. My position as Number 10 did not give me great hopes for a sound financial future.

Parker & Son was a family firm with an unwritten motto that the book-buying customer was king. When a customer entered the shop and asked for a particular book by name, the sales assistant would go to the relevant section and check to see if the book was in stock. If it was, it would be brought to the customer for inspection. If the customer decided to take the book, the author, title, and publisher would be written by hand on to a till slip by the assistant. The assistant would pull the big lever on the till and the top sheet would be given to the customer as a receipt and the bottom copy would drop down into the drawer below the till. Mr Powell collected these bottom copies every evening and he would spend the next day using the information on the slips to order the replacement books from the publishers. This was a sort of Electronic Point of Sale without the electronics!

If the assistant could not locate the book he or she would say, 'Why doesn't sir try Blackwells?' That did not mean that 'Sir' had to cross the street to visit Blackwells. It meant that somebody else would! The assistant would go to the trap door behind the till which hid the steep wooden staircase down to the basement and shout, 'Mick! One copy of Bloggs, *History of Blah Blah*—ten minutes'. He would then return to the customer and say, 'If you would like to take a seat or browse a while I will have a copy for you in ten minutes.'

This was the signal for me to drop my invoices and set out on a journey that I did up to six times a day. Most of the bookshops in Oxford had a reciprocal arrangement whereby books were exchanged without money changing hands. I never discovered exactly how the accounting system worked but assumed that they all settled up with each other once a month.

I had ten minutes to find that book! I would run out of the back door out of sight of the customer and make my way to Blackwells in Broad Street (often meeting a young Blackwell's runner going in the opposite direction on a similar mission to Parkers) and ask one of their assistants if they had the book. If they did I would pick it up, shout, 'Parkers' and then run it back to the shop.

If I was unsuccessful I had to run the following route: Thomas Woods in Broad Street (now the Paperback shop), Thorntons in Broad Street, and John the Bookseller in St Michael's Street. If I was still out of luck the last port of call (unless it was an OUP book when I would run to the OUP 'Depot' in High Street) was the dreaded Mowbrays Bookshop in St Ebbe's. I was not allowed to visit W. H. Smith because they were not part of the reciprocal agreement: the snobs at Parkers and

Blackwells did not consider them to be a *proper* bookshop. (Parkers sadly closed many years ago while W. H. Smith still thrives in the city centre!)

I would always arrive back at Parkers within the ten-minute deadline in various states of breathlessness depending on the length of journey I had had to make. It was very rare for me not to find the book that was required. I have often wondered since why the assistant did not pick up a telephone and ask whether the other shops had a copy of the book that they wanted.

In the summer of 1958 Mr Powell called me in and said that he was very pleased with my work and that I could, when I had finished my invoices, go into the shop every day and be an assistant. My reward was to be the promised extra £1 per week. I was now earning £5 per week and had decided that this was the place for me to spend the rest of my days. I had heard rumours that the Number One sales assistant was earning more than £10 per week and he was thought to be buying shares through the Stock Exchange. The printing thing was over for me. I was going to be a bookseller. I was going to be a Number One assistant.

That very day I arrived home to find a letter waiting for me on the mat. It had a strange crest in the top left-hand corner with a Latin inscription 'Dominus Illuminatio Mea' and the words 'Oxford University Press'. I opened the letter and it read:

19 August 1958

Dear Belson

I am pleased to offer you employment as a probationer Compositor Apprentice in this Press, upon the conditions, which are set out below.

Your probationary period will last for three months and if your work is satisfactory during this time you will be indentured as a Compositor Apprentice for five and a half years from the date of your joining the Press.

We work a five day week from Monday to Friday; you will begin work each day at 7.30 a.m. and break off from 12 noon to 1 p.m.: the working day will finish at 5 p.m. on Monday, Wednesday and Thursday and at 5.30 p.m. on Tuesday and Friday. You will be paid according to the following scale:

First six months 51/6
First year after six months 62/-
Second year 92/6
Third year 123/-
Fourth year 144/-
Fifth year 164/-
On completion of training 205/6

In addition you will receive a cost of living bonus in accordance with National Agreement.

You will be paid for the usual holidays and for an annual holiday under the terms of the National Agreement. It is a condition of this employment that you join the

Press Contributory Pension Scheme on reaching the age of 21. After a year you will be eligible for benefit from the Press Non-Contributory Sick Scheme. Will you please acknowledge this letter and say whether you accept these conditions.

I shall be glad if you will join us on Monday 10 November 1958, at 7.30 a.m. When you come you should report to Mr Hall at the Lodge, bringing with you your National Insurance Card and birth certificate.

I welcome you to the Press and hope that you will make many friends here, and be happy with us.

Yours very truly,

Charles Batey
*Printer to the University*

I was shattered about the wages and quickly told my parents that I had changed my mind about being a printer. I was certainly not going to turn down a chance of earning £5 per week at a place where I was ecstatically happy to leap into the unknown for a paltry £2 11*s*. 6*d*. After some hard talking from my parents which included phrases such as 'get an apprenticeship behind you, son' and 'they will always want printers' I was 'encouraged' to change my mind.

After an agonizing few weeks I had to face Old Mr Thomas and, with tears in my eyes, hand in my notice. The kindly old man listened to my story and wished me well. Two weeks later I left behind all those wonderful people that made up the staff of Parkers to be an apprentice to the Printer to the University.

# CHAPTER ONE

# Apprenticed to a Compositor

I ARRIVED at the Walton Street Lodge at 7.30 a.m. on Monday, 10 November 1958 to start work as a compositor apprentice. I stood underneath the arch and gazed into the beautiful classically 'Oxford' quadrangle that was once known as 'The Garden Quad'.

I later discovered that the buildings surrounding the quadrangle had undergone very few changes since 1859. An annex had been erected in 1873 near the middle of the Bible Side Wing (the South Wing) to house the new steam engine. The Cloisters had been originally open to the quadrangle but these were glazed up at a later date.

The pond was at first surrounded by railings and bushes and was famous for its golden carp. The pond itself was the source of water for the Press boilers and there was a beautiful willow tree spreading its branches over it. There was a border running the full length of the learned Side (the North Wing) and it was always filled with flowers.

There were two houses in the quadrangle: the North House and the South House. Over the years these had housed countless Managers, Controllers, and Printers.

Went this afternoon to Food Production Exhibition at University Press. Show announced to open at 2 o'clock. Gave it generous twenty minutes' start, then sauntered in—to meet one of the multitudinous surprises of my life. Had seen garden Quad before. Once, in springtime, with sunlight playing on bursting leafage and smiling its promise of still brighter days to come; once, under threat of thunderstorm, when grey masonry seemed bleached against background of gloomy sky; once in autumn, when hoary walls were ablaze with crimson glory. But never before like *this*! *Query*—Are Press men possessed of magical powers?

Before me was familiar willow, weeping in second childhood; yonder my old and handsome friend the copper beech, beaming brown benediction as usual, but on scene transformed. Flowers, fruit, vegetables—free gifts, competitive exhibits— adorned stalls to right and left, embellished grassy carpet in front. Beyond, on margin of waters, a concert platform—actually!

On nearer view of stalls saw card bearing well-known name and legend 'Highly Commended'. Quite true. Had commended that man myself (though not for skill of cultivator), and believed full justice done. Great mistake. Hadn't given him full

*The Garden Quad*

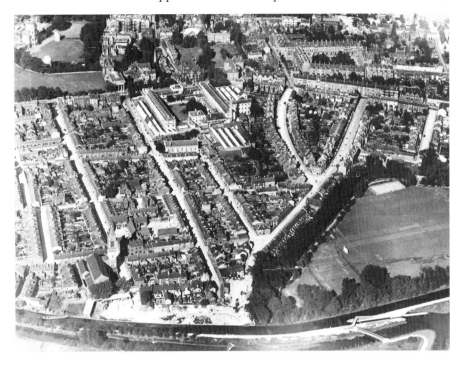

*Aerial views of the Press in 1920 and 1993 (the second photograph was taken by the author from the FOX FM helicopter)*

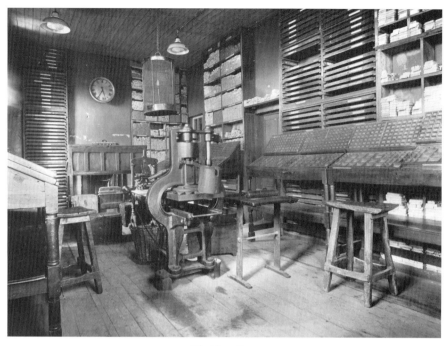

*The Type Store*

credit for versatility. Didn't foresee he would one day stay me with parsnips whilst U-boats sunk my lunch without trace.

Apples, tomatoes, celery, carrots, everything else—especially potatoes! Lost last vestige of fear of starvation.

Watched popular veteran's strenuous attack on nine pins. Watched ladies similarly employed. Enjoyed their exhibitions of skill. Indeed, enjoyed whole show thoroughly. Everybody and everything bent on making me happy. Invisible camera caught the rare symmetry of my umbrella, for delight of future ages. . . . Had to guess at name of doll! Guessed 'Winifred'. Quite sure that wasn't right: couldn't help it. Suppose I guessed 'Topsy' or 'Daisy': consequences serious. Shouldn't be able to explain vagrant fancy or dispel gathering storm. Safer to guess 'Winifred'— and lose the prize.

Anon., 7 September 1918

John Hall collected me and I was taken round the Quad and through the side door and introduced to the manager of the composing rooms, Ron 'Bomber' Harris. I was to learn that most people who worked at the Press had a nickname that was either witty or derogatory. Bomber informed me that during the next five-and-a-half years (if I was allowed to sign my indentures) I would work in every department in the composing rooms for about six months. He said that at the end of my apprenticeship I would become a craftsman compositor. I could then decide whether I wanted to leave the Press and become a journeyman compositor, or stay on and become a compositor, a proofreader, a caster operative, or a keyboard operator. The term 'journeyman' was used because printers were traditionally sacked as soon as they finished their apprenticeship and were made to move on to the next town and beyond in order to find work. They were then replaced by an apprentice who would be paid lower wages for the next 5 to 7 years before he too was sent away.

Bomber told me that I would not be allowed to sign my indentures until he was confident that I was 'suitable material' to be a compositor! He escorted me to the Lower Type Store on the first floor of the North Wing to meet my first Clicker (chargehand), Mr Fred Bolton. Mr Bolton was sitting at his antique desk next to a bespectacled gentleman by the name of Stan 'Sam' Coates. They were both sitting in carver chairs that had every leg cut to a different length. They had been cut to take account of the uneven sloping floor of the Type Store worn down over many years of shuffling feet. Mr Bolton, a Methodist Lay Preacher, was very tall and thin and spoke with a warm and friendly voice. Sam Coates was smiling and sported a hairstyle that was completely flattened by Brilliantine and parted perfectly down the middle of his head. I later discovered that he was one of the most knowledgeable and interesting members of the Press. He had begun his career in 1928 as an apprentice compositor working under piecework conditions and remembered the wagon and horses in tandem carrying the paper from Wolvercote Mill to the Press. When I arrived at the Press he had been a type-storeman for 30 years. As well as keeping all the compositors supplied with type and other materials he was the custodian of his pride and joy, the Fell ornaments and types and the flowered initials for which the Press became so famous.

Perched in front of Mr Bolton and Sam was 'Slug' Sawyer. John Sawyer was called 'Slug' because he had worked for some time on a Linotype typesetting machine and the name of the line of type that was cast was known as a 'slug'. He had started work at the Press as a boy of 14 in 1943. He was a specialist in the hand setting of Greek, Hieroglyphics, Armenian, Ethiopic, Coptic, Burmese, and Bengali. I was about to find out that I was to become one of Slug's 'Printer's Devils' (a name given to all apprentices in the printing industry).

It was in this department that I, like hundreds of apprentices before me, was to learn to get the feel of a setting stick and to run errands to get to know the geography of the Press. The room had rickety floors, old type-cases, and a cast-iron fireplace and it felt as if I had stepped back in time. There was an old watch stand in the corner where the night watchman would record his visits. The metal slot above it was still visible where he would hang the lantern that provided the only light available.

Bomber introduced me to all of them and told me that I was to be one of the errand boys in the Type Store and that it was my duty to serve these three men and

*The spiral staircase was only used for coming down*

do anything that they asked. He then left the room. Mr Bolton asked Slug to take me to the Top Store and teach me how to handset type into a stick. He said that I would learn about chases, formes, quoins, furniture, leads, points, and ems. I thought that he was talking a foreign language! He pointed to the spiral staircase in the corner: 'The Top Store is up there, Michael, but you can't go up there. Those stairs are only for coming down!' I thought that this was his little joke but later discovered that I would be sharing the Top Store with three other apprentices and that the spiral staircase was going to be a busy one-way thoroughfare. I would have to leave the Type Store by the door that I had entered and walk up to the Top Store, which was on the second floor of the North Wing, using the main staircase. When I was required to run an errand I would be called and expected to run down the spiral staircase, pick up details of my errand, run the errand, and then return to the Top Store via the main staircase. 'This way we will have no collisions', said Slug.

The Type Store was the place where all the Founders type was stored. The occupants of the Store supplied all the materials required for the Oriental Ship, or 'Top Comps' on the second floor of the North Wing and the Jobbing Ship on the first floor of the North Wing.

The Founders' type was cast, sometimes by hand and sometimes by machine, in the Foundry on the ground floor close to the present Fairway by typefounders

*Slug Sawyer checking stock levels
in the Type Store*

Len Bullen and his assistant Don Turner. They would deliver the type to Slug Sawyer in the Type Store after all the necessary preparations had been carried out. Slug would then arrange for the type to be handset into dummy pages before being tied up with page cord and wrapped in old sheets of printed waste paper. They would then be stored in their founts on shelves that stretched from floor to ceiling until a compositor required them. Sometimes the type of the most popular founts would be stored loose in large drawers set into the 'baulks' or 'stones'.

Mr Bolton and Sam Coates would spend their days reading through every typescript looking for accents such as acutes, graves, longs, shorts, umlauts, ligatures, diphthongs, queries, and dog's cocks (exclamation marks). These were known generically as 'special sorts'. They would make copious lists of the numbers of special sorts in the typescript and would estimate how much type and other material such as leads, furniture, and brasses would be required to set the entire book by hand.

If the type chosen was one of the rarer founts, such as 'Fell' or 'Miller', the compositors would never have enough type to hand-set the whole of the book so they would have to 'set and diss'. This meant that they would set the type until the supply was almost exhausted (or they had hand-set 8 or 16 pages) and then have the pages imposed into a chase, locked up with quoins (when it became a forme). It would then be proofed, proofread, corrected, revised, and printed. The compositor would then have to break up the forme and diss (distribute) the type back into the typecase before starting to hand-set the next 8 or 16 pages.

When Mr Bolton and Sam Coates had completed their estimates as to how much type was required for the particular book, the 'order' for the materials required would be sent to the typefounders.

Chief Typefounder Len Bullen joined the Press from London in 1913 and was apprenticed to typefounding under the legendary Sidney Squires. After fighting in the First World War he left the Press to join a London type foundry where he stayed until 1927. He returned to the Press for a further 5 years and was discharged owing to a shortage of work. He spent the next 16 months training at the Monotype Caster School. He told me this was the toughest period of his life. He was paid £1 *10s.* per week and out of this he had to pay 8*s.* 0*d.* for his rent. When he returned to Oxford it was to the Alden Press but he was later lured back to OUP. His father, grandfather, and great-grandfather had all been typefounders and it was in this capacity that he stayed until he retired in 1963. He had served under five Printers to the University—Horace Hart, Frederick Hall, John Johnson, Charles Batey, and Vivian Ridler. He was a craftsman and a gentleman and when he retired he was presented with a framed photograph of himself 'throwing a type' beneath which was printed his favourite poem written by Thomas Brown: 'I do not love thee, Doctor Fell, The reason why I cannot tell, But this one thing I know full well: I do not love thee Doctor Fell.'

To do their job compositors would require other materials besides type. They would need brass rules, ornaments, page cord, furniture, leads (picas, nonpareils, thicks, mids, thins, and extra thins). They would need to fill in an 'order' and they would get their apprentice to deliver it to the Type Store for processing. Sam Coates or Slug Sawyer would make up the order and it would be wrapped up in an old printed sheet of paper and taken to the foot of the spiral staircase. One of them would shout out the name of the next apprentice on the rota and the 'one-way' delivery service began. I was aware that I was working in a place steeped in history and wondered how many other apprentices before me had successfully negotiated that spiral staircase side saddle to the rapturous applause of their mates. I had heard that when 'Dukey' Richmond was the Clicker of the Type Store back in 1929, compositors would collect their diss from the Storeman and take it to the apprentices waiting in the Top Store. They would then bribe the apprentices to place the page of type back into store and the compositor who was working on piecework would be paid for diss that he had not done. Compositors would sometimes collect the diss from the Type Store and place it in their bags and during their lunch break would walk to the back of the Press in Jericho and throw the type into the Oxford Canal. One compositor threw so much type into the canal that he aroused the attention of the foreman dredger. Unfortunately for the compositor the foreman knew what 'Miller Sm. Pica' was and brought it back to the Press. The compositor was instantly dismissed.

My first day was a very lonely one because the other three boys were 'at school'.

*Len Bullen—Typefounder*

'School' was the term used for day-release further education which was paid for by the Press. I was to spend one day every week for the next five-and-a-half years at the College of Technology (now Brookes University) at the top of Headington Hill. I was shocked to discover this because I had thought that I had finished with desks and learning!

Night School was opened on February 8, 1853, with an attendance of twenty-eight boys. The promise of an excursion in the summer soon raised the number to seventy-five. At first the school was divided into four classes; subsequently into six. The subjects taught were reading, writing, composition, arithmetic, and elementary history and geography. These were varied as time went on, the two latter subjects sometimes being suspended in order to concentrate more attention on the others, or for the purpose of introducing drawing. An attempt to cultivate a taste for art was made by the formation of a drawing class out of ordinary school hours; but the scheme seems to have met with little success. One hour every evening was devoted to teaching. On Friday evenings subjects of recreative character were introduced, e.g. the reading of a story-book, such as Marryat's *Masterman Ready*, to the whole school; elementary instruction in music and singing; magic-lantern exhibitions; and lectures from time to time by members of the University. The Night School was discontinued around 1870.

The boys commenced work at a very early age, and but a few of those who sought employment at the Press have received even the rudiments of an education. . . . To have attended school five evenings in the week, after a 10½-hours working day, continuously for half the year, and to have repeated this from year to year, was an extraordinary test of endurance. The successful careers of many of the boys afford sufficient testimony to the good work achieved.

*The metal is melted down . . .*

*then poured into the mould . . .*

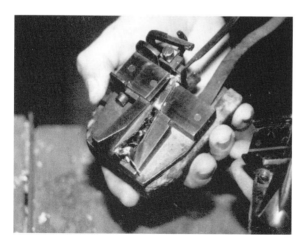

*. . . and the type is thrown*

Slug Sawyer took me to the corner of the room, gave me a setting stick, and told me how to hold it in my left hand and pick up the type with the finger and thumb of my right hand. He pointed out the case plan so that I would know which letters were in which box and he gave me a piece of 'copy'. He told me that he wanted me to set some type by following the copy. He taught me how to justify the line of type in my stick by using the different thicknesses of the spaces. He then taught me how to lift the lines of type out of the stick and how to place them on the galley.

After about an hour he said that he would leave me on my own to practise. His real reason for leaving was that he had heard something that I had not heard. It was a sound that I can still hear to this day from a hundred paces—the sound of the tea lady approaching!

Slug disappeared down the spiral staircase to begin the twice-daily tea break, which lasted for over half an hour each morning and a similar time every afternoon. Mr Bolton, Sam, Slug, and Don Turner (the Number Two type founder) began the ritual chewing over of the latest developments in the Type Store, the Press, and the World! This was all washed down with a cup of tea made in an urn and delivered to your door, frame, machine, or cubicle by Nan Humphreys or one of her colleagues. There was always a choice of special edibles on the lower shelf on the tea urn. One could choose cheese rolls, crisps, or large slabs of bread with thick black beef dripping lashed down with optional raw onion rings. The tea was always piping hot but came out of the urn ready milked. Nan's boast was that she would fill any vessel for twopence (1p). Many Press men drank their tea from 1-pint mugs. It tasted like washing-up water but I soon got used to it.

I could hear the jolly chatter going on downstairs and soon realized that I would not get my tea in the Top Store until the men downstairs in the Type Store had had theirs. I decided to sit on the baulk and enjoy a cigarette while I was waiting. Smoking was a habit I had picked up in Smokers' Corner whilst at school.

A few moments later there was a knock on the door and in walked Nan. She was a large maternal figure who knew that I was a new boy and had brought me a mug full of her special brew. When she saw me with a cigarette she nearly hit the roof! She explained that smoking was strictly forbidden in the Press unless your name was John Hall (I later discovered that he used to smoke a pipe in the Personnel Office). I quickly put out the cigarette when Nan explained that the punishment for being caught smoking was instant dismissal. The rest of the day was spent practising my new-found skills with type under the kindly guidance of Slug Sawyer.

The next day I was introduced to my new chums in the Top Store: Grin, Tadpole, Stalky, and The Baron who was the apprentice in the Top Composing Room. Grin was so called because he had more than a mouthful of teeth that gave

FELL PICA   M. BELSON
NOVEMBER

WHEN the first piece of 'copy' is received—and, it should
be reprint with not too long a measure—a stand should be
taken in front of the cabinet or frame. The feet should
be sufficiently apart to keep the body well balanced.
Naturally just a little to the left centre of the cases is the
correct position.

When travelling from box to box to pick type required,
always keep the left hand holding the stick as close to
the right hand as possible. A very creditable speed, without undue exertion, will be acquired. The worker will not
create objectionable habits of making contortions and
gymnastic displays with his hands and arms.

The spacing of the words in the lines must be given
care and attention. It will take a little time for the young
worker to be able to get into the habit of spacing every
line equally tight. To ascertain this correctly, place the
setting rule behind the line and push bodily, but gently,
forward, let the rule fall back, and the line should remain
suspended. The line shoulb not be spaced so tightly, but
that it will permit of it being moved easily. If the lines
are to tight there will be difficulb in removing them from
the stick when it is filled.

The difficulty to get accustomed to and overcome is
is the necessity for equal spacing. When setting solid
matter equal spacing is governed somewhat by the correct
dividing of words. More difficulty will, of course, be experienced with narrow measures, but with wide measures
these divisions would not be tolerateb.

Equal spacing is the term used to explain that the
spaces between the words in each fine must be of equal
width.

If instruction is given that the matrer is to be leaded
or double leaded, then increased width of spacing im-
proves the appearance of the printed page. Two thick

*The author's first hand-set galley proof, November 1958*

the impression that he was always grinning, Tadpole had a spotty face and rather a large head compared with the rest of his body, 'Stalky' was given his name following an incident behind the 'Oxford Old Style' type cases during a lunch-break frolic, and The Baron who lived in Kiddington Hall, a baronial mansion in the 'posh' part of Oxfordshire.

They decided that I too should have a nickname and I was renamed 'Noddy'. The reason was probably the fact that on one occasion I had cavorted through the Top Comps sporting a tea cosy on my head. The real reason was probably the fact that 'Noddy' was a simpleton!

---

*On piecework a man's income depended on his being able to do his work swiftly and efficiently without its having any adverse effect on quality. When copy was unclear even David was tempted to take on Goliath.*

A short compositor on piecework was standing on a box hand setting at his frame trying to decipher some appalling manuscript when an author who was very tall was shown into the department by the foreman. 'I suppose', said the tall author 'that I set you some problems, and I know by the proofs that you are beaten sometimes.' 'Yes, sir', said the little man in a quavering voice 'but don't forget that you are juggling with our bread and butter.'

---

The Press seemed an enormous place compared with Parkers and I wondered if I would ever find my way around. I realize now that all the running of errands not only gave me a sound knowledge of the geography of the Walton Street buildings but also allowed me to get to know every one of the 1,000 or so employees.

There were many tricks played on naive young apprentices by the older craftsmen. We would be sent on fools' errands to ask for striped ink, italic spaces, skyhooks, etc. I was once asked by Snuffy Hall to go to the Stereo to ask Mr Scroggs for a long weight. I made my way to his office on the first floor of the building that joins the South Wing to the South House and asked the manager for a long weight. Mr Scroggs said that he would and that I should stand outside his office and he would find me one. I stood there patiently for 15 minutes but then thought that he must have forgotten me. I went back into his office and asked him if he had forgotten that he was going to give me a long weight. 'I promise you it won't be long,' said Mr Scroggs with a twinkle in his eye. I returned to my post for another ten minutes or so until the proverbial penny dropped. I had had my long 'wait'! I was richer and wiser for the experience and for the rest of my years at the Press I showed no mercy to newcomers when it came to coddums.

The best piece of cod that I can recall was the time when fellow apprentice Fez Sherwood was told by his colleagues in the Top Comps that it was impossible for anyone to lie on their back on the floor and whistle 'God Save the Queen' while chewing a digestive biscuit. Fezzer said that he was sure that he could do it. The rest of the department could not believe their luck. They told him that the event should take place the following morning at 11 o'clock and that he was not to practise before attempting the impossible. Fezzer agreed to the conditions. Meanwhile, the men from the Top Comps travelled to every department in the Press to spread the word about the impending cod.

By 11 am the next day the Top Composing Room was filled to overflowing with people standing on the stones and frames to get a good view. A space was left on the dusty floor littered with scattered type and Fezzer was made to lie down. He started to chew on the digestive biscuit and to howls of laughter he attempted to whistle the National Anthem. What happened next is impossible to describe but suffice it to say everyone present was crying with laughter at the expense of one poor lad's *naïveté*.

---

*An 'in joke' for compositors in the 'Sam, Sam pick oop tha musket' vein written before 1926. 'Fashioned to raise a smile it caused a tempest too!' It is not clear why this particular piece of copy was so urgent but what we do know is that because they all worked together as a Ship no one could go home until the job was finished.*

### THE 'BILL' OF RIGHTS

The 'copy' was bad, and the clicker was sad,
And the comps. (in disgust) uncompliant:
Jaypee was morose, and Bilkollens verbose,
And good Mistawilpahkah defiant.
The 'ship grew insurgent: the 'copy' was urgent          5
And had to be set ere they dined.
With gestures dramatic and language emphatic
Bold Mistawilpahkah declined.
'Eh! What? 'Fore my dinner? Not ME!—for no sinner!
Nor yet for no reverend gent!                            10
My bit o' good cheer and my drop of Old Beer
And my pipe come in FIRST! This ain't Lent!'
''Ear, 'ere, Bill!' 'Good! Go it!' 'Oh, chuck it, Bill!' 'Stow it!'
'Now, Bill! Pick 'em up like a man!
There's nothing much in it. Buck up and begin it.'       15
And Mistawilpahkah began!!!

---

1 Clicker] Mr H. Harris. Could have been H. C. Harris who retired after 52 years' service as a compositor. He was awarded the Military Medal in the First World War and spent 30 years in the Jobbing Department.          2 Jaypee] Mr J. Parker retired on 17 March 1928 aged 74 years. He served the Press for almost 60 years!          3 Bilkollens] Mr Will Collins came to the Press in May 1906 and died aged 60 on Christmas Day 1930          4 Mistawilpahkah] This must have been Mr A. W. Parker who died on 24 May 1926. He was apprenticed 'at the case' in 1868 and held the then record of 57 years' service at the Press.

There was one errand that all apprentices used to enjoy and that was a visit to the 'Strong Room'. The Strong Room was an enormous Plate Store situated just off the main fairway that was sealed off at night and weekends by a massive metal safe door that would make the front door of Fort Knox look flimsy.

On the beautiful cast-iron shelving that furnished the department were stored all the line blocks, half-tones, woodcuts, stereo- and electro-plates that were used for printing illustrations and text together with all the documentation. The contents of the Strong Room were valuable because without them the Press could not undertake reprints. The shelves were so high that they had to be served by a metal walkway that could only be reached by a series of metal ladders. The walkway went all the way round the department at a height of about 5 metres.

Apprentices and craftsmen alike had, over a number of years, built up 'beds' of hessian bags of quoins on the upper walkway. They were used by the idle and bored for mid-morning, lunchtime, and afternoon sleeps. There was only enough sleeping room for four people at a time so 'berths' had to be booked in advance. This was done through the good offices of the clicker, George Pearce. George, who was the apprentices' friend, had an almost bald head with a monastic ring of ginger hair about 3 cm deep. He would ensure that the beds were never double-booked. He was known as the apprentices' friend because he would always give them a wake-up call in case they slept too long.

George had two assistants: Stan Davis and Harry Kimber. Stan was responsible for labelling all the stock and entering the relevant information onto index cards for future reference. When a book was to be reprinted the composing rooms would fill out an order form to request that the illustrations would all be ready by the time the type was ready for reprinting. If Stan and George had done their job properly they would be able to locate the material within minutes.

I could never work out then exactly what Harry Kimber used to do. He would appear and then disappear without notice from and into the crevices of the shelving like a ghost. He was incredibly old with long white hair and always wore a dirty black-and-white striped shirt with no collar. He also wore an enormous rubber apron, which almost reached the ground. There was an old iron Stanhope printing press in the corner of the department and it was one of Harry's duties to print out a copy of every block or plate that came into the department before they were stored on the shelves by the clicker and his assistants. He had worked in the Litho Department when he first came to the Press in 1909 and was later moved to the Warehouse. In 1915 he joined the Navy but returned to the Press in 1919. He worked in the washhouse and the 'Stick-Down' Department and there he stayed until he joined the Strong Room staff.

Apprentices had to work at least 6 months in every department during their apprenticeship and in January 1959 I left the Type Store and was transferred to the Clearing.

The Monotype Clearing Department was situated in the Fairway (now the Great Clarendon Street Reception area) and was run by the Clicker, Charlie 'Fatty' Foster. The job of the Clearing Department was to disassemble all the formes of type after a diss order had been issued. This meant that as soon as a book had been printed and there was no likelihood of a reprint, the type could be broken up for recycling. Fatty Foster, together with his staff comprising Thomas 'Pat' Wright, Bert Williams, Ollie Brooks, Clarence Humphrey (husband of Nan the tea-lady), Frank Isaacs, and an apprentice had the job of collecting the formes from the Monotype Department or the Letterpress Machine Room and bringing them back to the Clearing. They would then unlock the quoins with their shooting sticks and mallets, return the chases to the Stores, remove all the leads and furniture and either place them in racks behind them or sort them on to galleys, and then break up the type and throw it into bins.

While I was working on the Clearing Frank Isaacs operated the Metal Pot. It was an extremely dirty and smelly job and must have caused terrible health problems in later life to everyone who ever worked in there. The bins that had been filled with type by the Clearing Hands were then emptied into the melting pot. The metal was heated to about 1,000 °F, refined, and then cast into moulds when the ingots solidified at about 700 °F. The term 'refining' meant that the metal would be tested and additives brought the mixture up to a working standing that was 7½ per cent tin, 15 per cent antimony, and 77½ per cent lead. This breakdown ensured that although all three metals on their own melted and solidified at different temperatures, when they were mixed together they all solidified at the same time and temperature; this was called 'eutectic'. In the 1950s the Metal Pot was producing 26 tons of ingots per month. Each ounce of metal would be enough to make 20 pieces of type. The heat in the Metal Pot room was almost unbearable and the air was thick with lead dust. Frank always had beads of perspiration on his brow and he had to drink gallons of water every day to make up for the loss of body fluids. I wonder what modern-day Health and Safety Executives would make of this if the conditions were the same today?

The ingots were then taken away to the Casters and hung over the Monotype casting machines to be melted down to liquid metal again so that the typesetting process could start all over again. This was the mother and father of recycling schemes.

When Frank Isaacs retired an Indian called Oscar Steele took his place. He was a wonderful man with a love of cooking. When my father heard that I was working with an Indian he asked me to see if I could get a good curry recipe from him. I made the request next morning but Oscar said that he never used curry powder that had been bought in the shops because he always mixed his own spices. He said he would let me have some of his secret mixture the next day. The following morning he presented me with a delightful-smelling packet and told me

*The Metal Pot on the Clearing*

that there was enough powder for four curries and that I should be careful because it would be hotter than a Vindaloo. I remember thinking that my father, mother, brother, and I made four. This amount of curry would be perfect!

That evening my father started preparing one of his finest beef and mushroom curries and he added the secret mixture for four. We all sat down for supper and took our first bite. Within seconds there was no one left at the table. We were all in the kitchen fighting for the cold-water tap. All the sauce was drained off the curry and hot water was added. It was still too hot. Four times it was drained and watered down before any of us could begin to eat the meal.

The next day, with perspiration still on my forehead I told Oscar my culinary tale. He screamed out laughing: 'you are silly fool man, that was not curry powder for four people that was curry powder for four curries!'

When Oscar left the Press, Bryan 'Winky' Harper took over the Metal Pot but the conditions really affected his health and although he was later put on lighter duties he died of a heart attack soon after.

It was my job as the Clearing apprentice to ensure that the racks used by the compositors throughout the Monotype Department, the Monotype Annex, the Top Comps, and the Jobbing Department all had enough materials for the men to carry out their work. The quoins would be placed in the boxes that were scattered throughout the composing rooms, the lead racks and the furniture and lead racks had to be kept full at all times (a compositor who did not have enough materials when he was working on a bonus scheme was not a happy compositor).

Every day I would load the materials into my Number 8 truck and deliver the cargo. The Clearing truck had a house number '8' screwed to it and was much loved by every apprentice that came to push it. It was always handed over to the incoming apprentice with much ceremony and drama. Just like the running of errands for the Type Store, the Clearing work was another way for apprentices to get to know who people were, what they did, and why.

---

*Most compositors were just working-class lads and seldom gave much thought to the academic aspect of their work.*

A compositor was told to collect some work in his truck and while he was wheeling it [formes of imposed type] back to his department the foreman stopped him and asked him what book's material he was carrying. He looked down at the title [which would have been chalked on the chase] and said ''ARRY STUFFIN' 'IS BIRDS, Sir!'

---

As well as being the Clicker of the Clearing Fatty Foster was also the St John Ambulance Brigade First Aider. He always worked sitting down on a high stool and because he spent his whole day breaking up old type his hands were always jet black covered in lead, ink, and turps. People were always getting headaches, splinters in their fingers from the old quoins, and cuts and bruises from hitting their own hands with the mallets while locking up formes. Fatty (who also had a brother called 'Fatty' in the Letterpress Machine Room) would issue aspirins, use his bodkin and tweezers to remove splinters, and apply plasters all without washing his hands. There was no time for this nicety because Fatty too was working on a bonus scheme. The more type he broke up and recycled the more bonus he would get in his pay packet on the following Friday. To my knowledge there were never any cases of infection owing to Fatty's medical care. If anyone complained about the state of his hands he would say that you had to 'eat a pound of dirt before you die'. The problem was that we were not talking 'dirt', we were talking lead. I wonder now just how much brain damage was done to compositors over the centuries owing to intakes of lead?

Pat Wright was the opposite of Fatty Foster. He was a very small man who never wore an apron and never got his hands dirty. The strange thing was that he was doing exactly the same job as Fatty! Pat Wright made it his duty to ensure that all apprentices saved money every week. As soon as an apprentice arrived on the Clearing, Pat would ask him to fill in a DTS form. I remember asking him what a DTS was *after* I had signed it. He said that it stood for 'Direct Transfer Scheme'

*Sometimes monotony and depression would set in. This compositor (it could have been S. A. W. Goddard who worked at the Press from 1913 to 1958) only came to the Press for a job. He was not interested in the 'spread of learning' and only wanted a peaceful life. He would, like all compositors, have hated authors even though without them there would have been no books! Note the use of DV (God Willing); a popular phrase in constant use at the Press.*

## ALL I WANT

At six I rise up from my bed
And put my hat upon my head.
I run for the bus till nearly dead;
My breakfast's like a lump of lead.
My face is blue, my nose is red;
And all I want, if truth be said,
Is something to lie on when I'm tired
And something to eat when I'm hungry.

The author writes a nasty note;
He thinks he's got me by the throat.
He says I still ignore his quote,
Yet if you saw the scrawl he wrote
You would agree it gets one's goat.
And all I want, I stake my vote,
Is something to lie on when I'm tired
And something to eat when I'm hungry.

The clicker with a worried frown
Is all day jumping up and down,
And into the screaming telephone
Flings many a hasty verb and noun.
I'm sorry if I seem a clown,
But all I want, or may I drown,
Is something to lie on when I'm tired
And something to eat when I'm hungry.

It's Take a note for Mr. I).;
It's Send a call for Mr. C.;
It's Pass this back to Mr. E.;
It's Check this up with Mr. V.,
O.K., D.V., A.S.A.P.
Yet all they need, it seems to me,
Is something to lie on when they're tired
And something to eat when they're hungry.

and that it was operated jointly by the Press and the Trustees Savings Bank. Each week 2s. 6d. would be deducted from my now handsome wages of £3 2s. 0d. and deposited into an account in my name at the Trustees Savings Bank in Market Street in the centre of Oxford. The first Monday lunchtime after the first Friday that my 2s. 6d. was deducted I was in the queue at the TSB to make my first withdrawal! Pat Wright will always be remembered for helping hundreds of apprentices get into the habit of saving money rather than spending it.

He was classy little man who spoke beautifully and lived in a massive house called 'Half-Acres' in Adderbury Avenue in Iffley'. Rumours were that he had married a rich woman and did not need to work. He was a well-known figure in cultural Oxford, particularly in University rowing circles. He also sponsored the Pat Wright Cup Children's fishing competition that was held on the towpath of the Isis between Oxford's Folly Bridge and Donnington Bridge every year.

Pat had a little friend who used to live in the cellar under the North House. The cellar was the place where the composing rooms stored the formes of type after they had been printed and before being taken to the Clearing for recycling. The little friend was a tiny white-haired old lady with a nicotine-stained fringe who spent all of her day in the cellar smoking cigarettes and talking to Phoebe, the Press cat. (There has always been a stray 'Press cat' running around the building since time immemorial right up until the closure of the Printing House and to my knowledge they were all called Phoebe!) The only time the old lady left the cellar was to clean and 'see to' the ladies toilets and to talk to Pat Wright.

Another Clearing Hand was Bert Williams. He suffered from verbal diarrhoea and although in his seventies (it was rare for anyone at the Press to retire at 65) was as fit as a fiddle. He could outrun any of the apprentices and often did, particularly if they were cheeky to him and then tried to run away after taking the rise out of him for his silly chatter. Clarence Humphrey was a very jovial character who always seemed to talk in riddles. Most apprentices thought that he was mad.

Oliver Brooks was the legend of the Clearing. Olly was a white-haired old man with many a story to tell but he could, very quickly, become extremely violent and lose his temper especially if he thought that people were talking about him. He would even resort to throwing his mallet at people who really upset him. In his quieter moments he would tell stories that were a mixture of fact and fantasy. Pat Wright called these stories 'slings'. I cite below some of the slings that Olly slung on the Clearing from my records that were meticulously kept at the time. They are silly stories but when you read between the lines you can share the pent-up sexual frustration, racial ignorance, and the early stages of senility that were creeping up on this amazing old man.

## TALL STORIES (OR OLIVER'S SLINGS, 1958–9)

Years ago I was bitten by a pike. A woman once told me she had a ghost in her house,

*Pat Wright sings while Olly performs the Donkey Dance*

so I ran to her rescue and hit the ghost over the head with a stick. Lord John Sanger told me that he had sat up all night to put a hot poultice on a lion's back. I knew a man whose wife thought more of the cat than him. The cat ate the best fish while the man ate bread and lard. My wife's sister told me that there were so many dead bodies at Stoke Mandeville hospital that they were stacking them outside. I was there when a Salvation Army lassie, smelling strongly of whisky, was dismissed by the captain. In my younger days if you couldn't set up two galleys of 14 ems in one day, the clicker would say 'Olly, there's the door'. I was there at the circus when the lions came into the ring. The ringmaster told all the expectant mothers to leave or their babies would be born with lion's heads. In my dad's book about the circus I saw a picture of a man with a tongue 11 inches long and a man with donkey's legs that used to dance on the stage. I remember when the sun was so hot that you could fry eggs and bacon on the pavement. When I was courting my missus we saw a polecat and my missus screamed her head off, but I wasn't afraid of it! I went badger hunting a lot in my younger days. Did you know that badgers had two legs shorter than the other two so they could walk along banks at an angle? 'Ere, they don't half stink you know! When I worked in Chesham, a bloke I worked with was put in prison for 3 months for climbing a ladder to watch a pretty girl undress. After that the place caught fire and the Mono fell through to the casters. I was there in a London shop when a man told the shopkeeper that his prices were too high, so he picked up the scales and threw them at him. Years ago my brother was out shooting with bullets as big as marbles. Once he missed a crow and the bullet went through my shoe while I was digging the garden. I was there at a boxing match when Cordy Griffiths, a navvy, hit a Negro right over the ropes into the lap of the promoter. They called him Cordy because he always wore corduroy trousers. When I was 13 I went to a football match when a chap got so excited that he kicked my shins, so I got hold of him and pummelled his head in and *nearly* knocked him out! At an Amersham football match the crowd got excited and a cornet player got so excited that he hit the ref on the head with his cornet. When I was on stage at the Amersham Regal I used to make the women laugh so much that they all peed their drawers. Once when I was drunk I came out of the pub and shook hands with a copper, so he booked me and I was in prison for the night. When I was 29 I used to have a big black moustache and when I fancied a woman it used to twitch. All my friends called it the Adultery Moustache. I was there when a man suffering from nervousitis shook hands with a Negro and then ran a mile with fright. Once I knew a man who was 30 years old and very simple. Once a big bloke started hitting him so he ran indoors crying to his dad. A woman who was carrying a child was frightened by a dog. When the baby was born it had a dog's head and a human's body. It used to bark for its supper. When my cousin got married she ran back to her mother on the night of the honeymoon. I was only 9 years old at the time or I would have taken his place. Ha ha! I caught a man at Chipperfield's Circus training a lion with a red-hot bar. He said to me 'Don't tell anyone and I'll let you in free.' I was at Nottingham Goose Fair when the circus was there. The lion trainer was in the lion's den being shaved by a barber. The trainer kept his cigar alight. He could feel the hot breath of the lions on his neck. *I was there.*

Pat Wright would often get Olly to take part in the famous 'Donkey Song'. Pat would sing the lyrics while Olly danced round with his hands on his head flapping them as if they were donkey's ears and squealing out 'EEE-AW, EEE-AW, EEE-AW'.

There was one event that took place on the Clearing every year that was taken very seriously. It was the Clearing Carol Concert on Christmas Eve. During the afternoon Pat Wright would hand out the hymn sheets, that had been prepared and printed earlier in the week as a 'foreigner', to invited guests and other members of the clearing staff. He would also supply sherry and mince pies to the 'congregation'.

Often apprentices would try to sneak in to the service but they were soon chased off by the senior men. The reason for this was that apprentices thought the whole thing was a bit of a joke and saw it as an opportunity to try and disrupt the proceedings. They did not understand that the carol service was, for once, a serious part of Press life and the Clearing's way of reminding everyone of the true meaning of Christmas. The management allowed the service to take place in company time and always turned a blind eye to it. Sadly, they never used to attend either but that was just one example of the management/workers divide.

In April 1959 I was moved to the Monotype Composing Room to work with

Albert John (Peter) 'Snuffy' Hall. Snuffy was in charge of all the special sorts and accents (a term for all characters that carried an accent above or below). He had an encyclopaedic knowledge of typefaces and an unrivalled insight into the uses of all the special sorts and characters used in the Press. It was his job, besides training apprentices, to ensure that a plentiful supply of type and accents was always available when required by the compositors. Henry 'Henner' Rawlings and Bill 'Records' Pearce worked at the rear of the Mono office and it was their job to 'look out' for accents and special sorts by browsing through every typescript and compiling copious lists. The list would be handed to Snuffy who would ensure that by the time the typescript arrived on the compositor's frame there would be enough accents to enable him to complete the job.

Sometimes it was a question of simply asking the Monotype casters or the Type Foundry to produce common accents such as graves, acutes, cedillas, etc. but most times the accents were so rare that they had to be made by hand. The making of special sorts was a very skilful operation and an apprentice could spend all day making just one! Every piece had to be mitred and chamfered using a rotary mitre. Sometimes accents had to made in typefaces as small as 4¾ pt.

Snuffy was a craftsman *par excellence* and he would make the most complicated accents as if by magic. He was always one step ahead of the game and when an accent was very rare he would make up a few in advance and keep them in his multi-pocketed grey foreman's coat. Whenever anyone wanted one of these accents he would pull them out from his pocket as a magician would pull a rabbit out of a hat. Snuffy was truly amazing! Sometimes, when a special sort was particularly complicated, even Snuffy would be beaten and the apprentice would have to run to the Stereo Department to get a stereotyper to make the accent. They had the added advantage of being able to use blowtorches and solder to get the little bits of type to stick together whereas Snuffy and the rest of us had to rely on a thick gluey substance: we never knew what it was made of or from whence it came.

When I arrived at Snuffy's frame he asked me if I wanted to be a Grand Snuffer. I had no idea what he was talking about and so he pulled out from a drawer what looked like a very ornate medal with the letters 'G.S.' beautifully engraved on the front. He told me that it stood for 'Grand Snuffer' and that it was a medal that would be presented to any apprentice who could break the world record for snuff taking. I asked him what the record was and he said that I would have to have 14 ems (over 2 inches) of snuff ladled on to my forearm with a brass rule and that I would have to sniff it all up in one go. For this I would not only be the world champion but I would also take the Grand Snuffer's medal.

I agreed to the challenge and Snuffy summoned all the compositors together and told them about my world record attempt. I rolled up my sleeve and 14 ems of the finest Wilson's SP Snuff was placed on to my arm in a neat row that stood

*Manager Joe Ayres overseeing some of his compositors in the 1950s*

about a quarter of an inch high. On the count of three I sniffed up the lot in one go. There was about 5 seconds of complete silence where nothing happened and then there was an explosion that felt as if the roof of my head had became detached. Tears were pouring out of my eyes like waterfalls and I began sneezing uncontrollably every 2 seconds. I ran blindly up the gangway heading for the washroom and placed my head under the cold-water tap for about half an hour. The problem was that I could not then use the towels to dry my hair and face. The towels were on rollers and were only changed once a week. This was unfortunate because the towels were used by members of the department at the end of each work session, among other things, to clear their noses of the day's snuff input. I will not dwell on this subject but will leave it to the reader's imagination.

When I eventually returned to Snuffy as world champion to collect my Grand Snuffer medal I found everyone cruelly laughing at my stupidity. Snuffy said that the medal was a button that he had found down at the Oxpens after the circus had left town. The name of the circus was George Sanger's. I then realized that G.S. stood for George Sanger and not Grand Snuffer and that I had, yet again, been had!

What I suffered at the hands of Snuffy Hall and his gang seems sadistic as I relate it now but the mentality of working men generally and Press men particularly was such that they needed to rib each other just to create an 'amusing' interlude to break up the long hours that they had to work.

The Press folk could be very cruel to anyone that was in any way afflicted. Ken Archer was a member of the cleaning staff before being promoted to the post of internal messenger. Ken was a man with a heart of gold but his one fault was that he was easily upset. He was not to blame because when you consider what he had to put up with every second of the day while he was at work, it was a wonder that he did not have a mental breakdown. Because his surname was the same as the popular radio series, 'The Archers', every time that Ken entered the Mono everyone would whistle the signature tune. 'I s'pose you think that's bloody funny?' he would retort angrily every time. Of course, the more he 'bit' the more and louder the taunters whistled. Remember, this was not occurring in just one department. In every department of the Press, in every corridor, in the toilets, in the Quadrangle, and in the canteen he would hear the same tune ringing in his ears for more than 42 hours a week and this went on for years.

Another character who was the subject of much pain and torture was Percy. The difference here, though, was that Percy loved it. His job was to push his little truck around the composing rooms collecting up the side sticks, galleys, and quoins and storing them in his room where they would be ready for use again by the compositors and the caster operatives. He was very effeminate, small, and thin and would encourage the apprentices to hit him on the bottom with thin side sticks. The harder he was hit the more he seemed to enjoy it. He would often be seen running down the composing rooms being followed by two or three apprentices wielding side sticks and his boyish squeals of delight will be remembered by many. The University of Life now tells me what was going on with Percy but as young boys we knew nothing of such 'pleasures'. One duty that Percy always performed was the mock wedding ceremonies. When anyone was about to be married they were made to stand on one of the Stones in the Mono and Percy would preside over the ceremony. He would be dressed up in a black gown and always wore a mortar board and the terrified groom would be put through all kinds of verbal torment. When such a ceremony was advertised people would come from all over the Press to witness the event.

'Coddy' was a young compositor who got his nickname because he was truly the king of Cod. His whole life was devoted to taking the rise out of young and old alike. He could not only deliver the cod but could take it as well. He was involved in everything and he knew about everything. He knew all the scandal and all the

*Percy Williams 'officiates' at a retirement ceremony*

rumours and was often the ringleader. You always knew there was a particularly juicy bit of scandal coming up when Coddy beckoned you over with his first finger, there was an evil look in his eyes, and he said "ere . . . did you know? . . .'

It was Coddy who first introduced me to the sights of the capital—and I do not mean Buckingham Palace or the Tower of London! He would organize 'cultural' trips to London where we would tour the Soho area and its clubs. This was prior to the Wolfenden Report on prostitution and so the street corners and shop doorways were awash with ladies of the night. On my very first trip I was offered 'something my mother couldn't give me' and I have to admit that it was some time before I worked out exactly what this could possibly be.

Along with large groups of OUP craftsmen (and members of the management!) I would visit various clubs in Soho's Greek Street and Frith Street, the most popular clubs being Sunset Strip and The Queens. This was the first time that I had seen so many naked ladies in one room and I felt privileged to have been taken to these places by Coddy and his gang.

All the dens of iniquity had a House rule that only bone fide members were allowed in because of the 'explicit nature of the entertainment'. We all paid our membership fees but we did not use our own details; we used the names and addresses of all the leading management figures at the Press instead. Unbeknown to them they were all fully paid-up members of several seedy clubs in Soho and we hoped and prayed that the various clubs never contacted their illustrious 'members' at home.

I soon realized that there were two types of journeymen: one that taught you your craft and kept you on the straight and narrow, and the other that led you into muddier waters. I will always be in Coddy's debt for the latter.

Sadly, Coddy collapsed and died in the Litho Department in 1970 due to a massive brain haemorrhage, aged only 36. He had been suffering from severe headaches for many years and was diagnosed as having migraine. He left a wife and two children and because the death-in-service entitlements were poor his best friend, Cyril Cox, came up with the idea that all people at the Press who counted Coddy as their friend could make a payment of 1s. (5 pence) per week for 3 years. The appeal was launched Press wide and the response was amazing. Hundreds of people volunteered to make the payments and the management agreed to stop the money directly from the wage packets. This was a case of the Press 'family' looking after its own.

'Spikey' Hine was a compositor who got his nickname because of the frequent use he made of his bodkin. The compositor's skill was to be able to hand-set type into a setting stick and by adjusting the spacing—using quads, nuts, thicks, mids, thins, and extra thins—ensure that when the lines of type were imposed into pages they would 'lift'. Or to put it another way, when the forme of type was locked up with the furniture and quoins and removed from the stone, the type did not fall on to the floor as printers' pie.

Spikey would use his bodkin and a mallet to punch holes in the type. This would make the individual letters (or sorts) spread slightly and ensure that the line was a tight fit. The type was then rendered useless for anyone else to work with later. The introduction of the incentive bonus scheme around 1949 was the beginning of the end of true craftsmanship at OUP. The more work the compositor did the more bonus he would earn the following week. It is sad that I remember Spikey and many others like him for their 'bodging' techniques but it was difficult for apprentices not to copy them even though they themselves were not involved in the bonus scheme.

I do not want to move on from Spikey on a downer because I know from stories that have been handed down from the 'old days' that he was a popular member of the composing room and had been a fine craftsman in the days before bonus schemes were introduced. He had a great friend called Bernard Gooding, who would always compose a poem or a ditty in a hand-made card for any occasion. Two hand-written cards in my possession contain poems dedicated to Alfred Hine to celebrate his birthday on 21 June 1945 and 1948. They are mementos that I will always treasure. The are entitled 'Pal of mine' and 'May no discordant note be thine'. They show the bond of true friendship that was engendered at the Press by people that worked and played together.

## PAL OF MINE

Pal of Mine in Ages past
In 'Ship of Long & Co.,
How oft' did we in our distress
Hear many tales of Woe:
The work we had we often found                    5
Was never of the best.
And seldom had we share of 'Fat'
To feel that we were blest!
Tho' cash was never plentiful,
Nor money easy got,                               10
We had a 'wag' or two in 'Ship
Who cheer'd us quite a lot:
Their mirth-provoking antics
Halted oft' our wage to weep—
Presenting melancholia                            15
To set in very deep!
A member, very musical,
In summer oft' appear'd
On certain days in uniform—
And always loudly cheer'd:                        20
'Where e're could he be going?',
And to *know* was their demand!
But *ne'er* were they enlighten'd

*Alfred (Spikey) Hine*

By this member of the band!
No answer came from Bandsman                            25
As he slid into his 'frame'
And tho' he ne'er were 'ruffl'd',
He was always fit for game—
And much amus'd when 'side-page',
Short in statue [*sic*], made to don                    30
To show him how absurd could look
With cap and tunic on!
Well, the reason for my writing
Is to wish you, Pal, To-day,
Just ev'rything you'd wish yourself,                     35
And also that you may
Enjoy Good Health all thro' your year—
That many more you'll see—
And have the wealth to run your car
To dwell in ecstasy!                                     40
''Shipmate of *thine*'

2 the 'Ship of Long & Co] the companionship of which Mr Long was the clicker          7 Fat] the type
of work that paid well on piecework          14 our wage to weep] time spent acting the fool meant loss
of earnings for everyone in the 'ship          17 a member very musical] Alf Hine was a member of a silver
band that played all over the country. He would often wear his uniform to work because he would go
'straight from' work to the band's engagement.          29 side-page] the compositor working either to
the left or the right of him. On this occasion a short person who wasted time by cavorting round the
department wearing Alf's cap and tunic much to the amusement of all.          39 run your car] It was
unusual for Press employees to be running a car in 1945. Alf was always very proud to be one of the few.

## MAY NO DISCORDANT NOTE BE THINE

Cheerio!—and happy days
With leisure spent in Pleasant Ways!
Cash, enough—with some to spare
For anything you have a flair!
I trust that when at wheel of car
With Good Luck you may travel far—
If I am not mistaken, too,
To be on move just pleasures you!
And may you ever have Good health
To live and learn that this is Wealth!
When e'er I meet you in the Quad
Reminds me when so 'full of "cod"'
Were you in ages that are past
When from your 'frame' your wit would cast—
Methinks to-day you are the same,
Your eyes, to me, look 'fit for game'!
Trust years in plenty will be thine
My Back-Page 'Shipmate Alfred Hine!

Tarzan Harvey was another compositor who worked in the same row of frames as Snuffy Hall. He used to work on bibles that were often set in type as small as 6pt with notes that ran down the centre of the page in 4¾pt. He must have had the eyes of an eagle! Tarzan always had a friendly word for apprentices and was always there to give friendly fatherly advice. You could tell Tarzan your deepest darkest secrets and be sure that the matter would not become general knowledge later. This was always useful when apprentices needed to 'confess' to nefarious activities following trips to Port Meadow with a Press girl.

> *For years Port Meadow was used for many Press activities as was advertised on the notice board in 1927.*
>
> **Community whistling by the entire Press is to be inaugurated. Practices will be held on Port Meadow.**

During my time on the Sorts there was a national strike within the printing industry. This affected the whole country with the exception of the national newspapers. The dispute, which was over pay and the demand for a shorter working week, was organized by the Typographical Association (later the National Graphical Association). Printing in the UK operated a 'closed shop' system. That meant that if one wanted a job in printing one had to become a member of the trade union. Employers were not allowed to employ anyone unless they agreed to this condition.

Whenever there was an industrial dispute and a strike looked likely the management would always pre-empt the situation and not allow anyone to enter the Press. This was called a 'lockout'. This was rather cleverly and sensibly done to protect both sides. The Press took the view that all disputes would eventually be settled and that when that happened everyone could return to work knowing that there could not have been any 'blacklegs'. This ensured that there was never any bad feeling amongst workers when they returned and that the dispute would not rumble on into, perhaps, another strike because workers would not work with blacklegs.

When work finished on Friday, 19 June 1959, few would have forecast that no productive work would be carried out until 6 August. The complete failure of agreement between the two sides of the industry caused much material loss to individual workers, their families, and their employers, and considerable inconvenience to the general public who relied on the industry for all kinds of printing.

The claims put forward by the P&KTF in December included the following: 1. A reduction in the working week from 43½ hours to 40 hours, with a proportionate reduction in night shifts. 2. Wage rates for craftsmen to be increased from £10. 5s. 6d. to £11. 0s. per week. 3. Wage rates for women to be 66½ per cent, of the craft rate, rising from £6 to £7. 14s. 4d. Cost-of-living bonus to continue.

Meetings produced lengthy arguments from both sides but there was no sign of any agreement; no real progress was made, both sides refusing to accept the arguments put forward by their opponents. The Printing and Kindred Trades Federation claimed that the employers had refused to negotiate and had made no offer to meet the claims, even partially. Because of this the P&KTF refused to submit to conciliation through the Joint Industrial Council or by arbitration from outside. It was argued that the problems were too complex to be understood by any person other than from within the industry.

Complete deadlock having been reached by early in April the P&KTF decided to recommend the unions to ballot their members. The ballot papers were distributed and called on members to vote YES or NO on the following points: 1. A ban on overtime. 2. A ban on the extension of shift work. 3. A policy of non-cooperation in the workshop. 4. The withdrawal of participation in incentive schemes. 5. A ban on the introduction of new apprentices. 6. The tendering of strike notices subsequently if considered necessary. A large majority voted YES to all these questions.

The offer was as follows: 1. 42½ hour week on day work, reduction in the period of apprenticeship, and acceptance of adult apprentices. 2. An increase of 2½ per cent, on present basic rates. The union representatives made it quite clear that the offer was unacceptable. Production in the industry was stopped completely by Saturday, 20 June. The unions claimed that their members had been locked out but the employers claimed that strike action had been taken. Printing offices all over the country were picketed by trade union members.

Many attempts were made to break the deadlock during June and July, but little progress was made. The parties agreed that there should be a return to work on 6 August under conditions and wages operating before the dispute commenced. The unions should ballot their members on the proposed terms, and, if accepted within 4 weeks of the resumption, the improved conditions be made retrospective from 6 August 1959. All the unions with the exception of the National Society of Stereotypers and Electrotypers returned favourable decisions within the prescribed period.

The main features of the settlement were: 1. Reduction of the working week from 43½ hours to 42 hours. 2. Minimum grade rates to be advanced by 45 per cent, and clauses dealing with: *(a)* the use of craft skill to maximum effect. *(b)* the encouragement of shift work. *(c)* the cooperation of the parties in work study and methods by which production can be increased. *(d)* full cooperation between the parties in the adoption and development of new processes and new types of machines. *(e)* the transferability of apprentice vacancies, and alterations to the training period. There were also additional agreements with the Typographical Association and the Amalgamated Society of Lithographic Printers.

The only people who did have to work were the managers and the apprentices. The union allowed these people into the Press on the condition that they made no attempt to do any 'live' work. I was pleased to be allowed to go to work during the strike because it meant that I would still be drawing a wage every week. The men and women who were on strike received only a small handout from the union funds. Once it was clear that the strike was going to last for some time (it lasted six weeks) many people started looking round for casual work. The western bypass around Oxford was being built at this time and many Press people went to work road building. Every time I drive along that road now I think back to the Press men who built it and wondered whether the foreman ever found out who accidentally burned down his hut!

On the first day of the strike the apprentices were all called together by the managers and given menial jobs to do. 'Tooley' King and I were designated Canteen Cleaners. It was our job to sweep and mop the floor of the canteen every morning and every afternoon. This took us about an hour a day and left us plenty of time to get into mischief.

The weather during the strike was beautiful. It was hot and sunny every day. Because we had so much time on our hands after the first mopping session we decided that we would go to the Engineers' Yard to indulge in some sunbathing. The baling shed in the Engineers' yard was full of bales of shredded paper tied up with wire. The Tool and I dragged out a couple of bales into the sunlight and made ourselves a couple of sun-loungers. We took of our shirts and settled down for a sleep. Suddenly a booming voice rang out: 'Belson. King. What do you think you are doing?' It was John Hall and the boss of the Engineers, Frank Brown. We had no answer and we pushed the bales back into the shed and slunk back to our mopping duties. We were later reported to Bomber Harris and made to work in the frame outside his office where he could keep his eye on us.

We soon got fed up with this and realized that as long as we were hand-setting at the frame Bomber could not possibly know *what* we were hand-setting. It was then that I had the idea of setting up 'The Pirate Press'. We produced 'foreigners' for our friends and relations in the form of menus, visiting cards, letterheadings, etc. When the demand for foreigners ran out we systematically scoured the drawers and cupboards looking for things to hand-set. We found more than we bargained for! As we started rifling the various hidey-holes there were squeals of delight as each new discovery was made. We had uncovered not only many rude poems which had obviously been handed round from frame to frame for cheap thrills but also an amazing pornographic ring in the form of magazines from Scandinavia and thousands of black-and-white photographs all carefully numbered on the back for ordering purposes. The magazines and photographs kept us amused and quiet for weeks. Bomber must have thought that his tough regime had paid off.

When we had tired of the pornography we made our way to the roof of the North Wing. There was a trap door in the ceiling of the Top Comps which led on to the roof. We would climb up a ladder and lay sheets of double-demy paper

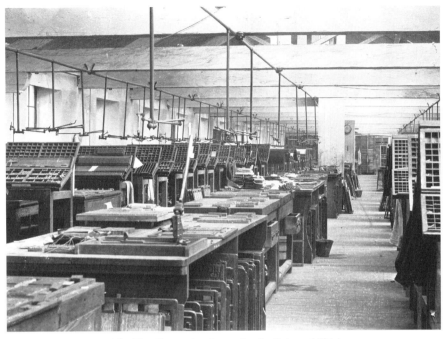

*The Top Composing Room (or the Oriental Ship)*

from the proofing press on to the hot slates where we would lie out and sunbathe. There was a very narrow gully running round the roof and we had to be careful that we did not slip because to do so would have been certain death due to the glass-roofed Monotype Composing Room that was two floors below us.

There was another good reason for being on the roof during this summer of 1959. The view from the roof was fabulous. I am not referring to the Wytham Hills or St Barnabas Church in Jericho but to the flat roof of the Radcliffe Infirmary. Although it was of little architectural interest to us it did have something that captured our attention. The attraction was the semi-naked nurses sunbathing on that roof. They obviously thought that they would be safe from peeping toms while they were there. They could not have known that one of our number had found a pair of binoculars in the drawer of one of the compositors whose window was facing the aforesaid flat roof.

The strike eventually ended and everything soon got back to normal and I continued to learn the rudiments of special sorts before being transferred to the Top Composing Room in January 1960.

Apprentices loved working in the Top Comps (short for the Top Composing Room or the Oriental Ship). This was the composing room where the Music, Egyptian Hieroglyphics, the Sanskrit, the Chinese, and many more languages were typeset by hand right up until the Printing Division closed in 1989. It was a

*Jack Webster—the apprentices' favourite*

favourite because the department was run by the popular Clicker known as 'Ster (Jack Webster). 'Ster was a fabulous man adored by everyone who ever worked for him and with him. He became the father, friend, and confidante of every apprentice. He was involved in every aspect of Press life particularly at the Stute where he or his lovely wife 'Bluebell' never had to buy a drink while one of his ex-apprentices was at the bar.

Jack could handset just about every language and dialect but his specialties were Indian, Bengali, Hindi, Gujarati, and Gaelic and in these he was arguably the world's finest compositor. All the compositors would stand at their wooden frames setting and dissing in complete silence until 'Ster would burst into song. This was the signal for the whole department to join in. The favourite song was 'Little Wooden Hut' which started with the lines: 'I wouldn't leave my little wooden hut for you/I've got one lover and I don't want two . . . ' My memory of these men and boys all singing in unison while they worked is one that I will treasure always.

Every time I went into 'Ster's office I used to wonder why he had a bowler hat on the shelf behind his desk. After a couple of weeks I plucked up the courage to ask why it was there. 'You don't want to see me wearing that, my boy', said the clicker. I found out later that it was the hat that was worn to the funeral when a member of the department died. Because of piecework it was impossible for everyone to go to the funeral so the clicker would take the bowler and represent the entire department.

Ron (Morty) Morton and Derek 'Der' Chaundy were the Music compositors. They were fine craftsmen but they had to live in the shadow of a legend. His name was Sid Cherrill and although he had retired long before I arrived on the scene his skills were talked about not only by everyone that ever knew him but by anyone that ever held a stick at OUP. Any photographs of music setting at the Press that

*The legend that was
Sid Cherrill*

you see in any archive today will almost certainly feature the hands of one of the OUP's greatest craftsmen, Sid Cherril.

Frank (Sirrah) Harris (so-called because it was his name spelt backwards) was a good hand compositor but was not recognized as having any particular language skills. What he did have, though, was a heart of gold. He became 'famous' in Press folklore because of his best friend 'Hoppity'. Hoppity was not a compositor but was a much-loved member of the Press. He (or possibly she) was a pigeon! Hoppity was not a normal common-or-garden pigeon. The pigeon was special because it had only one leg (the clue was in the name!). Sirrah was Hoppity's keeper for many years and would feed it corn and scraps from his window sill that looked out over the houses of Jericho. The pigeon was so tame that it would hop into the department much to the amusement of everyone.

On a Friday afternoon, Sirrah was also the department's 'de braarse' man and would call out 'where's de braarse' every 5 minutes until Clicker 'Ster made his way to the Counting House to collect 'de brarse' (the week's wages) for the department.

Roy Wheeler was a compositor who set some of the Hieroglyphics but sadly he died of cancer at a comparatively young age. His father had been a Linotype operator and taught the subject to printing apprentices on day-release at the College of Technology in Headington.

Arthur (Drago) Drage, who hand-set the Arabic and the Syriac, was an enigmatic character who would regularly corner apprentices in their frame to deliver one of his lectures on any subject that he chose! There was no way out and the boys could not escape from his clutches until he decided to let them go. He was a champion bar-billiards player and on my first morning in the Top Comps he challenged me to a game at the Stute during the lunch break. I had never played bar billiards before but decided to take up the challenge. When we arrived at the

Stute Drago said 'put a tanner in the slot then Michael'. I obliged with a sixpenny piece and Drago said 'off you go then'. In bar billiards you start with just two balls, one red and one white. The idea is for you to hit one against the other with the view of getting both balls down one of the holes. This is called the 'break'. If your break is successful you get to continue scoring until such time as you fail to drop a ball into a hole. At this point the opposition takes a turn and so on. I hit the white against the red and failed to score. 'My turn', said Drago and he went on to finish the game until the 'board' dropped without me revisiting the table.

'Loser pays', said Drago, 'put another tanner in!' The exercise was repeated three more times and I was not only 2s. down but also had not had any lunch. When I returned to work and related my tale of woe to the other members of the department they told me that Drago always conned new boys when they arrived at the Press and that he always enjoyed his 'sport' at gullible apprentices' expense. This was yet another lesson learned the hard way.

John (Backer) Bowley handset the Chinese, Cyrillic, Hebrew, and Arabic types and was by far the most popular craftsman compositor because he was young and could relate to the problems that apprentices came up against. He has been a lifelong friend of mine to this day and we still meet regularly with others for a meal to chew over the fat of the 'good old days'. Many years later when the hot metal composing rooms were closed down it was Backer who was the last compositor to hang up his 'stick'.

The granddaddy of them all was Henry (Comp) Deacon, the Hieroglyphics compositor. He was a tiny white-haired old man that looked to us young lads as if he was 100 years old. His son, Les, and his grandson, David, both worked at the Press as compositors.

'Now that leg with the little jigger on top—I often need that so I'll keep them together.' Mr Henry Deacon put down the page in type he was showing me, and produced a complete catalogue of hieroglyphic characters. 'That little man with the bow and arrow, we don't often get him, but I know I'll find him under "A". All the men are under "A", so they're easy; but it can be hard to know whether they mean a woman or one of these gods here.'

Mr Deacon has been setting hieroglyphs, the ancient Egyptian alphabet, for many years. *The Annual Journal of Egyptian Archaeology* is his work, and so are nearly all the reference books with hieroglyphic type. He cannot read what he sets, but years of experience have enabled him to move among the bewildering array of little cartoons with an affectionate familiarity. His copy comes to him handwritten, with reference numbers for some of the more difficult characters—for instance, a bird with a pointed tail is not the same as an almost identical bird with a square one—and for the rest he must use his instinct and his reference books. Hieroglyphics are not his only skill—he is equally at home with Coptic and Greek, and is also equal to reasonably simple music setting when there is a rush on. As he says 'We keep versatile up here.'

*The hands of a true craftsman*

'Up here' is upstairs at the Oxford University Press, where nearly all the hand-setting is done. Ordinary type, and many foreign alphabets, are now machine-set; but the Oriental languages are too complicated and too little called for to warrant elaborate equipment. Arabic, Hebrew, Sanskrit, Telugu, Kanarese, Coptic, Cyrillic—the list reads like something out of Marco Polo; and there are also classical Greek and Old German script, and mathematical symbols in endless variety, and, of course, music and hieroglyphics.

The compositors are not scholars; they cannot read most of what they set, but they learn new alphabets and even spell in them by skilled practice. Often it is not possible to make type of the simple kind used in our own alphabet; the multitude of points and elaborations mean that each symbol must be built up out of its components, and there are several hundreds of these.

Nowhere is this more true than in music setting, where each line and each space, every tie or slur or crescendo-mark is made of a mosaic of minute pieces. You can see the breaks if you look closely at music that has been set in type—the *Oxford Hymnal*, for instance. Very little music is set in type these days; engraving is rather quicker and more flexible, and can be better-looking. Mr Sidney Cherrill is in fact one of the last men in the country who specializes in setting music type. He is kept busy not on hymn-books any more, but on examination papers.

These also could be engraved, though with the letterpress that has to go in too it would be no more efficient; but the real reason why he does it is secrecy. There is no department for engraving at the University Press, and so this is the only way that the work can be kept entirely within the building. Mr Cherrill is fond of the story of a compositor's son (at Cambridge) who took first class honours in his tripos. The examiners were suspicious; he had to take a second, handwritten exam. He got a first again, of course; leaks are out of the question.

Mr Cherrill can read music, but does not read it as sound. He works, with his 20 years' experience, at remarkable speed; but even so, a single, reasonably complicated line of music may take him 20 minutes to set, although written by the composer in as many seconds.

Mr Cherrill and Mr Deacon are only two of many. Like their fellow workers they are craftsmen with an extra responsibility, for on their accuracy and discretion the academic life of Oxford quite largely depends. They, and the academic world, take it for granted: they do not even wish to master the learning they make possible. I hope they will not be embarrassed by this rare reminder of how much their skill means.

From 'Other People's Jobs: Setter of Symbols', reproduced by kind permission of the '*Oxford Mail and Times*' c.1950

All the old compositors in the Oriental Ship would tell the apprentices stories about the old days and would always remind us how lucky we were not to have to work on piecework. Names of legendary compositors were bandied about so often that apprentices felt that they actually knew them. Names such as Dave Faulkner who had been Jack Webster's predecessor and Mr Frimbley before him together with Albert Tooby, some of hundreds of compositors who had completed more than 50 years' service at the Press.

The piece-work system came to an end in the 1930s and Dave Faulkner explained in 1955 just before he retired how this complicated system worked for some but not all. He joined the Press in 1903 and in 1924 succeeded Mr Frimbley in charge of apprentices. During the Second World War he was appointed to take charge of the Top Composing Room (the Oriental Ship), a post he held until he retired. He passed away in December 1969 and it saddens me to think that I never had the privilege of meeting him.

Dealing with the compositors of some fifty years ago, before the advent of the monotype machines to the Press, type was hand-set and mostly at piece-work rates. It was not until l937 that piece-work was abandoned, with heartaches for some and blessings for others, and a set weekly wage substituted, which in turn has now been reinvigorated by a system of incentive payments. The piece-work system was worked by what was known as 'ships' (=companionships), each consisting of about nine or ten compositors who elected their own clicker annually. If he was considered unsatisfactory, he found himself at the next annual chapel being opposed by another candidate who had been persuaded to stand for the clickership at some underground meeting of the 'ship. In addition to the piece 'ships there was the Oriental 'ship, which used to work 'in pocket', and the Music 'ship, which was a 'stab. 'ship. Then there were two apprentice 'ships who were also on piece-work. At the annual chapel the election of clicker was not the only business—there was the election of 'ship's time-hand and a draw to decide who should do the regular work, such as examination papers, periodicals, and the *N.E.D.* (*O.E.D.*), parts of which were done by two or three 'ships. This latter business was carried out by the clicker placing in his apron an equal number of figures corresponding to the number of men in the 'ship. The clicker would then walk around the gathering and let each compositor 'have a dip' and take out a figure. Having done so he would then call out for figure 1, and the person holding it had choice of work for the coming year, figure 2 had second choice, and so on.

Besides the regular yearly work other jobs, of course, came along, and if they were not straightforward and could not be settled by the 'Prices per Thousand' scale, the 'lineage' would be settled by the men themselves. In this case the clicker called out 'Chapel up!' and the men gathered round a stone. At these meetings many men were ignorant of the true values of jobs, and had no regard as to whether it was, from the clicker's point of view, an economical lineage they were proposing so long as it was one profitable to themselves. After a good deal of discussion regarding the number of lines *less* than the scale a decision was made, and the question then arose as to who was going to do it. This was settled in the same way as the regular work, i.e. by means of figuring. It was not necessary for the men with the low figures to take the job if they thought the lineage was not good enough, and they could pass and those with the highest figures were let in for the job. The foregoing was the procedure of the piece 'ships. In the case of the Oriental 'ship the weekly wages of the members were fixed at a chapel meeting, and each individual was brought up to specialize on certain languages such as Hebrew, Arabic, Syriac, Sanskrit, Burmese, etc., and when a job dealing with one of these languages came along the 'specialist' was the one for the job, thus obviating the necessity of settling lineage and who should do it.

A clicker's anxious times were at Easter, August, and Christmas, when the men looked for a bit of bonus. This was done by the clicker balancing the compositors' charges against that which he himself had charged the House. If he was to the good, he divided it by the number of hours he had been charged and thus arrived at the bonus per hour. It may have been from 1*d.* to 3*d.* for every hour a man had worked since the last declaration, and was quite a considerable pick-up in those days. The House 'stab. 'ships did not share any bonus, but they had the advantage of not 'cutting the line' (going on short time) when work was slack, and were kept in work even if it meant spending the time on 'clearing'.

A companionship did not always live up to what its full name suggests. There were plenty of squabbles and plenty of 'green-eyed lobsters'. The individual 'ships themselves were variable in character—some cheerful with plenty of hilarity and good-natured humour, while others were composed of men staid and serious in their work.

Times were hard in the 1900s as the compositors were struggling to earn their living on piece-work rates but they still had time to have a bit of fun such as playing with the gas pipes and almost scalding their mates to death on the hot pipes! Albert Tooby remembers the good times and the bad during his long career at the Press from 1904 to 1956.

In the early years of the century, when a boy attained the age of 8, he was expected by his parents to seek employment to help increase the family income. My late father was very keen on my being taught a trade, and suggested that I should apply for work at the University Press, with a view to becoming a craftsman. He stressed that if accepted, I should ask to be allowed to work on the Learned side. And so it worked out.

COMPILED MARCH 1893 — REVISED MAY 1923

# COMPOSITORS

| King & Co. | Faulkner & Co. |
|---|---|
| 1 Akers. [10] | 108 Gilbert. [10] |
| 2 Trinder. | 109 Stone. |
| 3 Binham. | 110 Faulkner. |
| 4 Gerrard, W. | 111 Martin. |
| 5 Burgess. | 112 Jacobs. |
| 6 | 113 Isaacs. |
| 7 | 114 Trail. |
| 8 King, E. | 115 |
| 9 Shirley. | 116 |
| 10 Bowen, W. | 117 Hewitt. |
| 11 Payton. | 118 |
| 12 Starr. | *119 (Murray Dict.) |
| 13 | 120 Williams, T. |
| 14 | 121 Simms. |
| 15 | 122 |
| 16 KING, E. | 123 FAULKNER. |

| Chapman & Co. | Collins & Co. |
|---|---|
| 17 Garrard. [9] | 124 [11] |
| 18 Shuter. | 125 Remington. |
| 19 Kislingbury. | 126 Collins. |
| 20 | 128 Harris, H. |
| 22 | 129 |
| 23 | 130 Tooby. |
| 24 Harris. | 131 |
| 25 Thomas. | 132 Parker, J. |
| 26 Chapman. | 133 Parker, W. |
| 27 | 134 Sheppard. |
| 28 | 138 |
| 29 | *139 (Murray Dict.) |
| 30 | 140 |
| 32 Danford. | 141 Janaway. |
| 35 Tratt. | 142 Roche. |
| 36 | 143 Collins, W. |
| 37 | 144 Taylor. H. |
| 38 | 146 |
| 39 Vallender. | 147 COLLINS, W. |
| 40 CHAPMAN. | |

| Foster & Co. | Job. Dept. |
|---|---|
| 41 Jupp. [10] | 148 Ramsay. [22] |
| 42 Corner. | 149 Loney. |
| 43 Cann. | 150 Tayler, W. |
| 44 | 151 Sharp. |
| 45 | 152 Williamson. |
| 59 | 153 Johnson. |
| 61 | 154 Collett. |
| 62 Mann. | 155 Pinm. |
| 63 | 156 Lapworth, J. |
| 64 Harris, H. | 157 |
| 65 Stanley. | 158 |
| 66 | 159 |
| 67 | 160 Grundy. |
| 68 Clifford. | 161 Cox. |
| 69 Cox. | 162 Frost. |
| 70 | 163 Boore. |
| 71 | 164 Farrow. |
| 72 Foster. | 165 Griffith, E. |
| 73 | 166 Griffiths, T. |
| 74 Poulter. | 167 Nutt. |
| 75 | 168 Gerrard, E. |
| 76 FOSTER. | 169 Lapworth, H. |
| | 170 |
| | 171 Ellis. |
| | 172 Panting. |
| | 173 Hodgkins. |
| | 174 NUTT. |

| Mono. 'ship. |
|---|
| 77 } c/o Scroggs. |
| 78 } |

| Frimbley (app.) | Wild & Co. |
|---|---|
| 79 Clifford. [12] | *175 (Murray Dict) |
| 80 Bolton. | 176 Stone. [9] |
| 81 Allen, E. | 177 Tomlinson. |
| 82 Frimbley. | 178 Cook. |
| 83 Youngman. | 179 Walker. |
| 84 Allen, J. | 180 Hope. |
| 85 Brogden. | 181 Whitaker. |
| 86 Gage. | 182 Taylor, W. |
| 87 Rand. | 183 Wild. |
| 88 | 184 WILD. |
| 89 Hall. | |
| 90 Matthews. | **Not in 'ships.** |
| 91 Hamblin. | 185 Bowen, H. [5] |
| 92 | 186 Judge. |
| 93 | 187 George. |
| 94 FRIMBLEY. | 188 Goddard. |
| | 189 Smith. |

| Music 'ship. | Long & Co |
|---|---|
| 95 Cherrill. [9] | 190 Casemore. [7] |
| 96 Carter. | 191 Gooding. |
| 97 Copeman. | 192 |
| 98 Williams, H. | 193 Symmons. |
| 99 Dyer. | 194 |
| 100 Deacon. | 195 Harvey. |
| 101 Edmonds. | 196 Long. |
| 102 Bolton. | 197 Hine. |
| 103 Brooks. | 198 Lamb. |
| 104 Foster. | 199 |
| 105 | 200 LONG. |
| 106 | |
| 107 CARTER. | |

*The Companionships in 1923*
*(originally compiled in 1893)*

After about twelve months' employment boys had to undergo an examination in various subjects, success resulting in being apprenticed to a Compositor. Generally speaking, the first eighteen months of the apprenticeship was spent in the Type Store, where you were instructed in the classification of leads, knowledge of the various founts of type in use, the lay of the cases (both English and Greek), use of the stock list, and the papering and labelling of pages of type. This was real groundwork prior to entering the Case Room. There were two companionships for apprentices; the late Messrs Brown and Frimbley were in charge. Mr Brown (who was my clicker) was a sergeant in the local Volunteer Force and something of a disciplinarian. Every Monday morning you were expected to bring a clean white apron, put it on, roll up your shirt sleeves, and start work as if you meant business.

You were never allowed to rest your feet on the bed of your frame, and to attempt to sit on a stool—Great Heavens, that would be a serious crime! An apprentice started his case work in the frame with the clicker, under whose eye he remained until capable of working entirely on his own.

The period allowed for training was six months, at the end of which he was told that he would go on to piece-work rates. He could, of course, volunteer to go on piece-rate within the six-month period, especially if he thought he would benefit by doing so. Apprentices received 5s. per week of 52½ hours, plus a half of anything earned over 15s. There was, in addition, a House bonus. During the first three and a half years of the apprenticeship one received 6d. per week for every 25s., and 1s. 6d. per week for every 30s. and over credited. Later, one only received 1s. 6d. per week for every 30s. and over written. If my memory serves me right, if you attained the 30s. mark every week the bonus would be 37s. 6d. for one half-year and 39s. for the other. This was generally paid out at August and Christmas. Also there was a 'ship's bonus (which varied with the class of work) at Easter, August, and Christmas. Of course, if you were fortunate enough to get a full House bonus and 'ship's bonus you were 'Burlington Berty' until the funds became exhausted.

Some of the books used as copy were very valuable and great care had to be taken to avoid damage. They were placed in a box with a glass top, and proved very awkward to mount on the upper case. Apart from these books, copy was mostly handwritten—no typewritten copy in those earlier days!

There was the lighter side of an apprentice's life in print. Each frame was supplied with two gas jets on movable arms, which could be moved up and down and backwards or forwards wherever one wanted the light most. The fun would begin somewhat like this: a gas jet would be selected, and as soon as the clicker absented himself for a short space of time an apprentice would pull down one of the arms, place the jet in his mouth, turn the tap on, and blow. The result would be a gradual lowering of all the lights in the room. Then the rumpus began, but of course everyone was innocent! Most of the apprentices invested a penny in a nipple which they placed over the gas jet and which gave a crescent-shaped flame, a great improvement. In the winter months, when the heating apparatus was on, an apprentice would be 'scragged'. This meant that, at a given signal, one boy would be pounced on by the remainder and forced on to the steam-pipe until he yelled for mercy. Yes, they may have been hard times, but we had our fun.

The apprentice's job in the Top Comps was to ink up the proofing press every morning, pull the proofs for the compositors when they required them, and then wash-up the machine at the end of the day. In between these tasks he was expected to learn the skills of a hand-compositor setting Oriental, Fell, and Greek types. There were two experiences that happened on the same day while I was in the Top Comps that I will never forget. Backer Bowley had spent a week hand-setting eight pages of Chinese characters. This was a very laborious task because to make a Chinese character the compositor had to pick up several pieces of type that fitted together like an intricate jigsaw. Backer was an expert and was well pleased when

*John Bowley and James Campling show the Chinese how to handset Chinese!*

he set and finally imposed the eight pages before locking them up into a forme. He called me over and asked me to collect the forme from his rack and take it to the proofing press for proofs. I collected the forme from the rack in my forme truck and lifted it onto the press and pulled up the required number of proofs.

The formes were very heavy, weighing about 1 cwt. I gently lifted the forme down from the proofing press and slid it carefully back into the forme truck. When I arrived at Backer's forme rack I slid the forme over-confidently and rather roughly into the rack. The forme hit the back of the rack and bounced back out and the whole forme of Chinese characters (Backer's week's work) fell into a heap on the floor with a crash that still wakes me up in a cold sweat more than forty years on. I burst into tears like a baby as 'Ster and Backer approached the scene of the disaster. 'Ster put his fatherly arm round my shoulder and said, 'What's up old chap?' I remember blubbering something incomprehensible before he said 'Don't worry old lad you have just had your first printers' pie!' 'Printers' pie' was a term used to describe a pile of type that had been dropped on the floor or had been knocked over on the stone. Every compositor remembers his first printers' pie and the sickening feeling it caused in the pit of the stomach, and he would from then on always treat type with the greatest respect. Backer was not angry either; he was downright pleased. What I did not realize at the time was that Backer was, like all the other compositors, working on a bonus scheme. He had earned very good money for a week hand-setting Chinese and he was to be paid for it all over again because of my printers' pie.

I made my way back to the proofing press and started to wash up the rollers with turps and not a few tears and, as usual, my hands were covered in black grimy ink. I went to the sinks at the end of the room and dipped my hands into the barrel of cleanser that had the consistency of jelly. When you rubbed your hands together they would appear to get dirtier as the magic jelly started to lift the ink from your pores. I was just about to place my hands into the water when someone tapped me on the shoulder. It was Carol, the beautiful black-haired office girl from the Jobbing Department, who I had been trying to date for several weeks. She was wearing a tight black skirt and a crisp white cotton blouse. As she tapped me on the shoulder she said, 'Mick, I had a dream about you last night . . .'. Not believing my luck I spun round with my hands raised and printed a perfect black handprint on each of her breasts. Her blouse was ruined and she ran off in tears. I never did get to hear how the dream ended but if it was anything like the day I had had in the Top Composing Room perhaps it was better not to know!

In June 1960 I was moved to the Monotype Casters Department on the ground floor. There were nineteen casters in the room. Number 19 was operated by the apprentice and the other eighteen were run by nine caster operatives (each running two casters).

A Monotype caster was a magnificent feat of engineering and was said to contain more moving parts than any machine that has ever been invented. It was also the noisiest machine ever invented and the noise from all nineteen casters was unbelievable. To give the reader some idea of just how noisy they were, if a colleague came in to speak to you and placed his mouth two inches from your ear and then shouted as loud as he could, you would not hear what he was saying.

We were not supplied with ear protection or masks to filter out the lead fumes. I remember that when I went to bed after my first day in the casters I could still hear the thumping noise all night long. It took three or four weeks of sleepless nights before I got used to the noise. The art of lip-reading and sign language came into play and I soon became very good at it. I still remember the 'deaf-and-dumb' alphabet.

The casting machine was fed by an ingot of metal consisting of tin, lead, and antimony (the three main ingredients of type) that was suspended over the melting pot. As the molten metal was used up the ingot would slowly drop into the melting pot and top up the pot. The spools that came from the Keyboard Department were rolls of paper with thousands of holes punched through them. Every pair of holes punched in to the paper spool by the keyboard operator represented a letter, space, or punctuation mark. This information was in turn translated as the position that this letter could be found by the casting machine in the die-case that was positioned under the bridge.

The machines were very dangerous and there were hardly any guards on them. It would be very easy to lose a finger or even an arm or an eye. We were always taught to respect the machine and never to take risks by making adjustments unless the machine had been stopped or you had your arm resting on the bridge of the machine. This would keep your hands steady while making the necessary adjustments to the micrometer.

*Early pictures of the Monotype casters*

*A modern Monotype Casting machine in full flow*

Apprentices took no notice of these warnings and would make dangerous adjustments just to show off to visitors and would even play games on the machine such as 'hunt the magnet'. This game entailed one person hiding a small magnet somewhere on the caster while it was motionless and the other not only had to find it but also had to remove it while the machine was running. How stupid we were and how lucky we were not to have suffered some terrible injury.

The molten metal was being pumped into the moulds on the caster at about 700°F. It would solidify immediately before being ejected as type to make room for the next pumpful of hot molten metal. If the machine was running too fast (because the caster operative was trying to earn more bonus) the pump would push the molten metal into the mould before the previous piece of type had been ejected. The molten metal had to go somewhere so it would, without warning, spurt upwards towards the caster operative. This was known as a 'splash'. If it landed on your arms or face it would solidify as it made contact with your skin and very painful it was too. All caster operatives had scars on their bodies. Their shoes and clothes were silver and all the other Press employees knew caster operatives generically as 'silvershoes'.

*Harold Dotterill on the glorious Monotype Supercaster*

We had a little trick that we used to play on the visitors who were regularly brought around the Press by the official guide. We would drop a lump of cheese into the metal pot just as they leaned over the machine to inspect its intricate workings. The noisome odour beggars description but needless to say a visit to the sewage farm would have been more pleasant.

Cheese was not the only foreign body that could be added to the pot to achieve amazing effects. Fruitcake was good because the currants would explode and pop out of the pot like bullets and oil was even more fun because it would fill the room with acrid black smoke causing the visitors much discomfort.

One particular occasion that sticks in my mind was the day that we were visited by a party of Africans who had arrived at the Press in full tribal dress. They entered the department and there were gasps of amazement at the colourful spectacle. To see a casting machine produce type is a wonderful sight to behold and the Africans were all gathered round my machine to get a good view of the intricate machinery. I surreptitiously dropped a lump of cheese into the pot but before it could take effect I had a splash! Molten metal was ejaculating into the air with every thrust of the pump. The hot fragments of metal were landing on the tribesmen and with much hooting and hollering they started leaping about in pain. It was a war dance that I will never forget.

The foreman of the Casters was a kindly old man called Harold Dotterill who always wore a dark grey 'foreman's coat'. He was always on the move and spent his whole day running around at a strange angle with his head about a foot ahead of his body. It was his job to see that everyone had a continuous supply of work.

The engineer in the casters was George Richardson. It was his responsibility to ensure that all the casters were kept running. He achieved this by continuously stripping down each machine in turn and replacing any faulty or worn-out components. It was a never-ending job that was similar to painting the Forth Bridge. He would start every morning by putting on his white coat, laying out a small cloth on his bench, and opening his 'toilet' box. He would take out his electric razor (no one else had such a luxury) and shave himself. He would then dab a variety of creams and potions on to his countenance. When he had finished this ritual he would place everything back into the box. He would then start work.

Another caster operative who has stuck in my memory was the minute one-handed Reg 'Midge' Bellinger. In place of one of his hands he had a large metal hook. I did not then know how he came to lose his hand and was always too frightened to ask. I later discovered that he had started work at the Press in 1910 as a feeder in the Letterpress Machine Room and then as an apprentice under Mr A. H. Harvey. When Midge went to sign his indentures his boss, Mr G. Denton, remarked to the then Controller, Horace Hart, 'He's a bit small I'm afraid'. Hart replied, 'That's immaterial, most of England's great men have been small!' Midge volunteered for military service three times in 1914 and was rejected because of his diminutive stature. He was finally accepted and lost his arm in the battle of the Somme in 1916. He returned to work in the casters running two machines simultaneously with just one hand and a hook! Horace Hart was right; Midge was a great man.

'Fatty' Colmer was a jovial and friendly man who had an enormously protruding stomach that was so large that he had great difficulty getting close to his machine to make the necessary adjustments. Ron Dandridge was a super-caster operative who was also a brilliant cartoonist. Every time there was an incident of any kind at the Press, Ron would produce a wicked caricature for circulation. (There were several talented cartoonists at the Press who deserve mention because of their amazing ability to capture stories of Press life as the events happened: they were compositor Les Brogden, machine minder David Langford, and stereotyper Max Kibbey.) Ron is remembered for one of his many lunchtime visits to the University Parks to watch the Varsity cricket together with his workmates. He fell asleep in the grass and his 'friends' crept away leaving him to his slumber. He woke up at 1.40 p.m. (he should have been back at his machine by 1 p.m.) and had a lot of explaining to do! During his 'rollocking' his friends outside the office serenaded the sleepy victim with 'Dear Lord, and Father of Mankind, forgive our foolish ways'. Whether anyone dared produce a cartoon of

*The Jobbing Ship*

his sleep-in is not recorded! David Langford once produced a cruel caricature of me for a pantomime programme. I told him that it did not look anything like me. He said, 'Wait until you get older and you will see what I mean.' Thirty years on I have to say that he was spot on!

As Christmas 1960 approached I realized that my time in the Casters was soon to come to an end and that I would now have to spend some time in the Jobbing Department.

I spent the whole of 1961 in the Jobbing Ship, which was situated in the North Wing on the first floor. This was the department where the book jackets and covers, notices, business cards, the *University Gazette*, and other small jobs were handset and this was known as 'jobbing' work. The boss was a fierce little man known as 'Pant'. Arthur Panting was a very strict disciplinarian and all the compositors and apprentices were frightened of him because of his aggressive nature. He ruled the department with a rod of iron and would never let apprentices work overtime because he considered that because they were apprentices they were still only training. Apprentices in other departments were allowed to work overtime to enable them to earn a little more money each week. I remember 'Fezzer' walking into Pant's office one Friday afternoon after Pant had been round the department with the overtime list and asking 'Why am *I* not working overtime tomorrow?' 'Because I haven't bloody well asked you!' was the curt reply.

*Jasper Lapworth with his 'boy'*

The jobbing comps had told me that I would never get Pant to change his policy on apprentices working overtime. I devised a master plan. I went down to see Bomber in the Monotype Composing Room office and asked if I could work overtime for him. He must have felt sorry for me because he said that I could work on the following Saturday morning. I immediately went back upstairs and into the lion's den. 'Mr Panting', I said, 'I am working overtime tomorrow for Mr Harris in the Mono'. 'You're bloody well not,' he shouted, 'you're working for me tomorrow!' I had won the battle and the war and was probably the first apprentice to work overtime in the Jobbing Ship for many a year.

The policy in the Jobbing Ship was to place every apprentice in the custody of a compositor. This was the true meaning of the phrase 'apprenticed to a compositor'. My compositor was a wonderfully kind and patient man called Jasper Lapworth. I was Mr Lapworth's boy for the entire 12 months in the Jobbing Ship and in truth, even though he is long gone, I still am. Such was the influence that he had over my life. He was father, friend, and confidante and I adored him. I will always be grateful to him for what he taught me about the compositor's work and what he taught me about life.

One day, while Jasper was on holiday, I was sitting on a high stool at my frame, my feet resting on a half open case of type and eating one of Nan's beef dripping sandwiches (something that I would never dared to do had Jasper been there). Pant stormed out of his office in a rage and headed in my direction. 'Belson!' he screamed, 'You are committing three crimes! One, you should not be sitting down you should standing up and getting on with your work. Two, you should get your dirty feet off of the type case. Don't you realize other people have to put

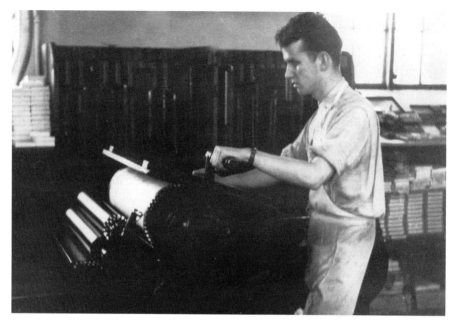

*The author 'on the press' in the Jobbing Department*

their hands in there? And three, the crumbs from that sandwich are dropping on the floor and by tomorrow this department will be crawling with cockroaches and rodents! Now get on with your work.' I did not work overtime again for three months; perhaps I hadn't won the war after all.

The work that apprentices were given to do in the Jobbing Ship was probably the most interesting and the most skilful part of a compositor's trade. Other composition departments in the Press were slowly being taken over by automation but the Jobbing compositors still had to do everything by hand in much the same way that it had been done by compositors for centuries. Everything was handset and put through the compositors' stick before being imposed into a chase and then proofed ready for the proofreader.

The Jobbing Ship had its own proofreader and the incumbent of the small office in the corner of the department measuring 2 metres by 2 metres was Gilbert Williams. Gilbert was the epitome of what a proofreader should look like. He was small, sat on a high stool, and was crouched over a Spartan desk with just a single metal lamp casting a bright light over it. The rest of the 'box' was in shadow. He had thick pebble glasses and his pristine shirtsleeves were held up by bright gold-coloured expanding armbands, he wrote on the proofs with his old pen that he dipped meticulously into the inkwell on his desk, and on his head he wore a visor to keep the glare away from his eyes.

It was the proofreader's job to carefully read through everything that was produced in the Jobbing letter by letter. Gilbert was fanatical about keeping up OUP's reputation and would ensure that every proof that left him had the hallmark of quality scribbled all over it. Some proofs produced by the fine Jobbing craftsmen were completely free of any errors but that did not stop Gilbert wielding his pen and ink. If he could find no mistakes he would always add 1pt space somewhere on the proof much to the annoyance of the compositors who were eager to move on to the next job. He was known as 'One point Williams' because of his pedantic antics.

Another nice thing about working in the Jobbing was the fact that as well as hand-setting, the book jackets, notices, etc. one was allowed to actually design them as well. Although there was a two- or three-man 'Layout Department' (what we would now call an 'Art and Design Department' with its banks of high-tech computerized technology and a dozen or so designers (not to mention the freelance designers working for the Press)) on the ground floor they never seemed to get involved in jacket design.

There were three reasons for this: first, the design of book jackets was pretty much symmetrical and followed the 'Oxford' look; secondly, the people that worked in the Layout Department were busy on other projects such as typographic page design; and thirdly, the compositors could 'feel' the design as they ran the type through the stick. The typographic design skills had been handed down through the apprenticeship system and there was no one more qualified to design what was to be the finished article. The feeling was at the time that they certainly had a greater skill in design than the arty-farty designers who came to the Press straight from college.

The truth was that these 'arty-farty' designers were in fact 'craftsmen' and unbeknown to me at the time, indentured to the Press.

Many memorable people worked in the Jobbing while I was there. The bookies' runner, Donna Cleaver; Jasper's bad-tempered brother, Harold; the watch and clock mender, Scally Allington; the shrew-like Ted Rogers; bushy eyebrowed 'Chi' Youngman; the quiet and studious Bert Greenman; the *Gazette* compositor, Ted Spalding; and the Linotype operators Den Parker and Ken Beckley (both Den and Ken went on to be the leading lights in the development of phototypesetting at OUP).

Linotype machines were first introduced in England in 1894 to set the *Financial Times*. They proved very successful for this type of work and just about every newspaper in the country adopted their use. They were brought into the Press in 1950 because it was thought, at the time, that they would revolutionize typesetting at the Press. Traditional mechanical typesetting was made up of three stages: the keyboarding, the typecasting, and the hand correction. The Linotype produced solid slugs of type one line at a time and the likelihood of a printer's pie was remote while setting was in progress and when the corrections were being carried out.

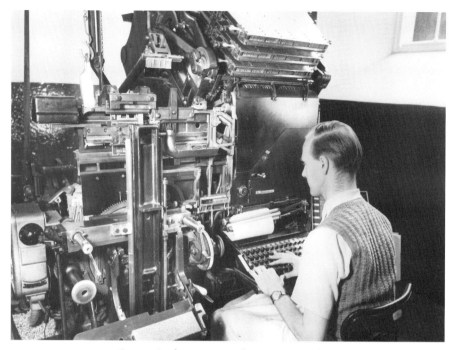

*Dennis Parker operating the Linotype machine*

The 'Linos' were used mainly to typeset *The University Gazette* and the Oxford University Hebdomadal Council Papers and proved no match for the already dominant Monotype machines.

The two clickers who deputized for Pant when he was away were Stan Parker (identical twin brother of Den) and Ted 'Chummy' Millard. Chummy—who got his nickname because he called everyone 'Chummy'. Many years later in 1998 when he, along with other Press pensioners, was invited by then Secretary of the Delegates, James Arnold Baker, to a pensioners' party. The idea was to allow all the 'oldies' a chance to see how things had changed since they had worked at the Press. I approached Chummy and said 'Hello Ted, do you remember me?' 'Of course' replied Chummy, 'How are you?' I said 'I'm fine, would you like me to show you round and try and find the exact spot where you used to work at your frame all those years ago?' 'That would be nice', said Chummy.

I took him to the first floor on the North Wing and counted the windows on the Quad side until we reached the office that was the nearest point to where Ted's first frame stood. We both reminisced about the 'good old days' and how we had worked together for that year in 1961. He was a little emotional so I decided to lead him back, through the old Type Store (now the corridor that joins the old building to the new building at the end of the North Wing) and along the fairway so that he could rejoin all the other pensioners who had by now formed a queue outside the restaurant to have their tea. We shook hands and he said 'Thanks for the tour Chummy, but who are you?' C'est-la-vie!

One little man whose job it was to fetch and carry and keep the department clean was Bill Fitzgerald. (He had a brother, Fred, who did exactly the same job in the main composing rooms and was a 'clone' of Bill.) He *always* wore a rat catcher cap and he *never* took it off while anyone was around. He would arrive for work very early each day wearing his 'travelling-to-work' cap and would open his locker and place his head deep inside it. He removed his cap as he slid his working cap on to his head. No one ever saw the top of his head, or knew why he always wore a cap, until Bill Butt, a bulky young apprentice whose hobby was to stir everyone up, met him on the North Wing stairs. The bad lad knocked Fitz's hat off to discover that he was not only completely bald but also had a very 'scaly' head. 'Fitz' was so angry that he didn't speak to *anyone* for weeks. The last time I heard of him he was still sitting in his front room all day and he was still wearing his cap!

January 1962 saw me moving to the Maths Ship for 6 months to learn the complicated business of setting mathematics under the watchful eye of the Clicker Jack Clifford, and his men Don Gibbons, Dick Kemp, Tony Hopcraft, Ernie Allen, and Fred Morgan. This was not a memorable period of my apprenticeship because I always hated mathematics at school and could never see much use for it. I soon changed my views on the subject years later when, as a journeyman, I needed maths to help me with the bonus scheme and ensure that I earned good money.

The Math Ship was lucky to have such fine craftsmen and they were all skilled in the hand-setting and correcting of four-line maths and some incredibly complex chemistry formulae. As an apprentice I knuckled down to the art and became fairly proficient by the time I had to move on to the Plate Imposition Department in June 1962.

This was the small department where all the half-tone plates that were printed in 1-, 2-, 4-, 8-, or 16-page sections on gloss or calendered paper were produced. This meant that the plates were imposed into a chase to make a forme and they were printed quite separately from the text. Half tones were rarely printed on text paper because the quality would not have been good enough. This is why most of the books produced in the days of hot metal printing used plate sections.

The Plate Imposition Department was no more than a stone and a few type cases in the corner of the Exam Ship which was situated next to the Production Department (now the area around the post-point in the Academic Division's ground floor of the North Wing) and manned by one clicker and his apprentice. The clicker when I arrived was Garvin Reeves, one of the Press's famous brothers (the other being Norman who worked in the engineers). They were famous for writing excellent pantomimes that were performed every year by the Press's football team for the OUP children's Christmas party.

Garvin was good at getting apprentices to work for him. He had a little silver box that contained tiny extra strong mints. These mints were highly addictive and apprentices would run miles on errands for Garvin just to be rewarded with one of those precious mints. When I completed my apprenticeship years later Garvin presented me with the silver box full of mints. I still have this treasured box on my desk at home.

After three months Garvin was moved on to take charge of the stores following the death of Snuffy Hall. 'The Fart' replaced him. The Fart was a nickname given to Keith Whettam. He was a larger-than-life character who loved his food and drink and it showed around his waistline. He had mastered the art of rubbing people up the wrong way and despite his know-it-all antics he was a very good and intelligent craftsman.

The Plate Imposition Department was attached to the Exam Ship. This was the department made up of about a dozen or so compositors and a proof-puller by the name of Alf Walker. The whole department was run by the Clicker, Mr Fred Matthews. Fred was a High-Churchman and a pure gentleman. He was always calm and never lost his temper and could see only good in everyone. He treated his apprentices like naughty young schoolboys.

Everyone called him 'Mr Matthews' and when one apprentice caught another doing something 'naughty' or using profane language he would 'dob him in' by shouting out something like, 'Mr Mattchews, [Michael]'s reading a dirty book, Mr Mattchews!' or 'Mr Mattchews, [Michael] said a dirty word Mr Mattchews'. Mr Matthews would run the length of the room and put his arm gently round the shoulder of the offender and quietly say, 'Come come now [Michael], there's no need for that'. The admonished would them immediately drop somebody else in the mire with, 'Mr Mattchews, Bill Butt's picking his nose, Mr Mattchews'. The whole cycle would start again and we would spend many hours watching this nice man running up and down the department trying to keep his boys in order.

One morning Mr Matthews came to work minus his eyebrows and everyone spent the morning trying to find out how he had lost them. He held out until lunchtime before spilling the beans. It transpired that just before he came to work that morning he wanted to find out how full his cesspit was. He could not see and did not have a battery in his torch so he lit a match to have a look. We then knew what had happened to his eyebrows!

One day while working on my stone carrying out corrections to the captions on the forme of plates I saw a vision. It was a beautiful fair-haired girl called Rosamund who worked in the Assessors Department. It was her job to assess the work that had been done by the compositors and the proofreaders and work out how much bonus they would be paid on the following Friday.

I was totally smitten and knew that she was the girl for me but I could not bring myself to actually ask her out for a date. I told almost everyone in the Press how

*Not bad for a tenner—
the author's 1939
Morris 8 Series E*

much I fancied her except her. Every time she passed my stone she smiled at me and still I could not summon up the courage to ask her out. I then heard that her friends had told her about my dilemma so she would pass my stone about every ten minutes to give me a sporting chance.

She obviously got tired of waiting and approached me at the bottom of the lift that used to serve the Exam Ship, the Jobbing Ship, and the Oriental Ship in the North Wing. 'Are you going to ask me out or what?' she asked. I mumbled something to the effect that I would love to go out with her. 'Good,' she said, 'we will go to the Town Hall tonight and watch the Wrestling. I have got the tickets just in case you said "yes".' I asked her how I would get her home. She said that it was not a problem because she would be coming in her father's car and she would pick me up and drop me off at my home after the date. I only knew one friend who had a car and it was unheard of for girls to drive, let alone deliver their dates back home. After the wrestling date I insisted that she dropped me off in a dark spot about a mile from my home just in case anybody saw me being driven by a girl. This was just the push that I needed. I was going to get myself a car and learn to drive in that order.

My brother, who worked for Barclays Bank, said he would give me £10 towards the cost of a car so I found a heap of rust in the form of a 1939 Morris 8 Series E for just £10. I had to go to the Baldons to collect it but Rosamund had to drive it home for me. The humiliation continued until I passed my test and was able to hold my head up again.

It was around this time that I decided that if I was to run a car, get married, and buy a house I was going to have to get some money together. It was clear that I was not going to get rich on an apprentice's wages so I decided to get myself a part-time job.

My mother, who worked as a dress-maker in Webbers department store in High Street, had told me that there was a Saturday job going in the transport department if I was interested. I jumped at the chance and arrived on the first Saturday morning at 8.30 a.m. dressed in a clean white shirt, tie, neatly pressed trousers, and a smart Harris Tweed jacket. I was sure to make a good impression.

Mr Stone, the transport manager, told me that the pay was £2 per day; an offer I accepted immediately.

He then set me to work. He pointed to the base of the lift shaft that was piled high with paper, showcards, and cardboard boxes and said: 'The lift will go up and down all day but it always stops 6 ft from the bottom. I want you to climb into the middle of all that rubbish and every time the lift goes past the floors above, people will throw their rubbish into the lift shaft. Your job, then, is to find the baler that is hidden in there and then bundle up all the rubbish into bales and they must then be secured with wire. Once a week a lorry will come and take away the bales that you have made and then you start all over again.'

At the end of the first day I emerged from the hellhole in a terrible state. The inside of my nostrils was black, my hands, face, and ears were filthy and I was totally demoralized. I was determined, though, to stick it out because of the extra money and I was a man with a mission. Every week I would arrive and I would begin my search for the baler before clearing enough rubbish to start the baling operation. People above knew that I was working in there and I do not know which was the most terrifying; the fact that all manner of objects were raining down on me (some things unmentionable!) or the fact that I was scared that the lift one day might not stop 6 ft above me and that I would be crushed.

Week after week I kept going but I could never clear the backlog of rubbish and would go home each Saturday totally exhausted. One Saturday I happened upon a tea chest that I had not seen before. It was covered by a large piece of hessian sacking. I went to move the sacking and was greeted by thousands of mice pouring down the sides of the tea chest like an overflowing tank of water. I was so sick and scared that the manager let me go home one hour early!

As soon as I passed my driving test I was allowed out of the pit and Webbers employed me as a furniture delivery man. I was allowed to drive enormous lorries that my driving licence would not cover today. I thought that I was king of the road and soon took on a driver's mate in the person of apprentice keyboard operator, Robbie Boyd. We enjoyed many hairy and scary moments together and were involved in several road traffic accidents and hundreds of near misses! The funniest incident happened while I was parked in High Street facing the traffic. I dropped the tailgate as a car was passing. The iron angle bracket on the corner of the tailgate opened the car up from bonnet to boot like a tin-opener. The driver was not amused!

When I moved to the Stones in January 1965 I handed over the Webbers lorry to Robbie Boyd and he then in turn took on keyboard operator Tony Bennell as his mate. When Robbie moved on, Tony took on the job with compositor apprentice Jeff Wareham as his sidepage. A few months later, owing to a chance of increased overtime at the Press, the OUP apprentices' connection with Webbers faded away.

*The Stones in the 1950s*

The stone was a heavy, shiny slab of flat metal about 3 yards square and 4 inches thick. The surface area (which was always kept spotlessly clean with turps and paraffin) was where the pages of type that the compositor had made up on to the galleys were slid off and imposed into 8-, 16-, 32-, 64-, and 128-page signatures. The pages were laid out in a set order, so that when they were sent to the machine room to be printed the sheet could be folded to form a section of a book. A large metal frame known as a 'chase' would be placed around the imposed pages and they were 'dressed' with furniture, leads, side-sticks, and quoins. Once the signature had been 'planed' and 'locked up' by hammering the quoins against the wedge-shaped sidesticks with a large wooden mallet the whole item became a 'forme'. Every part of the forme had a name: the backs, the gutters, the fore-edge, the heads, the tails, and the pellet. If the forme would 'lift' (i.e. the type did not fall onto the floor to form a 'printers' pie') then it would be transported to the Letterpress Machine Room for printing.

Many years later I worked with a young publisher called Matthew Hollis, who showed an incredible interest in printing in general and the compositor's work in particular. We had many talks over the proverbial pint after which he wrote the beautiful and sensitive poem printed below. I am sure that he had his own agenda for writing the poem but to my mind his grasp as an 'outsider' of what went on in the inside of a compositor's mind is breathtaking. It pleasures me to think that

*It's all here! Mallet, shooter, side sticks, quoins, furniture, chase, leads, bodkin, tweezers*

*The strange terminology used by stonehands is quite difficult to explain but an apprentice writing to his parents after his first day in a printing shop captured it beautifully:*

Printing is done with thin bits of lead with letters on top. When they are short they are called 'sorts', and the comps take them home in their pockets. When they don't, I have to sweep them off the floor. When the 'sorts' are all stood up in a cake it is called 'matter'; the iron table which they push it on to they call a 'stone'. The bits of wood which they pinch into the iron frame they call 'coins'. They call the chisel they do this with a 'shooting stick', and the iron thing they stand the sorts up in they call a stick—which it isn't. The chap who named these things must have been balmy.

And when a comp falls over a slab called a 'forme' it's called 'pie', and I have to shovel it all up and put it with the others. What makes comps swear is the bald-headed old bloke who draws Chinese pictures all over the proofs. He calls himself a 'reader', but you ought to hear what the comps call him!

From *The Record* (the monthly magazine of the Printing Staff of the Amalgamated Press Ltd., London), *c.*1933 there are still people out there who even though they have never handled a 'stick' can appreciate the beauty of the craft.

*from* THE STONEMAN

A type, mind, is a little man;
    a face, a beard, shoulders and arms,
   look—even the shank of a body.
        A. R. Spalding, *The Mannerisms of Type*


A true navigator, he could course
the old print works from memory—
decoding a world of picas and rubies,
of going to the case for brevier, bourgeois;
lining the back-to-front type, sort by sort,
or leading the galley for the optimum gauge;
before taking the chase to the stoneman
who'd dress it with furniture, sidesticks, quoins,
measuring the gutters, and locking the forme for press.

A world of infinite detail, he learned
to tell founts by the slightest flourish:
the kern of an f, or the spur on a G—
those stubby descenders of *Goudy*;
those *Baskerville J*s, *Fournier z*s;
and the crazed swash of *Caslon, Garamond.*
*He would scour the cases for dog's cocks, ampersands,*
*the Old Face of* Blado—Poliphilus;
drumming up scraps on the origins of *out of sorts,*
or how we take *upper* and *lower* case
from the height at which the type was stored.

To handle the language like that—
to lift, assured, each letter into place,
knowing it either clean or dissed
(one or the other, no in-between);
and throwing the frocked type for the recast
when the paraffin no longer did the trick.

And yet, more than aware of composing a line
that would soon be lifted and distributed,
so that nothing he worked would survive him
only its residue: imposed, in print, out of it.

In the same way, his men are scattered now, far flung
or melted down, leaving only the legacy:
of how as a young devil some wag would send him
for skyhooks, striped ink, an italic space,
or the old long weight. And what after all
did the o say to the 8, but *I like your belt.*

Extract from a poem by MATTHEW HOLLIS, *Reactions: New Poetry* (edited by Esther Morgan), (UEA: EAS Publishing for Pen&inc, 2000), 68–9

I did not like working on the Stones because it was heavy, dirty work and I thought that the stonehands were taking advantage of me. They were always asking me to run errands for them and then charging my time on their dockets as if they had done the work. This meant that I was always being told off by Lofty Deacon (the Clicker of the Stones) for not doing enough work. One day I blew my top at being asked to run these errands because I was close to the end of my apprenticeship and felt that I was learning nothing. I decided on a policy of non-cooperation.

Now that I look back on my time on the Stones I realize that I was wrong in behaving the way that I did and can probably put it down to worry. When apprentices were getting close to the end of their 'time' they started to wonder where they would end up when the music stopped. Wherever they were working when the time came for them to collect their indentures from the Printer that was usually the place where they stayed. I remember knowing that I did not want to end up on the Stones. I wanted to be a proofreader.

Among the Stonehands that I worked with there were some very amusing characters. Martin Harvey was a wiry white-haired man who was renowned for his

*Wally Connor—Stoneman*

*Apprentices singing
Christmas carols on the
Stones for the entertainment
of the Stonehands*

corned-beef sandwiches. Every day at the exact moment that Nan came round with the tea trolley, Martin would open his hamper. It was not a sandwich box; it was a hamper! It contained a loaf-load of thick corned beef sandwiches covered with mustard and they were generously shared with all the other stonehands. Every day was the same. Corned beef, corned beef, and more corned beef. Everyone was sick to death of corned beef but no one had the heart to tell him and it was better than having to buy lunch or bring in sandwiches yourself.

The stonehands, unlike other departments, always stopped work and sat on their stones to have their morning and afternoon tea. This was probably because it was one of the dirtiest jobs in the Press and the stonehands had to wash their hands before eating and drinking. Sometimes these breaks would go on too long and it fell to the Clicker to tell them to restart their work.

The office was in the centre of the Monotype Composing Rooms and it housed the manager, Ron 'Bomber' Harris, his deputy Bill 'The Perm' King, and the Stones' clicker Frank 'Lofty' Deacon. Bomber did not usually get involved with

*The proofreader's 'box'—the height of luxury!*

the mild misdemeanours of the stonehands and Lofty was too close to the men and they never took much notice of him anyway. The time to start work was left to 'The Perm'. Bill King, who had a beautiful head of bright ginger hair that appeared to be naturally set in tight rows of perms—thus his nickname—worked in the office overlooking the Stones.

Cokey Smith who was the wag of the department noticed that the angrier 'The Perm' got when they failed to start work after the break the more rows of perms showed over the top of the office window. Cokey would keep an eye out for the rising perms by calling out 'one perm, two perms, three perms, four perms, back to work lads!' If any stonehand had not started work by the time five perms were visible (which meant that he was now standing) they would receive a visit and a rollocking from a very irate Bill King.

Southampton Football Club supporter, Wally 'Tosho' Connor, Chalky 'Batters' White, 'Piccolo' Pete Charlett, Frank 'Much' Margetts, Tony Wharton, and Alan 'Dodder' Dodshon were just a few of the characters that adorned the Stones during my time there.

Even with all this fun I was not happy and the management decided to take me away from the Stones and move me to the peace and quiet of the Reading Department where they hoped that I would settle down.

My first day in the Reading Department was in February 1963 and was quite a culture shock for the now bolshy Mick Belson. There I found 44 men and women ensconced in little cubicles that measured no more that one metre square. Inside each cubicle was a slanting desktop, with a metal table lamp, a sheet of blotting paper, an inkwell, a pen holder and a box of spare nibs, a copy of *Hart's Rules*, and a high stool. There was no carpet on the floor and no roof to the cubicle. Above was the glass roof of the North Wing.

I was placed in the care of John Baker who had a special two-seater reading box with one seat for him and the other alongside him for his apprentice. I would have to read one page at a time by copy, making corrections with an old-fashioned pen and nib dipped in blue ink taken from the inkwell on my half of the desk and then hand the proof over to John who would over-read what I had done marking everything that I had missed in red ink. By the time I had read the second page John was ready to check it.

This was superb training of a quality that no proofreader gets today. When you made an error it was pointed out to you immediately and firmly. It was accepted by trainers that apprentices missed things through ignorance but once you were told of the error you were not expected to make the same mistake again. If you did you were likely to suffer the wrath of your trainer that often resulted in a rap on the knuckles with a wooden ruler.

By June 1963 my stay in the Readers was over for the time being and I was sent back to the department that I thought I had said goodbye to forever: the dreaded Stones.

I spent the next six months back on the Stones. My time in the Readers had made me grow up and had clearly settled me down. I was able to knuckle down to the job and was prepared to learn everything there was to know about imposition. When I was asked to run errands I did so with a willing heart and I made it my business to make friends with my enemies and actually quite enjoyed working with the stonehands once they had accepted me. I joined in all the departmental social activities, something I would never have done the last time I worked there.

In January 1964 I was aware now that I was only a few months away from the end of my apprenticeship and was desperately hoping that I would be transferred to the Reading Department. It was not to be. There was still one department that I had not worked in and that was the Monotype Keyboards Department. I did not want to go to the keyboards because it would mean that I would come out of my time there and that would be disastrous for my master plan. I protested but to no avail. I entered the keyboards as an apprentice keyboard operator with my old Webbers mate, Robbie Boyd, under Len Griffin.

It was while I was there that I became engaged to Rosamund and started

*The Monotype Keyboards in the 1950s*

*The author as keyboard apprentice*

looking round for somewhere to live when we got married. I decided that I would like to buy a house in Didcot, a garrison town half way between Oxford and Reading. The houses were cheaper there than in Oxford and we discovered that Blakes the Builders were building some decent houses on the outskirts of Didcot for £2,895. We reckoned that we could raise about £500 between us. Rosamund found £480 and I managed £20! This left us requiring a mortgage of £2,395. My parents had had their mortgage from the Woolwich Building Society in Oxford's Turl Street so they were the obvious choice for me. I made an appointment to see the manager during my lunch-break and asked him if he would lend me the money. He asked me how much money I was earning. I replied that I would soon be out of my apprenticeship and I would be earning £10 per week plus up to £5 bonus when I got 'top limit'. He said that he was not interested in what I *would* be earning but how much I *was* earning. I told him that I was earning about £8 per week. He said that if he lent money to everybody who said what they might one day be earning the Woolwich would soon go out of business and he could only lend money based on actual earnings. I was told to go away and not come back until I was earning the money that I said I was going to earn.

I went back to the Press that afternoon feeling totally dejected. I relayed the sad story to Rosamund and then to John Matthews, an apprentice who worked in the Stereotype Department. His advice was that I should go and see John Hall because he had done that when his building society rejected him and John Hall had fixed him up with a mortgage. He said that he was now the proud owner of a house in Wantage.

I went to John Hall's office in the North House and related my sad tale that I could not get a mortgage while still an apprentice. John Hall listened to my story and asked me the name of the building society. I said that it was the Woolwich. He told me in his quiet and authoritative manner that if I went back to see the manager the following day he could assure me that I would be offered a mortgage.

I called in to the Woolwich the following day and the manager welcomed me like a long-lost son. He said that a mortgage of £2,395 would be no problem at all and that the payments over 25 years would be £15 per month. I learned many years later that John Hall, because of his High Church connections in Oxford, had many friends. The manager of the Woolwich was clearly one of those friends but I will always be grateful to John Hall for getting me started as a landowner.

The foreman in the keyboards and the casters was a dapper little man called Frank Jones. He was good with apprentices and was always willing to help and explain the intricacies of the Monotype Keybord.

The keyboard was a machine that was run not by electricity but by air. Put simply, the operator would punch out the copy on his keyboard and this would release a jet of air that would puncture a pair of holes in a spool of paper that ran mechanically over the top and through the machine. The position of the two

*The Monotype Keyboard operators*

holes on the paper was relative to the position of that letter on the die case on the casting machine. The die case contained the letters that were to be moved over the moulds when told to do so by the holes in the spool of paper. The pump would then push the molten metal into the mould and the piece of type was created.

There were about thirty keyboard operators working in the large glass-roofed room. The job was very hard on the eyes and the concentration required was intense. All you could hear was the clicking sound of hundreds of fingers hitting the keyboard, the air forcing its way through the tiny holes on the spools of paper, and the ring of the bell that alerted the operator to the fact that he was coming to the end of a line and must justify it. Just like the hand compositor who had to adjust the spaces between the words to ensure that the line was filled out with equal spaces so the keyboard operator had to ensure that every line contained the exact amount of space to enable the caster to produce perfect lines of type.

Quite a lot of Press personnel lived on the Jordan Hill estate in North Oxford that had been built by the Press. The Keyboard Department had their fair share and there were always jokes put about by people who did not live at Jordan Hill that they would not like to live there because the only people you would see during the evenings and weekends would be the people you worked with. They claimed that residents could enjoy no privacy but this was hotly denied by all the people that lived there and statements such as 'you can walk down the street and never see anyone you know' or 'there is never any tittle-tattle' were commonplace. The second example was blown apart in the Keyboards one day when two Jordan Hill residents were talking quite loudly during a tea break. One said to the other 'Hey! Did you see the state of old so-and-so's wife's knickers on the line on Sunday?' The other replied 'I have never seen anything like it!' We never did find out how the conversation would have ended because 'old so-and-so' was standing

*'Perm, Buckers, and Bomber' (Bill King, Eric Buckley, and Ron Harris)*

behind them and he was not amused. That story ran and ran throughout the Press much to the embarrassment of all the parties.

There were some amazing characters who worked in the Keyboards. One that sticks in my mind was the unofficial Press photographer, Geoff Elam. Developer and fixing fluid always stained his shirt and trousers showing just how much time he spent in the darkroom. He also had two other hobbies; one was Big Band Music (his collection of records and tapes of the Glenn Miller era was massive and they were often borrowed by radio stations for their Big Band programmes); the other gave hundreds of Press folk hours of illicit pleasure and goes to prove what an enigmatic and complex character he was. I am sure one day someone will tell his story but it will not be me.

By April working in the Keyboards was taking a terrible toll on my eyes and I was suffering splitting headaches. It was probably caused by the glare of the lights and the concentration required for 8 hours a day. I asked to be transferred back to the Reading Department but met with very stiff opposition from Bomber and John Hall. They both thought that I was swinging the lead to get back to my beloved Readers and insisted that I stayed where I was. John Hall suggested that I visit an 'ophthalmic practitioner'. I looked at him quizzically and he said 'Get your eyes tested my boy!' I took his advice and discovered that the problem was nothing more serious than the fact that I needed glasses. I arrived back in the department with my new 'Buddy Holly' heavy black spectacles and became the subject of much ridicule. There were cries of 'Wotto four-eyes' and 'Give us a song

Buddy'. I was used to this kind of thing and I knew that they would soon forget four-eyes and turn their attention to someone else.

I was annoyed that the management did not believe me when I said that something was wrong with my eyes and decided to make a serious and active attempt of getting out of the Keyboards and into the Reading Department.

I thought that if they did not believe me I might as well pretend that the eye trouble was getting worse (even though the glasses had done the trick) and so I slowed down my work rate to a crawl, often spending hours draped over the keyboard with my head in my hands. My ploy worked and in April 1964 I was transferred to the Reading Department. I had to suffer taunts from everyone that it was strange that someone who could not see to operate a keyboard could see to proofread a book. I kept my silence and settled down to finish off my apprenticeship in the Readers.

# CHAPTER TWO

# Craftsmen and Specialists

'the harvest is the end of the world; and the rea*d*ers are the angels.'
from Matt. xiii. 39

*J. W. Embury joined the Press in 1869 as a boy in the Proofreading Department, left in 1878, rejoined in 1884, and stayed until he retired in 1928. In 1919 he wrote of what life was like at the Press 50 years earlier.*

When I first knew the Clarendon Press it was under the management of Mr Thomas Combe, with whom were associated Mr E. P. Hall, who had the oversight of the Bible Side; Mr H. Latham, who supervised the Learned Side; and Mr E. B. Gardner, who was chiefly concerned with the Publishing Office in London. The names of these four gentlemen appeared in all imprints.

Mr Combe was a very fine-looking old man, with long white hair and beard, piercing dark eyes, and a striking face and head which, it was remarked (after his death), bore a remarkable resemblance to those given by Michelangelo to the patriarch Moses. In the Press, and frequently in his walks in the north of Oxford, he wore a jacket of bright red flannel; and he generally had two or three dogs with him. One of the dogs was somewhat fierce, and occasionally flew at people in the cloisters and the gateway. One day he 'went for the postman—with serious results—the man of letters had to have his garments sewn up by the portress in the Lodge before he could proceed on his rounds. The favourite dog was a gentle creature called 'Jessie'. When Mr Combe built St Barnabas Church he caused Jessie's head to be carved opposite his own: it may still be seen there, on the base of the easternmost pillar in the north aisle.

Mr Hall took a great interest in the social life of both boys and men. The former attended a night school, and on Sunday mornings they came to the school in the Press, whence they were marched to the service at St Paul's—in later years, at St Barnabas. They had a drum and fife band, and there was a brass band for the men. Sometimes there were concerts and theatricals in the schoolroom; now and then there would be a lecturer. On one occasion Mr Hall announced himself to lecture on 'The Dignity of Labour'; but the employees, thinking they knew enough about labour without trying to see the dignity of it, left him without an audience.

When the men had their annual Wayzgoose in London or at the seaside, the boys had theirs at Nuneham. Every boy was given sixpence on starting; then they marched with the band to Folly Bridge, where they boarded the house-boat. At

Nuneham there was a tremendous spread for dinner, with plenty of lemonade made in a tub. (I remember seeing Mr Hall stirring it with his walking-stick.) There were all sorts of games and diversions: some of the boys would bathe; others hid in the nut-bushes and shied at the unprotected bathers with crab-apples. Coming back, there were songs and recitations on the top of the boat; some of the bigger boys put on short clays—much to the annoyance of Mr Combe, who hated smoking and would order a lad to throw his pipe into the river, giving him a crack on the head if he refused.

I was one of the reading-boys: we did little reading, but had to look after the readers' rooms in the mornings—dusting, sweeping, lighting fires, carrying up coals, and beating carpets. The latter task was very popular in the autumn, and was carried out in the orchard north of the Press. We got well under the apple-trees and beat the carpets with long sticks: it sometimes happened that the carpets went upstairs heavier than when they came down. . . .

It was in the Reading Department that I met someone who was to become my friend and colleague for more than 34 years. Cyril Edward Andrew (Cannonball) Cox came to the Press as a compositor apprentice in 1950 and after doing the usual rounds ended his career in the Printing Division as Head Reader before transferring to the Publishing Division many years later. I did not know it then but our careers and social life were to be inextricably linked. I was to follow him every step of the way. As he moved on from post to post I filled the vacant chair behind him. He once said to me 'Would you jump in my bloody grave so fast?'

### MORNING

Below my little narrow cell
Lie misty roofs of Jericho—
Blue roofs—and hark! the sacring-bell,
Sweetly un-English in his knell,
Of Barney's; while the sun, still low,
Has not yet blessed the roofs that glow.
Anon he riseth, and his gleam
Turns the red brick to ruddy gold.
The dull slates burn to azure, dream
Beneath the morning; and the bold
Lines of the chimneys, cast aslant,
Keen-edged, lie on the roofs. The chant
Of birds is faintly heard. There are
Woods towards Wytham, and their song,
There, makes music all day long—
Beyond the roofs, where tall trees are . . .
But roofs grow paler, and the morn
Dies to us as soon as born.

Anon. 1930

*Jericho from the North Wing before St Barnabas Church School was built*

The Head Reader was a man called Harold Boyce. He was the bandmaster and an officer in the Oxford Salvation Army and would sometimes wear his uniform to work. Cyril Cox's box was next to Harold's office and it was accepted by most proofreaders that the person who occupied this box would be the next Head Reader. Cyril would always vehemently deny that this would be the case should Harold ever 'pop his clogs'. We were half right because Cyril did indeed become Head Reader but Harold did not have to make the supreme sacrifice. He retired on his due date and is at the time of writing living happily in Dry Sandford.

### C.P. RULES AND SPELLINGS, BUT . . .

The author's whims you mayn't rebuff,
Though he may languish in a rut,
Nor may you change his quoted stuff—
It's 'C.P. rules and spellings, but . . .'

The Go-on Form's as plain as day,
It puts the orders in a nut-
Shell for the reader to obey—
Those 'C.P. rules and spellings, but . . .'

He double-quotes, he likes 'mediaeval',
And 'ise' for 'ize' (proverbial slut);
He's up to every kind of evil
　With 'C.P. rules and spellings, but . . .'

He writes in blue and green and red,
His punctuation's all to phut—
The gilt is off the gingerbread,
　It's 'C.P. rules and spellings, but . . .'

He strews his manuscript with caps
That would disgrace a school-boy 'howler'.
One consolation, reader chaps—
The 'cleans' are 'foul', but are not Fowler.

S.G.: *The Clarendonian* (1938), viii. 6

A friendly man by the name of Pat Duffy was Harold Boyce's deputy. When rollockings for sub-standard work had to be dished out Harold would often get Pat to do the dirty deed. Pat was too nice and would stand in the doorway of the reader's box clutching the 'bloodstained' proofs (proofs that had been over-read by the boss using red ink) and after a nervous giggle would say 'Harold wants you to look at these' and would then scuttle off back to his office.

At first I thought that Pat was timid but it turned out that he was a shrewd and highly intelligent man with a strong character and that he was to teach me a lot. His general knowledge was second to none. Pat's memories are printed below and

*Cyril Cox*

*Pat Duffy reading the Bible 'first proof'*

I make no apology for the fact that some of the things he mentions appear elsewhere in this book because they give us another perspective. For example, did 'Robbie' Burn say 'Bugger Batey', 'Bloody Batey', or 'Blast Batey' as he clocked in each morning and afternoon? Major issues such as these may *never* be resolved!

I first came to the Press in 1943 and was interviewed by John Johnson, my indentures being countersigned by Bertie Gray. As I had been at grammar school I had a year knocked off my time, but in true Press fashion it was the final year and not the initial extremely low-paid one. In fact I often wonder how I survived that first year, since the pay was 31*s*. 6*d*. for a 48-hour (5½ day) week. [The wages for the 5 years of an apprenticeship in 1944 was 31*s*. 6*d*.; 36*s*. 6*d*; 44*s*. 0*d*.; 51*s*. 6*d*.; and 59*s*. 0*d*.. Holidays and absences for sickness were both unpaid.] As I had no relatives in Oxford I was in digs in Cowley at £1, and also paid 5 days canteen dinners at, I think, 9*d*. a day for apprentices, plus 1*d*. for TA subs. I used to do a double paper round for 5*s*. and joined the Civil Defence Messengers who paid 2*s*. 6*d*. per month for bike battery lights that gave a surplus as a battery only cost 8*d*.

My abiding first memory was in the Top Comps which would be full of singing each day by several talented members of the old Minstrel Group: Bert Williams, Art Drage, and Jack Webster in particular. Talking of Bert Williams reminds me that he had a large allotment near Headington where he grew considerable amounts of produce that he sold to the Market greengrocers. He told me that in the 1920s he had bought a Douglas motorcycle that was always breaking down, so in the end he was so fed up with it that he dug a hole and buried it under the lettuces! So if any-one wants a vintage bike they need a metal detector on the ground where he worked.

Dave 'Fishy' Faulkner was in charge and my first job was to set by hand an arti-cle for *JTS* (*Journal of Theological Studies*) whose editor at the time had an aversion for using mechanical setting. The amount of expertise in such a small group was awe-inspiring, from Art Drage's knowledge of Indian languages setting, Sid Cher-rill's mastery of music setting using tiny pieces to assemble all the notes and staves, etc., even though he was so small that he carried a box with him to stand on when he had to reach the upper cases, and Jack Webster's Hebrew, not forgetting the complex piecing together of the elements of Chinese (with the added complication of vertical assembly!).

By far the strongest impression however was created by the very pronounced presence of Sammy Best, the resident proof-puller, who kept pigs on his allotment on Port Meadow and came to work straight from there! He always dressed in rem-nants of his 1914 army uniform from the trenches including full puttees. Inciden-tally, before the Second World War the comps were on piecework and the Top Comps room was illuminated by gas jets over the frames. If the workers needed a better light they had to buy their own gas mantles from the Type Store at 1*d.* each!

I must not forget dear old Fred Matthews in the Exam Comps who would be set-ting corrections to French papers and call you to go to the Type Store as he was run-ning out of 'Gillymotts'. When I first was sent for odd bits of type I found that Bernard Gooding (Sam Coates's predecessor) also spoke a different French from my schooldays, as he did not understand what Bourgeois was until someone told me it was pronounced 'Beejoice' at OUP.

I eventually preferred reading and settled there contentedly for some years under the fair but very strict regime of 'Ting' Harrison, successor to the famous 'Ned' Gass. The room at the top of the North Wing always reminded me of a monastery, with the inhabitants living a very solitary existence in their small cells. Later I discovered what a motley collection had finished up there, including a refugee German lawyer, a maths professor, a Quaker missionary who was proficient in at least ninety languages, teachers from several public schools, not to mention a dip-somaniac, and a claustrophobic ex-vicar who spent his day kicking the wooden par-titions of his 'box'. One thing always struck me, the very few readers amongst the older generation who had a family, or more than one child, and this before Marie Stopes!

I have an abiding memory of Ronald 'Robbie' Burn, a Classical scholar, ex-priest, and the first person to complete the 'bagging' of all the then-known Munros of Scotland, not retiring from the Reading Department until past 80 years of age. To celebrate his 80th birthday he climbed, with a companion, up Snowdon, only to discover that both had thought the other was carrying the sandwiches! After the war he fell foul of the Printer and was made to clock in with us, unlike the specialist readers who were treated as staff, and the time-clock having been moved most unjustly to the reading room at the top of three flights of stairs. His arrival at the clock would invariably be accompanied by a loud 'Bugger Batey!'

With the war in progress John Johnson firmly believed that his precious Press would be bombed, so for years he never slept at home but would be seen in his dressing-gown collecting his paper from the Front Lodge as we came through the gate. He had an eagle eye for small matters, once calling Ken Pinder to his office when Ken had been twice late in a week for one minute. Ken returned suitably chastened after being told 'This won't do Mr Pinder, this won't do at all!' What 'Johnny' would have thought of the later allowance of a cumulative ten minutes a week lateness I tremble to think. Yet JJ was fair and compassionate. When Gilbert Williams, later resident Jobbing Ship reader, came for interview he arrived late owing to wartime train delays and JJ offered him a bed in the Firewatcher's room, and Gil was surprised to be woken in the morning by JJ with a jug of hot water and tea and toast.

A pre-war job applicant arrived without appointment and JJ said he had no vacancy, but afterwards asked the man where he had come from. On learning he had walked from Brighton he changed his mind and engaged him. A Cockney character, Bill Farthing, told of his acceptance. He appeared before JJ hiding a hastily stubbed-out fag and sat down. 'You're smoking, my man!' 'No I ain't sir.' 'But I can smell it.' 'Well, I've got me boots on but I ain't walking.' JJ was quite amused and engaged him for his cheek.

One section of the readers was devoted to checking daily codes for the Admiralty. Proofs were carefully counted and proofed on special paper with thin hairs embedded as also used for ration books. The corrected pages were collected each day by a small van and in 1944 a large increase in work involved printing six months codes, to change three times a day, for the invasion of Japan. Fortunately they were not required. It always amused me that 'Ting' would not let anyone pass the barrier into the code area but at lunchtime we all left the room open and the cleaners could walk down there with impunity.

After the war an ex-naval type who was plainly suffering from stress would appear above one's head crawling precariously along the narrow wooden top of the cubicles. Percy Stone returned having served in the secret service but never discussed matters. Much later we had two refugees from Hungarian universities following the Rising, one of whom commented when the room was redecorated for the first time probably since the building of the Press that he had only once seen the peculiar shade of green which was used—in a lunatic asylum! From when the Press was built all rooms had been painted in a dull cream and Oxford blue.

A period which caused much amusement in the 1960s was when John Hall (Personnel Manager) appointed a female assistant (Mrs Salmon) and the girls in the various works offices took to wearing the fashionable miniskirts. Mrs Salmon issued an order that no girl was to walk through the Mono wearing one of these, as it was 'detrimental to production'. How they were to get to the Mono Office with material was a mystery, though some wag suggested that the easiest solution was for the girls to take them off!

I remember many examples of 'management madness'. On one occasion in the Counting House (the Wages Department) when checking the quarterly Petty Cash account it was discovered that there was a discrepancy of *6d*. Two people were instructed to work a Saturday morning's overtime to sort it out!

Later one of the compositors became friendly with a lady. He was working overtime one evening in the Top Room and had an assignment with her in the convenient loft above the Type Store. Unfortunately, John Hall was intrigued by the ladder as he walked through the department and on climbing found them in a compromising situation. Next day the lady was dismissed, but the fellow was only stopped his overtime pay!

Then there used to be a scheme whereby for no accountable reason people were awarded *2s. 6d.* rises occasionally. Harold Robinson in the readers always seemed to miss out so at last he tackled John Hall. After a while John got back to him: 'You are quite right Mr Robinson. You were overlooked. I will award you the rise and I will see it doesn't happen again.' As Robbie said, it never happened again!

When Vic Sugden was editing the *Clarendonian* someone wrote to him suggesting it might be a good idea if the shop floor people should send in suggestions for improving efficiency, which if adopted and proved could be rewarded financially. Vic thought it a good idea until one of the senior management vetoed publication with 'We can't have those people telling us how to run the place!'

The proofreader would then, after a suitable time lapse, take the proofs back to Harold and try to explain why he or she had missed so many errors, the most popular excuses being, 'I had a headache that day', 'the type was too small', 'I kept getting interrupted', 'it was too cold in the department that day', etc. Harold would then look up from his desk, shake his head (in total disbelief), and then let out a really big sigh. The interview was over.

I got fed up with these regular visits and decided that the best form of defence was attack. On one occasion when I was being shown a bloodstained proof I said to Harold, 'It is obvious that I am no good as a proofreader. I want you to transfer me back to the Comp Room.' He capitulated immediately and replied 'Oh no Michael, we cannot let you go, you are much too valuable.'

Apprentices attending day-release training at the Oxford College of Technology in Headington were often a tadge wild once they were free from the clutches of their bosses. The apprentices from OUP were not so lucky because the English Teacher was Harold Boyce. We would sit quietly getting on with our work while the apprentices from other firms in the city, who did not know of Harold's elevated position at OUP, would run amok. He was unable to control them and his life had become a misery. He took me to one side after a particularly riotous session and begged me for my help. Although no firm promises were made as to my future prospects a nod was as good as a wink to a blind man! I brought all my leadership skills to the table and convinced the mob to call off the dogs of war. After my little chat they behaved like little lambs. I had cracked it and I thought that I would never have any more problems with him. This was a major miscalculation on my part.

*The Bindery's Richard Brain is 'banged out'*

I officially ended my apprenticeship in the Reading Department on 10 May 1964, 5½ years after starting work at the Press. I was now a journeyman and had to make the trip to the Printer's office, which later became the Library Conference Room, to collect my indentures from the Printer to the University, Vivian Ridler.

It was customary for all apprentices to be 'banged out' as they made the trip to and from the Printer's office. Sometimes they would be loaded into a trolley and paraded around the Press and into the Quad and sometimes they would be followed all the way with hordes of people carrying chases and banging them with metal side-sticks. This was a very noisy affair for compositors but it was worse for machine minders and bindery men who had to suffer the indignity of having ink or glue placed in unmentionable places. Printers in London and other parts of the country would sometimes strip the new journeyman of all his clothes and bind him up before parading him round the print shop.

On my appointed day I prepared myself for my trip by planning a route to and from the Printer's office that no one would expect so that I did not have to undergo a banging out. I thought I was being clever at the time but now regret it because I lost the chance to take part in a traditional ceremony that had taken place thousands of times before in every print shop in the world.

I made my way to the Printer's office using the back stairs and was met there by Vivian Ridler, John Hall, Ron Harris, and my dad! My father had been there when I signed my indentures and he was there again 5½ years later to see me collect them.

Vivian Ridler was without question the finest Printer in living memory. He really cared for his staff and all of the employees at the Press had deep respect for what he stood for and his unquestionable knowledge of the gentle art of printing.

When Vivian Ridler retired in 1978 my fellow editor of the *Clarendonian*, Harvie Willshire, wrote:

> Vivian Ridler was born in Cardiff in 1913, and shortly after his birth his parents moved to Bristol where he spent his youth. He was educated at the Bristol Grammar School and it was towards the end of his time there that he first became interested in printing. His curiosity was aroused when he noticed that the typefaces used in his schoolbooks differed in design, and this prompted a quest for more knowledge about the printing process. It was an extension of this interest that led him and a school friend to buy an Adana printing press and a small amount of type with which they produced letterheads and similar pieces in their spare time. Eventually they acquired better equipment and began to print small books under the imprint of the Perpetua Press. One book was chosen for exhibition among the fifty best books of 1935. The Printer still keeps this press going in his back garden.
>
> Now that his future was destined to lie with the printing industry he became apprenticed to what was then the firm of E. S. and A. Robinson (now part of the Dickinson Robinson Group). He used to cycle to work, and he says that one of his most vivid and pleasant memories of the daily ride was the delicious smell of hops from the brewery near Bristol Bridge and the equally delicious smell of tobacco from a factory further on, both accompanied by the groan of the trams which regularly pursued him along the road.
>
> It was during this time that he became involved with John Johnson, when the latter visited Bristol to lecture on jobbing printing. It was as a result of this meeting

*The Work Study Group*

that Johnson invited him in 1936 to help Charles Batey, then the Assistant Printer, at the University Press. Later he moved to London to establish the Bunhill Press for Theodore Besterman. During the war he served in the RAF, mainly with a mobile fighter squadron.

After the war, as one of his chief interests had always been the design of print, he was appointed the first tutor in typography at the Royal College of Art and typographer to Lund Humphries & Co. of Bradford. He was also elected a Fellow of the Society of Industrial Artists.

Vivian Ridler rejoined the University Press as Works Manager on 1 April 1948, becoming Assistant Printer a year later. He was appointed Printer in 1958. Over the years he has played an active part in the affairs of the Industry, both locally and nationally. He was a founder member of the Institute of Printing, examiner in typographic design for the City and Guilds of London Institute, and in 1968 became President of what was then the British Federation of Master Printers. He was awarded the C.B.E. in the New Year's Honours List two years later.

The Printer has been in office, an office that must rank among the highest in the world of print, for 20 years, during which he has seen many changes both to the industry in general and to Oxford University Press in particular. When asked what he thought were the most significant changes to have taken place during his time he picked out four that came immediately to his mind. First, the steady transition from letterpress to litho in what had been a predominantly letterpress house; second, the erection of the new buildings to provide a new litho department and to cope with the growing demands of the bindery; third, the alteration in the system of management by the introduction of a board of directors; and finally the bringing together of the publishing divisions alongside the printing division on the Walton Street site. The change he most regrets, although it was inevitable, was abandoning the collotype process in 1968.

---

*Jim Chatting explains the intricacies of the bonus scheme.*

After the Second World War in the late 1940s there was a great deal of catching up to do by way of printing and the amount of work available was in excess of the number of printers employed by the Press. The first Incentive scheme at the Press was in the Letterpress Machine Room *c.*1949 when in order to achieve greater productivity a scheme was devised in House based on the Make Readies and number of sheets run.

To establish values time studies were taken. The Job operation or process was first broken down into defined elements that could vary both in number and in time taken to perform them. Some complex jobs involving a large number of elements to complete one cycle could take several hours to study. Letterpress Make Readies on large Perfector machines was an example of this. Various elements of work were studied and these were studied by different studymen on a number of different operatives when this was possible. The expected possible range of work was covered for a particular department or section.

Analysed, charted, and graphed to give a pattern of element frequencies and time that was required for a particular element and with the addition of allowances for personal needs and contingencies the result was a Standard Minute (SM) value. These standard times were combined to give an overall value for an operation. In some departments (for instance in the Bindery) the three dimensions of a book had a bearing on the speed with which it was processed and so extensive SM tables were needed by the Assessing staff to credit the appropriate SM's for the work done. As far as possible for easier understanding the SM values were kept to as small a number as was consistent with the accuracy required.

Bonuses were calculated from the SM's earned, waiting time, if any, and the hours worked in a particular week including reconciling wrong clock card entries, missed entries, and missing daily work sheets, or dockets as they were known. Assessing work was carried out by a number of mostly female assessors, though some tradesmen were involved for a time.

The scheme got under way in October 1950 with the Composing Room Maths Ship, which was considered at that time to be the most difficult to assess, the first section to start. At Christmas 1950 the Mono Keyboards and Casters followed and over the next few months it was introduced progressively in the Composition area.

Originally there had been some quite strong resistance from the Machine Room and Bindery Chapels to the introduction of an Incentive Scheme but now they could see more money being earned to the Comps as a result of the productivity scheme the Machine Room asked for it to be extended to them. The Bindery also requested inclusion and this was done over a period of time. At a later stage the Litho was included and with the application of the Engineers in 1957 the scheme was completed.

Various updates and maintenance changes were made to this scheme and it continued until the new Printer David Stanford came on the scene in 1983. A radical new approach was made at this point. The original schemes had mainly been on an individual basis but a completely new scheme based on a departmental basis was formulated and this meant all the members of the department shared the same rate of bonus depending on the productivity of the whole over a period. This scheme when fully implemented took fewer people to run, when compared to the fifteen to twenty required in the first scheme due to the very detailed assessing required in some departments. Of course the numbers in the Printing House had also considerably reduced from 1950 levels.

I married Rosamund on 19 September 1964 at Combe Methodist Chapel outside the walls of the Blenheim Estate. The week before the wedding my reading box had been decorated with flags and buntings and my colleagues in the department gave me a rousing send-off. After our honeymoon in Torquay I returned to the Press without a penny in the world. I had no money in the bank, no money in my pocket, but my wife had a five-pound note that was given to her by her Aunt. We knew then that there was only one way to go and that was up. I was going to

*Bonus supremo*
*Jim Chatting, JP*

work every hour that God sent me and I was going to hit the top limit on the bonus every week.

The bonus scheme at the Press was quite a complicated business. The maximum bonus one could earn was 50 per cent of one's basic wage. To obtain this one needed as much to master the use of a slide-rule as to work fast. This is where Cyril Cox came into his own. Maths at school that seemed so pointless in its *pure* state became incredibly easy under the guidance of Cyril Cox when it was *applied* to earnings.

Every operation: reading by copy; reading by eye; press reading; revising; reading foreign matter; reading maths; reading dictionaries; all had a value. This value was time. You had a certain time to do a certain operation. If you were given, say, 20 minutes to read a page of a dictionary and you managed to read it in 15 minutes then you would have 'saved' 5 minutes. These were called 'saved minutes' or 'SMs'. Every saved minute was paid for at half the going hourly union rate for a proofreader up to a maximum of half your weekly rate. If you tried to earn more than you were allowed your bonus would be 'stabilized' or capped as we would say now.

Cyril's slide-rule technique ensured that as soon as the stabilizer had kicked in and you could see that you could not earn any more money you would stop work. It was quite common for proofreaders to stop work on a Thursday for fear of having to 'give the firm some money'. The readers' 'values' were very loose, much to the annoyance of the compositors, machine minders, and binders whose values were much tighter.

This ridiculous situation left plenty of time for fun and games every time the Head Reader and his deputy left the room. The most popular games were scrabble, hangman, general knowledge quizzes, horseracing, and cricket.

Scrabble and hangman were played on a league basis and readers would visit each other's boxes on a home-and-away basis. Invariably there were disputes over whether a word existed or not and visiting players would stomp back to their own boxes muttering curses about their opponents. After one game of Scrabble I did not speak to one of my best friends, Harvie Willshire, for 3 months over a dispute as to whether 'pi' could be used. He said that Greek letters were foreign and not allowed under the 'no foreign words' rule whereas I claimed it as a mathematical symbol. Cyril 'U Thant' Cox stepped in eventually and banged the children's heads together!

Falling out with Harvie was a silly thing to do because he was one of the fastest proofreaders in the department. He would always finish his work way before everyone else and would become bored. He would walk round the department reading through everyone else's proofs using a blue pen to avoid the dreaded bloodstained proofs from 'The Duff'. When the proofreaders were working on dictionaries or the thousands of names in the *Oxford University Residents' List* we all relied on Harvie to check the alphabetical order for us. He did this with consummate ease and great accuracy and his kindness meant that everyone was able to stop work early and have some fun!

Examination papers for Oxford and Cambridge Entrance, Oxford Local, Liverpool, Welsh, Malayan, West African, etc. had been typeset, proofread, printed, and bound at OUP for many years and there was only ever one breach of security at Oxford. The culprit, who was later dismissed, simply stole one paper and gave it to his son who was about to sit his O-Levels. His son could not have been very bright because he passed it round amongst his chums and even showed his teacher! The OUP had the responsibility of working on secret codes for the Ministry of Defence during the Second World War so by tradition we were good at keeping secrets.

For the proofreaders at the Press, the reading of the examination papers meant high wages. There was a lot of white space in an examination paper and when the work-study people asked for sample pages to measure we always ensured that only the solidly set ones were given to them. Many examination pages had vast amounts of spaces and dot-leaders. We were paid as if they were full pages.

The Head Reader or his deputy would often bring round heaps of examination papers for proofreading. The first thing we would do was to sort them out into levels of 'fatness'. If there were only a few lines on every page or lots of foreign matter we would keep them. If they contained solid pages of English we would wait until the coast was clear and then drop them back into the boss's out-tray in the hope that someone else would do them! This would often backfire on us and we ended up doing the difficult work all in one go without the luxury of having any 'fat' to set it against. The foreign papers were good because all we needed to do was mark the foreign language with a red pen in the margin and get one of the specialist graduate readers to read it for us. Not only did we get paid for reading something that we did not have to do but we were also paid an extra allowance because it was 'foreign'. There were also extra allowances if the work was alphabetical, had footnotes, contained maths, or the copy had any handwritten marks on it.

Horseracing was very popular on Saturday afternoons while we were working overtime and being paid at double-time rates! We would place our bets with the bookie's runner in the Jobbing Department and then take our portable radio set out to the Top Composing Room so that we did not disturb our proofreading colleagues who still had to work on a Saturday.

On one such occasion on a Saturday afternoon Cyril Cox and I had each chosen a horse that happened to be in the same race so we decided to hedge our bets and share any winnings between us. We took the portable radio out to the deserted Top Comps, placed it on the baulk, and turned it up to its maximum volume. It was a steeplechase and both of our horses were coming towards the last obstacle neck and neck. We both took up our riding positions and with imaginary whips galloped round the stones with screams of 'go on my son' and 'get over it you bastard'. As the two passed the winning post first and second at 10–1 and 5–1 we started a lap of honour round the department only to draw up our horses suddenly as we came face-to-face with the Head Reader who had been standing in the doorway and had witnessed the entire race. Harold looked at us both long and hard, sighed, shook his head, and walked away.

There were certain jobs that came round every year such as the *Residents' List* mentioned above, *Oxford University Calendar*, *Crockford's Clerical Directory*, etc. and this always meant lots of overtime for the Reading Department. At these times Harold would come round with the overtime list and would stand in the doorway of your box and say 'morning, noon, and night'. This was his code to let us know that overtime was available for Saturday morning, Saturday afternoon, all day Sunday, and two hours on Monday night.

It was on one of these Sundays that the readers decided to hold a cricket match in the department. All the boxes in the centre of the room had been demolished and this left a wonderful open space. At 12 noon a set of stumps were chalked on the wall of Harold's office and the pitch was paced out. The bat was a piece of wood taken from an old packing case and the ball a tightly rolled-up bundle of paper. All the readers took up their positions in the 'field'. I was fielding in the slips and Cyril Cox was at mid-on as Allan Aslett marched to the crease. The bowler was William Walter Westwood Hardacre, a Yorkshireman, whose slow off-breaks were legendary. Wally came into bowl and Aslett stepped forward and whacked the ball straight over the bowler's arm to be caught by . . . Harold Boyce standing in the doorway wearing the full braided uniform of a Salvation Army bandmaster. We were *all* copped and with much shame and embarrassment we quietly slunk back to our boxes on the boundary. Harold let out his customary sigh and with a shake of his head turned and walked out. There were no comebacks because, I suppose, if he was going to sack anyone he would have had to sack the whole 'team'.

> *In answer to a query by a Press Reader regarding the insertion of a hyphen, the author, who perhaps felt that the Reader's initiative should have been used, wrote:*
>
> **'Please do what your rule book, rule-book, or rulebook says.'**

There were some strange people that worked in the Reading Department and there was none more weird than Ronald 'Robbie' Burn. His story makes rather unpleasant reading and so I would implore any readers with a weak constitution to turn over the page now. He was employed as a graduate reader in the Reading Department, specializing in Latin and Greek. He was a small angry grey-haired bearded man who unfortunately had a deformed back and dressed like a tramp. He was angry because he had been pulled up for always being late for work. He was made to 'clock in' like all the craftsmen proofreaders by Charles Batey, the then Printer to the University. Specialist proofreaders were treated differently from craftsmen proofreaders who had served an apprenticeship. They were paid a monthly flat rate according to the Burnham Scale for teachers and they did not have to clock in. Craftsmen proofreaders were only paid half the amount as a weekly flat rate and had to earn the other half on the OUP's incentive bonus scheme and they had to clock in. They would, of course lose money every time they were a few minutes' late.

Robbie would turn up every morning (often late), ram his clocking-in card into the machine and spit out the daily curse, 'BLAST BATEY'. The card would never be put back into its slot but thrown on to the floor in disgust. He would then make his way to his double box at the far end of the Reading Department. He always wore filthy smelly clothes and climbing boots. At weekends there would be tied around his body everything except the kitchen sink. There was a kettle, saucepans, a primus stove, a knapsack, and climbing ropes. His journey through the department sounded as if a one-man band had visited it! We understood that he liked walking and mountain climbing but it was to be many years later that I discovered the real story behind this remarkable man (see Pat Duffy's (above) and Leofranc Holford-Strevens's recollections below).

His box contained literally thousands of scholarly books all covered in dust and the conditions inside his 'office' were disgraceful. He had some disgusting habits which included the saving of his own sputum which he kept in sealed jars on the window sill and urinating in milk-bottles and keeping them under his desk because he was too lazy to walk down the stairs to the toilet. At lunchtime he would leave the Press at about 12.15 p.m., cross the road, sit on the wooden bench next to the number 3 bus stop, and wait for the Lucys Iron Foundry Boys from Walton Well Road to walk by on their lunch break. Robbie had worked it out that as the Lucys Boys were eating their packed lunches and fruit on their way to the city centre they would toss the apple cores and crusts into the bin hanging on the bus stop post. As soon as they had gone past Robbie would dive into the waste bin and would then settle back down on the bench to enjoy his *al fresco* lunch!

---

A well-known music critic is noted for his witty replies to queries made by the proofreader. In one of his books he was discussing the *Midsummer Night's Dream* music of Mendelssohn, and said that in the music one could almost hear Bottom's 'Hee-Haw!' The reader queried a lower-case 'h' for the 'Haw!' When the proof came back, written in the margin was: 'Dear Reader, You probably know the language better than I do.'

---

The Reading Department was made up of half craftsmen readers and half specialist readers. We worked in almost perfect harmony: the craftsmen passed on their technical printing knowledge to the specialists and explained what could and could not be done with type; and the specialists passed on their academic knowledge of language, grammar, etc. There were also some 'dilutees' employed: these were people drafted in from the dole queue. The management thought that because they could not find craftsmen readers any more they would take people from off the street, train them up, and in a couple of weeks they would be proofreaders. The plan failed and the part-time drummer, the clerk, and the candle-stick-maker all found their way back to the dole queue. The only exception was John Harvey. Although not the best proofreader in the world he was certainly the most entertaining. His monologues were legend: the best being his Field-Marshall Montgomery and Adolph Hitler.

There were many specialists in the Reading Department and some stick in my memory more than others. Other than Robbie Burn mentioned above there was Mr Czarlinsky who read the Slavonic languages. He had been some sort of cultural attaché at one of the embassies and would not suffer the noise and disruption caused by the younger proofreaders in the department and was often heard cursing in his native tongue. I could never understand what he was saying but I don't think he was too keen on me.

James Fettes looked and acted like an undertaker. He always appeared solemn and the other readers would make jokes behind his back claiming that he was really a vampire and did not sleep in a bed but would hang from the rafters. He was tall and thin and had a very pointed nose and he always appeared to have a sneer on his face. He wore a black overcoat and a scarf throughout the year: even on the hottest days of the summer; the scarf never left his neck. I later got to know him properly and found him to be one of the most intelligent, kind, and witty men that I have ever met.

Fanny Williams read most of the French texts. She was a formidable woman who spoke with a 'posh' accent had a decibel level that would now be considered a health and safety hazard. If we had a query concerning French we had to visit Miss Williams to be greeted by a loud 'What do you want young man?' We would whisper our queries for fear of anyone else in the department knowing how crass our question probably was. 'Speak up', said the wicked old woman, 'I can't hear you!' We then had to shout out our query so that everyone in the room would be aware of our 'stupidity'. She would then proceed to broadcast the answer to everyone while the poor soul nearest to the epicentre had to endure the embarrassment and then be subject to much ridicule from his chums.

How glad we were when the Press employed two more young ladies: one to read French and German, the other to read French and Arabic. One was Genevieve Hawkins: the other Jillian Atherley. I remember being so relieved as I took my first French query to Genevieve to discover that although she too had a

*Genevieve Hawkins was Editor of the*
OU Gazette *from 1977*

'posh' voice she greeted me with a warm smile and answered my query allowing me to walk away with dignity. I later discovered that she was terrified of me because of my reputation as a wide-boy and that her warm smile was probably fear! She became one of my best friends at the Press and we have shared a very special relationship ever since. Jillian later married fellow proofreader Colin Baldwin. It was the first time in living memory that proofreaders from the same department had got married

Miss Mary Grosvenor was a specialist reader in Hebrew, Chinese, Italian, and French but would also help out the Classicists when they were busy. She seemed to have spent most of her time at the Press working on the *Patristic Greek Lexicon* as a writer of many of the articles, reviser, editorial assistant, and proofreader. She will be remembered not only for her work on the great book but also her friendly and helpful manner towards the non-academic craftsmen readers and compositors. As James Fettes said when Miss Grosvenor retired, 'her tact which puts you at your ease when you feel that your query must be elementary to the expert is a rare enough quality, and this was not lost on compositors . . . she was not designated as one of those "queer readers"'!

A great character was Archibald 'Alf' Buck (or Bucky as he became affectionately known). He had been a classics teacher at a public school and was a wizard at cricket keeping wicket well into his 60s. When he retired from the teaching profession he joined the Press. He was a cantankerous old man and would not suffer

*Dr Naish—
a gentleman
and a scholar*

fools gladly. If he made a correction on a proof he expected the compositor to get it right first time. If they failed in their duty he would scream out at the top of his voice such things as 'you dozy bastard', 'you bloody cretin', 'use your fucking eyes!', etc. Had anyone else used this sort of profanity they would probably have been sacked but when Bucky swore with his beautiful public school plum voice it sounded almost like poetry. Harold Boyce would always ignore Bucky's outbursts as if they never happened.

When Mr Buck died an enormous crowd turned up at the Crematorium to see him off. It was announced that Bucky had set aside enough money in his will for everyone who attended the funeral service to have a drink on him. The designated pub was in Forest Hill and immediately after the service Cyril Cox and myself hitched a lift in Commercial Director Richard Russell's car to get to the pub before the rush.

Cyril made his way to the bar and ordered three pints of ale. The problem was that the man who was holding Bucky's beer money had not arrived and the barman knew nothing of the bequest. Cyril forked out for the three pints with his own hard-earned cash. Unaware of this personal financial tragedy for a poor OUP proofreader the highly paid Commercial Director held his pint in the direction of Heaven and cried 'CHEERS BUCKY!' Poor Cyril nearly choked on his.

Dr John Naish was a scholar and a gentleman. He, like Robbie Burn, was allowed to have a double box to work in. Dr Naish was a brilliant linguist in more than eighty languages in their printed form including many of the African dialects. He was said to have mastered one every 3 weeks! Oddly enough, he was an avid reader of the *Daily Mirror*! His reading box was covered from floor to ceiling with his priceless book collection and he would sit at his desk in a small area that was not covered. He was a man for whom time stood still. He, like all the specialists, and unlike all the craftsmen readers, was not on the bonus scheme and did not have to worry about how much work he did during each day.

If I had a query regarding one of Dr Naish's languages I would run down to his box and knock on the door. 'Come in', would be the kindly reply.

'Ah, Dr Naish, could you just tell me . . .'

'Hello young man, how are you today?'

'I'm well, Dr Naish, thank you, but could you just tell me . . .'

'Do sit down, young man.'

'Thank you Dr Naish but I just wanted to know if this should be an asper or a lenis . . .'

'Do you know, many years ago when I was in India . . .'

It was at this point that you realized that the bonus scheme and money was not everything and you would just sit back for an hour or so and listen to this wonderful old man's stories of life in the Raj and other tales of mystery and adventure from all over the globe.

Leofranc Holford-Strevens came to the Press in August 1971; an event that no one who worked at the Press at the time will ever forget. He came as a specialist proofreader but the advance publicity had said that the man was so clever and knew so many foreign languages that they couldn't find a place for him within the University. When he arrived he was the epitome of an absent-minded professor. He was very dishevelled in his dress, wore a pork-pie hat at a jaunty angle, and somehow managed to read *The Times* while walking down the street and missing lampposts by inches. He talked very fast and at such a high intellectual level that none of us knew what he was talking about. He would tell us classical jokes and would be crying with laughter long before he got to the punchline. When he finally delivered it none of us could understand the joke but because of the joy it was obviously giving him, we would all fall about laughing as if we had understood. Later Leo was to meet a beautiful and brilliant American musicologist and

*Leofranc Holford-Strevens: unique*

the meeting of great minds led to marriage and they are living happily ever after!

Leo's memories are a fascinating insight as to how *they* saw *us*! As in Pat Duffy's memories (above) some things are repeated. This 'Bugger/Bloody/Blast Batey' issue will not go away!

On 2 August 1971 I joined the Printing Division of the Oxford University Press as a Graduate Reader, employed to read proofs in classical and foreign languages. The Head Reader was Harold Boyce, a stalwart of the Salvation Army band, on whom I left a lasting impression by explaining, when another reader raised a query no one else could solve, that men's and women's hockey was played to different rules. His deputy at that time was Pat Duffy, whose skills extended to running me up a badly needed set of bookshelves for my study at home; when he changed department his place was taken by Cyril Cox. There were other young graduates, most of whom came and went; not all, fortunately, like our Arabist, Richard Ball, a fellow member of the Chess Club, who having converted to Islam and renamed himself Rashid was murdered somewhere in Nigeria. (Through the Chess Club I met another murder victim, Wellington Tshazibane, a temporary employee of the Publisher who came to the rescue in a team match and whose name I saw a few years later on a monument to persons killed by the South African police.) There also were memorable older figures like A. W. Argyle, theologian and writer on New Testament Greek, Archibald Hector Buck, a former schoolmaster at Christ's Hospital, knowledgeable in Latin and Greek but even more so in cricket and rugby, who hated his Christian names and whose favourite word rhymed with his surname; Olgierd Czarlinski, a Polish diplomat before the war, our specialist in Russian and Italian, who had the good fortune to be in St Peter's Square when the election of a Polish pope was announced to the astonished Roman crowd.

Graduate readers enjoyed staff status, drawing a monthly salary rather than a weekly wage supplemented by a bonus; as staff, we were exempt from clocking in and out, though I was told of an older man who had so much abused that privilege as to lose it, ever afterwards muttering 'What a pity' as he fulfilled this servile ritual. On the other hand, as a result of agitation by a radicalized graduate who had already departed, we were required to be members of the National Graphical Association, then a powerful force in printing but far less interested in its book trade members (let alone graduates) than in newspaper workers, particularly those in Fleet Street, whose wages (deliberately inflated by the likes of Beaverbrook in order to impoverish the competition) gave the public a false impression that printers elsewhere were rolling in money. One year, indeed, the union accepted the overall increase offered by the British Federation of Master Printers, but insisted on a redistribution far less favourable to the book trade than the employers' offer, 3 per cent instead of 7 per cent.

Like other readers, we worked in the early 1970s on the second floor, clambering up fifty-nine stairs to reach it; behind us were the skilled compositors who did the really difficult work beyond the capacity of the Monotype Keyboards downstairs; they were known as the Top Comps, not only because they worked on the top floor. They were true craftsmen, who through years of experience could set exotic languages without knowing them; it was no more than a wandering legend that had one of them recognize an error in Urdu copy because he had to make an abnormal hand-movement between cases, but although I knew Russian and the Father of the Chapel, who regularly set it, did not, he put me to shame by his ability to read it in handwriting, which I knew only in its textbook form. At the far end of their shop was a lift, intended for formes and other heavy objects, with a notice 'Authorized personnel only'. Once I asked a comp who counted as authorized personnel; he replied 'You work here, don't you?'

Being on the top floor, we readers took no part in the disgraceful scenes on Christmas Eve of my first year. In those days, work continued till 5 p.m. on 24 December; but certain of the Bindery girls, after a good lunch-hour's drinking, reportedly made themselves available to the lads downstairs, who were not too sozzled to queue up for their turn. Absences in the Bindery the following September were abnormally high. After that, the entire Printing House was given the afternoon of Christmas Eve off. This was in addition to the closed week already in force between Christmas and the New Year; one year the Comps' and Readers' Chapel protested, asking for three extra days of holiday instead, but the management, which claimed that it needed the time for maintenance, was supported in its refusal by the Society of Graphical and Allied Trades, which represented the Bindery. In other words, the Comps and Readers, who were mostly men, found two days of family togetherness quite enough, thank you, but the women of the Bindery were happy to have husbands and handymen about the house.

When in the mid-1970s the Publishing Division was moved from London to join the small Clarendon Press operation, it gradually took over the top floor, which was converted into a corridor of offices promptly called Death Row. A lift was installed, albeit second-hand and prone to breakdown, in order to save the publishers' tender legs; it is still there today. The printing workers were moved to other parts of the building, and repeatedly moved, partly as the Publisher expanded, partly so it seemed at managerial whim, as walls were put up and knocked down as if the Works Director, when he was a little boy, had been refused the building set he had so badly wanted.

The Press had, as it still has, its own shop, which in those days to judge by its opening hours was curiously uninterested in selling books; perhaps that is why it was unofficially known as the Depot, having been that in the nineteenth century. There was also a social club, the Clarendon Press Institute ('the Stute'), now the Institute for Chinese Studies, and a Press Fire Brigade, run with mighty eagerness by the Commercial Director, who organized regular drills. Printers and publishers alike, we would get up, put on our coats, and troop out to the assembly point; on one occasion the shopkeeper in front of whose premises we had gathered took the impromptu crowd for a student protest and demanded it go somewhere else. Meanwhile the fire brigade was scurrying over the building in search of a red lamp representing the fire; once the Publisher's tea-lady pooped the party by telling them it was in her cupboard.

When I joined the Press, the Printer made the money and the Publisher lost it; but things were about to change. The Printing House could always be relied on for a first-class job when the work was difficult and complicated, but for work of a less challenging nature it began to prove too expensive. In 1972 the then Printer, Vivian Ridler, whose heart was so much in fine printing that he had turned away more mundane journals, summoned a meeting to assure us that the future was secure; Stella Brewster, a senior graduate reader, caused a sensation by telling him to his face that he did not know what was going on, but unfortunately did not deign to enlighten him herself. Nor indeed did even she know that the days of the large printing factory paying union rates on a prime commercial site would soon be brought to an end by computers in front rooms.

For a time, the Printer expected rich rewards from Africa, above all Nigeria, for which we turned out schoolbooks; 'a great market', he said. 'What the kids don't tear the termites eat.' Indeed, the Nigerian leader, General Gowon, was very willing to do business with Great Britain, which had stood by his country during the Biafran War; unfortunately, willingness to order was not matched by willingness to pay either OUP or anyone else. (At one point two years' worth of imports were waiting in container ships off Lagos harbour for bills to be settled.) We also set examination papers for African countries, not because they lacked the skills, but because they could not trust their own printers not to sell the questions in the market. (In one firm, it was said, workers had been required to take off their clothes at one end of a corridor and put on overalls at the other, reversing the process when they left; unable to smuggle out a paper, they simply memorized one question each.) So desperate were children and their parents for this knowledge that on one occasion the padlock on a crate of examination papers bound for Ghana was tampered with on board ship; at Accra, when the ship was being unloaded, it was naturally that crate which fell from the crane. Papers all over everywhere, a bonanza new order for Oxford. The Press seemed unwilling to believe that these orders would come to an end when political leaders decided that such dependence on the former colonial power was a national disgrace. While they lasted, however, they were an opportunity for the Top Comps to display their skills in setting unusual characters, and for the Commercial Director to visit Africa in the manner of a great lord. In sad contrast to the papers from other African states, those from Uganda, badly presented and full of elementary errors, showed how low the country had sunk under its dictators. (When I joined, we also set papers for Malaysia; but once Malaysia and Indonesia had agreed on a common spelling for their language, we lost the contract to the Dutch. Perhaps we should have taken this for a warning that not even former colonies owed us a living.)

In 1978, five hundred years after the first book was printed in Oxford by Theodoric Rood (who misprinted the date as 1468), both Publisher and Printer celebrated just as much as if it had had anything to do with them. The Publisher threw a party in the Quad, at which according to the programme a singularly uninspired song was sung in honour of Herr Rood; the Printer gave his employees a wayzgoose consisting in a trip to Alton Towers, and had them all photographed for a commemorative booklet. Meanwhile, the national economy was entering crisis mode: an apparently generous wage settlement in 1979 was devalued by the inflation it was meant to counter. The next year, power in the BFMP passed to hardliners determined not to concede such a rise again; the NGA was happy to respond by calling the strike it was determined to hold before the coming unemployment weakened its position. Bemused pickets stood outside the Press building, though they had no quarrel with the management; a passing militant from Ruskin, misreading the situation, delivered an unsolicited lecture in a Glaswegian accent on the need for the 'waurkan class' to do something or other and went off, leaving one astonished apprentice saying to another: 'He must be some sort of socialist.' After a fortnight the counter-militants at the Master Printers, whose zeal had exceeded their intelligence, admitted defeat; the strike went on for another week before the union found the grace to accept their surrender.

None of this can have helped the Printer in the recession of 1981, though at first it was the Publisher who was harder hit, surviving only through the profits of the branches; soon afterwards it was the Printer's turn to suffer compulsory redundancies. It was clear that the writing was on the wall, if not for the Printing House as a whole (which in fact it was), at least for graduate readers, whom the union would regard as taking the bread from its real members' mouths; when, early in 1984, a vacancy arose in the Publishing Division, I applied for it and got it, thus escaping the total cull of graduates in 1986.

Compositors said that you had to be weird to be a proofreader spending your whole life cooped up in a little box. 'Germs' was no exception. He was a graduate reader who was terrified of catching germs off anyone or anything. He would never visit anyone who had a cold and would open doors only after ensuring that he had his hand covered with tissue paper.

Craftsman reader Ron Evans spent a lot of his days plotting how he could get rich by doing the football pools. Head Reader Harold Boyce got fed up with noticing that every time he passed Ron's box Ron appeared to be staring at his football coupon. He crept up on the unsuspecting victim and said, 'I want to talk to you about the football pools, Ron.' Ron replied, 'Yes I know, Harold; bloody hard luck about Blackpool beating Burnley one nil!'

One reader would borrow money from everyone in the department and always pay them back on Friday. The following Monday he would start borrowing again. No one could understand his financial strategy until we all realized he was putting his wages in the building society to gain interest and was living off our money. Another reader would spend every minute of his lunch hour in St Giles' in the hope of catching a glimpse of some female student's stocking tops. Harold Robinson was so fat that he only just fitted into his reading box. He always appeared to be asleep and when challenged would shout the standard readers' reply, 'I am not asleep, I am just resting my eyes!'

The only fight ever recorded in the Reading Department was one between an enormous Irish ex-policeman and a tiny disabled Geordie. They were scuffling together in the Geordie's one metre by one metre box in a dispute over whether or not to have the window open when the Salvation Army Head Reader was sent for to sort it out. Unfortunately, he said that he was 'too busy to attend to fighting proofreaders'! He probably thought that it was a fair match anyway but left it to Cyril Cox to separate the warring factions.

Frankie Bolton's main job was to press read the Hebdomadal Council Papers that OUP produced for the University. They had to be read by a first-proof reader and then Frankie would check them marking his corrections in red so that the boss could see how many mistakes the first-proof reader had made. He was a tiny man with thin features and spectacles that just about managed to stay perched on the end of his nose.

He was a very fast reader and we could hardly keep up with him (the first proof operation taking much longer than the press reading by eye). When he had caught up Frankie would visit the first-proof reader and ask if he could take some unread proofs away. I would say that he could not have them because his red marks would look as if I had missed them. He promised me that that would not happen and that he would write the corrections in blue so that it looked as if I had marked them. I agreed to allow him to take my unread proofs back to his box. A few minutes later I heard him calling out to the Head Reader, 'Harold, What's this man doing here, he's missed hundreds of mistakes'. I was fuming but an hour later he came back to my box for some more unread proofs. I told him that I was not pre-

*Dinky Piper reading for 'Press'*

pared to allow him to take any more proofs away. He said that he was very sorry for what he had said to the boss and that it would never happen again. Like a fool I released another handful of unread proofs only to hear him do exactly the same again. I was being watched by all the other readers who were much amused at my embarrassment because the same thing happened to all proofreaders until they caught on to Frankie's foibles!

There was Cyril Don (Dinky) Piper, a Press Reader who was proud to work at OUP following a distinguished war record where he had been commissioned in the field. He was a dreadful snob and treated first-proof readers as if they were second-class citizens. I suppose we were really, because Press Readers were paid an extra half a crown per week. The test that Dinky had to pass was even simpler than my intelligence test had been.

> I was supposed to be good at spelling [at school] and it was arranged that I should present myself at the University Press to be interviewed as to my suitability for employment there. Unexpectedly I was ushered into the presence of the Controller, the famous and forthright Horace Hart. After looking me up and down he suddenly asked: 'There is a man mentioned in the Bible called Pharaoh, isn't there?' 'Yes, Sir, there is,' I replied. 'All right, then' he said, 'take this piece of paper and this pencil and write down his name. And I did—correctly! (Many a time during my career as

a press-reader I have come across the mis-spelling 'Pharoah', even in theological works.)

The result of the interview was that Mr Hart told me to report the following Monday morning to start work as a reading-boy in the Reading Department. And that is how I came to the Press on 9 March 1908. A reading-boy had to sit at a reader's elbow and read the copy (sometimes poor manuscript) to him, putting emphasis on capitalization, italics, and all punctuation, while the reader made the necessary corrections on his galley proof. Of course there were breaks in this procedure, as when the 'old' reader (they all seemed old to me in those days) dozed off for half an hour and I could slip away and find another boy to have a chat with. Reading-boys acted as messengers and errand boys for the department. One important job was to go round the composing rooms, calling at the hand-presses to collect the copy and first pull of proof for delivery to the Head Reader. . . . Of the twenty or so readers the majority were ex-compositors with records of careful craftsmanship, there being not more than half a dozen specialists in Greek and Latin, including a Frenchman, a Swiss, and a German—Herr Gustav Wolff—who always stood to attention when spoken to by any member of management; outside he carried a rolled umbrella at the trail, a habit acquired from carrying his rifle so in a Jaeger unit of the German army. Bibles were set by hand and read in a separate little department situated on the top floor of the south wing, and there were, of course, a couple of machine revisers tucked away in an odd corner of the machine room. The Head Reader of those days was 'a character'. His use of English was deplorable; for instance on catching a reader looking at a newspaper or otherwise not concentrating on his proof he would dig his elbow into the victim's ribs and say, 'Ullo, I've caught 'ee then, have I?', or 'What are you a-doing of?' He was a compulsive belcher and snuff-taker, and his waistcoat and 'dicky' (stiff shirt front) were covered with brown dust. He never carried a snuff-box himself, but when offered a pinch by a crony, and he had many, he would push his fat finger and thumb into the box and extract half the contents at one go.

Oriental press-reading was done by J. C. Pembrey, a self-taught scholar who towards the end of his days, when over 90, did work at his home in Walton Street. It was one of my jobs to carry proofs backwards and forwards from him, and I can see him now with his lovely smile and wearing a smoking-cap, opening his front door to me.

I have an amusing memory of a reader from the north of England who came to work at the Press. He had no knowledge of university procedure, and on being given some first-proof reading (a list of names for a college bursar's records) asked the Head Reader the name of the job. He was told quite correctly 'University Dues'. Imagine the amusement caused when his work schedule was handed in at the end of the week with one of the items reading: 'First proof, 3 slips, 14 hours, "University *Jews*"!'

After this first spell in the Reading Department, I was officially apprenticed for seven years to be trained as a compositor, and joined a companionship of other lads in one of the composing rooms, where we came under the supervision of a fully competent and strict middle-aged craftsman. Yes, he *was* strict, for if we made mistakes in composing—it was all done by hand in those days—or correcting, we were made to put it right while he stood over us and watched. No doubt this training stood us in good stead in later years, and I recall many of our most outstanding craftsmen, the majority of them no longer with us, who were trained in this hard but correct way.

Bert Pollard was a craftsman first-proof reader who was always friendly towards new people when they arrived. He had started work as a compositor in Jersey before the war and served in the RAF before joining the Press in 1946.

There were two pedantic readers who worked in neighbouring boxes and they were known as 'the box of matches'. Their names were Bryant and May (Bill Bryant a craftsman Press reader with an amazing eye for detail and Mr May a Jewish scholar who proofread all the Hebrew).

The doyen of all proofreaders was the legendary Arthur 'A–Z' Young. Arthur was a tiny man who would walk into his 'box' every morning and proofread non-stop all day at an amazing speed. He had started work as an apprentice reader and sat in the same chair for more than 60 years. At a time when 40 and 50 years' service was commonplace Arthur's 60 years earned him a reward from the management of . . . an armchair!

I was becoming disillusioned with my lot as a proofreader because of the eyestrain caused by up to ten hours a day scrutinizing galleys and pages of minute type sometimes as small as 6 point. The little box that I worked in had no natural light other than that that found its way to my desk from the skylight. I had no one to talk to and my nerves became very frayed and then my health started to deteriorate. My doctor prescribed medication to calm me down and things seemed to be getting worse every day. One day I confided to a colleague about my problems and he said that he too was on medication for a nervous disorder. I realized that I could not carry on like this or I would end up in an asylum. I started to look around the department and realized that they were all 'nutters' and that if I stayed there I too would become a nutter.

On the ground floor was a department that was known simply as 'Editorial'. Once a typescript had been checked for special sorts etc. by a member of the Type Store, it was sent to the Editorial Department for cast-off and copy-editing. The cast-off involved the counting the number of words in the typescript to determine how many pages the book would make. This information was vital for costing purposes. The other part of the job was to mark-up the copy for the typesetter.

When I arrived at the Press the Editorial was run by Esmond 'Essy' Fathers (sometimes 'Dad' Fathers!). He had joined OUP in 1912 but left to serve in the Oxford and Bucks. Light Infantry but he was badly wounded in Ypres in 1917. It was considered to be a 'Blighty wound' so he was returned to England for treat-

*Down to seven: the last picture taken in the Reading Department*

ment. He rejoined the Press as a proofreader in 1919 and studied French, Latin, and Greek at night-school. He moved to the Editorial where he was to head up that department and went on to train up a man who was to become a legend at OUP—Fred Stewart.

When Essy retired in 1963 Fred inscribed a prayerbook: 'To E.H.F. on retirement as a small token of my deep appreciation for thirty years' ever-ready advice and guidance'. Both 'Essy' Fathers and Fred Stewart leave behind a legacy of 'Oxford' style that people now can only dream of. It was said of both of these men that you 'ignored their advice at your peril'. 'Graves' and 'Turning' are words that now spring to mind!

I made an attempt to get out of the Readers and asked Fred Stewart, the Clicker of the Editorial Department, if I could work for him. He told me that he thought I was a wonderful chap with a great sense of humour. He was sure that I would be an editor one day but that he could not have me working with him because he would not be able to stand all my 'silly chatter'!

I was doomed. I started to become very noisy and disruptive in the department and often annoyed the people in the adjoining boxes who were trying to work.

In June 1967 the news broke that Harry Clifford had died. Harry was a rotund little man who had worked in the Machine Revise Office in the Letterpress Machine Room with Ken Pinder and the clicker, Steve Eddles. Ken Pinder had just left to work at Pergamon Press leaving Harry and Steve to cope with the heavy workload. Now with Harry's death the situation in the Machine Room had become very serious.

This was the chance that Harold Boyce was waiting for. He could now rid his department of Mr Noisy! He came into my box and said that owing to Harry's death he would like me to go and work in the Machine Revise Office. He said that Steve Eddles was 'not a young man' and that I would then be in charge when he retired. I asked him if I had a choice. He said that I had no choice and that I was going. I asked when he wanted me to go. He beckoned to an apprentice who had been waiting with a truck down the corridor and said, 'immediately! You go now and the apprentice will deliver your things within the hour.' He thought that he had had the last laugh and that I was history. Little did he (or I) know that one day I would return to the Reading Department and become Head Reader.

*The first female apprentice was Sophie Huelin*

# CHAPTER THREE

# Machine Room Fun

I ARRIVED in the Machine Revise in June 1967 carrying only a pen and reported to the Senior Machine Reviser, Steve Eddles, who went on to complete 51 years' service. Steve was a tiny man with a stiff leg. During the Second World War he had been wounded superficially in the left leg by shrapnel, was stretchered away, and put down in a 'safe' area. Unfortunately for Steve, while he was lying on the stretcher, he took a direct hit on the other leg. His leg was shattered and he was to remain disabled for the rest of his life.

The Machine Revise Department was a little office that jutted out into the Quad. It had once housed an engine that used to pump water from the pond to cool the letterpress printing machines. It was (and still is) the best office in the Press because of the view of the copper beech tree. Every day of the year brought a new colour scheme into view that was pleasing to the eye and which climaxed every autumn. Steve pointed to Harry's sloping desk and high chair that overlooked the tree. This was to be my home for the next few years.

Steve was a very complex man who was very kind and generous when mixing with his colleagues socially. It was quite a different matter when he was at work, particularly when things went wrong. If you made a mistake and Steve got wind of it he would make sure that everybody knew about it—including the boss! He was of the old school and found it hard to adjust to the new breed of apprentices that came to work at the Press. Shortly before he retired, three machine room apprentices came into the office for us to check their revises. 'Put them on the table, boys', said Steve. They threw the revises on to the table but they all fell on the floor. One of the three—Rupert 'Rhubarb' Evans—bent down and picked them up and handed them to Steve. 'Thank you, young man', said Steve. As the boys left the office Steve commented: 'Did you see that, Michael? The revises went on to the floor and the white boys did nothing, but it was the "savage" that picked them up!' When I told Rhubarb later his legs went to jelly and he collapsed with laughter.

As one of the first black apprentices at the Press he had to put up with a lot of racist jokes from some of his small-minded colleagues. It was not meant to be cruel and he took it in good part but it would not be tolerated by anyone today. Rupert was a fine cricketer and went on to play for Oxfordshire for many years.

Every day was spent checking revises. Before beginning to print from a forme of type the machine minder would pull one proof and fold it up into a signature. The proof would then be given to his assistant, who was known as the 'feeder', to take to the machine revise office. It was the machine reviser's job to check that the pages had been imposed correctly and that the type had not been damaged during transit from the Composing Room to the Machine Room.

The machine reviser's job carried a great deal of responsibility because he was the last person to check the proof before the printing began. It was his signature that was put on the proof to say that it was perfect. If the machine reviser found any errors or broken type known as 'batters' he would mark them on the proof. The machine compositor would then collect the proofs from the box outside the machine revise office, assess how much type he would need to correct the forme, collect the type from the composing room on the opposite side of the building, and then make the necessary corrections while the forme was still on the machine's bed.

In the time I worked in the Machine Room the compositor was a man called Jim Allen. He was a wiry character who ensured that there was always enough work for him to work overtime every night. He achieved this by hiding in the toilets most of the day and only coming out during the late afternoon to start correcting the type. There were lots of machines but they could only print when the revises had been checked and the type had been corrected. The rest of the time was 'waiting time'. It was not unusual for a machine minder to pull up proofs in the morning, send them to be revised, and spend the rest of the day waiting for Jim Allen to do the corrections. Jim would spend two hours overtime carrying out the corrections and the machine minder could not start printing until the next morning. All this waiting time was catastrophic to the machine minder and his feeder and they would lose money on the bonus scheme. The bonus scheme was very tight in the Machine Room and there would often be flare-ups that ended in ferocious arguments and worse.

The machine revisers on the other hand enjoyed a fabulous bonus scheme. I do not know who was responsible for working out the figures but to say that they were generous was an understatement. The moment I arrived at my new desk and saw what was expected of me I knew that I was in for some rich pickings. The years in the Machine Revise Department were to be the happiest of my life.

The first day in my new job went by very quickly. The only problem was that I had not done enough work to earn any bonus on the incentive bonus scheme. I mentioned this to Steve Eddles who said, 'Don't worry Michael just charge 64 pages of *OED* (the *Oxford English Dictionary*), that will be worth 6¾ hours to you'. I couldn't believe my luck and I charged the work that Steve had done. The same thing happened the next day so I started to get worried. I asked him to explain his generosity. I discovered that the machine revise values were so ridicu-

*Norman (Manny) Mansfield*

lously generous that there was not enough time in the day to charge all the work that he had being doing since Harry Clifford's death. He was worried that I would spill the beans and that his little secret would be rumbled. He need not have worried on my account.

Bonus values were worked out on the en content of a page of type. This calculation (though not strictly accurate) can be explained simply. Every page was measured to find out how many characters there were and this was known as the en content. The more ens there were on a page the longer we were given to check the page. Because the type on the *OED* was so small it resulted in thousands of ens on each page. The machine revisers were allowed 202 minutes to check 32 pages of type. This task would have been heavy going in the days of hot-metal type when every character was a separate piece of type and could easily fall out of the forme or get damaged. The reviser would have had to check every letter carefully with a fine toothcomb, but technology had begun to change and the plates were made from a single sheet of plastic. They were pliable, strong, and rarely would there be a chance of any character going missing.

The management had not realized how this change in technology affected the values and the 202-minute job would take less than 10 minutes! One would have to do only 30 minutes work a day to get the maximum bonus that was 50 per cent of the weekly wage. If the reviser did any more work then he would not be paid for it. This was the disincentive of an incentive bonus scheme. Why work any more than you had to? The money started to roll in because of this loophole in the bonus scheme. Both Steve and I had to work maximum overtime to try and use up the spare minutes that we were building up. The added joy came from the fact that the time spent on overtime was supplemented by even higher bonus because the top-limit bonus was based on overtime earnings as well.

*My heroes Ron Veal and Harry Thornton*

There was one worrying period, though, when the compositors and readers were called out on strike over a union recognition matter. The machine revisers too were made to go out on the strike that was to last just over a week. The Machine Room and Bindery continued working because they were not involved in the dispute. The Machine Room at that time was working double-day shift-work and this meant that the *Oxford English Dictionary* was being churned out for 16 hours each day.

When the strike was over and we returned to work there was a mountain of revises covering the office floor. The manager of the Machine Room, Norman Mansfield, entered the office and declared that every page had to be revised before he was prepared to let the sheets go into the Bindery for folding and binding.

Despite our protests he declared that the job must be done and that we should work every night, all day Saturday, and all day Sunday until the backlog had been cleared. The evening overtime was paid at time and a quarter rates, the first four hours on Saturdays were paid at time and a half, and the Saturday afternoons and the all-day Sundays were paid at double time. It was getting better and better and there was still the 50 per cent bonus to be added! I remember thinking that if this was Harold Boyce's idea of punishment for being disruptive, let the beating continue. I would keep my bonus slips in my drawer under lock and key. They showed that I had earned 'top-limit' bonus every single week since I came out of my apprenticeship except one. The reason for this one-week slippage was because I had been struck down with appendicitis one afternoon and rushed to the Radcliffe Infirmary for an emergency operation and I had not had time to fill in my daily worksheet or 'docket' as it was known. It was the information on the docket that was used to determine the level of bonus earnings. A week after the operation I was back at my desk earning the big money.

There was a great character working in the Letterpress Machine Room who was a barrack-room philosopher with a slant on life and stories that could bring anyone to their knees with uncontrollable laughter. I am not sure how the following stories will translate into cold English but suffice it to say that you really had to be there and listen to the man to appreciate the humour of which I will never see or hear again. It may help to know that although he never talked about it until a few days before he retired, he had a most unpleasant job to do while serving in the desert during the Second World War. This involved amongst other things walking behind the tanks and digging up the crushed remains of humanity that had been run over by the tank tracks. The things he had seen and done probably accounted for his hiding behind his special humour.

His job was a machine manager on a DPE Rotary letterpress machine and every day before starting work he would call his disciples together to meet at the end of his machine. There was a massive shiny table used for checking the printed sheets as they came of the end of the machine. He would place his incredibly large set of scissors on to the centre of the table and after ensuring that all of his colleagues were evenly spaced around would spin the perfectly balanced device. The object of this exercise was to, in his words, discover who was going to be the '**** of the day'. Sometimes the '****ometer' (the scissors) would spin for what seemed an eternity before coming to rest and pointing to the poor soul that had to carry the title for the rest of the day. This all brought about much raucous laughter from everyone present and the day started as it always did in the Letterpress Machine Room with much happiness. On Fridays it was '**** of the week' and on the last day of the month, '**** of the month'.

During a local government water and sewage dispute we were all told to make sure we boiled our drinking water. He arrived at the Press from the Abingdon Road as usual and on the second day of the strike declared that the 'turds were floating down the Thames under Folly Bridge like baby crocodiles'. Now that was poetry! As was his philosophy that if a young man scratches a line on the headboard every time he makes love to his wife during the first year of their marriage he will never live to strike them through!

His colleague on the next machine was rumoured to have been particularly well blessed. This had never been confirmed until one day they were side by side in the urinals. He looked over the dividing partition and made the statement that became legend in the Letterpress Machine Room: 'I'm buggered! With your length and my width we could rule the world!'

We became very clever at covering our tracks when things went wrong. If a job had been printed and contained serious errors the management would instigate an inquiry as to who was to blame. When a culprit was found the bonus he had earned when doing the job would be taken back from the following week's wages. For obvious reasons the workers were not keen on this system so as soon as a mistake had been discovered everyone involved in the 'crime' would pull together to ensure that no culprit would get caught. If it was a machine reviser's error then the proofs would all mysteriously disappear; no proofs, no proof! If the machine minder was at fault the story was the same. He might have left his mallet or his shooting stick on the bed of the machine and forgetting it was there start the machine only to batter large amounts of type. Machine revisers and Machine Room compositors would rally round by collecting new type and putting the matter right. The warehouse men, such as Stan Kitchen, Barry Barron, Maurice Legg, or Alan Manger, would supply extra paper from their secret store when minders had ruined some work or discovered that they had not printed enough copies. Feeders would clean up after other feeders when things went wrong with the inking of a machine or the ink had dried on hard. Everyone pulled together to ensure that no one lost out because they had made a human error.

There were many occasions in the Machine Revise Department when my mistakes could not be covered up. If I had missed a serious spelling error the already printed flat sheets would be stacked outside my office to remind me of the error. A team of feeders would be brought in to put the matter right. One would scratch out the offending letter/word with a sharp scalpel, a second would use an eraser to smooth out the scratching, while a third would stamp in the new letter/word using a piece of type and a broken piece of inked roller. It was a humiliating and sobering feeling to see the results of one's mistakes in such graphic terms every time one left one's office.

Sometimes the mistake would not be discovered until the book had been printed and bound and the entire stock would again be stacked in front of the Machine Revise office for more psychological punishment.

I did not always get caught out. There was one memorable occasion when we were printing the 'Red and Black Bible'. I discovered that I had missed a terrible error. The bible was being printed on one of the rotary presses and the print run was many thousands. The rotary machines used two sets of APR plastic plates; one for the black and one for the red. The words to be printed in red in the New Testament were the words actually spoken by Jesus. To achieve this the stereotyper had to rout out all the red words in one set and all the black words in the other set. There was a verse that should have read 'Jesus said "blah blah" and "blah blah"', but the stereotyper had routed out the 'and' in one plate and left it in the other. The result was that the verse read 'Jesus said blah blah and blah blah'. By failing to spot this early enough I had changed the whole meaning of the sentence and thought that I would be damned by theologians for ever.

If I had admitted my mistake the entire Bible would have had to be reprinted at a cost of thousands of pounds. I decided to keep my guilty secret and to this day nobody has ever noticed.

I had a lot of time on my hands in the Machine Revise Department because of the loose bonus scheme so I would run little raffles. I would walk round the department selling raffle tickets at 10 pence a time. I could buy sidewinder watches from a wholesaler for £1 each so I always included a few of these to give the raffle some 'class'. A typical list of prizes would be three sidewinders, four bars of cheap Swiss chocolate bars, and six packs of Wagon Wheels. The total value of the prizes was about £5 but I would sell about £10 of tickets each day. This was very lucrative and still they wanted more. I discovered that the most popular prizes after the sidewinders were the Wagon Wheels!

I decided to hold daily Wagon-Wheel-eating competitions in the Machine Revise office. The rules were that two (gullible) people would first buy half a dozen Wagon Wheels each from me and then they would be timed as to who could eat the most in 5 minutes. They were full of marshmallow and very difficult to eat without appearing to foam at the mouth, particularly when being eaten under race conditions. The results were hilarious and the person I appointed the winner would be given three free Wagon Wheels (I had carefully worked out the profit margins). I would then declare the winner as the Wagon Wheel Champion of the World. Minutes later I would be contacted by some other young lad who was keen to hold this title. I would sell him half-a-dozen Wagon Wheels and the whole process started again. This became so popular that I had to limit the competitions to four a day because they had become a spectator sport and I was frightened that Manny Mansfield would put a stop to it.

One day I had run four Wagon Wheel competitions and two raffles and the department was crying out for more. I had no more prizes to offer so I went to visit Ralph, one of the feeders, who ran a small shop at the end of the Machine Room selling mostly chocolate, condoms, washing up liquid, and disinfectant. I asked him if he had anything that I could raffle. He said that I could look in his locker and take anything that I fancied and that I would just need to give him the profits from the raffle. I went to his locker and selected the prizes. The raffle took place an hour later and all the prizes were distributed. Ralph appeared in my office and I thought that he had come to collect his share of the spoils. He was not a happy lad. I had raffled his best leather gloves and the winner would not part with them.

There was a golden rule that had been negotiated with the Letterpress Machine Room mangement by Gerry Fulton, the then Father of the Chapel (later House Father). It was agreed that members of the management would never enter the workers' toilets. This meant that anyone wanting to skive for a while could go to the toilets and not have to live in fear of being caught out by the boss or any of his foremen. If a member of the management team wanted someone to do a particular job and couldn't find him in the normal hidey-holes, they would walk to the toilets, open the door about two inches, and shout out the name of the person they were after.

Because of this guarantee of not being caught, the toilets were used for all sorts

*The Machine Room toilets were a no-go area for the management*

of activities. Smoking was, of course, the most popular pastime and it was not uncommon to see men taking their tea down to the toilets with them while they enjoyed a smoke. Then old chairs were taken in and a table quickly followed these. A pack of cards arrived and the famous Machine Room card schools were born. The most popular games were 'three-card-brag-nothing-floating', Chinese brag, and pontoon and many fortunes were won and lost on that makeshift table. Sometimes, when the stakes got very high and there were three players left in with no one willing to stack, the word would spread around the department and every-one would shut down their machines to come and watch.

When all the machines stopped working, the manager, understandably, got agitated and would send his foremen out to hunt for the missing staff. The fore-men knew where everyone was but there was Gerry Fulton's negotiated rule: 'no bosses in the bogs!'

There was a notice in all the OUP toilets that stated 'Conditions are now such that smoking is forbidden in these toilets.' It was some years later that I discovered that this was not just another 'No Smoking' notice. The words 'Conditions are now such . . .' were an insight into the lavatorial history of OUP. In the early days the Printing House did not allow smoking in the factory because of the fire risk due to inflammable paper, inks, and cleaning fluids but they did allow smoking in the toilets because they were of the chemical variety. The smell was so disgusting that it was making people sick and the cigarette and pipe smoke helped make conditions just about bearable.

When water toilets were finally installed the management considered that 'Conditions are now such . . .' was not necessary. Smoking at the Press was banned from that day and the ban (although totally ignored) continued until the closure of the Printing Division.

For many years Press workers were not allowed to have toilet rolls. The management and staff toilets had rolls of proper toilet paper but the workers had to use off-cuts of paper from the machine rooms. They measured 6 inches x 4 inches and were sometimes shiny. They were kept in little open-topped wooden boxes that hung inside the toilet doors. I do not need to highlight the problems experienced because of the management's little bit of inhumanity to the workers.

After much hard bargaining it was Gerry Fulton who made the breakthrough and the workers were allowed 'Izel' toilet paper (each sheet preprinted with the message 'supplied by the management—now wash your hands'). The management needed to keep the divide going and decreed that they and staff members' toilets were to be supplied with soft toilet paper. Gerry once told me as I was praising him for the many things he had achieved as the leader of the union that he would probably only be remembered for his services to the lavatorial needs of Press employees. I disagreed at the time, but in writing this I realize that this was the first thing that I thought of when thinking of his achievements.

When Steve Eddles retired I assumed that I would become Chief Machine Reviser. This was not to be. Head Reader Harold Boyce, had got wind of the fun that I was having in the Machine Room and sent another proofreader over to work with me. His name was Roger Nettlefold. Harold brought him over and made a big point of the fact that Roger would be Senior Machine Reviser and that I would remain Junior Machine Reviser. I was devastated for several reasons. First, the Senior Reviser got an extra five shillings a week, secondly, Roger did not have a clue what the job was about, and thirdly, Harold asked me to teach him how to do the job!

Luckily, Roger was an easy-going individual and was very embarrassed by his sudden rise to fame. He said that as far as he was concerned we would just work together as equals. Our years together were amazing and we had a lot fun. Much of which can never be told.

All the paper that was delivered to the Machine Room came on wooden pallets. The wood that was used to make them was of very high quality and often tongue-and-grooved. The paper stacks themselves were topped off with hardboard. Everyone who worked at the Press would take this 'scrap' wood home to build sheds, trailers, loft flooring, etc. Roger and I made it our business to be first in the queue if there was really good wood to be had. Stan the Storeman had a large crowbar that he lent us to pull out the nails before packing the wood up ready for transport home. Initially we would do the 'work' in the lunch-hour but as more and more high-quality pallets arrived we found that the demolition was taking large chunks out of the afternoon. I recall one very hot day the truckers arrived with about twenty pallets outside the office. Roger and I both removed our shirts and started work with the crowbar. We obviously lost track of time and the office door opened at 3 p.m. and in marched Manny, the Machine Room manager. There we were standing in the centre of the room stripped to the waist and covered in sweat surrounded by a mountain of wood, hardboard, nails, and sawdust. He stood for a moment in total disbelief and, looking over to the pile of revises that were waiting to be done, said, 'When you two have got time perhaps you could do a few revises.' That was it!

Steve Eddles, before he retired, had been an officer in the Press Division of the St John Ambulance Brigade and was also the First Aider for the Machine Room. I had always watched what he was doing and he would give me little jobs to do such as administering aspirins for headaches, removing splinters, and handing out plasters. The management did not bother to appoint another first-aider because I 'appeared to handling most emergency cases quite well'.

One afternoon I heard a lot of shouting nearby and wondered what all the fuss was about. I was soon to find out. The door burst open and in came Peter Kitchen, the feeder on the large Timpson rotary printing machine. He said that a builder had fallen through the roof narrowly missing the machine's open-topped gas oven which was used to dry the ink on the paper. Fearing the worst I grabbed the entire contents of the first aid box and ran round to the side of the machine. What I saw there horrified me. The builder had fallen from the scaffolding on the second floor of the South Wing, bounced onto the first-floor scaffolding, falling on and through the wired safety glass roof above the rotary machine, hit the side of the oven and fallen right on to the concrete floor by the side of the machine. (Had he fallen left he would have been cooked alive in the oven as there would have been no way of getting him out.)

I could see that the back of his head had been cracked open and blood was gushing from the wound. There were severe lacerations to his body, arms, and legs. I placed a double wad of lint over the wound and applied direct pressure to it just as I had been taught by Steve Eddles. The blood still kept on coming so I doubled the wad of lint and somehow managed to start bandaging his head. The man opened his eyes, started to raise his head and in a soft Irish brogue said, 'Don't worry about me, 'oil be all roight in a moment just as soon as oive had a cup of tea!' It was at this point that OUP's official nurse arrived. She had been told what had happened and had brought with her a roll of sticking plaster! Eventually, the ambulance arrived and my patient was taken away but not before I had been praised for my first-aid skills. Ironically, it was soon after this that I was told that I was no longer allowed to give first-aid as I was not qualified. Had that missive been applied a day or so earlier my Irish builder would probably be dead. He had a fractured skull, a dislocated collarbone, and severe lacerations to the body.

When Roger had a chance of a proofreading job nearer his home in Abingdon he left the Press. The management decided to wind-up the Machine Revise office in the Machine Room and I was to return to the main Reading Department that had, while I was away, moved on to the ground floor.

I was given a corner position in my new department and a hatch was cut through into the Fairway. The Machine Room feeders would get the revises to me by sliding them through the hatch on to my desk. When I had checked the revises I would place them back through the hatch where the feeder would collect them.

I realized what had happened. They had found a way of controlling me and I did not like it! I was cut off from my Machine Room mates. No more raffles or Wagon Wheel competitions, no more timber salvage. I could hardly take part in all those activities when back in the peace and academic calm of the Reading Department.

There was some good news though. The readers were no longer in little boxes but had nice desks with low screens around them. Also Head Reader Harold had diverted his attention to copy-editing and had all but allowed my buddy Cyril Cox to take over the running of the department as Assistant Head Reader. This meant that every time Cyril was out of the office or on holiday there was no one to answer the phone or give out work to the readers. Cyril decided that I should be the one to deputize for him in his absence.

When the time came for Harold Boyce to retire Cyril Cox was appointed Head Reader. All the proofreaders and editorial staff were pleased with this not unexpected promotion because Cyril's attitude towards the people who worked with him and for him was quite different from Harold's. Cyril had a wicked sense of humour and this brought out the best in people.

Everyone then wondered who would be appointed as Cyril's deputy when Cyril moved to the Filmset area. New technology had struck again and the hot metal, stereotype, and plastic plates were heading towards extinction. Filmsetting techniques required a different approach to copy-editing and proofreading and Cyril had been seconded to spearhead the next generation. I watched as Bomber Harris, Harold Boyce, and Cyril held their meeting in Cyril's glass-panelled office to choose the new deputy. They kept nodding in my direction and I was thrilled when I was sent for and told that I had got the job. Bomber said that it was my last chance and that I should 'behave'. Harold smiled at me and said, 'You'll be all right'. Cyril just gave me the thumbs up.

I knew that the days of commerce were over forever. The team was in place and the roller coaster of Cox and Belson at OUP set off on its fabulous journey. I was not going to blow it now.

The Reading Department was split in two under Cyril's overall control. Cyril ran the filmsetting proofreaders and I ran the hot-metal readers. We started off with about fifteen staff each. I was responsible for five graduates in Classics and Mathematics and ten craftsmen proofreaders. I remember sitting at my desk looking out at all I surveyed and thinking to myself, 'You ain't done bad for a secondary school kid with no qualifications.' I did not know it then but there were even better things to come.

As time went by and the new technology was fast replacing the old, Cyril started to transfer my readers to his department because that was where the bulk of the work was. After about a year the number of people that I was responsible for dwindled to two. It was obvious that it was time for us to amalgamate the two departments. We worked incredibly efficiently together and managed to have lots of fun for many years.

Filmsetting was not as successful as it could have been at the Press because the management always treated it as a toy rather than a tool. The technique was always treated as a research and development project. When the first filmsetter had been introduced to the Press it was placed, not close to the other typesetting machines, but in a tiny room at the back of the canteen under lock and key. Half a dozen people were chosen to experiment with the technology and everyone else was kept well away from the room.

As apprentices we had attended the Printing Technical College at Headington on a weekly basis. There they would teach us all about the new technology and the lecturers told the OUP apprentices that they were lucky to have the filmsetting machine at work because others could only read about it. What the lecturers did not know was that the management would not allow hot-metal apprentices anywhere near the new machines. I was keen to just get a glimpse of the new technology but I was caught before I could enter the door. I was turned back and told that if I ever tried to get into that room again I would be reported. This management policy of stopping apprentices from looking into the future was, in my opinion, the thin end of a wedge and a philosophy that would one day destroy what we had. Eventually, new apprentices who had no knowledge of hot metal were allowed in to the filmsetting area and their training began.

The OUP Printing Division was failing to make money and the typesetting costs were rising to extraordinarily high levels. The Publisher could get the work done outside the Press for much less so it was no surprise to anyone that the amount of work started to decline. The Publishers wanted to make a profit on their books and they could not do this when typesetting and printing at the Press was so expensive.

Publishing, too, had their problems. Because they were no longer using the Printing Division and their army of copy-editors and proofreaders, editors were desperately looking for freelance staff. The Publishing Division approached Cyril with a view to him leaving the Printing Division to set up a centralized copy-editing, proofreading, and indexing service. After lots of heart-searching Cyril made the leap from Printer to Publisher as Chief Desk Editor.

I was called into the office and offered the post of Head Reader. I accepted even though the job was no longer a 'staff' position and I was not technically one of the management team. I was disappointed at first until I realized that my average wage including my bonus was to be my new flat rate. This meant that I would be paid overtime rates on that new flat rate when I came in to supervise the Readers and Editors when they worked overtime. Things were looking up . . . or so I thought.

# Underground Commerce

IT WAS generally known that if you wanted to buy any article or purchase any service you could get it at the Press. There were retail shops, club books, betting shops, football pools, banking and other money-lending facilities, contraception services, pornographic lending libraries, watch and clock repairs, and much more all operating under cover sometimes with and sometimes without the knowledge of the management.

There was a shop in every major department where employees could purchase just about anything. Readily available on demand were tins of paint and paintbrushes, car tyres, gallon containers of disinfectant and washing-up liquid, watches and clocks, chocolate bars and crisps, orange juice and Coca Cola, condoms, sex toys, photograph albums, note-pads, garden ornaments, and spring-flowering bulbs. One could also order items of clothing such as shirts, coats, gloves, and shoes all for next-day delivery. All these items were not just brought in each day to order, they were nearly always held in stock in cupboards and lockers. One man had a full-blown walk-round supermarket in a lock-up cage in the cellar below the Letterpress Machine Room in the South Wing whereas other small-time operators would retail things such as watches, chocolate bars, and condoms from their drawers or lockers in the various departments around the Press. The items for sale throughout the Press were not stolen but were purchased cheaply from local wholesalers. Once a man tried to sell tins of paint around the departments but colleagues smelled a rat when they realized that the only colours that were available for purchase were dark blue and cream. Strangely, these were the colours that adorned every wall in the Press!

As an apprentice my first venture into sales was with two of my fellow apprentices, the Baron and the Black Dove. The Black Dove had heard that some allotments in North Oxford were being taken over for building. He said that on the allotment there were loads of corrugated tin sheets on the shed roofs and tons of rhubarb waiting to be removed for us to sell round the Press at a handsome profit.

The first job was to do some market research. The three of us went round every department asking if anyone wanted to buy any cheap corrugated tin for 1 shilling a sheet or some delicious rhubarb for sixpence a bunch. From more than 600 people canvassed we found two takers! They were 'Cap S Walker' from the Keyboard

Department (so called because his rotund shape when viewed from the side looked like the letter 'S') and Ernie Harvey from the Monotype Casters who said that they would take some of each. We told them that their order would be executed that evening.

The Baron had a Ford Transit motor caravan and he drove the Black Dove and me to the North Oxford Allotments. It was very dark autumn evening and it was raining when we arrived at the site. After stumbling through the long wet grass in the dark to find the rhubarb and the corrugated sheets we started to load up the motor caravan with our booty. There were a couple of important things we had not taken into account when we set out on this venture. First, rhubarb that is so beautifully sweet and delicious in the spring turns stringy and disgustingly sour by the time that autumn comes round, and secondly, corrugated tin that has been left out in all weathers on a disused allotment for a couple of years becomes very rusty and fragile after a short journey in a van.

Our first port of call was Ernie Harvey's house at Cutteslowe in North Oxford. We tried to make the delivery but every time we pulled out a sheet of tin from the motor caravan the sheet disintegrated into pieces and fell on to the pavement. Ernie was not impressed but we found four sheets that were 'not too bad'. He offered us two shillings for the tin if we threw the rhubarb in for free. At this point in time the deal seemed more than generous. We took the money and ran.

Our next call was Cap S Walker's house just off the Iffley Road in Oxford. As luck would have it Cap S was out at a meeting. (Keyboard operator Philip Walker was the NGA Father of the Composing Room Chapel and House Father and was always attending trade union meetings.) His son (who also worked at the Press) answered the door and we carefully unloaded our fragile load into his front garden together with the rhubarb.

The next morning all hell broke loose when we attempted to collect the cash from Cap S. He had arrived home later that evening to find a heap of rusty tin on his doorstep and a pile of inedible rhubarb and he was not a happy bunny. We, as a company, decided to waive our remuneration and considered ourselves lucky that we did not suffer any physical abuse. Our tally for the evening was two shillings but we had to give it to The Baron for the use of his motor caravan and the petrol it consumed.

The Black Dove and I decided to start selling shirts at the Press. He had seen an advertisement placed in a national newspaper by a company called 'Mendac Shirts'. They were looking for agents to sell their shirts in factories. We purchased a load of shirts and started selling them 50 per cent cheaper than similar shirts in Oxford shops. The trouble was that the shirts had been starched too much to make them look good in the cellophane packet. When the punters put the shirts on, they found that the starched collars were like razors and several people suffered lacerations to their necks. When they complained we told them that when they washed them all would be well. Alas, after washing, they became very limp and lifeless and the stitching started to come undone. 'Coddy' Foster was particularly annoyed when he tried to pull his shirt off over his head and the collar came off in his hands! The Black Dove and I decided that we would end our business partnership and go our separate ways. He went on to study ventriloquism and left the Press to become a successful stage comedian and ventriloquist, the high point being an appearance on BBC television in the famous show entitled *Sunday Night at the London Palladium.*

Betting was a very important pastime at the Press. There was a network of agents throughout the building representing all the Football pools companies. One could bet with Littlewoods, Vernons, Copes, Zetters, William Hills Fixed Odds, and Spotting the Ball coupons. All the agents (of which I was one) were paid commission of 12½ per cent of their weekly collection. Some agents made an awful lot of money from the football pools because just about everybody in the Press 'did the pools'. They saw the pools as the 'only way out'. One of my hundreds of clients invested £100 per week on just one perm and I collected £12.50 per week in commission from him alone!

Gambling on the horses and the greyhounds was another major pastime enjoyed by Press gamblers over the years. When I first came to the Press in 1958 I had never placed a bet on a horse and did not know how to write out a betting slip. Gambling at the Press and at all the factories and shops in Oxford was illegal. A local bookmaker had half a dozen 'bookie's runners' at the Press who took 10 per cent commission from all the stake money. They all had leather bags that had a time-clock lock on the top. When I wanted to place a bet on the horses or the greyhounds I would write out the details of the bet and the stake on a plain piece of paper, write my nom-de-plume at the bottom of the slip, and then wrap the cash stake up in the slip. My nom-de-plume was 'Fishy'. I would then take my bet to the bookie's runner who was 'Donna' in the Jobbing Department, 'Chip' in the Mono, or Reg in the Bindery who would drop it into the bag (there was a 'runner' in every department). Before the start of the first race the runners would close the bag and the time clock would automatically lock it. After work in the evening the runners would take their bags to the betting shop and the bag would be opened using a special key. The bets would then be sorted into winners and losers. The winning slips would have the winnings wrapped up in the slip with the nom-de-plume written on the outside. The runners would then distribute the packages when they arrived at work the next morning. This was all carried out under a veil of secrecy and you had to be in the know before you would be allowed to place your bets.

The secrecy became a farce as poor old Donna became increasingly deaf and would shout instead of speaking normally. His frame was right next door to the Jobbing Department's glass-panelled office. The manager, Arthur Panting, was an officious little man who ran the Jobbing Department with a rod of iron and was feared by everyone but universally acknowledged as being very fair. If he had known what was going on under his nose he would have instituted disciplinary proceedings that would have led to instant dismissal for the bookie's runner and the itinerant gambler.

Punters from smaller departments that did not have their own resident bookie's runner would send their apprentices to the Jobbing Department and make their way to Donna's frame to secretly place their department's bets. I remember taking the bets on one occasion from the Oriental Ship to Donna's frame by creeping down the back stairs out of Pantin's view. I whispered to the now completely deaf Donna, 'Here are the bets for 'Ster's [Jack Webster's] Ship'. At the top of his voice he shouted, 'Speak up boy. I can't hear you. If you have brought some bets just put 'em in the bag.' Everybody in the department whistled 'piano' and the manager's head shot up trying to spot the wrong fount in his department. I ducked down behind Donna's frame and waited for calm to return to the department before crawling back up the stairs to the relative safety of the Top Comps.

When the old runners retired the betting operation was taken over by a couple of lads in the Bindery. They owned greyhounds and one was even a croupier in a local casino. They turned small business betting at the Press into a major operation and never refused a bet. They also never failed to pay out.

Money lending was also big business in the Bindery and hundreds of pounds changed hands everyday at extortionate interest rates. The rates were as high as 10 per cent per week. I cannot even begin to what that means in terms of APR!

> *The Press received an unusual request from a lighthouse keeper in the Far East (perhaps he too had heard of OUP's underground shops):*
>
> To the Clarendon Press, Oxford England,
>
> Your name and address have been hardly recomanded to me by a cetan friend of mine that you are the best manufactire in the cety of England ans so that to must fowerd me one of your biciyles catalogue to me.

Watch and clock mending was a popular pastime for some entrepreneurs. The three that I came into contact with were Lofty, the Stones' supervisor in the Mono Office, Scally, the proof-puller in the Jobbing Department, and Kitch, a feeder in the Letterpress Machine Room.

Lofty was a massive man who had enormous fingers. He would take watches apart and put them back together again handling the minute workings of a small watch with the dexterity of a brain surgeon. All this was done in his lunch hour whilst sat at his desk. Scally was good on alarm clocks and could mend any timepiece that was put in front of him in minutes, often washing the innards of the clock with turps from the tin under his proofing machine. Kitch was more refined and found that lighter fluid solved most watch problems. The advent of battery and digital watches soon put the Press watch-menders out of business.

Chris Woodward, who was to become my father-in-law, ran a successful Christmas poultry business for more than forty years. He had been an apprentice compositor before the Second World War when he left to join the RAF where he was awarded the Oak Leaf and was Mentioned in Dispatches. After the war he decided not to return to the Press but to take up farming. He kept in close touch with his many friends at the Press and supplied them with turkeys and capons every Christmas. The birds were much in demand and every year people were clamouring for them. It became quite a social occasion on collection day which always took place in the Stute on Christmas Eve. Most of the managers at the Press were customers so he never had to keep his birds under wraps! He gave up farming in 1962 and returned to the Press as a compositor in the Exam Ship and the business continued to flourish right up until his death in 1993.

There were many businesses outside the Press that did very well because of Press patronage. The first of these was a little shop (now a private house) opposite what was the Clarendon Arms (now an annexe to the Press). The old lady who ran the shop only appeared to sell three things: newspapers, cigarettes, and snuff. Because OUP employees were not allowed to smoke inside the Press buildings the only way they could get their required dose of nicotine was to take snuff. Wilson's finest S.P. Snuff was dispensed into quarter ounce portions and wrapped up in small paper cones after being weighed meticulously on brass scales. Just about every employee at the Press would stop off in the early hours of the morning to pick up their daily paper and/or their daily fix of snuff.

Snuff taking was a social but rather disgusting practice. Whenever a 'snuffer' met another snuffer anywhere in the Press one would invariably start to rub his thumb and first finger against the breast portion of his apron. This cleansing of the ink and lead dust from his fingers was the start of a ritual and an unwritten signal for the other to produce his snuffbox. The box would be taken out of his apron pocket, opened and offered to his colleague. The colleague would take a pinch and wait for the owner of the box to take his pinch. Then without any need for words of thanks they would both place the brown powder to their noses and sniff simultaneously. The experienced snuff-taker would never sneeze but would pull out a filthy piece of rag from his apron pocket and blow his nose into it. Some particularly dirty characters would blow their noses on their aprons. This ritual happened up to twenty times a day and I will not go on to describe the state of the rags, the aprons, and (this is the worst bit) the roller towels in the washroom that were only changed once a week. It was quite common for some mean compositors to deliberately let their thumbnail grow very long so that, when offered snuff, they could shovel up a massive amount of snuff and instead of putting it up their nose would tap it into their own snuffbox.

A few yards away from the snuff shop was Slasher Moore's hairdressing salon where his son still operates today. Bill Moore a.k.a. Slasher was a lovely bald-headed man who could only cope with four haircuts an hour so it was imperative that if you wanted to have a haircut during your lunch hour you had to be in the first four when the lunch-time bell rang to stop work at midday. Everyone used to wait under the archway to the Quadrangle for the bell to ring before the stampede began.

The problem was that everyone was running for different reasons and you did not know whom you were running against. It was obvious that they were not all running to get to Slasher's. Some people were running to get to the Stute first so that they could book one of the snooker tables or the bar-billiards table. Some were rushing to get to the bar for a drink because the queue could be so long that by the time you got a drink it was time to return to the Press. Some were running to Hilda's residence. Hilda was a prostitute who operated from a little terraced house in Great Clarendon Street and her services were very much in demand during the lunch break. We know how many haircuts that Slasher could do in an hour but the number of tricks that Hilda could do in the hour was never recorded! A guide perhaps would be the fact that one Press employee would go home for lunch and on his way back to work would park his moped outside Hilda's abode and he would always leave the engine running!

Opposite Slasher's barber's shop was Reg Wonnacott's clothing emporium. Mr Wonnacot was a gentleman's outfitter who catered for the sartorial elegance of all the Press's male employees. He sold aprons to compositors and binders, overalls to machine minders and feeders, as well as coats, jackets, trousers, hats, shoes, and socks. The reason that everyone purchased their clothes from Reg was that he would let you take the goods home to try them on first and would then let you pay for them weekly without any charges for interest or let you bring them back if they did not fit. There was never any written agreement to sign and no records were kept. He simply trusted you and to my knowledge that trust was never betrayed.

Another business that did quite well out of the Press was Del Nevo's fish and chip shop just a few hundred yards away. Mr Del Nevo had several fish and chip shops in the area but the Walton Street shop was the jewel in the crown. It had a back room that was packed with scrubbed wooden tables with long benches on each side. People who did not wish to eat in the Press's canteen would run to Del Nevo's to get a seat and be served by 'Auntie' with cod, chips, bread and butter, and a cup of tea for just 1s. 9d. (c.8 pence). When we worked overtime and were feeling flush with money we would push the boat out and upgrade the cod to haddock or plaice for an extra 9d. (3 pence).

Joe's café was just a few doors away from Del Nevo's and it was popular with people who were working overtime at the Press. There was an agreement between the management and the trades union that if an employee was asked to work overtime on the same day he would be entitled to 9*d.* tea money. The union rules also stipulated that before any man could work overtime he must take a statutory half hour break.

The first choice for tea was usually the canteen because the dinner ladies would fry up all the leftover vegetables from that lunchtime into a massive bubble and squeak and serve the crunchy slightly burnt mixture to the overtime workers with a fried egg on top for, would you believe, exactly 9*d.* This meant that the Press did not effectively have to pay for tea money because the leftover food would have been thrown away had it not been consumed by the overtime workers.

The second choice was Joe's café because of its legendary bacon sandwiches and a cup of tea for just 1 shilling. We considered that it was worth paying the extra 3*d.* because it gave us the chance to stretch our legs and get some fresh air before returning to the Press for 2 hours of overtime.

# CHAPTER FIVE

# Comps, Printers, Binders, and Nuts & Bolts

*The Composing Rooms*

JOHN JOHNSON, when he was Printer, used regularly to walk round the printing works to check that everyone was working properly and efficiently. One afternoon, in the composing room, he passed a proof-puller who was leaning against his proofing machine idly swinging his mallet. 'Have you no work to do, my man?', barked the gruff J.J. staring at the rack full of formes waiting to be proofed. 'Oh,' said the proof-puller, 'I was keeping those for overtime!'

Many years before I joined the Press the composing rooms had originally been split into two sections, the Learned Side handling all the bookwork and jobbing

*Chip Beal at the frame*

*Ron Foster 'making-up' the Bible*

work in the North Wing and the Bible Side producing the hand-setting of Oxford's bibles in the South Wing. In 1895 there were 128 journeymen working in the Jobbing Ship, the Oriental Ship, the Bible Ship (still in the Bible Side), and the Ships of Brownjohn & Co., Cross & Co., King & Co., Mullis & Co., Owen & Co., and the Machine Revisers. There were forty-one apprentice compositors 'at case' and eighteen boy probationers waiting for a decision as to whether they were to be indentured. There were twenty-two proofreaders on the Learned Side and five on the Bible Side, of whom one was R. L. Gass, the author of the reminiscences that appear in the Preface above. There were proof-pullers, pressmen, photographers, clerks, warehousemen, cleaners, various 'other boys', and of course the foremen and managers. The total number of employees in the composing rooms amounted to about 290 men and boys.

By 1914 the Monotype Department had been set up and the Bible Ship had been reduced to about seventeen compositors, readers, and just one apprentice. As mechanical typesetting took a hold at the Press there were around 258 people working in the Learned Side. But the geography and the way that pages of type were produced had changed dramatically. The Reading Department had expanded to thirty-one and there were two people working there then that I was

*The Cardboard Comp was brought in by compositors to help during a bonus payment dispute*

to work with when I arrived in 1958. They were Arthur Young and Esmond Fathers. The Photographic Department had trebled but there was still a hardcore of eight Ships run by Chapman, Harris, Hewitt, Simms, Taylor, Wild, and of course, the Oriental Ship, the Jobbing Ship, and the newly formed Music Ship. (It was to be quite a few years later before the introduction of the Maths Ship and the Exam Ship.) The largest expansion came, of course, from the new kids on the block; the Monotype Department, the Monotype casting machines and, later, the Monotype Keyboard Department. It was this process that was to change the face of typesetting forever. The Monotype Department had been placed in a purpose-built 'greenhouse' behind the North Wing and in 1914 it housed fifty-five compositors and caster operatives.

When I started work at the Press the composing rooms had been reduced to the main Monotype Composing Rooms, the Mono Annexe on the ground floor of the North Wing, the Jobbing Ship on the first floor, and the Top Comps on the second floor. In the Mono Office was the Composing Room Manager, Ron (Bomber) Harris and his deputy, Bill (The Perm) King. Also tucked into a corner were the Stones' clicker Frank (Lofty) Deacon and a couple of ex-compositors whose job was 'looking out'. Their job entailed them spending the whole day looking through proofs that had been 'pulled up' by the compositors to see if anything was missing! The Ships were still there but harder to spot. There were correction comps, make-up comps, stonehands, maths comps, the storemen, and proof-pullers.

One compositor that will not be forgotten was the 'Cardboard Comp'. He was brought out to help during a dispute over a bonus issue and was operated by page cord. He asked for no wages or bonus and caused no trouble but still he was mysteriously abducted during the night following the dispute. Fingers were pointed at likely management suspects but, like Shergar, his little cardboard remains were never found.

In the Mono Annexe were the compositors who dealt with all the examination papers. They were known as the 'Exam Ship' under the clickership of Fred Matthews and were a self-contained unit making up the examination papers, imposing them, proofing them, and carrying out all the corrections before sending them to press. There was also a small Ship that made up and imposed all the plates and half-tones for illustrated books. The Jobbing Ship on the first floor was another totally self-contained Ship under the foremanship of Arthur Pantin. The Top Comps on the floor above was made up of the Oriental Ship and the Music Ship. All the above Ships dealt only with hot-metal type but things were about to change.

The Monophoto typesetting system was introduced into the Press in 1960. Linotype keyboard operator Ken Beckley was given the task of ensuring that the 'new technology' (based largely on the old Monotype system) was a success. Nobody at the Press understood the Monophoto quite like Ken so I have plagiarized his description of how it all worked. He was a good friend of mine and would probably be horrified at my oversimplification of the process.

The Monotype Corporation had been experimenting with filmsetting before the Second World War, and their efforts culminated in a prototype machine being demonstrated at the London IPEX in July 1955. Briefly, the method of producing the final film product from the 'Monophoto' machine was as follows: Each character or symbol was housed separately in the film-matrix negative case (equivalent to the die-case on the Monotype caster). When the keyboard operator tapped a key two perforations were made on the spool of paper. When the spool of paper was transferred to the filmsetter these two holes acted as a signal for the positioning of the film-matrix case, thus allowing the desired letter to appear over an aperture ready for photographing.

A beam of light was then passed through a condenser lens to the film-matrix and on to an optical flap; the light then passed to a pair of prisms and onto a projection lens or iris diaphragm, from which the beam was again deflected onto a pair of travelling mirrors; the light was then deflected from one mirror to the opposite mirror and then reflected upwards onto the film mounted in the film drum. Thus the image of the character positioned by the holes in the spool of

*Ken Beckley 'licking and
sticking' (filmset makeup)*

paper over the aperture was reproduced on the film. When all the film had been exposed the film-drum was removed from the machine for development.

The 'Monophoto' machine ran at 9,600 revolutions per hour (160 revolutions per minute)—but, unlike the 'hot-metal' caster, it worked at this constant speed irrespective of whether 6 pt. or 24 pt. was being set: there was no slowing down for the larger type faces.

Whereas up to photography stage the 'Monophoto' machine was mechanical, the handling of the product of the machine became largely a matter of manual dexterity, especially if the 'stripping film' method of make-up was employed.

When stripping film was used a high-contrast photographic emulsion on a very thin sheet of membrane, was carried on a temporary base which was removed during make-up. A working layout was prepared on which spacing, type sizes, and general page arrangement were indicated. The layout was squared up to a 6 pt. quadrille grid mounted on to a make-up table and fastened down. A plasticized transfer sheet was placed over this and also fastened down. The stripping film was laid on to the transfer sheet and lined up vertically and horizontally to the grid using a Vernier gauge in conjunction with the 6 pt. grid lines to ensure accuracy; when satisfied that the film page was laid down squarely the stripping film base was peeled away thus leaving the membrane adhered to the transfer sheet; it was

*Manager Tom Chandler
checks the running sheets.
The machine minder is
Albert Saxton and his
feeder is Jack Fellows*

then pressure-rolled into contact with a squeegee rubber roller to ensure flatness and to remove any air bubbles which might have formed. The page was then ready to be proofed in the dry-developing proofing machine. When the page had been finally passed for press and all necessary corrections made, the membrane was coated with a special adhesive and a sheet of Kodatrace rolled into contact with the membrane. The transfer sheet was then peeled away from the membrane thus leaving the membrane bonded to the Kodatrace. The page was then ready for plating or contacting according to the printing process to be used.

## Machine Rooms

Bill (properly William George) Clements started work in the Machine Room on 5 November 1909 aged 13 years. He always said that printing was his life. It was part of his family's life as well, because his mother, daughter, cousins, and all his in-laws all worked at the Press in the Bindery, Warehouse, and offices. Bill fought in the First World War and was awarded the Military Medal. On his return to the Press after the war he became Father of the Chapel and served his fellow workmates with distinction for many years. He retired from the Machine Room aged 73 years.

The Press was renowned for the number of people that clocked up long service. When Machine Room Clicker Jack Thomas finally left the Press in 1973 it broke a record of his family's 160 years of *continuous* service—and they were all called 'John'! His grandfather found employment with the Press as a machine minder in 1841 where he too rose to the rank of Clicker after more than 50 years' service. His son joined the Press as a machine minder in 1886 and he too notched up more than 50 years. Our Jack went on to complete 50 years and I guess that is a record that will never be broken.

The manager of the Machine Room during my time at the Press was Norman

*The Pre-make Ready's Tony Hopcraft imposes the plates onto honeycomb before loading it onto Arthur Axford's Miehle Perfector, with Bill Hine c.1930*

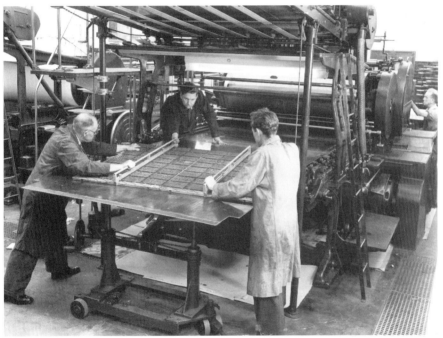

Mansfield. He was the firmest and strictest manager in the Press but was respected and admired by everyone that worked for him because he was always fair and never bore a grudge. When a mistake was made he would leave his office like a fireball and weigh into the perpetrator of the 'crime' with such ferocity that even those not involved would run for cover. When the 'rollocking' was over it was over! A few moments later he would be chattering most amicably to the man that he had just ripped into, about his garden, his family, or the state of the weather.

*Laurie Taylor adjusts electroplates on the honeycomb base*

Norman Mansfield had managed the machines of the once mighty Letterpress Machine Room for 25 years and at his retirement there was much wailing and gnashing of teeth at the loss of such a fine manager.

> *People from all over the world wanted a chance to train at OUP as a letterpress printer:*
>
> Cape Province, South Africa
> 10 July 1956
>
> Dear Sir,
> I beg to apply in your printing press to get a thorough training in the year 1957, as a boarder.
> Kindly reply me sir within two shakes of a dog's tail as I am anxious for printing next year. I can be very glad if you can send me your hand book information.
> Yours faithfully

Norman Mansfield had taken over from Tom Chandler around 1953/4. His deputy had been Joe Borthwick and the foreman was Gilbert Tyrell. In 1951 there were sixty printing machines at the Press including the Platens (or Croppers as they were known to the machine men) under the foremanship of George Hope. The Lithographic Machine Room was run by Jim Coles. By the 1960s Norman

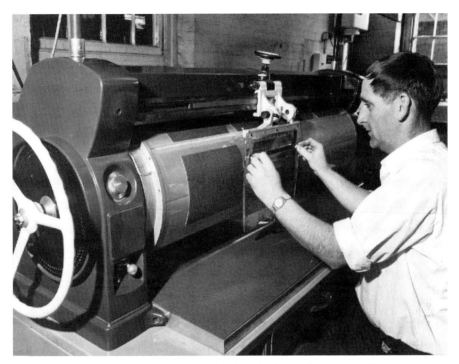

*Brian Holloway imposing APR (plastic) plates in the Pre-Make Ready Department*

Mansfield was assisted by Gilbert Tyrell, Jack Thomas, and Arthur Axford in the Colour Room (as the Croppers was to be renamed).

Norman Mansfield's job was to programme the loading of the machines while liaising with the Production Control Department. He was also responsible for the Stereotype Foundry under the foremanship of Ken Scroggs.

Gilbert Tyrell and Jack Thomas were responsible for the quality control, the giving out of the work, checking the running sheets, and the control of the paper and ink availability. They also had to keep up links with the Paper Office and the Composing Rooms, and organize all the pre-planning materials.

The Pre-Make-Ready Department also came under the control of Norman Mansfield and his team. The department was run by Les Deacon with his staff of Tony Hopcraft, Keith Whettam, Fred Woodcock, Rodney Masters, and Frank Young. They were responsible for the imposition of the stereo plates and electro-plates (later Dycril and plastic plates) on to honeycomb bases.

Percy Boswell and Fred Clifford ran the Paper Office and when they retired they were replaced by a chemist, Keith Fissenden. As the technology in other parts of the Press was changing apace, so it was in the paper business. The machines became faster and faster and the condition of the paper and its relative humidity became more and more important.

*Gerry Fulton was 'Imperial House Father' in 1974*

There were many 'characters' in the machine room. One was the bookie's runner, Jim Allen. Much to the amusement of his colleagues Jim passed his driving test on the eighteenth attempt! This was probably an OUP record. Machine feeder Ted Cripps collected the Vernons football coupons not just around the Press but all of Jericho! Trucker 'Curly' Thomas, with his mop of red curly hair, was always ready to stand up on a pallett and entertain his colleagues with a song and a dance. Often this would be accompanied by the vocal 'trumpet' of another Jericho resident, Eric 'Nobby' Clarke.

Just like apprentices throughout the Press the machine room boys would play their own tricks on their colleagues. They would plant stink-bombs under the check/break pedal of the machines so that when the feeder pressed the pedal the bomb would break and a dreadful smell would emanate and cause much discomfort to all in the vicinity. Thin slices of old composition rollers were cut up and put into their colleagues' sandwiches in place of the meat when they were out of sight. This again was quite an unpleasant experience.

The large Timson rotary machine had a large drying unit that was in fact an oven. The printed paper passed through the naked flames to dry the ink instantly before the sheets were folded. The paper would often catch fire when the machine slowed down or stopped so the operatives had a large fire extinguisher containing nitrogen to put out the fires. Machine feeder Peter Kitchen liked to use the nitrogen jet as a punishment for unwelcome visitors. The hot oven was an ideal place

*Peter Hazel feeding the Victoria Platen (early 1950s)*

for warming up fatty cake, steak and kidney pies, and other foods and the area was a magnet for the fatty cake pirates.

*Mary Owen remembers her time in the Lithographic Machine Room:*

I started work in the Bindery on 14 August 1939 folding the end-papers and pasting tapes on to the backs of books for 9 shillings per week. I lived in Abingdon so half of my money went in bus fares. The Litho Department became very busy and so many bindery girls were moved there to help with the war effort. The main work in the Litho at this time was the printing of codes and decodes for the forces. Very hush hush. Even the waste-paper baskets were locked away during our 30-minute lunch breaks. At the age of 16 I was expected to work until 8 p.m. on three evenings a week. After the war we printed lots of music and the two collotype machines in the department printed the Oxford Almanac every year. I loved working at a place that published and printed books and even though I left OUP in 1949 I still have many happy memories.

The Letterpress Machine Department was reducing in size as the Lithographic Machine Room was increasing. The Letterpress management had attempted to compete with the lithographic process by using Dycril and APR plates. Many books were printed using this system such as the thirteen-volume *Oxford English Dictionary*, the *Shorter Oxford English Dictionary*, and many bibles and prayer books. But the system just prolonged the inevitable and in 1979 the Letterpress Machine Room folded. Some machine minders and feeders transferred to the

*Albert Saxton printing the*
Coronation Bible *in 1952*

Lithographic Machine Room and were retrained. Foreman Brian Holloway was also transferred to the Litho under Jack Sinclair who in turn had earlier taken over from Jim Coles and his popular foreman, Wilf Bradley.

### The Stereotype and Electrotype Foundry

This department of the Press enjoyed a wonderful view over the Quad. On my first ever visit to this rather gorgeously dirty and addictively smelly department I was met with strange galvanized sinks full of chemicals and large sheets of thin metal plates hanging from the ceiling. The air was thick with lead dust and at a long black metal bench facing the Quad was a row of dark-coated men with filthy hands holding blowtorches aimed at slabs of metal. The stereotypers that I remember were Harold Saxton, his son Terry, Ron Buckingham, Fred Burden, Ron Mobley, John Matthews, and John Dally.

 This, then, was the 'Stereo' whose manager during my time was Ken Scroggs. Ken had joined the Press in 1921 but left soon after he had completed his apprenticeship in 1929. He returned in 1949 after having gaining much foundry experience on the *Liverpool Echo* and at the printers Eric Bemrose. He was appointed manager in 1951 a post he held until he retired in 1971.

> *The flong was the moulding material used for casting stereo plates and they were made from sheets of paper and paste. The Press used wet flongs until about 1952. Dry flongs were used in the newspaper industry but were considered not to be suitable for use at the Press. The verses printed below were penned by Commercial Director Richard Russell's mother who was amused by the word 'flong'. Although the sequence of operations are hardly correct the poem entitled 'The Stereotypers' Flong-Song' caused much amusement when it was published in* The Clarendonian *in 1977.*

> We fling the flong and scatter
> The wet flongs o'er the type,

*The Timson Rotary operated by Bernard Booth, Trevor Luke, and Bill Horan*

> For dry flong would be flatter,
> And lacked the rounded shape.
>
> We mix the paste and roll it,
> And shape it with a song;
> When it's just right to hold it,
> We fling our far-flung flong.
>
> We're happy stereotypers,
> We do no process wrong,
> And to the linotypers
> We send our well-loved song...

The men in the foundry were responsible for making electro plates and stereo plates, for mounting blocks (text-figures and half-tone illustrations), and for creating special sorts (the rare accents and breathings that were not readily available in the type cases or that could not be made easily by the compositors). Stereotyping was a duplicating process for the production of bookwork where although quality was not considered to be as good as traditional letterpress printing directly from type it was used at the Press because the plates did not wear out as quickly as type. Electrotyping was a higher quality platemaking process and was also used at the Press.

*The Stereotype Department*

*Ken Scroggs checks a plate in the Stereo*

## The Collotype Department

The collotype process, the people that worked in this department, and what they did was always a mystery to me but Derek Honey captures life in the Collotype Department perfectly.

> I started work at the Press in 1954 as an apprentice Collotype and Lithographic printer. I signed my indentures in the presence of my father and the Printer, Charles Batey, and as part of my training I spent one day a week at college, first in Oxford and later in London. The rest of the week was spent learning my craft. I was to specialize as a Collotyper.
>
> Collotype was a facsimile form of printing in which no screen was used to reproduce perfect copies of works of art. The base was of two-inch plate glass that was ground to give it a rough surface then coated with liquid gelatine and a light-sensitive chemical—usually potassium bichromate—at high temperatures. When it cooled and the gelatine was hard, the plate was exposed through film or glass, creating an image on the plate. The theory was simple. Depending on the density of the image, the gelatine hardened to varying degrees. The more that it was exposed to, the harder became the gelatine and therefore rejected water but accepted greasy ink. The perfect image was therefore obtained by the varying degrees of hardness and the softness of the gelatine. The plate was then washed out in a bath of water to re-soften the gelatine until it was ready for press.
>
> The press operator was a highly skilled man, for each colour and hue of colour had to be printed separately—there was no process colour printing on this process—and he had to match the colour of the print to the original painting. Because of the humidity and varying heat only a few copies were printed at a time—on a flatbed press—before the plate would dry out and the operator would then have to etch the plate with glycerine to soften the gelatine again. Some days only twenty copies of each colour could be printed which made collotype a very expensive process. The end print was often nearly as expensive as the original painting, and may have become collectors' items.
>
> After a few years training I became the collotype platemaker and my laboratory was situated in the old cellars of the Press in a specially built dust-free environment. I used an old carbon arc lamp to expose the plate because it produced perfect white light and the temperatures in the oven room could reach 130 degrees Fahrenheit. To avoid dust from one's clothes getting on the plate while coating it (with your fingers!) the platemaker would have to work naked!
>
> Collotype was the perfect process in its day but with the advent of higher resolution screens in lithography, and the much faster speeds obtainable, the writing was on the wall.

## The Bindery and the Warehouse

In the 1955 the manager of the Bindery was the 'strict but fair' 'Johnny' Johnson who ruled with a rod of iron and his foreman was a man called Harry Clifford.

*Top Floor Handwork Section. In later years known as the Una Carter Memorial Room*

*Staff operating the Smyth Horne Three-Wing Casing-in Machine*

There were also three clickers: Reg Chalmers, Alec Fortescue, and Jim Coggins. Johnny's office had many windows that looked out over the entire department and each of these windows was given a number by the bindery workers. Each had a perfect view of a particular area of the Bindery and so the numbering system was very useful to pass round information quickly as to which group of people were under surveillance at any given time. Later, Reg Chalmers was appointed the Manager and Alec Fortescue and Jim Coggins continued to act as the foremen under him. When he eventually retired his job was taken over by Martin Slade who went on to be Director of Oxuniprint at the time of the closure of the Printing Division.

The real business of the Bindery was once explained to me by craftsman binder Chris Hale. Chris had originally wanted to work on the railways as his father and grandfather had done, but was 'forced' by his parents to take up an apprenticeship at OUP. 'You need to get a good apprenticeship behind you' was the rallying call that many young men were told as they left school, 'They will always want printers!' Now where had I heard that before?

In the early 1960s new machinery started to appear in the Bindery and almost immediately its success was being measured with the increased mass-production of books without the loss of quality that was feared by the pessimists. It was not just the new machinery that made the binding at OUP the envy of the world, it was the craftsmen and women that operated them. The cloth-cutting machine was run by the 'famous' Peter Stone. Famous, not for cutting the cloth that was wrapped round the cases of the books but for his piscatorial prowess. He was internationally known and respected in the sport and was author of many books and articles on the subject. He was also an expert taxidermist and many OUP collectors have fish and pets that were 'stuffed' by Peter Stone. The case-makers were George Rawlings, Jackie England, and Alan Purvey. George was renowned for his singing at the Bindery wayzgooses and it was considered to be a poor outing if they had not been treated to a selection of his songs. The favourite rendition was 'Any Old Iron' when he would swing a fob watch round on a chain and let it go so it crashed to the floor and fell apart, much to the amusement of the assembled crowd.

The flat printed sheets were collected from the machine rooms by warehouse trucker Curly Thomas and were taken to the Folders. This was a section with about thirty staff under foreman Ron Fidler. After the sheets had been folded they were sent to Frank Smith and his staff of six or seven to be gathered. When the gatherers had completed their task the 'signatures' were sent for sewing by Ethel Harvey (later Kath Fulton, wife of the Imperial House Father of the Chapel). The sewers employed forty to fifty women at this time. Once the books had been sewn they had to be 'nipped' (squeezed together to release the air) to the final spine width. There were four nipping machines run by Jack England, Ted Eeles, Don Hicks, and Don Walton.

*Hand-feeding sections on to the saddle of a Smyth Semi-automatic sewing machine*

*General view of the sewing section in the 1960s. Note the machines being driven by overhead Shafts and belts*

*Alec Fotescue on the Berry Press with Les Hookham in the background in the 1950s*

*Inspection and jacketing of the Shorter Oxford English Dictionary*

*General view of the Inspection and Dispatch Department under the supervision of Aubrey Beesley*

*Geoff Nicholson operating the Smyth Pressing unit on the Binding Line*

*Percy Best: Warehouseman and entertainer*

The books were sent to the guillotines for cutting. It was a wonder that any work was done at this time because of the mostly good-humoured political banter. (Wally Butt was a staunch Conservative, Bert Camm was a Liberal and an Oxford United supporter, and Bert Cox was a labour man and an Oxford City supporter.) The books were then glued so that the books held together. Chris Hale's glueing machine, though, was always covered in human hair. This formed part of a weird collection of locks of hair donated (sometimes voluntarily) by visitors to the machine.

The next stage was the 'rounding and backing'. This was done by Arthur Gray when he wasn't cake-making and icing for anyone in the Bindery that needed this service. The triple-lining machine would add gauze to reinforce the spine and this was operated by Bert Janaway. He was a very short man and he was a fast talker and a fast walker. He would call everyone 'son' regardless of their age or position. When the gauze had been added the book had to be 'cased in' with cases supplied by the Case-making Department. This was done by motor-cycle fanatic Bill Cooper and Les Hookham (father of proofpuller Peter 'Shook' Hookham). The books were then pressed in a contraption that looked like a wine-press before being sent to the Packing Department. Aubrey Beesley was the foreman (and a leading light in the Press Fire Brigade) and was in charge of sixty women packers. The dust-jackets were placed round the books before being boxed up and sent to the Jordan Hill Warehouse where they were then the responsibility of Bill Kirkley and his staff. The books were then ready for distribution to bookshops throughout the world. Later the Warehouse was closed down when the Press built the high-tech warehouse in Corby, Northamptonshire.

In the Bindery one name became legend not only at the Press but also to many people all over the world: he was Uncle Percy. For more than 40 years Percy Best visited the Wingfield Hospital in Oxford organizing fetes, raising money for the hospital, and visiting sick children as Uncle Percy. He became a 'Mr Punch' in his own right with his 100-year-old puppets before joining the International Brotherhood of Magicians. He would perform every year at the Press children's Christmas party with his show followed by lots of magic and balloons.

---

*In 1926 warehouseman C. Beesley remembers his early days at the Press when he joined in 1866. Mr Combe's influence on the wayzgoose left an impression on him as it had on J. W. Embury's reminiscences in Chapter Two above.*

I well remember my first appearance as an employee of the Press, when I was eleven. I began in the Warehouse and under the foremanship of Mr J. Hughes. With other boys I had to walk continually round and round a table, gathering consecutive sheets into complete books. Our working day commenced at 6 a.m., the breakfast interval was from 8.15 to 9, the dinner-hour from 1 to 2, and the day's work ended at 6 p.m. Those 10½-hour days, which brought in 25s. 6d. per week, were not wholly monotonous: the foreman saw to that. It was his custom to give to each of us daily two doses—never *less* than two—of 'light refreshment', administered with a foot length of catgut taken from his frock-coat pocket for the purpose, and applied—wherever he could hit. It was meant as a cure for 'shammocking', or idling.

There was a night school for Press boys, with a kindly schoolmaster in Mr. W. Parker. On Sunday mornings also we had to attend school, and to march to St Paul's church and take our places in the gallery. The vicar at that time was the Rev. Alfred Hackman.

On Good Friday we received two hot-cross buns, on Christmas Day two mince-pies. They were tabled in the schoolroom, and we filed round the table twice, taking *one* bun or mince-pie each time.

Each of us was provided with a card for recording the weekly twopences we paid: the Press contributed the same amount, and at the end of the year the grand total was laid out in clothing at the Queen Street shop of Messrs. Seary and Co. Mr Thomas Combe, the chief manager at that time, was most anxious that we should spend our wealth wisely. He used to say to us, 'Tell your parents to buy corduroy trousers; they wear well.' I wore them.

The great event of the year, for the boys, was the trip we had at Wayzgoose time. We paraded in the Quad, and, led by our Fife & Drum Band and with banners and flags flying, marched through the town to Folly Bridge. There we boarded the *British Queen* houseboat and the *Lord Nelson,* and off we went to Nuneham. There was plenty to eat and drink, but as the weather was generally hot Mr Combe showed a fatherly concern about our liquid refreshment: we were *not* to drink direct from the river! He would have a very large tub placed on the river bank, and when it had been almost filled (from the river) he first put into it a large packet of powder, and then thoroughly stirred it with the walking-stick he carried; after that, he pronounced it wholesome drink for the boys. Of its taste and colour I will say nothing, nor venture an opinion whether it owed anything of either to the walking-stick. Apart from this Drink Question, we always had a fine time; and when we arrived at Folly Bridge again, about 9 p.m., there was a crowd waiting to see the Press boys land. We played 'When Johnny comes marching home', we gave three cheers for the management, and then we 'merry, merry boys' dispersed to our homes.

Compositors found the Bindery a bit of a mystery. We knew, of course, that they bound books but compositors were never allowed to enter the department for two reasons. First, there was no reason why we should go there. We set the type before sending it to the machine rooms for printing and we had no contact at all with the Bindery. Secondly, there was something there that we all wanted—girls! The Bindery was swimming with them and the upsetting thing was that the Bindery boys seemed to be having all the fun! The rumours would run riot about 'goings-on' in the cellars but they were only rumours. Linda Wharton gives a clue:

> I worked at the Press until 1973 when I left to have my baby. I worked in the Bindery with Alec Fortescue and Jim Coggins as my foremen. I worked on a brand new machine with Geoff Probitts in charge and it was there that I made friends with Irene Stansfield fron Northway. She was one of triplets and her brother Derek and her sister Sandra also worked at the Press.

*Members of the Examination Dispatch department in 1984*

We had lots of fun working together and I think that it was because of that that I was moved downstairs to the folders. They couldn't stop us from seeing each other though. We just went to the loos the long way round: me upstairs to Irene and her downstairs to me.

I worked on most machines in the folders where Ron Fidler was the foreman. He was fair and I always got on with him. I remember one day I was wearing a mini dress (and I mean mini) when the Bindery manager, Reg Chalmers, was showing visitors round the department. For some reason they spent a long time looking at my machine. The next thing I know I get called to Ron's desk and he had a fatherly chat with me about my knickers. He said that he had had a complaint from the Union woman, Betty, who had had a complaint from some of the other women in the folders.

Well, I listened and then went home and took all my skirts 'UP' to 12 inches long (or should I say short?). I went back to work next day and one bloke said that I was only wearing a belt. For a joke I started to unzip it and offered to take it off for him. He decided that it looked better on. It is funny but as I told Ron, I had looked in the Union Rules and could not find nothing that said anything about not showing my knickers, so what had it to do with the Union?

Another time when the contractors were in, Irene and me went down the tunnel to eat our lunch (yes, it was our lunch that we were nibbling). Ron got a call from John Hall, the personnel manager, asking if the girls in the tunnels could stop screaming because it was disturbing his lunch! I told Ron that it wasn't fair because it was the boys that were screaming. I just hope that no one took any pictures!

In the Book Repair section Alf Price was a specialist in leather work and hand-tooling and also taught his craft at the Printing College in Oxford. He spent much of his time repairing books for college libraries and hand-binding festschrifts. He was responsible for the binding of the Coronation Bible that was used in 1953 at Westminster Abbey. He was a legend in the world of hand binding and finishing and his death in 2002 robbed the OUP and the printing and publishing world of a true craftsman. The first three words could have been describing him.

Gold, pure gold, hand beaten into a sheet so thin that it quivered as I passed by, lay on the work-bench ready to be transferred to the morocco binding of a Bruce Rogers Lectern Bible, such as the one recently bound for the new Coventry Cathedral. It was pleasing to watch as with deft handling of his special tools Alfred Price in our Bindery transformed the Bible into an object of lasting beauty to grace the pulpit of one of our churches.

One of the few remaining craftsmen in this country capable of hand binding and finishing a book, Mr Price is proud of the fact that he comes from a family of skilled craftsmen and craftswomen. His mother and sister have associations with the book-binding trade, while his brother works in the British Museum Library. Apprenticed at Zaehnsdorf, Ltd., of Shaftesbury Avenue, Mr Price later worked as a designer and gold finisher at W. T. Morrell before joining the Wigmore Bindery as foreman in

*Alf Price was a true craftsman. The world of binding is poorer without him*

the Finishing Department. During this period he worked on numerous books for HM the Queen and members of the royal family, and gave demonstrations at the British Industries Fair and PATRA exhibitions at Earls Court. With well-merited pride Mr Price showed me some examples of his craftsmanship—delicate inlays of wafer-thin coloured leather set in intricate patterns in the bindings of volumes such as Tree Tops, a copy of which was presented to the queen and another to Prince Charles. The Duke of Edinburgh's speeches, made here in Oxford, were bound in vellum by Mr Price.

The sun glinted on lines of gold tooling—lines that shimmered and appeared alive and ever-changing in shape as the book caught the angles of light. Mr Price demonstrated how the pattern is first drawn out on graph paper. This pattern is then tipped into position on the cover, and the complete design is impressed through the paper into the leather with a heated tool—one of the many that hang in racks behind Mr Price as he works at his bench. Each tool is designed for working its special pattern of lines, curves, crowns, etc. The impressed pattern is then carefully painted with two coats of 'glaire' (a preparation made from the white of an egg), the first coat being allowed to dry before the second is applied. A light film of grease is then spread over the surface. Fascinated I watched a sheet of gold leaf placed on the design and pressed in with the heated tools. This gold leaf is so thin, I learned, that thirty-two sheets of it would be no thicker than a single thickness of newspaper sheet.

On a bench nearby lay hanks of brightly coloured silks that will be woven by Mr Price into the headboards of our best books. Strips of exotic scarlet Levant morocco

*A busy Post-Packing Department with Jack Guy, Dot Millard, Harold Brown,
and Elaine O'Driscole*

and Persian morocco lay side by side with goatskin and homely leather. In a corner
of the room lay a family Bible, two centuries old. It had come here to be repaired
and rebound as nearly as possible to match its original binding. It is good to know
that the skill and materials that will go into its renovation will last for another two
centuries, and that the standards of craftsmanship on which our reputation
depends, are in good hands.

When the new rotary printing machines were about to be installed in the Litho
Machine Room above the Bindery, bindery-man Terry Chaulk had a dream. He
dreamt that the Bindery ceiling would collapse under the weight. He told everyone about the dream and this caused a mild panic among the workers. He also told
the Bindery overseer that if anyone was killed or injured he would spill the beans
to the local press. Needless to say there was no incident but on the day of the
installation the Bindery was empty!

## The Maintenance and the Service

The Press did not run itself. The organization could never have survived for more
than 500 years if it had not been for the engineers, the carpenters, the painters, the
boilermen, the ink-makers, the electricians, the cleaners, the chefs, and the tea-
ladies to keep the wheels of industry turning.

In 1960 the Boilers, too, came under the scrutiny of the modernizers when three new fully automatic boilers were installed to replace the old Lancashire Boilers. The new boilers were oil-fired and each one was capable of producing 4,300 lb. of steam an hour, steam that was pumped all around the Press.

William Green of the Engineering staff from 1856 to 1881 could not have known that he was to become a record breaker after he completed 25 years' service. He had seven sons: William a compositor who served for 12 years, Joseph an engineer 60 years, Albert, Frank, and George in the warehouse 46, 17, and 49 years respectively, Walter a machine minder 18 years, and Frederick a machine feeder 5 years. Joseph had three sons. William, a machine minder, Percival, an engineer, and Lionel, an engineer, who notched up 25, 51, and 34 years respectively. Lionel's son Maurice was a proofreader who completed 20 years. A total of 380 years!

---

*The following watery reminiscence explains just how the water that cooled the engines etc. actually got to the Press at the end of the nineteenth century.*

When I started work at the Press in the Engineer's Department in 1878 the water supply was one of our chief difficulties. There were only two City water-taps in the works—one just inside the lodge gates and the other at the south-west end of the Bible Side building on the middle floor. There was a pump over a well sunk in the Machine boys' playground, between the east end of the Bible building and the 'Clarendon Arms'. We got the water for the steam engine and boilers and other work, including washing, from Worcester College Pond. This pond is fed from the Oxford Canal and is not fit for drinking purposes. Two cast-iron pipes, six inches in diameter, conveyed the water to the Press across the grass-fields that are now Walton Crescent and Richmond Road. A pump on the steam-engine (in a room now used as the Machine Room office) was connected to one line of pipes to pump water for the engine. From the engine the water went to feed the steam-boilers. The other pipe was connected to a large pump under the Machine Room floor and was driven from the shafting; it pumped water to the pond in the Quad for storage and to supply two small pumps connected with the water-tanks over the top of the staircases at the south-west end of the two main buildings-these were officially used for washing type forms [*sic*] and plates, and for the Printing-Roller making room; unofficially apprentices dangled their feet in them during heat-waves. The tanks were not large enough to store a quantity and sometimes there would be a shortage of water during the day, while frequently soon after the engine was shut down not a bucket of water or a fire-extinguisher of any kind would be available in the building in case of an outbreak of fire.

The pond was once, some twenty years ago, very nearly the cause and scene of a fatal accident when Mr George Denton, crossing the Quad one dark evening, stumbled over the stone coping and fell into the water. He was luckily rescued in time.

The pumping of the water from Worcester Pond gave trouble sometimes as the pumps would bring up fish too big to pass through, and they would get fixed under the valves and put the pump out of action. This meant shutting the engine down and stopping the machinery to get them out—a fishy job!

In 1884 the large City water-mains for the fire-hydrants were laid round the Quad and the outside of the main buildings and to the rising mains inside to the three floors. Then there was a further move made for an improved water-service, and a large number of water-taps and washing-sinks were installed. In 1887, to commemorate Queen Victoria's jubilee, and perhaps as an encouragement to 'Drink more Water', a drinking-fountain was fixed on a wall near the middle of the Machine Room, but this was not a success. It had a cast-iron plate with the date 1887 and the University crest on it, and a metal drinking-cup attached to a chain; it was not inviting and soon fell into a bad state, and eventually was removed. I well remember hearing the jokes made about it to the effect that had it been connected up to the refreshment house not many yards away, which at that time advertised the Beverage Brewed from Malt and Hops (no substitutes used), it might have had a chance of success.

From 1946 to 1978 Les Strange carried out the plumbing and heating of the Press. The miles of water pipes, steam pipes, and gas pipes all mysteriously disappearing into walls and then suddenly darting underground into the cellars were all part of Les's world. He knew where they all started and he knew where they all went! He was single-handedly responsible for the boilers, the heating, the water supply, and the drainage and he coped with it all with apparent ease. He also had time to help others with their home plumbing problems. I was useless at DIY so he plumbed in my first washing machine without leaving the Press. Each day he gave me one instruction or piece of pipe and I would not be given the next item until I reported back to him next morning that the piece had been fitted correctly. With the aid of diagrams and old taps and pieces of pipe the washing machine was up and running in a fortnight!

A popular member of the engineering staff was Bedford Thomas. He was from St Vincent and was arguably one of the noisiest people ever to work at the Press. He was a great character and spread mirth wherever he went. My abiding memory of Bedford was the time that I entered the sinks area of the Oriental Ship one evening whilst working overtime. They were enormous sinks and Bedford was sitting naked in one of them covered in lather. He was going out that evening 'straight from' and did not have time to go home for a bath!

## The Painters and Decorators

The painting requirements of the Press were similar to that of the Forth Bridge. As soon as the painting of the walls, doors, and cupboards had been completed the process started again at the beginning. Jock the Painter and his trusty Ken are the first ubiquitous white-aproned painters that I remember. They only had two colours to deal with: Oxford blue and Cream. Every wall in the Press was painted in these colours; blue at the bottom and cream at the top. When these painters left

*Bedford Thomas—bathing beauty*

the service of the Press the painting was taken over by contractors but it was soon felt that the Press needed its own painters again for the smaller jobs. George Dent, a Geordie, and Robin Webster were employed as the new painters and George stayed until the closure of the Printing House when he was transferred to the publishing staff. Robin was deaf so it fell to George to teach everyone the 'deaf-and-dumb' language so that we could communicate with him.

## The Carpenters

These were a popular bunch of workers for many reasons. As well as being skilful carpenters and cabinet-makers they were always available to give tips to others to help them with their DIY. They also knew the location of wood offcuts and these were always taken off the premises. The management ran a 'chit' system whereby workers could take away these oddments without the fear of being accused of stealing. Carpenters would often leave their bags unattended and the old screws, nails, and nuts and bolts that had been discarded were quickly rifled. Ivor Trafford once told me that he left the bags on purpose so that this could happen and lighten his load. He also suspected that I was his best 'customer'! The daddy of all the carpenters was Stan Webb. He was a superb craftsman and a wonderful person to know. He had a wide range of interests but what he was most famous for was the fact that he was superintendent of the Press Division of the St John Ambulance Brigade, an organization that he served for many years. There are too many other carpenters to mention by name but Ivor Trafford, Colin Richens, Keith Winkworth, and Malcolm Deeley stand out as being craftsmen of the highest order.

---

*There was plenty of heated debate in 1950 when a decision had to be made whether to re-gravel the Quad or plump for the revolutionary tarmac!*

Having waded, at various seasons, through a mixture of mud and slush in the Quadrangle for over fifty years, and having seen members of the Cleaning Department patiently washing down traces of the same mud on stairs and passages ... I was amazed to read A.J.B.'s letter in *The Clarendonian* as I relaxed after my Christmas Dinner. To suggest that gravel should again be used in the drive surrounding the lawn when the opportunity comes to replace the surface with clean asphalt, as is proposed, is just about as progressive as to suggest that the country should go back to old-style macadamized roads instead of our present ones. How would the Quad be *marred* by asphalt? I fail to see. We have moved with the times, and should continue to do so.

I should also like to think of my young successors as striding briskly to, or past, the cycle sheds after work, on a well-drained asphalt drive, able to walk into their homes without spoiling their expensive carpets by walking on them with mud-stained shoes.

*The Bicycle Sheds*

The bicycle sheds have been in the Quad since God was a boy (or so it seems). In 1927 it was feared that the bicycle sheds would take over the Quadrangle; or even worse that it would be covered in and developed as part of the factory. The Press had signed a contract with a builder in 1914 to cover the Quad. Luckily, this contract was never fulfilled. The anonymous writer clearly had a crystal ball but would, I am sure, be delighted now to have witnessed the concrete bicycle sheds being smashed up and taken away in the skip. Now, about those cars and vans . . .

> With the first snowdrops came a bicycle shed. Stanchions rose from a concrete bed to receive the burden of a roof, like a huge sepulchre slab, and one more wall had found a grave, that bicycles may be housed.
>
> Now none will deny the usefulness of a bicycle, that most gentle palfry of the mechanical age, and there must be few that would challenge the right of a bicycle to its shelter; but the entombment of that grey wall by the persistent bicycle must not pass without lament. And who knows but that, when next year's snowdrops open so secretly their petals and the quadrangle once more demands our greater thanks, another wall may not have fallen to the emphatic tinkle of the bicycle-bell? There have been many Jerichos. And if the gentleness of the bicycle can hide such potency, what of other and mightier machines. . . . The insidious expansion of England's green land goes on before our eyes, grown dull by use. All the more reason, surely, that we should cling with jealous hands to the grey walls and the green turf that together make for our working hours a setting that can be boasted by few other factories, if by any other.
>
> Let us therefore make the coming of the bicycle-shed the occasion to record our affection for our quadrangle. And let there be never a whisper, nor even a thought, that perhaps the sons of our apprentices' sons shall in their time hear the rhythm of the Wharfdale, the whirr of the rotary, or the rattle of the casters where are now green grass and the song of the blackbird. We have one wall left to us; let no bicycle shed stand between it and the sunshine. The bicycle is a gentle, friendly machine, but, like all machines, it is without discretion.

*The Cleaning Staff*

The Press was cleaned daily by a team of 'suckers'. They got this name because as well as the usual brushes, mops, and dusters used to clean the Press they also used enormous trailing pipes that vacuumed up rubbish and pieces of type that had been dropped on the floor. The flexible pipes (often 10 metres long) were attached to a suction system that was driven by a motor housed in the cellars. One of the most famous suckers was 'Sid the Sucker'. To watch Sid work was a little like watching a sundial—there was never any apparent movement.

It was quite easy for lazy people to get away with doing next to nothing and

John the Cleaner (known as 'Mr Clean') was no exception except that he never did *any* work. Whenever a group of cleaners were seen together with their overalls covered in grime, Mr Clean's overall would be sparkling white.

> *One day in the Clearing Department on 8 March 1979 at precisely 2.36 p.m. it happened.*
>
> All production ceased and the crowds gathered to witness the phenomenon. An uneasy and eerie silence descended over the area when, from the midst of a swirling dust storm, a gentle scratching sound was heard. Suddenly there was a flash of brilliant white light and seasoned printers who thought that they had seen everything had to look again. Yes! You've guessed it—Mr Clean was actually *seen* pushing a broom!

## The Tea Ladies

One of the most memorable tea ladies was 'Nan' Humphrey who pushed her tea trolley around the Press for 14 years. The tea was kept in a large cream-coloured tank on top of a large wooden trolley. Inside the tank was a strange-tasting mixture of tea, milk, and sugar that would be dispensed into the mug of your choice for just one penny. On the bottom shelf were large lumps of crusty bread, cheese, and raw onions. Crisps were introduced later but the management had these withdrawn because greasy fingerprints were getting onto the books in the Machine Room and the Bindery. Later, tea and coffee vending machines replaced the tea ladies but the Press was a less colourful place because of their introduction.

## The Drivers

Chauffeurs and van drivers all have their place in Press history. One such van driver was Ron Pavier. He came to the Press as a chauffeur in 1936 but later became the Press van driver making all the local deliveries mainly to the University. When he retired his colleagues penned a poem in his honour.

> No more the hand of law to heed,
> No more the limit to exceed,
> No more the need to fret and sweat,
> As you must hump that old *Gazette.*
> No more to climb those flights of stairs
> To seek them in their private lairs;
> No more the rain-swept streets to roam
> To see if that Professor's home.
> No more those Council Papers send
> That dreary task is at an end.
> Drink deep and simply smile and say
> 'No more a need to go that way.'

Walter Ernest Gregory was the Press van driver who ran regularly between the Press and Jordan Hill Warehouse in North Oxford. He started work at the Press in 1915 driving a Foden steamwagon and he never had an accident in 47 years of driving. When he retired he had clocked up 250,000 miles! He was extremely deaf and would often guess at the answer to a question rather than admit his deafness. It was common practice in the Bindery to check with Walter the time of his next run to the warehouse. One day the office girl called out 'Hello Walt, how are you today?' He replied 'Ten to three!'

### The Tannoy

The only telephones at the Press were in the managers' offices and because everyone was constantly moving around the Tannoy (loudspeaker system) was the only way of keeping track of everyone. If you were missing from your work-station for more than a few minutes the treacherous Tannoy would call out your name and you would have to go scuttling back to your department running a gauntlet of cheers from your colleagues.

The only people not affected by the Tannoy were the proofreaders. It was thought that the disruption would cause concentration levels to diminish and this in turn could cause the readers to miss vital errors. The readers of course took full advantage of this ruling and were often quite difficult to find.

The voice of the Tannoy was always a cultured one and this would cause much mirth from the working-class lads on the shop floor. There was even a sort of secret code that could be worked out from the order in which the calls were made, for example, 'calling Mr Hall [the Personnel Manager]' immediately followed by 'calling Mr Fulton [the Father of the Chapel]' would almost always lead to speculation that there was Union trouble brewing.

The Tannoy was also a source of relieving boredom and there were childish comments shouted out for nearly every call: 'Calling Mr Harris', 'Call him what you like!'; 'Calling Mr Fissenden', 'It must be raining, she said "it's pissing down"'; 'Calling Mr Archer', everyone whistled the signature tune to 'The Archers'; 'Calling Mrs Salmon', 'She's gorn fishing', etc.

### Security

Before the arrival of electronic surveillance cameras and swipe cards you would have thought that it was pretty easy to get in and out of the Press undetected. The Press Lodge Porters, as they were then known, were always smartly dressed in an OUP uniform and peaked cap. Nobody escaped their eagle eye until a somewhat bewildered lady who found her way through to the foot of the Jobbing Department stairs said to me 'Excuse me, could you please direct me to Cronshaw Ward?'

Cycling in the Quadrangle was forbidden and lodge porters were often seen and heard chasing miscreants and screaming 'get orf yer bike'. Both Ken Hudson (son of the then Lord Mayor of Oxford) and Eddie Turner (now a police officer!) were apprehended by the lodge porter for having the audacity to ride their *motorbikes* round the Quad on their first morning at work. Interestingly, some 13 years later when Ken left the Press to become an insurance agent he retraced his route back through the Lodge but this time obediently pushing his bike and being serenaded by twenty-six Monotype keyboard operators singing 'We'll keep a welcome in the hillsides'. Prophetically, he did return through the hallowed Lodge only to be stopped by one of his ex-colleagues who asked 'Are you better now?'

In the 1970s many people left the Press to work at the Cowley car factories for almost double the wages that they were earning as skilled craftsmen. Wags thought that it would be amusing to put up large signs at all the exits with 'Gate 15', 'Gate 16', 'Gate 17', etc. Our uniformed and humourless lodge porters soon removed these.

There were far too many Lodge Porters to mention them all here but Smoky Joe will always be remembered for his cigarette ash. It must have been a pretty boring job sitting on the Lodge all day (particularly the Rear Lodge) so when Bryan Winter lit one of his many daily cigarettes he would never remove it from his mouth while he was smoking. Because of this still-life the ash stayed on the cigarette right to the end. It was truly remarkable as the ash bent at unbelievable angles and yet still remained intact. It should have been listed as one of the Wonders of the World. Everyone was horrified when Smoky Joe gave up the weed and the entertainment ceased. He was re-christened 'Smokeless Joe'.

## A Moving Business

In the 1970s the engineering, carpentry, and building staff were kept extremely busy because of the movement of plant and new machinery. It was organized by the then Works Director, James Campling, who himself declared the upheaval as 'a somewhat bemusing and ponderous game of musical chairs'. But the whole thing became a farce because if there was any planning it certainly did not show. Machines and staff were moved from pillar to post every few months. One litho machine that was ordered was so big that the management got the engineers to take it apart and the builders to knock down a wall to allow it in. After the wall had been rebuilt they decided that the machine was in the wrong place and it had to be dismantled again and moved again. It appeared that no one knew what he or she was doing and that Campling's 'bemusing and ponderous game' was far from being a game and no one was laughing (except, perhaps, the engineers, builders, and carpenters who feasted on the overtime for years!).

*James Campling: prime mover*

*Another printing machine on its way out*

*The old Boiler Room chimney . . . going . . going . . . going . . . gone!*

# CHAPTER SIX

# Clubs, Sports, and Diddlums

A S YOU would expect from an organization with more than a thousand employees there were many clubs and groups where Press folk could meet in the evenings and weekends and play sports and relax in each other's company outside working hours. The nub of this social activity was the Clarendon Press Institute and later the Jordan Hill sports complex in North Oxford.

The Stute, as it was affectionately known to Press employees, was first used as the OUP social club in 1893. It was built for £5,000 and was the focal point of just about every Press activity, both sporting and social. The building was set in the grounds of Beaumont Palace in Walton Street on the site of the old Workhouse that was moved to the Cowley Road in Oxford in 1860.

> *At the formal opening of the Institute, in September 1893, the Bishop of Oxford (Bishop Stubbs) in the course of his inaugural speech took occasion to refer to the site on which the building had been erected:*
>
> This piece of ground had gone through some wonderful vicissitudes. At first it seemed to have been part of a great palace, then a sort of monastery; then it was known by the title of 'Rats and Mice Hill', and afterwards had a workhouse built upon it. When it was not good enough for a workhouse it was sold to Cardinal Newman, to found a Roman Catholic institution upon; but the Cardinal dropped it, apparently like a hot coal. It then came into the hands of the University, and I believe that the establishing of the Institute was the first time since the workhouse was abolished that the site had been used. Those things might be an allegory; there might be marks of ups and downs, progress and retrogression. At all events, when it was 'Rats and Mice Hill' it must have got to the bottom of its stage. Now it was to be devoted to a great and excellent purpose . . . it should be a sort of lay church, for the workers of the Press to make the best of the faculties God had given them.

In speaking of the ground being out of use from the removal of the Workhouse until the building of the Institute, the Bishop may have left use for cultivation out of account. As a matter of fact the ground was 'used' for many years as a vegetable garden by a Mr Jacks, a Scottish packman, who lived just opposite.

Further details concerning the site were contributed to the local press at that time by Horace Hart, from which it appears that the Workhouse site and garden, comprising about five acres, were sold by the Oxford Guardians in August 1864, and bought by Ambrose Smith of Walton Street for £8,000. The consignment is dated January 1865. The purchaser immediately resold the ground to the Revd Dr J. H. Newman of Birmingham, who, abandoning the idea of building a Roman Catholic College in Oxford, soon sold the ground again, this time to the University.

The first meeting of its members took place in July with Horace Hart presiding and the first Institute Council was formed. The Stute was run by an elected Council almost up to the closure of the Printing Division. The opening ceremony had taken place on 16 September 1893 and the inside of the building had been decorated and the rooms were 'gay with flags and flowers'.

There was a library, a dramatic society, a debating society, a vocal society, and orchestra, and whist and cribbage tournaments were arranged. It was just what Press employees needed; a real social club, one that was to cater for the social needs of Press employees for many years to come.

The Stute was a magnet for apprentices and they could easily get their hands on alcohol because older colleagues would purchase drinks for them. This was not so easy during the lunch-breaks but in the evenings (particularly Fridays) all roads led to the Stute.

While I was an apprentice Mrs Hale played the piano in the bar every Friday evening and everyone would join in with the singing while others performed their party pieces. One man's weekly monologue on the 'Death of Nelson' was not to be missed. There were cheers as every week he would 'die' in his inebriated state among the sawdust on the floor.

Lee Jackson, the Bar Steward, would give away his snuff and sell scrumpy cider in nips on the condition that apprentices did not exceed his limit of three. This was always ignored and at closing time Walton Street was littered with (literally) legless apprentices and lads suffering from the effects of the cider. I was lucky because the railings outside the Stute led to the first lamppost that was also the number 3 bus stop. Luckily, the number 3 bus stopped just a few yards from my house.

There was a major renovation in 1975 that transformed the billiard rooms on the lower ground floor into a self-service restaurant. The old TV room became a coffee lounge and lounge bar, and the Council Rooms and Library became 'official business dining-rooms'. The whole place was gaudily decorated and the working-men's club atmosphere with foaming beer, pickled onions in crisp packets, and snuff freely available behind the bar was no more. The regulars could just about tolerate all this but there was worse news to come. The management was not satisfied with destroying the ambience that had served the workers for so

*The Press gave the employees' children a party every Christmas*

many years—they changed its name. The Stute became 'The Clarendon Press Centre' and from that moment it was never to be the same again.

The Band and Vocal Society was formed in July 1852 after Thomas Combe announced that he had purchased a 'certain number of brass instruments'. A nucleus of a band had been formed and over the next few months the membership rose to fifteen necessitating the purchase of more instruments. They performed many concerts and in 1854 the Vocal Society was inaugurated with the Instrumental Society to become the Band and Vocal Society. They worked harmoniously together giving concerts at Christmas for several years. At the first concert the conductor hedged his bets by announcing to the audience: 'In placing this programme in the hands of the audience, the members of the University Press band and Singing Classes beg to claim their indulgent consideration. It is only about a year and a half since the Band was formed; at which time every individual composing it was entirely unacquainted with the instrument he now plays. . . . In consenting to give a concert they do not come forward to challenge criticism, but merely to show, for encouragement to others, how much may be accomplished in a very short time by zeal and perseverance.' According to Cocker they had no reason to worry because the concert was an outstanding success.

It never failed to amaze me what Press people got up to in their spare time. In 1951 the Country Dancing Club at the Institute was fairly well supported every Monday but they were always on the lookout for new members, encouraging them to come and get a 'graceful swing into your body by Country Dancing'. Later they introduced English Sword Dancing lessons and encouraged people to come along because 'no-one minds how many mistakes you make'!

**Clarendon Press Institute, 1919**
*Twenty-sixth Anniversary of Foundation*

## PROGRAMME

A Comic Drama, entitled

### 'All that glitters is not Gold'

By the Dramatic Society

*On Wednesday, September 17, at 7.30 p.m.*

#### CHARACTERS

| | |
|---|---|
| Sir Arthur Lassell | Mr. B. GOODING |
| Jasper Plum | Mr. G. CARTER |
| Stephen Plum | Mr. H. S. WHITE |
| Frederick Plum | Mr. A. DAVIDSON |
| Toby Twinkle | Mr. H. SHEPPARD |
| Harris | Mr. G. BEAL |
| Servant | Mr. W. WILKINS |
| Lady Leatherbridge | Miss H. WEBB |
| Lady Valeria Westendleigh | Miss G. LAUNCHBURY |
| Martha Gibbs | Mrs. H. SHEPPARD |

Guests, Millhands, &c.

ACT I.   Scene: *Hall in Jasper Plum's House at Bristol*
ACT II.   Scene: *Drawing-room*

Selections by the Institute Orchestra

*Probably the first Dramatic Society's show after the First World War*

The Press boasted a minstrel band, called 'The Clarendon Press Minstrels': a society that would not be allowed in today's politically correct climate. The fact remains, though, that Press employees who could sing, dance, or play a musical instruments were drawn to this society where they would 'black up' their faces using burnt cork and take part in sketches and songs to entertain their colleagues. On 9 and 10 April 1920 the Minstrels were assisted by the Clarendon Press Orchestra. It was described as an 'extravaganza' and the audience were delighted by, amongst others, B. C. Walker's 'Good old Yorkshire pudden', Horace Alcock's 'I do like an egg for tea', and Bert Walker's 'Dat fal lil' feller with his Mammy's eyes'!

*The minstrel shows nearly always took place at the Stute and would play to packed audiences. The 1921 show appears to have been a great success.*

The Clarendon Minstrels have again scored a distinct triumph. Persistency refused to be baulked by difficulties and disappointments in seemingly endless procession, and the success was well and truly earned. Notwithstanding 'compet-

*Cyril Cox, Mick Belson, and Garvin Reeves 'Busy doing nothing' in the Press Pantomime 'Alice in Wonderland', 1966*

ing shows' elsewhere there was a good house on the first evening. The Large Hall was crowded on the following evening; and in the afternoon there was an audience of some five-hundred close-packed, delighted, appreciative juveniles, whose spontaneous outburst of cheering at the close of the performance was doubtless gratifying to the 'coons' (and others) who had entertained them. Among those 'others', normal as to complexion but imbued with like enthusiasm, Mr W. Long, the conductor, is to be congratulated on the result of his skilful coaching, for the singing was especially pleasing; while Mrs Percy Taylor filled the role of accompanist admirably. The popular 'Bubbles' was well sung by Master Stanley Judge, while sundry little nigger boys manipulated pipes and soapsuds in the background; and Mr Alf Gibbons, the 'human nightingale', scored every time with his rare powers of whistling.

The entertainment was often repeated in local hospitals and the records show that the Minstrels performed at the (now Nuffield) Orthopaedic Hospital, the Cowley Road Hospital, and the Warneford Hospital.

The Clarendon Press Institute was used for many activities and there were not

JANUARY, 1919.

# THE
# Clarendonian

The Quarterly Magazine of the employees of
**THE CLARENDON PRESS, OXFORD**
Issued by the Council of the Clarendon Press Institute
and conducted by the Institute Library Committee ∽∽

OXFORD: Printed at the Clarendon Press
by Frederick Hall, Printer to the University

*The cover of the first*
Clarendonian

many more popular activities than the Ladies' Keep Fit Classes in 1938. Interestingly men always ran the classes! The last sentence, though, baffles me in the review of the 1938 display!

> Each Monday night the [Press] ladies perform all sorts of weird and wonderful exercises in the Institute to the strains of Brahms, Beethoven, and Irving Berlin. Mr Janaway has trained them to an extremely high standard of efficiency. From a display point of view they are well worth watching, and the physical benefit they have derived from the exercises you will be able to judge for yourself when they give a display. Night starvation to them is now a thing of the past . . .

The Clarendon Press Dramatic Society was formed in December 1861 and opened with a performance of *The Merchant of Venice* at the Star Assembly Rooms in Oxford. Over the years there had been many dramatic societies formed but the

*Early Press Cricket Club*

*Quincentenary Cricket Team, 1978*

last one, and arguably the most popular, was the Ancient Order of Pantomimers which was set up to produce an annual pantomime for the Stute's Children's Christmas Party. It all started in 1959 when a group from the Football Section got together to perform an adaptation of *Babes in the Wood*. The pantomime's popularity grew and the shows, all written by engineer Norman and compositor Garvin Reeves (the 'Brothers Reeve') were soon performing three performances each Christmas for the next 15 years. They were so successful that many would-be Press thespians clamoured to join. There was only one rule and that was that only men were allowed to enter the Order. It was thought at the time that the introduction of women would 'only bring trouble'. This form of discrimination never caused problems because there were always plenty of people willing to wear a frock for the cause. By 1974 the Order had lost some members through untimely deaths and it was felt that it was time to hang up the costumes and bow out at the peak of their success.

Information about what was going on at the Press was vital to everyone and *The Clarendonian* was the mouthpiece. It was a magazine that was independent of the Press and published by the Council of the Clarendon Press Institute. *The Clarendonian* was first issued in January 1919 and was sold at 3*d.* per copy. There were twenty pages of Demy 8$^{vo}$, plus cover, and records show that the bill for printing the first four issues in 1919 came to £65. 14*s.* 6*d.* During its life it was under the control of fourteen editors and co-editors. The first editor was Allpress Hinson, and he held that post for the first thirty-four issues. In 1922 the price was put up to 6*d.* per copy, but this seems to have had an adverse effect on the sales and the price reverted to 3*d.* after four issues. October 1926 saw a change in format and size to Crown 4$^{to}$, and the first issue of the new size was free to all members of the Press as an inducement to becoming regular subscribers.

In January 1928 Mr Hinson gave up the editorship because of failing health and *The Clarendonian* came under a succession of editors. Mr Davidson was followed by Miss Fanny Williams, co-editors Miss Viney and Miss Brereton, Miss E. Ward, and Miss Wilson. By 1940 wartime shortages brought the regular publication of *The Clarendonian* to a temporary end. A special eight-page 'War-time News Sheet' issued in 1942 listed the names of 209 Press members who had joined the forces. A 'Victory News Sheet' was published in 1946 containing the names of the 256 members who had joined the Forces and the eighteen men who had died on active service.

In March 1947 the Printer (Charles Batey) took over the publication of *The Clarendonian*, the size reverted to Demy 8$^{vo}$, and the magazine was circulated free of charge to all members and pensioners of the Press. Eric Muncaster held the post of editor for seventeen issues, followed by Harold Boyce for a further fifteen issues. The next editor, Victor Sugden, took over with the March 1955 issue, and continued to edit the magazine until George Perry took over. When George Perry

*Quincentenary Bowls Section, 1978*

*Three members of the Running Section*

*The Tennis Section*

retired in 1977 the editorial baton was passed to co-editors Mick Belson and Harvie Willshire and later Mick Belson and David Brown. They continued to publish this wonderful magazine until just before the closure of the Printing House.

The other main focal point of Press social activities was the Amalgamated Athletic Clubs (OUPAAC); the umbrella organization that governed and financially supported all the various clubs and sections at the Press. There had always been sports clubs at the Press. The various sections would play their sports in a 'very carefree manner'. Cricket and football would be played on Port Meadow and rugby enthusiasts would beg or borrow the grounds and kit from local clubs. The people involved in cricket, tennis, bowls, swimming, rifle shooting, hockey, cycling, rowing, and running were drifting from fixture to fixture in a very haphazard manner. In 1885 it was decided that all Press sports clubs should elect their own officers and be self-financing. This was fairly successful for a while but in 1894 the Council of the recently built Clarendon Press Institute suggested that all the clubs should amalgamate. The Stute was to be the clubhouse and each section would elect two representatives to form the Institute Council.

The Jordan Hill sports ground opened in 1925 but the original pavilion was not built until 1934. The money to build the pavilion was raised by the workers at the

*The Press Golf Society*

Press but the Delegates of the Press gave a financial helping hand towards the end to ensure that the project was a success. The Clubs were very popular with Press employees and were all well supported. Workers could engage in competitive hockey (men's, ladies', and mixed), cricket, football, golf, running, rifle shooting, bowls, cycling, fishing, swimming, and water polo. At the time of writing the cricket, football, golf, running, and bowls sections are still operating although there are very few Press employees making up the teams. The OUPAAC has now allowed members of the public to join in the sporting activities so it can no longer be regarded as a 'Press' institution.

The Press Piscatorial Society was formed early in 1902. Although no minute books or records survive of the early proceedings we do know that one Mr W. L. Roper and Mr A. Lusty were among the first to attend the early meetings. The society started after a few Press men had got together over a game of cards and a challenge was made that one fellow could catch more fish than the others. As a result of this challenge a group of Press personnel decided to meet at King's Lock for the first match.

They got a lot more than they bargained for on that first morning because as soon as they had set up their tackle they discovered a dead body floating in the river. They had to call the police who in turn had to call an ambulance to take the corpse away. This dampened the fishermen's spirits somewhat but Press humour being what it was they returned to work the next day to be ribbed by their work-mates that all they could catch was 'dead-uns'!

*The 1956 Cup Winning Team*

Top left to right: *Doug Maas; Harry Smith; Ray Church; Ron Hartwell; Terry Foster; Mick Cooke; Tony Hopcraft; Dave Cook*
Middle left to right: *Ken Walker; Sid Hayle; Ted Papal; Tony Stretton; Nobby Clarke; Cyril Cox; Ron Mobley; Jack England; Charlie Morgan; Brian Ashmole; Dick Townley; Norman Appleton; Ron Thomas; Alf Jeffries; John Hall; Bill Wilkins*
Bottom left to right: *Mick Foster; Aubrey Owen; Ron Lewendon; Den Hewlett; Malcolm Poulter; Bob Potter*

In spite of this shaky start the society was formed following a meeting at the Stute and the subscriptions were fixed at 2*d.* per month. It was decided by the newly elected committee to call themselves a 'Piscatorial Society' rather than an 'Angling Club' because 'we are a learned Press and the more common word "angling" would therefore not apply'. The first official competition took place opposite Kennington Island on the river Thames (now known as Rose Island) in July 1902.

After a day's fishing the society members would always 'finish off' with a visit to the nearest pub where they would exchange yarns about the proverbial one that got away. This tradition was religiously followed until the society disbanded following the closure of the Printing House. Publishing staff formed a new club in 1997 under the name of the 'Oxford University Press *Angling Club*'! This new club at first attracted many members and they became affiliated to the OUPAAC for a while.

*The Quincentenary River Swim from Folly Bridge to Iffley Lock, 1978*

In the early 1900s it was quite common for the Press anglers to be bidden farewell out of pubs such as The White Hart at Fifield with a trumpet fanfare by a grateful landlord. Travelling by horse and carriage the fishermen found that they could travel much further afield to such places as Appleton, Newbridge, Bablock-hythe, and Buckland. The first Buckland trip was memorable because the horse bolted as it approached the village of Appleton. It was only stopped when it hit a lamp-post outside St Frideswide's Church and all the fishermen were thrown out of the carriage. The records show that they all escaped serious injury and lived to fish another day.

Once the horse-drawn carriages gave way to charabancs the members discovered new places to fish; Tadpole, Radcot, Day's Lock, and sometimes they would travel by train to far-away places such as Culham (less than 10 minutes from Oxford!). The first ever visit to Tadpole became legend because the society members netted over 1 hundredweight of fish.

One hot summer's day the society held a competition at a gravel pit near Stanton Harcourt right next to a refuse tip. Novice angler and machine room assistant Inky Parsons decided to seek advice from the Bindery's expert and internationally renowned angler, Peter Stone. Peter told Inky that he should try floating crust because it was a lake full of carp. Inky arrived armed with a French stick and began fishing. He was not having much luck and decided to walk along the bank to consult Peter Stone once more. Before he had reached the guru he was overtaken by a scruffy mongrel dog carrying his French stick much to the amusement of all the other fishermen.

*The Swimming Committee of 1985—Mick Belson, Sam Goodlake, Frank Deacon, Frank Goodgame, Don Loader, and Printer to the University Eric Buckley*

The swimming club began in the Merton Street baths in Oxford in 1929 before moving to Temple Cowley baths in 1939. The Press boasted a fine water polo team and also ran life-saving classes. These classes were abandoned in 1938 owing to the 'interference of overtime'! The swimming sessions were free and bathing costumes and towels could be hired for 'a nominal fee'. Only men were allowed to join the club even though the Swimming Committee was in favour of admitting women. After some years of heated debate the General Sports Committee of the Press gave in and allowed women 'the privilege' of joining their male colleagues in the pool.

The Swimming Club was always very popular and there were three annual events that were always well supported. They were the Annual River Swim from Folly Bridge to Iffley Lock, the annual swim from Medley to Folly Bridge, and the Annual Gala. Participants would start to train many months ahead for all three events. The Folly Bridge to Iffley Lock race would start from the boathouse at 7.30 a.m. and with the swimmers covered in grease they would launch themselves into the cold waters of the Isis. Their objective was to be the first swimmer to touch the 'Bull's Nose' at Iffley Lock nearly 2 miles away. In later years they were rewarded with a hot breakfast, coffee, and brandy after they were pulled out of the water.

When Eric Buckley joined the Press as Printer he accepted an invitation to become the Swimming Section's President. He made sure that he was always on

*Swimmers at Folly Bridge waiting for 'The Off'*

the riverbank by 7 a.m. to check the quality of the brandy that would later be offered to the swimmers when they arrived at the finishing line following the Annual River Swim. When the Printer married his American wife, Harriet, he convinced her that she should also attend. She was a beautiful woman who reminded me of Lauren Bacall. When she arrived as dawn was breaking I thanked her for getting up so early. She lifted her dark glasses and drawled 'Honey, I haven't been to bed yet!'

The Cycling Club was formed in 1933. On one occasion they pedalled to Whipsnade arriving at 1.30 p.m. just in time for lunch at The Chequers. They spent a couple of hours at the zoo before setting off for Aston Clinton for tea. They arrived back in Oxford around 9.30 p.m. 'totally exhausted'. They attended weekend camps on the Isle of Wight and enjoyed a full programme of cycling trips every weekend throughout the year.

The OUPAAC, together with the Stute, would run the interdepartmental games allowing people who were not particularly skilled in a sport to have a go by representing their departments once a year. There were always cups and other trophies to be won and displayed with pride in the departments after the games. During the winter months the interdepartmental games would continue indoors with whist, darts, dominoes, shove-halfpenny, and skittles all washed down with plenty of beer, cheese, and chutney. These were known as the 'Winter Olympics'.

In 1917 a part of Port Meadow was given over to allotments and Press folk were not slow in obtaining plots of ground to help home food production during the First World War. It was decided in 1918 to form a gardening club with a view to

*The Press Ladies Football Team with referee Ron Bushnell protecting his assets*

holding a Food Production Exhibition in the Quadrangle. It was judged a great success, was called 'The Food Production and Flower Show and the Horticultural Society', and continued for many years.

*This poem written was written by a member of the association in 1919 soon after the First World War:*

> The printer man, when print began
> Pursued both pelf and pleasure,
> Arranging types and sampling swipes
> In wide or narrow measure.
> In later years, with types and beers
> He still contrived to stick it;
> Whilst leisure hours increased his powers
> Of sport—including cricket.
> But recent days constrained his ways:
> All games were out-of-daters;
> He chucked the lot, to hatch his plot
> And lift a ton of taters.

When I first started work in the Machine Room I was to learn many things about gardening from Jim Hedges who was the star of many Food Production and Flower Show events particularly with his chrysanthemums. It was his encourage-

*The Oriental Ship win the Winter Olympics at the Stute*

ment that prompted many a young apprentice to take up gardening. During tea breaks he would hold seminars on subjects such as pruning, budding, rooting, and mixing your own weedkillers and fertilizers by buying the ingredients separately and mixing them yourself at a fraction of the cost. These things I still do today. He even taught us how to kill wood pigeons by wiring peas that had been soaked in water and then scattering them on the ground so that the pigeons would choke to death.

In the early 1800s the Press had a fire engine and certain members of the staff took part in fire drills and were rewarded with coupons, cashable at the Insurance Company's charge. There was little in the way of disciplined drill and they were not supplied with uniforms.

The Oxford City Brigade made persistent appeals to the University and College authorities to provide the buildings under their care with more adequate protection against fire. As a result of these appeals up-to-date equipment, fire plant, new water mains, hydrants, etc. were installed. It was a Mr J. De La Mare who approached the Controller (Horace Hart) on the subject, suggesting the formation of a 'Volunteer Fire Contingent for the Press'. Within weeks the University Press had the makings of a Fire Brigade with more than fifty members.

In 1840, and at later dates, the Press fire engine is mentioned among others as assisting at fires in the City travelled as far afield as Eynsham and the men were often seen to show extreme bravery.

OXFORD UNIVERSITY PRESS

## VOLUNTEER FIRE CONTINGENT

❧

# PROGRAMME

of the thirty-fifth

## Annual Prize Competition

## and Demonstration

to take place at the Press on

*Saturday, June 26, 1920, beginning at 2.15 p.m.*

❧

The Prizes gained in the above Competition, as well as
those awarded for the Quarterly Competitions, will
be presented by the Rev. the Vice-Chancellor
at the close of the proceedings together
with Long-Service Medals

---

# ORDER OF PROCEEDINGS

❧

**2.15**   **Roll Call.** Inspection of Brigade by Chief Officer
Symonds of the City Brigade and the Controller.

**2.30**        **I. One-Man Drill.**

**Object of Drill.**—To show how quickly one man can get to work upon
a supposed Fire with the Press Fire Plant.

At the signal each competitor will fix stand-pipe and key to hydrant, run
out and connect two 50-ft. lengths of canvas hose, and fix branch-pipe.
The branch-pipe must be put in belt when carrying second length of hose.

Four Prizes are awarded, as well as a fifth and sixth
Prize kindly contributed by Capt. Symonds and
Messrs. Barlow & Alden respectively. The First
Prize carries with it the Championship of the
Brigade and the Challenge Cup.

**3.15**        **II. Four-Men Engine Drill.**

*Four men with four lengths of delivery hose, two branch-pipes,
and two lengths suction.*

**Object of Drill.**—To show how quickly four men can get to work upon
a supposed Fire with the Press Fire Plant.

**At signal for MAKE-UP:—**

No. 1 takes off branch on near side, makes up farthest length, buckles up
off-side length, brings in the two lengths of hose and makes up fore-
carriage.

No. 2 takes off branch on off side, and makes up two lengths of hose.

No. 3 disconnects off- and near-side connexions, makes up near-side length
of hose and stows gear.

No. 4 locks levers, disconnects delivery hose on near and off side, replaces
caps, disconnects suction hose and stows it.

---

**4.15**    *Distribution of Prizes and of Long-Service
Medals.*

The following is a list of the Members of the Brigade entitled to Long-
Service Medals :—

| | | | | |
|---|---|---|---|---|
| Superintendent E. HUNT | 34 years' service | = | Silver Medal and 2 bars. | |
| Engineer J. GREEN . . | 34 | ,, | = | ,, ,, |
| Fireman J. GRIFFIN . . | 33 | ,, | = | ,, ,, |
|   ,,   W. ROPER . . | 29 | ,, | = | ,, and 1 bar. |
| Foreman J. TYRRELL . | 24 | ,, | = | Silver Medal. |
| Fireman C. FOSTER . . | 23 | ,, | = | ,, |
|   ,,   F. CLIFFORD . | 22 | ,, | = | ,, |
|   ,,   F. COX . . . | 21 | ,, | = | ,, |
|   ,,   S. BEST . . . | 20 | ,, | = | ,, |
|   ,,   H. WELLER . | 19 | ,, | = | Bronze Medal and 1 bar. |
| Asst.-Eng. H. PARSLOW | 18 | ,, | = | ,, ,, |
| Fireman E. FITCHETT . | 18 | ,, | = | ,, ,, |
| Asst.-Eng. P. GREEN . | 16 | ,, | = | ,, ,, |
| Fireman G. TAYLOR . | 16 | ,, | = | ,, ,, |
|   ,,   A. HINE . . . | 16 | ,, | = | ,, ,, |
|   ,,   W. GREEN . . | 10 | ,, | = | Bronze Medal. |
|   ,,   R. CLIFFORD . | 10 | ,, | = | ,, |

❧

*During the afternoon the Press Orchestra will play the
following selections :*

| | | | |
|---|---|---|---|
| MARCH . . . | 'Gladiator's Farewell' . | . | *Blankenberg* |
| OVERTURE . . | 'Le Diadem' . | . . | *Hermann* |
| SELECTION . . | 'Bishop's Songs' . | . . | *Volti* |
| WALTZ . . | 'Autumn Leaves' . | . . | *Lincke* |
| INTERMEZZO . | 'La Cinquantaine' . | . | *Gabriel-Marie* |
| SELECTION . . | 'Maritana' . | . . | *Wallace* |
| WALTZ . . | 'Night of Love' . | . . | *Lincke* |
| MARCH . . | 'Sons of the Brave' . | . . | *Bidgood* |

---

**At signal for RUN-OUT:—**

Having completed the Make-up each Crew will go to the clothes stand,
and remove helmet, belt, and tunic. At the signal the Crew will dress as
speedily as possible, and proceed to get to work on the RUN-OUT.
Belts, tunics, &c., must be properly fastened before crossing the line ; otherwise fines will be inflicted.

### TEAMS.

*(Order of going on.)*

| ( 1 ) | ( 2 ) | ( 3 ) |
|---|---|---|
| R. CLIFFORD (Capt.). | H. WELLER (Capt.). | P. J. GREEN (Capt.). |
| E. GODDARD. | L. GRIFFIN. | P. BENNETT. |
| G. LAPWORTH. | A. HINE. | F. COX. |
| E. FITCHETT. | R. LEWIS. | J. THOMAS. |

| ( 4 ) | ( 5 ) | ( 6 ) |
|---|---|---|
| G. TAYLOR (Capt.). | J. TYRRELL (Capt.). | H. PARSLOW (Capt.). |
| W. BROWN. | C. FOSTER. | F. CLIFFORD. |
| C. HUTCHINS. | W. ROPER. | E. NURSER. |
| R. NEW. | J. LAPWORTH. | S. BEST. |

| ( 7 ) |
|---|
| W. GREEN (Capt.). |
| J. GRIFFIN. |
| F. J. AYRES. |
| C. PIPER. |

(Prizes are awarded to the first two Teams.)

**4.0**        **III. Demonstration Drill.**

**Object of Drill.**—To test the efficiency of the Brigade, both as to
skill and expedition, in the use of the University Press Fire Plant, and
to show what would happen should a fire break out in a particular
department during the daytime.

**A Fire is supposed to have broken out during working hours
in the Houses on the first floor.**

The members of the Brigade are assumed to be at their various places of
work in the building. The alarm is given and the various Groups of
Firemen assemble at the Archway of the Quad, bringing gear with them.
There the Groups will receive instructions from the officer in charge.
Some of the men will work from the hydrants in the Quad while others will
use ladders at the first-floor windows.

---

*The programme for the 1920 Fire Brigade Annual Prize Competition*

*Stan Parker and John Bowley—victorious in the table tennis doubles*

After a fire in St Aldate's in 1870, in which two women were burned to death, the Oxford City Volunteer Fire Brigade came into being. It was at this time that Thomas Combe handed over the charge of the Press engine to Captain Fane and Engineer Thomas Green; and it remained under the charge of the City Brigade (though not removed from the Press except for use or for repairs) until the process of time imperceptibly handed back the 'charge' to the Press.

In the 1920s the OUP Fire Brigade numbered about thirty men, some of who were also members of the Ambulance Division. The uniform worn then consisted of a double-breasted tunic buttoned up to the neck and a flat peakless cap and it made them look like German infantrymen. The Volunteer Brigade has its roots going back to 1835 and became a member of the Oxford and District Fire Brigades Association when it was formed in 1908. This organization had been originally set up for university, college, and industrial brigades within 5 miles from the centre of Oxford.

The Delegates installed a fire engine at Walton Street in 1830 when the move from the Clarendon Building had been completed: it was manned by volunteers. The first Press fire in which it was involved was on the Bible Side in 1838 but this manual pump assisted at fires in the City; and it was pulled, by horse, to the 1854 fire which devastated Eynsham.

The Clarendon Press Volunteer Fire Brigade took part in annual competitions and were held from 1836 right up to 1988. The City Brigade looked to the Press for help with major fires and this cooperation came to its peak during the Second

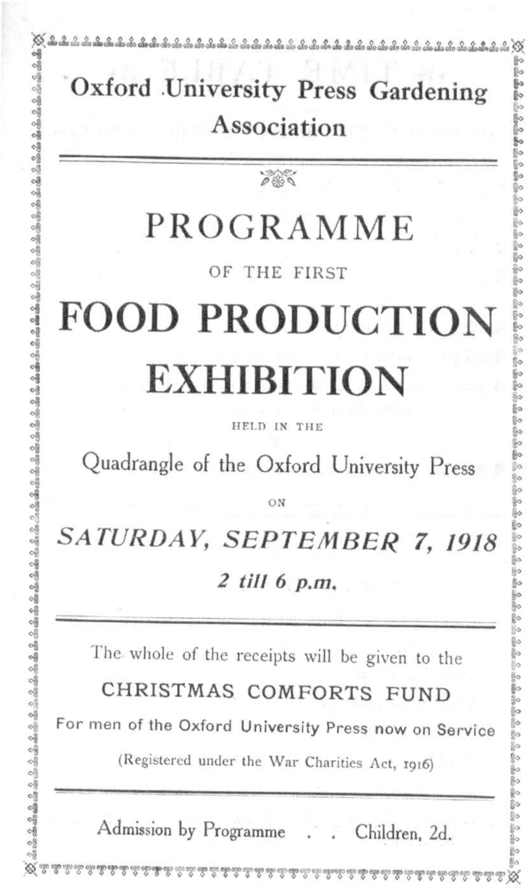

Oxford University Press Gardening
Association

PROGRAMME

OF THE FIRST

FOOD PRODUCTION

EXHIBITION

HELD IN THE

Quadrangle of the Oxford University Press

ON

SATURDAY, SEPTEMBER 7, 1918

2 till 6 p.m.

The whole of the receipts will be given to the

CHRISTMAS COMFORTS FUND

For men of the Oxford University Press now on Service

(Registered under the War Charities Act, 1916)

Admission by Programme . . Children, 2d.

*Vegetables, flowers,*
*tea, and a concert*

World War. The Press was fully committed to government printing, including codebooks. John Johnson, as Printer, was also the Brigade's Chief Officer, and slept at the Press throughout the war. The Brigade, by day, night, and weekend, would man two of the City's pumps. The Press was responsible, through its ARP wardens and its St John Ambulance Division, for civil defence for all its premises (including Jordan Hill) as well as other codebook operations at the Press annexe in Juxon Street, and at Mansfield College.

The Press Brigade went from strength to strength and won many trophies for its skills in competitions against other private brigades and many Press firemen were retained by the Oxford City Brigade. In the final years the profile of the Brigade was raised dramatically when Commercial Director, Richard Russell, took over as Chief Officer. Although he was a member of senior management he was well liked and trusted by his men having served several years on the shop floor as a management trainee.

*Winners of the Gardner Challenge Cup for the Junior Four-Man Manual Engine Drill,
8 June 1929*

Aubrey Beesley, who joined in 1923, became the first person from the Brigade to be Chief Officer, the three preceding Printers having held the title. He took over in 1945, retiring thirty years later! The 1929 cup-winning crew of Percy Boswell, Gilbert Tyrrell, Aubrey Beesley, and Andy Chalmers was a typical quartet. Percy went from the Forwarding Office to run the White Paper Office; Gilbert became the Assistant Manager in the Letterpress Machine Room; Aubrey was a bindery foreman; Andy was the bindery engineer (during the war, when branches—nozzles—were scarce, he made two from bits of brass and copper bedstead).

Things did not always go right. At a fire in the film store in the old slaughterhouse behind the original Litho Department poor Harry Thornton arrived first on the scene only to find that the lengths of canvas hose that were stored nearby had perished so they burst when he tried to extinguish the fire. Even the City's crew did not have an easy time of it because they had to lift a car off the hydrant in Walton Crescent before they could attempt to extinguish the fire.

The most destructive fire at the Press was discovered on the evening of 18 July 1974 in the Examination Ship by a night watchman. The Oxford City Fire

*Press fire fighter, Trevor Luke*
*during drill practice*

Brigade attended with five appliances and it was 7.30 the following morning before the last machine left the site. There was much structural damage to the department and the surrounding area and a lot of type and equipment was lost. Miraculously, many of the proofs of the examination papers were out of the building so that they could be reset without loss or embarrassment to the customers.

*Richard Russell remembers with affection the men under his command.*

David Ledger was one of the keenest of all our firemen, being with us for some thirty years, and winning the Singleman cup thirteen times. However, he was often the victim of a sort of Fireman's Murphy's Law. If something unlikely happened it was always ascribed to Ledge. Stan Topp was the most loyal of Second Officers, but on the odd occasion he was known to go in the wrong direction. Alan 'Dinky' Dawson was an admirable fireman, but in his large black helmet he looked like a black-top mushroom. It was these people, with others including Phil Radmore, who were brilliant when the drier on a web-offset press caught fire one lunchtime. The insurers said that their prompt work, before the arrival of seven local authority appliances, reduced the damage by £100,000. Paul Thompson, David Ledger, Trevor Luke, and John England provided a full crew of retained firemen to man an appliance at the City fire station. There was a fire-men's strike in 1980 and, while we could not take on a public role, we hired a van for our mobile pump and gear so we could look after Press property without upsetting TUC protocol.

I once asked John England why he wanted to join the Brigade. He said it was a form of social purpose towards his colleagues and the Press, and he liked the mod-est forms of uniform and discipline. His predecessors did have those glorious hel-mets, but perhaps all firemen, deep down, get a boyish pleasure in squirting water.

Another important organization was the Press Division of the St John Ambu-lance Brigade. In 1908, in the days of horse-drawn trams and gas lighting, a few Press employees got together and decided to form an OUP section of the Brigade. Horace Hart gave permission for this to happen and the first meeting was held on 30 October. The Division was registered on 21 January 1909 with over twenty members. A Ladies Nursing Division was added soon after and this increased the strength of the organization. During the First World War the Division worked long hours and together with the Press Fire Brigade met the convoys of wounded soldiers and provided comforts for them on their way to local Hospitals. During the period of the war the division transported over one hundred and five thousand people.

Martin Slade, who was for many years Divisional Officer and Superintendent of the Division looks back with pride on this vital part of Press life:

*Richard Russell—
on his way to a fire?*

*One of the last pictures of the OUP Fire Brigade*

The members of the Division provided a much-needed first-aid service for their colleagues and were responsible for maintaining the equipment in the first-aid boxes situated in all sections of the Press. Members met weekly on a Tuesday night in the Stute reading room for training and they took a yearly examination carried out by Dr Mure of the Pressed Steel Company. The Division was also inspected by the County Commissioner of the Brigade as well as attending a yearly outing either to London to see a show or a trip to the sea. In later years some training sessions were held jointly with the Fire Brigade and we trained on larger incidents by releasing people from lift shafts or working in total darkness in one of the tunnels which run under the Press.

For a good number of years the Division had a divisional doctor, Dr Robertson, who presented a cup to the winner of the annual first-aid competition. Following the death of Dr Robertson the division had a student doctor, Dr Stanwood, who later qualified and stayed with the division until he was eventually posted to a Birmingham Hospital. The Division was also responsible for training hundreds of first-aiders on the annual first-aid course when the Division brought in another doctor from the Pressed Steel company, Dr Barnes.

First-aiders would be on call within the Press dealing with small incidents and from time to time larger ones such as heart attacks and strokes. In the Bindery first-aiders had to deal with serious cuts on guillotines and on one occasion had to release a member of staff from a sewing machine when the back of an arm was pierced by a set of needles. Christmas Eve was the most difficult time for members when staff returned to work in the afternoon from the pub and some were not fit for work. After discussions with management about the danger of staff having a serious accident it was decided to close the Press for the Christmas Eve afternoon.

*The Editor of the* Clarendonian *at the children's Christmas party keeping in touch with Nurse Webber*

As well as operating within the Press the Division attended the children's Christmas party and had to contend with over two hundred children—not for the faint hearted! Members also worked for the Brigade outside the Press at fetes, point-to-points, theatres, and cinemas, and for many years received no remuneration. There had been many discussions by management that the members should receive an honorarium for their work but it was refused. Finally members did accept £25 a year which was later increased to £200.

During the final years of the Printing Division, Health and Safety Legislation increased and the numbers in the Division declined. The Division approached the management with a proposal to draw up plans for a first-aid room, which was accepted and implemented. Due to the increasing number of staff occupying the Walton Street site the Press had to employ full-time nurses, who helped with training and the Division re-formed the long time defunked nursing section. The work of the Division continued to decline in the Press but members were still called upon to work in the first-aid room when the nurse was absent or needed extra assistance.

Although the work was serious and important we still had a good laugh. One can recall just two of many incidents. There was the case of the guy who would always

*Some of the membvers of the Clarendon Press Ambulance and Nursing Division with their Superintendent Stan Webb (left)*

take other people's chocolate and his colleagues decided to take out the bar of Cadburys chocolate and replace it with a bar of Exlax. Fortunately, I was warned what had happened and to expect some results. It did not take long before I was called out and when the victim told me how he had a bad bout of the runs I did my best to sympathize and suggested perhaps it was something that he had eaten. I never told him what really happened. The other incident was when our Personnel Manager told me he had the runs. I unlocked the medicine cupboard and said I had the very thing that would help to reduce his obvious discomfort. As I picked up the bottle the label fell off. I administered the medicine and as I was returning the bottle to the cupboard and about to re-fix the label I spotted to my horror that I had given him medicine to make him more loose. I was very close to having a fit of the giggles but just managed to blurt out that if this did not do the trick then I had something stronger. When he left the first aid room I fell about laughing; not I'm afraid a good role model for a first-aider.

The Division closed in 1985, some 70 years after its formation.

The Press had its own Health and Safety Committee made up of representatives from the management, the unions, and other interested parties such as the Press Fire Brigade and the Ambulance Division. They regularly visited all departments ensuring that the Press was a safe place in which to work. The highlight of the year was the Health and Safety Dinner held annually in the Stute.

I had heard that the dinners were always rather jolly affairs with excellent food and plenty of free drinks always available. As joint-editor of the *Clarendonian* I plotted to get myself an invitation on the pretence that I would be reporting on

*Dr Barnes from Pressed Steel, Mr Thomas, County Staff, and the Divisional President,*
*Vivian Ridler with a batch of recently trained first-aiders*

the event for the magazine. The meal was wonderful and was followed by a very amusing Health and Safety film entitled *The Plank* starring, among others, Ronnie Barker and Eric Sykes. Although the film was funny it had a very serious safety message running all the way through it. Everyone took their seats, the lights were switched off, and the projector started to roll. The film had only been running for about 10 minutes when the projector started to play up. Immediately the Personnel Manager leapt to his feet and switched on the harsh fluorescent lights. He was somewhat shocked to discover how many firemen and the odd *Clarendonian* editor had somehow managed to acquire a pretty young nurse on their laps. This did not go down well with the management that was present and although there was probably no connection the *Clarendonian* was never again to be represented at the Health and Safety Committee Dinner.

The Ex-Servicemen's Association was formed not to cater for the social needs of its members but to foster the spirit of comradeship and singleness of purpose which unite men of all Services who lived and fought together under the stress of war. The members would meet at their Annual Reunion Dinner but more importantly they would ensure that there was a good turnout each year in the Quadrangle on Armistice Sunday to honour the memory of the fallen in two world wars.

The OUP employees were a very generous bunch when it came to supporting people less fortunate than themselves. A branch of the National Farthing League was formed to raise money for Dr Barnardo's Homes by collecting farthings and

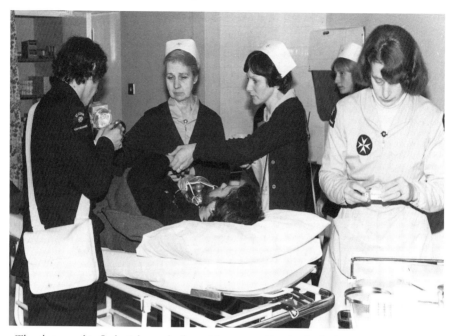

*The photographic flash picks up the first-aid team working in the dark on a training exercise with the Press Fire Brigade*

small change each week throughout the year. Every department was involved and the money was donated annually to Barnardos. In 1955 £24 10s. was raised.

There was another organization that was well supported by the Press workers. It was 'The National Committee for Provision of Holidays for Unemployed Workers in Distressed Areas'. Every year there would be a collection. In 1938, for example, the breakdown of the collection was as follows:

| | £ | s | d |
|---|---|---|---|
| Warehouse | | 10 | 9 |
| Engineers' Department | | 6 | 3 |
| Printer and Printer's Staff | | 5 | 3 |
| Photographic Department | 3 | 4 | 0 |
| Bindery | 2 | 10 | 9 |
| Monotype Department | 1 | 17 | 3 |
| Composing Rooms and Store | | 6 | 0 |
| Jobbing Department, Pressmen, and Type Foundry | | 9 | 0 |
| Stereo and Electro Department | | 6 | 6 |
| Machine Room | 2 | 6 | 0 |
| Reading Department | 1 | 14 | 0 |
| TOTAL | 13 | 15 | 9 |

It is important to remember that when a Press employee was taken sick the only weekly income would come from the State but this was not payable until he or she had been sick for one week. A common cold could cost an employee a whole week's wages. This was where the sick clubs came into play. Members would pay a weekly sum to as many sick clubs as they could afford and when they were ill the clubs would pay them a fixed sum in cash on a daily rate. At the end of the year (either at Christmas or the summer) the sick clubs would add up the income, take away the benefits paid, and, after a small honorarium to the Treasurer, distribute the residue back to the members.

The Mono Benevolent, the Stute Slate Club, the Caxton Convalescent Home, PMA (Printers Medical Aid), Benevolent, Provident, and the Typographical Association Sick Fund were just some of sick clubs (some local and some National) that supported Press workers when they were off work through sickness or injury.

### THE CAXTON HOME

When I went to the Caxton Home,
Far from the madding crowd to roam,
I saw my WELCOME on the mat;
The Master said, 'You must get fat!

'No worry here for you,' said he.
'For three full weeks from that you're free;
To enjoy life—that is your fate.
In dining-hall please clear your plate!

'I'll ring the bell for you to rise,
You'll not be late if you are wise;
Your breakfast will be piping hot,
Do as you're told, and eat the lot!

'When time is up 'tis sure I'll weep
If no results acclaim your "keep"!
I want to see you've gain'd in weight,
If you have not, you'll earn my hate!'

The size of plate I had to clear
At first nigh made me shed a tear;
But Limpsfield air soon put me right,
Then I could clear the whole at sight!

In three weeks' time I was weigh'd out;
The food I'd had had made me stout!
To scales I went amidst a hush,
And what I'd gain'd, it made me blush!

The Master and the Matron too
Said, 'Justified is ev'ry sou
That we have spent upon your "keep",
There is no cause to hate nor weep!'
. . . . . . . . .
'Tis hop'd that we'll endow a bed,
So please may it be a *long*'stead?
Because if short, you're put about
When at the foot your feet hang out!

My bed was short, but I was not,
To *me* it seem'd just like a cot!
If what we send is five feet four,
Then six feet two will sleep on floor!

A.B.G. [Bernard Gooding]

The Mono Benevolent sick club was run just for compositors, whereas the Stute Slate Club was run by the Committee of the Clarendon Press Institute. The PMA was run nationally to provide spectacles and other medical aids for members. The Benevolent Fund was another local sick club and they put up good healthy prizes for the Benevolent Fund Draw in 1938: 1st prize was a box of chocolates, 2nd prize was 25 cigars, 3rd prize was 100 'State Express' cigarettes, and 4th prize was 100 'Churchman' cigarettes. They ran regular draws to raise money because particularly in 1937, 'there were very heavy calls made upon the fund'! I wonder why?

The Provident Society was set up around 1873. At the 49th Annual Meeting of the society on 16 January 1921 it was announced that there were 344 members and that the subscriptions collected during the year amounted to £645 19s. 6d. They had paid out £300 15s. 8d. in sick benefit and £34 4s. in funeral benefit. After the expenses of £11 0s. 6d. had been deducted, the committee declared a bonus of 1s. 9d. for each 2s. benefit paid for, and had carried forward the princely sum of £31 6s. 1d. to cover the period before the next week's payments were due.

The TA Sick Fund was run by the local branch of the Typographical Association for the benefit of all printers in the Oxfordshire area.

Another popular club was the OUP Book Club. An elected committee originally ran the club with a Chairman, Treasurer, Secretary, and a network of collectors that collected weekly subscriptions. Later the club was taken over by the management and employees could elect to have a fixed amount of money deducted from their weekly wages. They could then order books from the Press Depot (now called the OUP Bookshop) in the High Street as soon as they had made their first weekly payment. There was no limit as to the number of books that one could purchase or how much one could go over one's budget. It was buy now, pay later, with no interest charges for credit. The club closed when wages reached a stage when people could afford to purchase the books they wanted for cash.

Every department at the Press had a 'diddlum'. These were savings clubs that would be run by one 'trusted' member in each department. Some were Christmas Diddlums and some were Summer Holiday Diddlums. The treasurer would declare that a unit was, say, *6d.* and members of the department would stipulate the number of units that they thought they could afford to pay every Friday. The treasurer would open an account at either the Post Office or the Trustees Savings Bank and all the moneys would be paid in on the following Monday lunchtime. If an employee paid 2 units of *6d.* every week for 50 weeks he or she would collect £2 *10s. od.* (£2.50) either at Christmas or on the Friday before his or her summer holiday. The Treasurer, however, kept all the interest that accrued on the account throughout the year. This was known as his 'bunts' and was his reward for all the work that he had put in during the year collecting the money. Often stories would appear in the newspapers about diddlum treasurers in other parts of the country absconding with the diddlum funds, but to my knowledge there were never any crooked diddlums at the Press.

*The Press Bell Ringers*

# CHAPTER SEVEN

# The Wayzgoose

**D**EPARTMENTAL outings (or wayzgooses) were always very popular with Press employees until the 1960s. By then everyone had their own transport and the lure of a trip into the country or the seaside in a bus had lost its appeal. This was a great pity because these annual trips gave workmates the opportunity of playing together as well as working together. Meeting socially in the evenings or at weekends became more difficult as Press employees moved away from the vicinity of the printing works to live in the suburbs of Oxford. Also the Press's social club, which was known as the 'Stute', was situated in Walton Street and was usually only frequented by people who still lived close to the Press in the Jericho area of the city.

Wayzgooses (which were sometimes paid for by the management and sometimes self-funded) were often to 'far-away' places such as Thame, Aylesbury, Cheltenham, Bath, or the many southern seaside resorts. It took all day to get there and back. The same trip nowadays can be achieved in a couple of hours by car or train.

Prior to 1851 the wayzgoose was an afternoon affair at a local inn that was usually followed by a supper. Here I offer some charming descriptions of some of these outings after 1851. The compositors and apprentices from the South Wing had a lot of fun in 1854:

> On Saturday, July 15, the men and boys employed on the Bible Side of the University Press enjoyed their annual holiday. The former, through the liberality of their employers, etc., and by an arrangement with the Great Western and the South Western Railway Companies, were enabled to spend a day or two on the sea-shore, arriving at Portsmouth about noon on Saturday and returning on the Monday evening following. The various institutions and objects of national importance (and of such especial interest at the present moment) which Portsmouth so eminently affords were eagerly visited; rambling and bathing on Southsea beach; the military parade of a garrison town, and the music of its regimental bands were much enjoyed. Trips across to and round the Isle of Wight, excursions across the Island and along the beautiful shores of the back or southern part of it, and to Southampton, were pleasantly and healthfully made; the holiday closing on Monday evening with a sight of Her Majesty and the Royal Family going out of the harbour of

Portsmouth on board the Fairy, followed by the Elfin and the Royal Yacht, accompanied by the firing of cannon from the Victory and the Platform Battery, and all returned much gratified. The juvenile portion of the establishment, numbering upwards of a hundred, were treated with an excursion to Nuneham. Marshalled in military order, in which they showed the good effects of the drilling lessons they receive, they marched out of the Press at an early hour to the music of their own drums and fifes (with which they have attained an efficiency that, as we heard it remarked, would not disgrace 'the reg'lars'), and preceded by the handsome banners recently presented to them. After traversing the principal streets they embarked on board the Nelson at Christ Church Meadow. Arrived at Nuneham, the happy party speedily availed themselves of the privilege of careering over the extensive park and delightful grounds, and in engaging in various healthful games. In the afternoon, by the kind permission of G. V. Harcourt, Esq., M.P., the private gardens and conservatories were visited, where they were equally astonished and delighted with the splendid fruits and flowers, which bear witness to Mr Bayley's admirable skill and care. Of course creature comforts were not forgotten, and after a day of uninterrupted enjoyment, closed by a dance on the greensward, the party re-embarked and, amid the alternate strains of vocal and instrumental music, pleasantly effected the return voyage to Oxford, where they separated after giving vent to their feelings of grateful satisfaction by a series of cheers for everybody who had contributed to their festivity—more especially for their kind and generous friends Mr and Mrs Combe.

When the machine feeders set out in the summer of 1924 they were soon to be in trouble with the law. I love the 'interchange of observations'!

With the weather favouring us, our party of twenty-nine set out at 1.15 on 12 July, from the Institute and by char-a-banc, to visit Cheltenham. We were quickly passing through the beautiful country around Cumnor Hill and Tubney, and at Fyfield a short halt was made. It was intended that the next stop should be at Cirencester, but on reaching Faringdon we found the signal against us—the arm of the Law was outstretched: things looked black, and there was nothing for it but to stop and listen to the policeman. A four-seater, it appeared, had had some difficulty in passing us a mile or so back. However, after some interchange of observations we were allowed to proceed. At Cirencester some of us visited the fine old church. Moving on again we were soon enjoying the glorious view from Birdlip height, and then descending (with little need of power) to Cheltenham and the Corner House for a most appreciable meat tea. Returning by way of Northleach (where we spent a quiet hour and a half) and Witney, we reached Worcester College at 11.15, well content with the trip.

The machine minders on their outing enjoyed a *substantial* meat tea.

Having chosen Marlborough as their destination this year, the machine minders' party, numbering forty and including Mr. Rogers, set forth from the Institute at 1 p.m. on 19 July, paused briefly at Steventon, and then by an hour's run through the lovely scenery of the Berkshire Downs arrived at Newbury at 3.30 and halted for half an hour. There followed another beautiful ride, through the Savernake Forest, and the travellers entered Marlborough at 4.45, quite ready for the substantial meat tea awaiting them. After tea the town was surveyed at leisure. The return journey began at 6.30, was broken for an hour at Swindon, and continued to Fyfield, where there was a sociable and harmonious interval of an hour or so. The compliment of a toast was paid to Messrs E. Town and W. Buckingham, by way of celebrating the completion of their apprenticeship. Songs were sung by Messrs S. Judge, C. V. Winstone, and others, but the 'star' turn was unquestionably the monologue with which Mr W. Legge delighted the company. There remained one ride more, and the party reached their starting-point again at 10.45.

Surprisingly, nature and culture were the order of the day for the Warehousemen.

On 26 July, at 12.15, four-and-twenty Warehouse men began their journey to Cheltenham, proceeding via Woodstock to Chipping Norton. Here it was necessary to equip the char-a-banc with due protection against rough weather, as we had run into a heavy storm. Happily the storm was brief, and there was no other rain heavy enough to be inconvenient. The next stage took us through some charming scenery, leafy lanes, woods, and rough country, where magpies were seen, and owls, and rabbits; and then, suddenly, into view of some wonderful open country, rolling hills, fertile valleys—surely one of the fairest prospects in England. Onward to Andoversford, and thence to Cheltenham and down the fine Promenade to the Cadena Cafe, where an excellent tea was provided. After tea the party dispersed in groups to explore the town. The Spa was visited by some; and the Museum, containing among its interesting exhibits the Corporation gold plate; and the Art Gallery, where are works of Dutch and Belgian old masters. Leaving Cheltenham at 6.45, and halting for half an hour at Northleach, where the fine old church was inspected, we ran by way of Witney and arrived in Oxford about 10 p.m., a happy party, having enjoyed every minute of the trip.

Companionships too had their own Wayzgooses. Foster and Co. went first to the races and then to that well-known tourist attraction—Woolworth's!

Saturday, 27 September, was the date, and Newbury Races (as usual) the attraction. Starting at noon in most delightful weather, we arrived at the approach to the racecourse about 1.30, and were much astonished at the number of cars and coaches, and much amused by a coach-load of Bristol ladies, who were dancing to the accompaniment of a tambourine. Our next hundred yards occupied about twenty minutes, but we were in the Ring in good time for the first race. We left for Reading at 5 p.m., and the happy faces did not suggest that we were any the worse for the fun, financially or otherwise. After a first-rate meat tea at the Reading 'Hotel Co-op', Mr Foster expressed the hope that all had had a good time, and he hoped also that the excursion would be repeated next year, when they would all be invited again. Mr Joseph Parker, the veteran of the party, proposed a vote of thanks to the organizer of that day's enjoyable trip; and Mr Foster cordially responded. A further hour was spent in Reading, most of the party making their way to Woolworth's. The journey was resumed at 8.45 and completed at 10.30, all having had an extremely pleasant time.

What a terribly refined bunch they were at the Jobbing Department's wayz-goose even though the weather was 'unkind'.

Marlborough was the chosen destination of the fourth annual outing of this depart-ment on 1 July. There were threats of stormy weather, but no reflection of gloom on the faces of the travellers, when the start was made soon after one o'clock. At Abing-don, the first stopping-place, the War Memorial was viewed and older haunts and friends revisited. Then onward through Ilsley and Newbury. The drive across the Downs provided fresh air in plenty. Newbury's neat appearance made a favourable impression, and the short interval spent in looking round was enjoyed. Onward again, through Hungerford; but as the famous Savernake Forest was entered rain somewhat discounted the pleasures of the ride. A few miles beyond the Forest lay Marlborough and an excellent repast (for which all were ready) at the Aylesbury Arms Hotel. After tea the College was visited, as well as other places of interest. Starting for home at six, there was an hour's wait at Swindon, which town did not show to advantage in the prevailing dampness. Then a long, quick run via Lechlade, and Witney was reached in time for a final refresher. On dispersing at the Institute at eleven all were agreed that notwithstanding unkindness on the part of the weather the outing had been very enjoyable.

Press organizations as well as departments would organize their own wayz-gooses and the Fire Brigade had a 'joyous day' in 1924.

Our party, which included Mr R. W. Chapman, the Controller, Mr K. Sisam, and Captain Symonds, set off from the Press in two cars soon after 8.30 and travelled by way of Eynsham and Witney to Northleach for the first half-hour's halt. Then across the hills to Cheltenham, where the sunshine was in good going order, and thence through Tewkesbury (an interesting old place, well worth a longer stay) and across the Severn at Upton, arriving at Malvern for lunch just after 12.30. After lunch, and the toast of 'The King', and a vote of thanks to the host for his excellent catering, some explored Malvern, some climbed the hills, and some, less inclined for warm work, pursued a gentle quest for shady nooks. Soon after three o'clock the way was resumed with the rather long drive to Chipping Norton, for tea; and on such a day the ride across country via Evesham, the famous Broadway, Moreton-on-the-Hill, &c., was most enjoyable. Over the tea tables (at the White Hart) the Hon. Secretary made some pleasant remarks on the Annual Competition, and, on behalf of the Brigade, Supt E. Hunt proposed and Engr. J. Green seconded a vote of thanks to the Secretary to the Delegates and to the Controller for the outing; and Mr R. Hurst, speaking for the Old Members, thanked the Controller for the invi-tation extended to them that day. Cordial responses were made by the President (Mr Chapman) and the Controller. The homeward ride was broken for an hour at

Woodstock, some making melody at the Thirsty Traveller, some availing themselves of the opportunity for a stroll in the famous Park; and the joyous day ended at the Institute just before ten.

The Ambulance Division's wayzgoose of 1926 seems to read like a circular route map and there does not appear to have been any juicy scandal to report:

On 18 June the Division, accompanied by Mrs R. W. Chapman and sixteen senior members of the Nursing Class, journeyed by way of Dorchester, Shillingford, Wallingford, and Goring to Pangbourne, where the first halt was made. Thence the route ran over the Chilterns to Nettlebed and Henley, where there was another short stay; and then onward to Marlow for lunch. At Marlow members were interested to find a regatta in progress. After lunch the journey ran through High Wycombe to Princes Risborough, for tea at the Buckingham Arms. The homeward ride was by way of Aylesbury and Thame.

The Monotype wayzgoose of 1926 seems to have been an altogether jollier affair. The necessary 'halt' before Benson would have been caused by excessive drinking at the Stute before the coach arrived to pick them up.

A Monotype party, forty strong, made their way through Benson (not without a halt), Henley, and Wargrave to Burnham Beeches, arriving half an hour before tea time. On the homeward ride rain was falling when the party reached High Wycombe at 6.45, and an hour or so was spent in like manner at Stokenchurch. Some unsuspected talent was revealed, and among familiar artistes Mr J. W. Embury delighted all, including local listeners, by reciting 'Bendigo of Nottingham'. On the way home the rain failed to quench community singing, which was kept up until the arrival at the Institute at eleven o'clock.

It was not just the large departments that enjoyed an outing in the summer. Small groups of three or four would go out together for a wayzgoose.

The editorial staff of the *Clarendonian* has had its outing. It walked to Godstowe Trout by way of Binsey Perch, and came home by bus.

Politically correct women's liberationists should look away now! I was worried about the writer's final thoughts until I realized that a woman wrote the piece.

Our Bindery girls are rightly a source of pleasure and pride. Whether we see them neat and deft at their work, or smiling and graceful as they dispense tea at the Fire Brigade Display or at the Flower Show, they are refreshingly radiant as flowers on the stem. They in fact contribute so much to our enjoyment that we heard with peculiar pleasure of their proposed trip to Windsor on 29 June [1929] . . .

Two charabancs set out from the Institute at 1 p.m. on the Saturday, which after a scowling morning suddenly burst into radiant sunshine. Fifty girls were aboard, shepherded by Mr Dearlove and Mr Foster, with Miss Hutchins and Miss Fry as shepherdesses . . . after a noble tea . . . powder puffs were discriminately applied . . .

*The St John Ambulance Division taking a refreshment stop on the way to the seaside*

Then on to Wallingford where we stopped for tea refreshments, music, and dancing. The evening was fine, and the piano was taken into the garden, where it was a pretty sight to see those young girls among the roses.

At 10 we left Wallingford and came home, singing lustily . . . all the girls did look very nice, [the writer] would like to borrow the patterns of some of their frocks.

The Staff Women's outing of 1935 sounds as if it was a lot of fun (if 'ardour' needed cooling before 2.30 p.m.)!

A much-discussed scheme materialized on Sunday, 30 June, when some of the girls on the Staff went for their first outing. Brighton was the spot selected (chiefly because there was a cheap excursion). It being a very hot day, we were glad to have the opportunity *en route* of cooling our ardour with Wall's ices, thanks to the vendor with unerring aim who chanced to be on a distant platform while the train was held up. After lunching on the train we arrived at Brighton about 2.15, there to receive a cordial reception from our friend Mr. Howes. The party then drifted seawards; some tested the power of Brighton's speed-boats, others preferred to discover what the renowned Black Rock had to offer (chiefly drinks—iced and harmless!). In the early evening we united again for a hearty meal, after which snaps were taken to celebrate the great occasion. We were all very pleased with ourselves when we eventually left Brighton, and the day was voted a great success, every one clamouring for a repetition of the experiment.

The 1936 Engineers and Typefounders' outing appears to have started fairly quietly but the waters at Bath clearly revived their singing voices.

This year we made for Bath via Severnake Forest and Devises, reaching the old City at about 5 p.m. Several members visited the Baths, while others sampled the waters; and at dinner everyone did justice to a splendid spread, with the result that the seats on the coach were filled rather more than on the outward journey.

We came back via Chippenham and Swindon for lubrication of the vocal chords, which hitherto had been remarkably silent. From then the party was distinctly vocal, though harmony was not always present. One member was very emphatic about his love for a white rose, while the others, more patriotic, preferred *Rule Britannia*.

The following year the 1937 Engineers' and Typefounders' outing seems to have been a pretty relaxed affair with lots of thirsty choristers on board the charabanc singing exactly the same songs as the year before.

> Outings good and outings bad,
>   Outings merry and outings sad,
>     Outings quiet and outings tough,
>       And still the lads haven't had enough.

And so with tradition behind them and the prospect of a good time in front, a coachful of care-free individuals set out on 5 June.

Having 'gone west' on the previous outing, south-east was chosen, with Guildford as the objective, and this was reached after a glorious trip through scenery which only Surrey can provide. Thirty-two thirsty members made full use of the short time at their disposal, and the return journey was made via Newbury. Here a stop was made for dinner, and the occasion taken to present Mr W. Cooper with a small present on his retirement from the Press.

From then onwards several members certainly proved themselves eligible for inclusion in the Choral Society, and the white rose which bloomed with such profusion last year was again loudly extolled, this time ably supported by a 'human trombone'.

However, fools were suffered gladly, and Oxford was reached shortly before midnight; and so ended another most enjoyable day.

Even though the outings were held at the weekends the men were not free from the discipline that they faced at work as Fred Hart discovered when he was 'reported' for having fun in 1949!

The weather was perfect as we set from the Institute on our way to Brighton . . . We stopped for lunch just outside Reading and Fred Hart soon got into trouble. He was reported for performing a trapeze act on a rope suspended from a tree, 'the young scamp'.

Brighton has many things to offer for entertainment; the lads chose the girls, the less active—deck chairs, and the anglers—the Aquarium. . . . To finish a grand day, we had a first-class programme of entertainment . . . and so to the sound of lusty, maybe husky, voices we made our way home.

The proofreaders thought they would try something less cultural in 1954 but still found time to check out the local cathedral. Well, they were 'learned' proofreaders!

The Readers again broke with tradition by choosing a seaside visit for the annual outing. However, they made amends by spending a certain amount of time in Wells, where most of the party took the opportunity of looking round the Cathedral. Weston-Super-Mare was reached in time for lunch, after which each was left to his own devices for an hour or two. For one it was a sea-trip, for another a snooze on the pier or a scout round the shops for 'something for the wife'. (Who was the gentleman walking along the street surrounded by a cloud of smoke, who nearly swallowed his cigar when he turned to see a Press fireman at his shoulder?)

The party on reassembling, carefully stowed away the parcels and sticks of rock, and settled in their seats for the run back to Swindon, where a very attractive evening meal was waiting. And then there remained little else to do than examine the interiors of various hostelries here and in Faringdon—and, of course, to have a drink and a yarn in the excellent company always present on these occasions.

Like all Press awaydays the reports always gave detailed timings. The machine minders in 1954 were no exception.

At 7.45 a.m. on Saturday, 26 June the Machine Minders set forth on the annual outing by coach to Bournemouth. Refreshments were carried and a stop made near Winchester for the usual snack, always enjoyed by everybody. Resuming our journey we arrived at Bournemouth at 11.15, which gave time for a walk round and, maybe, a 'tonic' before Luncheon at 1 p.m. It was an excellent meal, served at the Cadena Café, and we afterwards dispersed, each to seek our own pleasures, meeting again at 5.30 p.m. for the return journey, via Salisbury, to Lower Woodford for supper. Our stay amidst these delightful 'country surroundings' was all too short, and we continued our journey at a good speed to reach the outskirts of Newbury for the last round up. The rest of the journey seemed to pass all too soon, and Oxford was reached about 11.30 p.m. The weather was fine, the company first class, the outing a success. May we have many more of them.

The Machine Room Feeders had their own wayzgoose in 1954. Neither the Feeders (the labourers) nor the Machine Minders (the craftsmen) would ever have considered joining forces for an outing even though they worked together on the same machines throughout the whole year.

For the 46th annual outing the machine feeders decided on an inland tour, which included Tintern and the Wye Valley. The party left the Institute at 7 a.m. on a morning which looked none too promising. However, the sun broke through and everyone's spirits rose. The first halt was called just the other side of Gloucester, when considerable inroads were made into the contents of the boot. The roadside breakfast is always a special feature of these outings. On once again as far as Symonds Yat to drink in the glories of the views over three counties and of the great horseshoe bend of the Wye some four hundred feet below this vantage point. After a further halt to sample the waters of the local brewery, Tintern was reached just before mid-day and, after an excellent lunch at the Wye Valley Hotel, some repaired to the bar to implement threats of extermination on the dart board, some renewed acquaintance with 'The Moon and Sixpence', while others explored the possibility of salmon fishing or took a look round the abbey ruins. Then followed a pleasant run back to Gloucester for tea, after which the journey to Eynsham was resumed, though not until 'Beano' and 'Bib' had been found and restored to their sorrowing brethren. The Star Inn was reached on schedule at 8 o'clock and, after a welcome supper, the company settled down to good English beer and a sing-song, with Jack Fellows performing nobly at the piano. At last, and only after the landlord had effected a gallant rescue of his lady from the coach, the final stage of the trip was commenced, the Institute being reached at 11.45 p.m.

Andy Chalmers ran the bindery wayzgooses during the 1960s and these were always well attended but they were arranged just for the men. Apprentice binder, Chris Hale, would organize the 'alternative' bindery outings to such places as Southend and Brighton. This attracted all the hot-blooded bindery boys mainly because of the bindery girls who were also invited. Many bindery romances and marriages started after the alternative outings and it was not uncommon for the birth-rate to increase following these outings. How different was the Bookbinding Department's outing in the 1920s and were they too as 'merry as a marriage bell' and 'contented'?

The excursion of 1 July will long be remembered in this department as the first joint outing of the girls and men. About equal in number and eighty-five in all, the company set out at half-past twelve and made for Woodstock, where there was a halt; and then, refreshed and photographed (by pre-arrangement), enjoyed another swift run, through the beautiful country of Oxfordshire and Warwickshire to Stratford-on-Avon, where forethought had ensured a first-class tea. After tea there was a general ramble in search of relics and memorials of the great Shakespeare, whose works have given so much employment to the Press. A large party chartered a motor-boat, desiring to compare the beauties of the Avon with those of the more familiar Thames. The homeward ride began at seven, and the weather, though unkind, failed to dull the spirits of the company. At Banbury, supper was served in excellent manner by Mrs Mosley of the Crown, and then an impromptu concert was presided over by the esteemed overseer, Mr S. Dearlove, who was supported by Miss Hutchins and Mr Clifford. Everything went merry as a marriage bell. There was no time for speeches and we arrived again at the starting-point (the Institute) at twelve o'clock, the company dispersed to their homes happy and contented.

I ran several wayzgooses to Newbury racecourse in the 1970s. The forty-two coach tickets were snapped up in minutes every year as soon as the date had been announced. Regulars would pay a small sum each week throughout the year and this would pay for the coach fare, the entry into the race-course, and all the victuals they could eat and drink. On one trip the evening was made complete by a visit to Faringdon where the Crown Inn put on a fabulous dinner followed by time spent in the Casino at the back of the hotel. The chief croupier worked in the Bindery so we were welcome to spend as long as we wanted getting rid of any winnings that we might have made at the races. Sadly these racing wayzgooses were the last to be held at the Press. Those who took part will remember always with great affection a time when people at the Press worked hard for each other and played hard with each other.

> Some three or four score years ago
> Our train was homeward winding
> When, suddenly, occurred a bump,
> And brakes were harshly grinding.
> (Interval of half an hour)
> The guard came, walking down the line,
> A voice was loudly crying,
> 'Why stay we here so long a time?'
> Said he, the face espying,
> 'How can we give the "Right away",
> With danger signal glowing?'
> 'Kamflarge that dial! then we may
> At once be homeward going.'

# CHAPTER EIGHT

# Retirement and Death

LONG service at the Press was the norm and when I arrived on the scene in 1958 I discovered that the top eighteen employees' service amounted to 950 years! So fantastic is this achievement that I will name them all. They were Bertie Kitchen (Machine Room) 60 years, Arthur Young (Readers) 56 years (he went on to complete more than 60 years!), Harry Lapworth (Jobbing) 55 years, Henry Deacon (Top Composing Room) 54 years, George W. Webb (Staff) 53 years, Harold Robinson (Readers) 53 years, William Masters (Machine Room) 52 years, Bertram Gray (Staff) 52 years, George Lapworth (Bindery) 52 years, Walter Clifford (Compositor) 51 years, Alfred Hine (Compositor) 51 years, Leonard Bellinger (Machine Room) 51 years, with Frank Carter (Machine Room Feeder), Stanley Copeman

*Three printers: Ridler, Batey, and Buckley*

*The pensioners enjoyed a party every year and the management footed the bill*

(Compositor), Frederick Smith (Keyboards), John Williams (Staff), Frank Horwood (Bindery), and Miss Clara Wilkins (Bindery) all clocking up 50 years.

They were all frocked in one way or another and I list as many as I could find interspersed with retirement appraisals, obituaries, and pictures. The list is based on my own research and from valuable notes handed down to me from George (I Was There) Perry before he left the Press. I had no access to OUP's records other than the ones supplied to me by the Personnel Department during my time as editor of *The Clarendonian*. When publication of the magazine ceased around 1985 my source of information dried up. I have been greatly helped with the checking of my dates by Pensions Manager Jean Crawford and the Press Archivist, Martin Maw. For their help I am sincerely grateful. Much care has been taken in researching the Roll of Honour and the author regrets any errors or omissions. Any information should be sent to <onthepress@aol.com> or visit this book's website at <http://www.onthepress.co.uk>. In the event of a revised edition I will be able to put the records straight!

## ON THE PRESS ROLL OF HONOUR

Abbreviations: b. = born; j. = joined the Press; l. = left; rj. = rejoined; r. = retired; d. = died; PFB = Press Division of the Fire Brigade; SJAB = Press Division of the St John Ambulance Brigade; Stute = The Clarendon Press Institute; AAC = Amalgamated Athletic Clubs

1891    **SGT JOHN GILL** j. December as Porter and Timekeeper. Served in the Royal Artillery for 21 years and later with the Hants Military Academy as a drill instructor for 15 years. Grandfather of Mrs I. Wheeler r. July 1906. d. October 1915

*Sgt John Gill*

1906  **JOHN THOMAS I r.** j. 1847 machine room overseer. d. 11 March 1921;
**T. L. Aldridge** r. d. 28 April 1932 aged 86

> *If ever there was any doubt that the OUP's reputation for high quality today is because of what has gone before, surely this obituary of Letterpress Machine Minder Jack Thomas I who died in 1921 will convince the most sceptical.*
>
> On the 11th of March there passed to rest one of the last of the Old Brigade of fine craftsmen who during a long period of years worked unfailingly to produce from this Press the highest product of typography that could be obtained from the material then available. Nothing but the best would ever satisfy John Thomas, and this principle he always sought to instil into the successive generations of printers who came under his supervision and training. He started his career at the Press when he was only ten years of age, in the year 1847, and with the exception of a short period of six months he was employed here until he retired from active service in May 1906—a spell of nearly sixty years' service. Even in the early days of his work he manifested the same care that was characteristic of him in later years, for it is on record that he was sent to the Great Exhibition of 1851 by the Firm as a reward for being the best layer-on at that time. In temperament he was ever cheerful and willing to participate in good-natured chaff—sometimes at his own expense; and he was ever willing to share his unique knowledge of the best methods to be used to cope with the many intricacies in dealing with the handling of thin Bible and India papers. He possessed a wonderful memory, and could tell without reference the extent and size of any Bible or Prayer Book issued by this Press. . . . His chief hobby was gardening, and the manner of his passing was just such as he would have desired. On that Saturday morning, whilst working on his allotment, he was overcome by weakness, and at four in the afternoon he passed away, peacefully, at the ripe old age of eighty-five.

*John Streaks certainly left his mark on the Press:*

In the autumn of 1921, when the long first-floor room on the Bible Side was vacated by the bookbinders and cleared for warehouse use, there was found on the splay of one of the southern window recesses an inscription, in pencil and in a schoolboy hand, thus :

*John Streaks came to the Press in January 1816.*

At that distant date the long room was partly a gathering-room (east end), and partly a composing-room under the supervision of Mr Joseph Arnett; and John Streaks was twelve years old. The young recruit was not to remain permanently among the cases. After one or two 'moves' (common on juvenile general service) he found his metier in the stereotype department. There he served through his novitiate, graduating as a craftsman of more than average ability. For a few months in 1868–9 he worked in London, on the staff of Messrs J. and B. Dellagana, but with the exception of that short interval the Press stereotype department was his place of business until he retired from business altogether. He succeeded to the control of the department in 1873 or thereabouts, when Mr Thomas L. Aldridge relinquished it to become chief reader of the Bible Press. Each of these new appointments was to endure for more than thirty years: Aldridge retired in 1906, and John Streaks two years later.

In the earlier stages of his career, when character as well as craftsmanship was in the making, it was John Streaks's good fortune—he always counted it so—to be thrown into close association with T. L. Aldridge, who was about nine years his senior. Aldridge had been apprenticed at case (Bible Side), and subsequently moved to the stereotype department and rose steadily to the command. It was in those earlier years, and from 'Tom' Aldridge, that the young John Streaks received his first promptings to explore the treasure-fields of literature, and in his latest years he still acknowledged his indebtedness and paid tribute accordingly. . . .

To his qualities as a servant of the Press, as a colleague, and as an overseer, there was ready testimony on the occasion of his retirement, on 31 March 1908, when a farewell and presentation ceremony took place at the Institute, the Controller (Mr Horace Hart) presiding. In making the presentation, the Controller said that amongst the diminishing number of those whom he found at the Press when he came, a quarter of a century back, there was John Streaks, in the same office, doing his work in precisely the same way. He was a workman of the old type. His name might appropriately have been John Blunt or John Bull. They all knew of his perseverance and John Bullism, as well as of his great skill as a craftsman. He was a quiet and dogged man, believed in getting his own way, and at the same time was very popular among the men. There was not, he believed, a solitary employee who had not a good word for the friend who was now leaving them. He had conducted his department with remarkable skill, and on behalf of the ruling powers at the Press he assured Mr Streaks they were very sorry for him to go.

1907    **W. T. Osgathorp** left the Press service. j. 1880s. Member of the PFB, Stute Council, and Cricket Club. d. 1 April 1927; **J. de La Mare** r. j. after service with the *Oxford Times* and the *Oxford Chronicle*, became a clicker in 1982. Originator of the PFB

1908    **G. Hawkins** d. j. *c.*1872 from Stephen Austin as an Oriental compositor. Served on Oxford City Council from 1890 to 1893. Later served as a Justice of the Peace; **JOHN STREAKS** r. after 16 years' service. j. January 1856 aged 12. Stereotyper. Became manager 1873. Amateur actor of considerable talent. d. 5 April 1920; **T. Fitchett** r. j. Type Foundry in February 1854. d. 9 November 1928 aged 86 years.

1912    **T. W. Prosser** r. j. 1854. Overseer under Bartholomew Price

1913    **W. Doe** r. from the Machine Department. d. 13 July 1935

1914    **R. Gass** r. j. 1864. Bible Reader. Three sons worked at the Press. d. 24 December 1926 aged 87 years

1915    **J. H. Mansell** r. j. November 1862 aged 14 years. Apprenticed as a compositor and worked in the Oriental Ship. Was transferred to the clerical staff in 1878 and was put in charge of the Counting House. He was the first secretary of the PFB, secretary of the Stute, and secretary of the Cricket Club. He was secretary of the Provident Society for 40 years and treasurer of the AAC for 15 years. d. 1929; **G. Denton** d. j. 1867 aged 10 years. Apprenticed in 1871 as a compositor. Became assistant to the overseer in the Learned Side Composing Room under T. W. Prosser. In 1892 he was transferred to the Central Office where he remained until his death. He attended both Sunday School and Night School and later became a teacher. He devoted his spare time to the study of music and in 1874 was teacher to the Boys' Drum and Fife Band. He played the bass trombone and could also play the flute and viola. He was the founder member of the Press Orchestra and was also its conductor

1916    **W. Rowbottom** r. j. 1904. d. 27 November 1932; **WILLIAM SAXTON** r. Machine Room. d. 13 June 1937 aged 84 years; **Joseph Castle** d. Chief Engineer. His son, William Castle took over the job when his father retired

> When William Saxton retired from the Letterpress Machine Room in 1916 it was the end of the line for 'Bill's Goose Club'. Bill would collect cash each week throughout the year from all of his faithful members and they in turn would be presented with a goose at Christmas. The geese were all fed and bred on Port Meadow.

1918    **J. C. Pembrey** d. Was well known to three generations of Oriental scholars. In 1847 read Wilson's *Sanskrit Grammar* for press and in 1916 Macdonnell's *Vedic Grammar*; **Ernest (Jack) Masters** d. j. 1888. After a few years in the Machine Room he was appointed as a proof puller in the Middle Composing Room on the Learned Side. During the First World War he was a 'keen follower of events' he was 'delighted at the slaughter of Germans and was always pleased to read of more and more being "done in"'; **Richard Faichen Aldridge** d. j. March 1869. Served first 2 or 3 years of his apprenticeship in the Stereo Department. Became manager of that department on the retirement of John Streaks 1908. Original member of the PFB; **William Asby Goodger** d. Overseer of the Composing Room on the Bible Side for 9 years before moving to the Bindery and the Warehouse. Was sometime chairman of the Stute Council. His father worked on the Warehouse staff and his grandfather worked in the Front Lodge

1919  **A. Green** d. after 46 years in the Warehouse. Father worked at the Press before him and two nephews and three brothers were working at the Press in 1919; **William Noel Willoughby** d. from the Lithographic Department. Killed while cycling in a tragic motor accident

1920  **G. Richardson** r. Machine Room. d. 20 February 1934; **J. Money** r. Machine Room; **Harry Draper** d. j. from Wolvercote Paper Mill at 16 years of age and remained in the Engineering Department until he died; **John Webb** d. j. *c.*1885 as a compositor. One of the first members of the Stute Council. Chairman of the AAC from 1902; **Richard Garrick Jones** d. as a result of ill-health brought on by experiences in the First World War. j. *c.*1906 as a compositor; **Frank A. Sheppard** d. aged 57. He spent all of his working life as a compositor. His father and brother also worked at the Press; **J. V. Fitchett** d. Apprenticed as a compositor 9 September 1895 and joined the Monotype Staff 4 November 1906. Father worked at the Press for more than 50 years and three brothers also worked at the Press; **Miss C. Gulliver** l. Bindery after 12 years' service to enter the nursing profession in the USA; **R. W. Chapman** succeeded C. Cannan as Secretary to the Delegates; **Thomas Curr Hewitt** d. Spent 40 years at the Press as a music compositor, proofreader, and instructor of apprentices and Orientalists; **John Couling** d. j. June 1870 aged 12 years as a layer-on. He was later employed as a proof-puller in the Machine Room; **M. J. Griffin** r. Emigrated to Australia. Member of the PFB for 33 years winning the Challenge Cup seven times. Played cricket for the Press and d. in Australia on 12 December 1951 aged 88 years

1921  **J. Bumpus** d. He had worked at the Press in the Bible Warehouse from 1888 until Christmas 1919. r. through ill health; **F. George** d. aged 76 years. Served apprenticeship as a compositor on the Bible Side transferring to the Learned Side in 1864. Worked on Williams's *Sanskrit Dictionary* (published 1872). Later employed as corrector in the Machine Room until failing sight forced him to return to the Learned Side. r. 1901; **George William**

**Cook** d. aged 66 years. j. 1874 as a proofreader. Stayed for a year, spent a year in London before returning to the Press. He was responsible for the *Oxford University Gazette* from January 1903; **William Thomas Edens** d. j. from Parker's Printing works January 1909 as a compositor in the Jobbing Department; **J. Castle** d. Controller of Wolvercote Paper Mill from 1883. r. 1917. j. *c.*1860 as an apprentice in the Engineering Department under his father who was then Chief Engineer. Left the Press to work for Napiers but returned shortly after to become overseer in the Machine Room. He then went on to Wolvercote Paper Mill; **G. J. (Jack) Tyrrell** d. j. *c.*1887. Apprenticed as compositor on Bible Side. Member of Dramatic Society, SJAB, and the PFB

1922    **Charles F. Hutchins** d. j. 1 January 1911 and renewed his apprenticeship in 1914; **William Richard Barton** d. aged 82 years. j. *c.*1855. l. 1856. rj. 1869 and after a spell in the Warehouse was transferred to the Stereotype Department when electro-typing was introduced to the Press; **George Alder** d. after 50 years service. Worked in many different departments including the Entry Office, Machine Reviers, and the Machine Room; **T. E. Taylor** d. j. as a messenger, later compositor, and by 1898 was a clicker. Played rugby for the Press and a member of the Stute Council; **G. Burden** r. j. Warehouse in *c.*1870. d. January 1928; **William E. (Bill) Gillam** d. l. aged 20 years to take up farming in Australia; **E. C. (Ned) Armstead** d. from the Composing Rooms j. from Pitt Press, Cambridge March 1891; **Miss Rose Wyatt** d. aged 22 years from the Bindery; **Walter Hales** d. aged 21 from the Bindery

1923    **John William Beesley** d. aged 29 years. j. 30 September 1907 and later apprenticed as a machine minder. Injuries during the First World War led to discharge. l. October 1921. Many members of his family worked at the Press including his father, J. Beesley of the Bindery; **William Starr** d. aged 63 years. j. April 1888 but stayed only 3 months. rj February 1892 in Oriental Ship and became a specialist in Arabic; **Charles Davis** d. aged 42 years. j. 1911 from the Regular Army to which he was recalled in 1914. rj. July 1919. Cricketer of renown, scoring over a thousand runs (including four centuries) and taking fifty-seven wickets in the 1913 season playing only Saturday afternoon matches. A man of many parts, played a good game of billiards, could hold his own at boxing, and was a 'better-than-average gardener'; **George Carter** d. j. 1888 after serving his apprenticeship with the *Oxford Times*. Clicker of the Music Ship in 1911. Member of the Dramatic Society

1924    **C. R. Hobbs** r. j. 1890 as a compositor. Member of the Stute Council and secretary of the Mutual Help Society. Played a female part in the first performance staged by the Dramatic Society on 18 January 1894. d. 27 March 1950 aged 84 years; **M. R. Williamson** r. j. February 1879 and spent most of

his service in the Jobbing Department. d. 31 October 1948 aged 91 years;
**G. H. Payton** r. after 56 years' service working in the Oriental ship specializing in Sanskrit; **P. H. Martin** d. r. February 1924 after more than 40 years'
service. Early member of the Stute Council and original member of the
PFB. Sometime President of the Provident Society. His son was employed
at the Press but enlisted before the First World War and died after hard-
ships at KUT; **John Noble** d. aged 59 years. l. 1923 after 16 years' service;
**W. G. King** d. r. 1904 after 14 years' service; **William White** d. aged 72
years. j. 1868 as a compositor apprentice. Secretary of the local Typographical Association; **William Castle** d. j. *c*.1867 and apprenticed in the Engineering Department under his father Joseph Castle. Became Chief
Engineer when his father died. r. December 1916; **A. H. Frimbley** r. rj. May
1891. Worked at the Press for 3 months shortly after completing his apprenticeship. Six months later commenced the supervision of apprentices, a
duty that was to last for 33 years

---

*In 1926 poor Machine Room feeder Richard Knapp appears to have had a short and
miserable life.*

One of the boys we welcomed home from the War, Richard Knapp was destined
to fall to a more insidious assault than shot and shell. At the age of thirteen he
enrolled at the Press and for a few years fed Wharfedales. In hope of doing better,
he went to the G.W.R. engine-sheds as a cleaner; but finding his progress hindered by imperfect sight he returned to the Press, working in the Lithographic
department for a time, and then again in the Machine department until the outbreak of War switched him off to sterner work elsewhere. On demobilization in
1919 he returned to the Machine department and fed Miehles and loaded self-
feeders until his health gave way utterly and hopelessly. He faced his dreary
prospect with a courage and patience that held through two years of pain. He died
on 18 March, aged thirty-seven, leaving a widow and son. 'Dick' was a likeable
fellow: ever ready to 'do his bit', and to help any one in any way according to his
ability; straightforward at all times; and regarded by those who knew him inti-
mately as 'One of the Best'.

---

1925    **Thomas Ramsay** r. j. 1891. Was closely associated with the Provident Soci-
        ety, the Hospitals Fund, the Mutual Help Society, and the Stute Council.
        d. 26 March 1935 age 81 years; **T. A. (Alec) Symmons** r. after more than 40
        years' service. One of his sons, Alexander was also employed at the Press;
        **H. W. Akers** r. j. 1873, worked elsewhere from 1881 until he rj. 1883. Mem-
        ber of many committees both outside and inside the Press. Took an active
        part in the Provident Society, the Mutual Help Society, and the Benevo-
        lent Fund. d. 28 December 1940; **Joseph Allen** r. after 38 years' service. j.
        1887 and worked in the Warehouse throughout his service. In October 1903

he discovered copies of the Bible printed in 1833 that were a facsimile of the 1611 Bible. d. August 1929; **William Herbert Brown** d. j. September 1899. Member of the PFB; **Arthur Richard East** d. r. from the Letterpress Machine Room after almost 40 years' service in 1916; **G. Wain** l. Machine Room where he had worked for *c*.40 years. d. 1929 aged 53 years; **B. E. Griffith** r. j. May 1875. Succeeded A. Soanes as Printer of the *Oxford University Gazette* in 1884 and Editor in May 1916. b. 1847. d. 3 April 1932; **Miss Mabel W. Kimber** d. aged 20 years. Had been employed in the Bindery Department

1926    **Edward Drummond Willett** d. l. September 1912 after 27 years' service in the Type Foundry to become landlord of 'The Gardeners Arms' in Plantation Road, Oxford; **William James Weller** d. aged 36 years. Served apprenticeship as a machine minder. Member of the Piscatorial Society; **H. Bellow** d. j. 1864. In charge of the Pressing Room for 50 years up to the strike of 1922. He was always noted for his punctuality. b. 1847; **Miss A. West** r. after over 43 years in the Bindery. Member of the original Bindery staff. d. 1 November 1958; **RICHARD KNAPP** d. aged 37 years. j. aged 13 years. His progress was hindered by bad eyesight so he worked in the Lithographic Department and then the Machine Room. Demobilized from the First World War in 1919 and returned to the Machine Room. b. 1890; **A. W. Parker** d. Apprenticed as a compositor 'at case' in 1868. Born in 1856 he served for 57 years; **A. H. Harvey** d. aged 53 years. Apprenticed with Butler and Tanner, before moving to Eyre and Spottiswood, and then Hazell, Watson and Viney. j. November 1900 as deputy manager in the Machine Room; **Miss I. L. Smith** d. j. 1914 in the Bindery at the age of 13 years. Prominent member of the local Girl Guide Movement; **E. King** d. aged 69 years. He initiated *The Clarendonian: The Magazine of the Craftsmen of the University Press, Oxford* in 1919; **H. Osborne** d. r. 1921 after spending his working life in the Composing Rooms. A notable athlete, cricketer, and oarsman

1927    **G. A. Ball** d. j. as a compositor and was later moved to the Monotype Staff. b. 1871. Spent *c*.40 years in service; **H. E. Beesley** d. r. 1922 owing to ill-health. j. May 1904 aged 14 years. Member of the Stute Council and also served on the original *Clarendonian* committee. member of the SJAB; **H. W. Gerrard** r. j. 1888. Compositor specializing in Coptic, Russian, and music. d. 14 September 1940; **Henry Froude** d. aged 86 years. He succeeded Mr E. B. Gardner as manager of the London House in 1874. r. 1913; **G. Stone** d. aged 40 years. j. as a compositor apprentice *c*.1900. Member of the SJAB and the PFB; **W. Neale** d. aged 22 years. Was injured at cricket practice by pricking his foot with a spike. He died in the Radcliffe Infirmary 5 days' later. A keen sportsman he also played football for the Press; **E. J.**

*James Gilbert at case*

**Money** r. j. 1865 as a machine minder. Member of the first Stute Council and was for a time Chairman of the Hospitals Fund and member of the Provident Association Committee. Played cricket and bowls for the Press; **JOSEPH PARKER** r. aged 74 years after completing 60 years' service;

> *In 1867, at the age of 14, Mr Joseph Parker came to work at the Press. He left on Saturday, 17 March 1927 after completing 60 years' service almost to the day*
>
> There is less cod in the Middle Composing Room now, and it is missed; for besides being the prince of leg-pullers Mr Parker was one of the most popular and best-known characters in the Press. Past and present members of the 'ship gave him a smoking cabinet on the morning he left; and the affection and respect felt for him were voiced by the clicker . . . and the father of the Chapel. At twelve o'clock Mr Parker was given a very thorough 'jerry', initiated by the Music 'ship.

1928 **B. Moss** r. j. Warehouse staff in 1901 after service in the Police Force. d. 1929; **W. Sheppard** r. j. in 1874 aged 13 years. In 1882 was one of the first four men to work on the *OED*. d. 1939; **J. C. GILBERT** r. after almost 48 years' service. Spent 44 of those years working on the *OED* lifting his first 'take' on it in 1882 until it reached its last stages in 1926. d. 1938; **William Jones** d. aged 50 years. j. Engineers in 1912; **G. Green** d. aged 62 years after 48 years' service; **J. W. Embury** r. j. 1869, l. 1878. rj. 1884. Chairman of Stute Council and a member of the Dramatic Society. d. 1946; **J. Rogers** r. aged 75. Member of Piscatorial Society and former member and President of Provident Society; **C. Hewitt** r. j. in 1879 and worked continuously on the Learned Side. Member of PFB in the First World War and the Minstrel Troupe; **W. Farrow** r. j. in Jobbing ship 1892 d. 2 December 1947 aged 85 years; **W. Cooke** r. j. in 1870 at 12 years of age. Spent 47 years of his service as Press-man in Top Composing Room. d. 22 January 1941; **J. Howkins** r. employed in Engineers Bible Staff and at the Ink Works, Juxon Street. d. 21 March 1934; **L. Stevens** worked in Machine Room, rescued Mr A. Farthing from Hinksey Pool and was presented with certificate from the Royal Humane Society and a silver watch by his colleagues to mark his courage and gallantry; **J. A. Robbins** r. j. 1884 became overseer of the Composing Rooms in 1897; **W. Binham** r. after 30 years' service. Oriental specialist and expert in Bengali; **J. M. Buck** r. b. 1850, j. 1894, with his service at Read, Crisp and Moore (later Clowes & Sons) at Beccles he completed 50 years' service. d. 1931.

---

*With tongue in cheek this is one of the saddest stories I have ever read. The passing of Dr Fell in the Quad in 1928 was not only a sad affair for his many admirers but there was mystery surrounding the death. There are many today that think that the porter 'dunnit' but I am with the 'death by dahlias' school. The cause of the death must remain for ever open. Was it just retribution on the illicit consumer of the dahlias? . . . Or did he simply expire into the night, as though friendly Death, hovering over the garden, had plucked him as it were a rose? Dr Fell was, of course, the Press tortoise!*

Our old friend—whose loss we, alas, now deplore—was of a temper firm, though not morose, determined as his cousin of proverbial fame. Who might behold Dr Fell, so many blades of grass undauntedly surmounted, so many flower beds traversed, essay his perilous passage across the gravel to the rockery on the learned Side—liable at any moment to be picked up by a thoughtless hand and returned to the grass whence he came—who watched this more than epic striving, this impetus, this conquest of countless obstacles, may remember a notable warrior. Not Roland was bolder nor Oliver more sage. Like many another warrior he was a daring marauder: the dahlia bed was in a state of siege, lettuce leaves were spread before him in vain to placate him. The gardener found in him an honoured ally who might at any moment—who, indeed, did—turn into an unprincipled foe; until that lovely June evening when easy Death found him in the rose garden, and the porter found his corpse. Truly might we say, this was but the shell, the spirit of Dr Fell haunts the rose garden yet.

1929    **T. W. Scroggs** r. after 45 years' service. Served apprenticeship as a compositor. Promoted to assistant foreman in the Composing Room and foreman in 1910. d. 1935 aged 64 years. Two sons also served at Press (see 1968 and 1971); **John William Kitchen** r. after 55 years' service. j. aged 13 years as a machine feeder on Scotch platen machines. Went on to work on counting and paper wetting; **G. A. Wolff** l. after 33 years' service in the Reading Department on the Learned Side. j. 2 May 1896 as French and German reader. When he found Italian and Spanish were necessary, he taught himself these languages in his spare time; **F. T. Richmond** r. j. in September 1885. Appointed to Type Store when C. E. Bowen left that department. Later returned to the Jobbing Department but in June 1909 was appointed to take charge of the Type Store; **C. Beesley** r. j. in 1864 aged 11 years. Was sick visitor to Provident Society for 30 years and founder member of Gardening Association; d. May 1933 **G. Ostler** d. j. as compositor from *Oxford Times* in 1885. Moved to Reading Department after a few years. The last 3 years of his life were devoted to compilation of the *Little Oxford Dictionary*. He also worked on the *English Dialect Dictionary*; **J. S. Walker** r. j. in 1885. Worked on Liddell & Scott, *Greek Lexicon*, Johnson. *Bantice Language*, and many Oxford Classical Texts. d. 7 February 1973; **G. Thomas** r. d. 1 August 1940; **E. Rogers** r.; **F. G. Beale** r. d. 10 January 1933; **H. J. Harris** r. after 44 years' service. Librarian at Institute for a number of years during which time, as Secretary to the Library Committee, he arranged for a series of Lectures at the Stute. These were popular and one was given by Horace Hart. d. 7 September 1929; **E. W. Blanchard** d. aged 42 years. Member of the Reading staff; **F. Thomas** r. after 52 years' service. d. 3 October 1934. Member of PFB from its formation.

1930    **F. Price** r.; **E. Winstone** r. Reading staff; **H. S. White** r. j. 19 March 1886. Played rugby football and cricket for the Press. Active on Athletic Sports Committee, founder of Piscatorial Society, and an early member of both the Bowls Club and the Dramatic Society. d. 4 June 1937 aged 73 years; **F. W. Barnard** r. after 39 years' service. For most of the time he worked in the Jobbing Department but took charge of the Warehouse Department *c.*1918. Secretary of the Rowing Club and was associated with other Press organizations, including gardening, war-time Christmas Comforts Fund, the War Memorial, and the Benevolent Fund. d. 21 February 1955; **F. J. Cook** r. j. as a compositor on 19 May 1884. Later appointed proofreader on the Bible Side and then moved to the Counting House November 1887. Formed Stute Library and was Secretary to Benevolent Fund. d. 17 March 1949; **J. W. H. Wright Snr.** r. after almost 60 years' service. Was an exceedingly accurate reader of Greek manuscript copy, with, although probably unable to translate, an unerring eye for proper accents and positions. d. 6 April 1939 aged 81 years; **P. Lamb** d. aged 58 years. j. 1880s. Served apprenticeship on the Bible Side and worked there until 1916 when he transferred to the Monotype staff; **L. Burrell** r. after working in Machine Room. d. 1 December 1937; **T. E. Cleaver** d. b. 1857, j. 1880s after serving apprenticeship at the *Oxford Chronicle* and spending 2 years in London. Completed 48 years' service at the Press; **W. Collins**. d. aged 60 years. j. May 1906.

1931   **F. J. Forest** r. after 52 years' service. d. 17 February 1948 aged 83 years; **E. Hunt** r. from Engineering Staff after 53 years' service. For 35 years was in charge of the engine and boilers. Founder member of PFB. d. 1959 at 94 years of age; **T. Kench** d. aged 61 years. Was a founder member of the Bindery where he served for almost 40 years; **E. A. Tucker** d. aged 62 years. j. 1904 as a compositor. Responsible for starting subscriptions at the Press to the Caxton Convalescent Home; **H. Sheppard** d. aged 68 years. He spent all his working life at the Press; **W. T. Webb** r. from the Warehouse Department having spent the whole of his working life at the Press. d. aged 68 years on 4 July 1933; **W. Hine** r. from Reading Department. j. 1879 as a compositor apprentice. Transferred to the Reading Department in 1906. For more than 40 years, both as a compositor and a reader, was associated with *New Oxford Dictionary*. d. 15 November 1950; **C. W. Rising** d. j. March 1900 as a proofreader. Spent great part of his service working on examination papers; **G. Haggard** d. aged 75. Worked for a time as a compositor and later for *c*.12 years as a proofreader. l. during the First World War; **G. Attfield** d. 24 December after more than 40 years' service to the Press of which 25 were spent in the Monotype Department; **H. Weller** r. after 51 years' service. In his younger days he was one of the best all-round sportsmen in Oxfordshire. Played cricket for the Press and was active member of the PFB for many years

1932   **F. Bascombe** r. j. 1890 at 17 years of age in the Counting House. Appointed entry clerk in 1901. Played bowls for the Press. d. 1954. Member of the Stute Council from 1918 to 1922; **D. G. Andrews** r. j. 1908. Served on committees of the Gardening Association, Benevolent Fund, Hospital Fund, and the Stute Council; **F. A. Phipps** r. j. 1877 whilst still at school as a 'half-timer'; **J. W. Mundy** d. aged 80 years after leaving Press service where he operated a hand-press some years earlier; **W. T. Jacob** d. aged 38 years. Apprenticed at the Press. Member of the Clarendon Press Minstrels and the Dramatic Society; **W. King** d.; **W. Morgan** d. aged 71 years. Was in Press service in the 1880s and left to become a professional singer. Was a member of D'Oyly Carte Opera Co. for about 20 years. rj. Press service during the First World War. l. early 1920s; **F. Wakelin** r. after 41 years' service. d. 1946; **H. C. Thomas** d. aged 58 years. j. 1907; **C. E. Bowen** r. j. October 1881. A compositor, he was later transferred to the Forwarding Office. Founder of the Gardening Association, member of PFB, and a gymnastic instructor at the Stute. Played rugby football and association football for the Press. d. 15 March 1954; **A. E. Rivers** r. from the Letterpress Machine Room after 52 years' service. Played rugby football for the Press and was a member of the Piscational Society. d. 1946; **R. Hurst** d. after 45 years' service at the Press aged 66 years. Former member and Chairman of the Stute Council and a member of the Clarendon Press Minstrels troupe; **Miss L. Gomm** r. after 40 years' service When she joined the Press the Bindery staff comprised of two men and a few girls. When she left there were 250 girls. d. 7 May 1937

1933    **F. Nutt** r. after 42 years' service. Spent last 20 years in the Jobbing Department. Founder of the Press Cycling Club in 1897. d. 25 August 1949; **W. Judge** r. j. January 1878. Founder member of PFB and the Clarendon Press Minstrels. Played rugby football for the Press; **F. Chapman** r. after more than 40 years' service. Played cricket for the Press. His grandfather, 'Old Andrew', worked at a hand-press at the Press when it was housed in the Clarendon Building. d. 1947; **G. A. Gobby** d. aged 44 years. j. September 1923; **E. Bates** d. aged 66 years. j. 1923 after working for many years in London; **F. W. Smith** d. j. White Paper Warehouse in January 1905; **H. E. Poulter** d. aged 60 years. j. November 1885; **W. Taylor** r. j. March 1879 and spent the whole of his working life in the Composing Rooms; **H. A. Grant** r. after 45 years' service at the Press. Member of the original Minstrels troupe and the band where he was a violinist of some skill, being much in demand to play at Dances and concerts at the turn of the century. d. 8 July 1933; **A. Timms** r. j. 1899. l. 1904 to join the Royal Berkshire Regiment. rj. June 1914 but was recalled to the Colours on the outbreak of the First World War. Was said to have been only Press man to take part in the Battle of Mons. Wounded at the Battle of Loos he was discharged and returned to Press in 1916; **F. F. George** r. after 53 years' service at Press as a compositor. His father also spent his entire working life at the Press as a compositor. d. 1940; **F. J. Allen** r. j. February 1860 in Letterpress Machine Room. Member of the Drum and Fife Band. d. 11 February 1938; **T. H. Price** r. After early service in the Bible Side Warehouse (which he joined in March 1884 aged 14 years), he was apprenticed as a hand-pressman. He printed the only book to be printed at Bodleian Library (see 1921); **H. T. Towersey** r. j. November 1891 after working in Aylesbury and High Wycombe. For many years he helped to typeset the *New English Dictionary*. d. 31 March 1935 aged 67 years; **Miss L. L. Hutchins** r. after 49 years' service Member of the original Stitchery which later expanded to become the Bindery. In May 1918 she was appointed to take control of the girls' section; **H. Long** r. after many years service with Morley Bros. and 19 years service at the Press in the

Bindery. d. 1940; **W. H. Street** r. j. the Warehouse Department 9 March 1889. Transferred to Jordan Hill in January 1926 to take charge of the new Warehouse

---

*Thomas Wallen was presented with a wallet full of money, an armchair, and a pipe when he retired in 1935 but he probably had a job getting the armchair into his 'capacious' pocket!*

Preceded by his father and two brothers at the Press, Thomas Wallen began in the Machine Room in 1883. His rotund figure suggested, and his character did not belie, stability; for twenty-six consecutive years he was entrusted as Treasurer with the funds of the local branch of the national Union of Printing and Book-binding, and Paper Workers, and was a collector of numerous Press funds. In the latter role his habit of committing all the money he received to that capacious apron pocket was a source of wonderment to onlookers and conjured up visions of an intricate sorting-out anon.

---

1934    **J. Biggs** r. j. 26 January 1885. Played cricket for the Press and was a member of the PFB and the Minstrels. d. 1947; **H. J. Denton** r. aged 74 years. j. February 1873. For almost 20 years he was overseer of the Bible Composing Room. During his service, when a certain Bible was required, it was type-set in 3 months with the help of forty compositors from the Learned Side. Member of the Drum and Fife band, the Brass Band, and the Orchestra. d. 15 March 1937; **W. Jacobs** d.; **T. Howkins** d. aged 56 years. j. January 1891 as an apprentice stereotyper. l. October 1918 to take charge of Stereo Department in Aylesbury. Played cricket and football for the Press; **F. R. East** r. j. August 1905. Apprenticed in March 1906 in Stereo Department and left the Press on completion. rj. November 1920; **J. V. I. Gantillon** j. 1923 as Chief Oriental Languages proofreader. His widespread range of linguistic studies was remarkable and he was a specialist in at least half-a-dozen languages and more than a passing acquaintance in a dozen more; **D. Roche** d. aged 52 years. j. 7 January 1907. Member of the Stute Council and former member of the old Minstrels; **W. G. Carter** r. after over 50 years' service at the Press, all spent in the Electro and Stereo Department; **H. Horn** d. aged 53 years. j. the Photographic Department 4 October l895. He was later appointed Manager of the Collotype Machine Room; **J. P. Cann** d. aged 66 years. j. as a compositor in October 1911; **A. H. Sharpe** d. aged almost 62 years. j. as a compositor 27 January 1908. Played cricket for Press. Was Father of the Chapel and died in the Monotype Department in the arms of A. R. Plaister

1935    **F. W. Cooper** r. after 52 years' service. Member of PFB and SJAB for 19 years. d. 27 November 1940; **THOMAS H. WALLEN** r. j. Machine Room in 1883 following his father and two brothers. d. 12 October 1953; **H. E. Mapleston** r. j. July 1888. Secretary of the Piscatorial Society and Member of the Stute Council, becoming its General Secretary for 12 years, and later its Chairman. d. November 1937; **W. B. Long** r. j. 1 October 1883 as a compositor. Secretary of the Press Musical Society for 12 years and member of the Minstrels. Auditor of the Stute for 35 years. d. November 1937; **A. G. Loveland** r. after 37 years in the Electro and Stereo Department. One of the first members of the Piscatorial Society; **G. F. Soden** d. aged 52 years. j. August 1895 in the Machine Department. Played football for the Press; **John C. Loney** r. j. as a compositor in 1877. Member of the Dramatic Society. d. 28 April 1949 aged 86 years; **W. L. Roper** r. from the Machine Room. j. 1883 as 'half time' boy at 2*s.* per week. Member of PFB and SJAB. Last 'half-timer' to retire. d. 2 June 1957; **A. E. Skinner** r. j. Warehouse Department 27 May 1887; **W. G. Loney** r. j. 18 August 1879 and spent his whole working life at the Press except for a few months in 1895. Apprenticed as a compositor he spent almost 50 years as a proofreader. d. 27 January 1941; **C. W. Martin** r. from the Reading Department. j. 1901 after experience in other printing houses including Cambridge University Press. Member of the Dramatic Society for 19 years and was also a member of the Stute Council; **T. L. Griffiths** r. j.1884. Transferred to Jobbing Department under J. de la Mare when it was formed. When Horace Hart began the 'Fell' revival Griffiths evolved many beautiful borders and ornaments; **J. W. Holliday** r. after 44 years' service; **E. L. Gass** r. after 52 years' service. j. October 1883. For 17 years was the Head Reader in the Reading Department; **H. Lapworth** r. j. as a compositor 24 January 1885. Transferred to Jobbing Department October 1888, and became overseer in 1906 in succession to J. de la Mare. Honorary Secretary of the PFB for 14 years and member of the Stute Council; **J. W. White** r. j. 22 August 1892 as a compositor. Took over the first keyboard on installation of the Monotype Department and remained in the Keyboard Department for 25 years; **W. H. H. Tayler** r. j. 19 January 1885. Spent most of his time on the *Oxford University Gazette*. At one time he was captain of Rowing Section. d. 1947; **A. Chandler** r. j. from Parker & Son 1 July 1901. Worked in the Keyboard Department for 20 years, before moving to the Reading Department. He retired from the Machine Revise Office in the Letterpress Machine Room; **F. E. Bryan** d. j. 1885 and served his apprenticeship in the Counting House. Press cashier from 1915. Played cricket for the Press and was treasurer of the Stute and the AAC; **H. J. Bowen** r. j. 1883 Member of PFB and SJAB. President of Musical Society and auditor to Stute and the Provident Society; **J. H. Bayliss** r. j. 1885. Worked at first on a hand-press and later was apprenticed as a machine minder; **F. J. Cox** d. j. Machine Room on 14 September 1891 and was later transferred to Engineers. Played cricket and football for the Press and was a member of PFB

---

*It almost beggars description to think that compositors could hand-set type as small as 4 and 5 pt. in such terrible conditions in 1938. The strain on their eyes must have been awful.*

Arthur Hodgson had been an apprentice in the Bible Side Composing Room in the days when compositors would set Brilliant and Diamond Bibles with the aid of a naked gas-jet. He remained there till the room was closed in 1917, having been in turn clicker and store-keeper for a number of years. His knowledge of the old Bible and Prayer Book types was remarkable, and he rendered invaluable service on many occasions with the Prayer Book cancels necessary when changes occurred in the Prayer for the Royal Family.

---

1937   **Miss B. M. Denton** r. j. November 1915 as the first woman to be a member of the staff on the Printing side. After a few weeks service in Examination Department she was transferred to the Correspondence Department; **A. C. Hine** r. j. Bindery 1895. Member of many committees including the Benevolent Society; **Herbert Richard Goddard** l. as a hand compositor owing to ill health. j. January 1901. His brothers William and Stanley worked in the Letterpress Machine Room. d. 31 March 1950; **W. A. Tomkins** d. j. 1919. l. after a short time and rj. 1928. Played cricket and football for the Press; **J. Bowen** r. after more than 50 years' service. Member of PPB and the Dramatic Society. d. 1946; **W. E. Traill** r. j. *c.*1912, after working as a ships' printer and also in other houses, as a 'stop-gap' and stayed 25 years; **H. F. Cook** l. to work for Alden Press. j. 30 June 1919 and was apprenticed as proofreader; **J. R. Collier** r. j. 1 May 1912 as a compositor; **H. W. Barrett** d. after 18 years' service having been ill since May 1931; **C. J. Hellyer** r. j. 30 September 1907. d. early 1948 aged 76 years; **C. Ives** r. having spent all his working life at the Press except for a short spell in London. Played football for the Press and was the centre of a controversy over a penalty kick shortly after this new rule was introduced into football; **W. Cooper** r. j. February 1887; **A. Lovegrove** r. j. 5 April 1904 and employed as a proof-puller. Came from Morris's of Shoe Lane. d. 11 January 1942; **John Thomas II** r. j. on 11 May 1886 and was never late during his whole working life. Bowls player and member of both the Stute and the AAC. d. 18 March 1962 aged 89 years; **A. J. Bowen** r. after 58 years' service aged 72 years. Apprenticed as a compositor in July 1900 he was transferred to the Counting House and ultimately promoted to Chief Estimator. Member of PFB. An all-round sportsman he, with his brother, gave gymnastic instruction in the Stute. Member of the first Stute Council and later became its Treasurer. d. 1946

1938    ARTHUR HODGSON r. Served apprenticeship in the Bible Side Composing Room and had a remarkable knowledge of the old Bible and Prayer Books type; **T. Rees** r. j. August 1896 as a compositor and became a Reader in 1905. d. 29 January 1939; **E. Walker** r. j. in the Electro and Stereo Department October 1887. d. 23 July 1952; **C. H. Hodgkins** r. j. 30 September 1907 in the Jobbing Department. b. 6 December 1872. d. 3 July 1968 aged 95 years; **W. R. Bird** r. j. April 1912 as a collotype plate maker. d. 25 September 1939; **W. J. Dyer** r. j. October 1907 as a compositor from Bemrose of Derby after being apprenticed at Butler & Tanner in Frome. Spent many years working on music. d. July 1950 aged 77 years; **C. T. Rand** r. after 53 years during which he was never late. j. March 1885 aged 11 years. His wife worked at the Press for 31 years, three daughters have been employed, and in 1938 his son remained. d. 20 April 1959 aged 85 years; **J. H. Scott** d. j. 1916 and was engaged on dispatching proofs. Later became a forwarder; **P. Cooke** r. j. February 1884 joining his father and two brothers, all of whom had life service at the Press. He was a hand-press printer. Prominent footballer, member of the PFB, the Stute Council, and Secretary of the Stute Slate Club. d. 19 March 1948; **H. Redhead** d. after an illness that he had suffered since July 1931. j. December 1908; **F. Cox** r. j. 20 January 1900 with a break between 1917 and 1925. d. 8 December 1954; **MRS NELLIE GULLIVER** d. Bindery; **W. H. Gardner** d. aged 44 years. j. 1907. Proof puller in Jobbing Department; **G. H. Hellyer** r. j. November 1907. Played cricket for the Press; **F. P. Clifford** r. j. November 1886. Apprenticed as a hand-press man he was later transferred to the platens. Member of PFB for 41 years. d. 6 March 1958; **P. G. Simms** r. j. before 1887 when he was apprenticed as a compositor and later became a proofreader. Played cricket and football for the Press. Only Press cricketer to score a century in an Airey Cup-tie. Last played for the Press in 1922 in first match between OUP and CUP. d. 3 June 1948

> *Not everyone who worked at the Press was well known to all and sundry but they all got a mention, however small, in* The Clarendonian *when they retired or when they passed on.*
>
> 'Nellie' Gulliver, who worked in the Bindery before her marriage to Harry Hunt, a builder, passed away in November 1938.

> *'Ned' Harris's retirement in 1939 highlights the hard times that the boys suffered at the hands of the teachers.*
>
> Mr Edwin Harris, familiarly known as 'Ned', commenced work at the Press in June 1884, having received his education from the hands (perhaps in more ways

than one) of that stern disciplinarian, 'Gaffer' Moss of St Paul's School, Juxon Street. On completion of his apprenticeship in June 1891 he was transferred to the Jobbing Ship where he worked until March 1894, when a reduction of the staff in that department necessitated his removal to Mullis & Co.'s 'Ship in the Upper Composing Room, of which he was later to become Clicker. In February 1904 he went to the Reading Department, and successively as machine-room reviser on the stone, then back to his old 'Ship under 'Teddy' Taylor, Mono reader, and then assistant in the Composing-rooms and Checker of corrections, a position in which he remained until his retirement, having served the firm for 54+ years. Also, during the difficult years of the war he had control of the *Oxford Magazine* in the absence of the editor.

As Secretary of the Institute, although his outward appearance perhaps gave an impression of an easy-going disposition, yet he was most methodical and a stickler for law and order. In those days election to the Institute Council and offices was exceedingly keen and he eventually narrowly lost his secretaryship to J. Brown, who, as Clicker of the Apprentices, was supposed to have had some advantage. He was a member of the Press Dramatic Society, taking small parts, and in *Blackeyed Susan* his portrayal of the Admiral presiding at the court-martial on the gallant William (J. W. Embury) and his *dénouement* and final summing up with the words, 'He is free!' caused at the time the usual amount of 'cod' which is supposed to be the inherent prerogative of printers.

And so, on 13 January 1939, came the last farewells. The Printer made his valedictory speech and handed to him a wallet and notes as a parting gift from the Staff, and 'Ned', in replying, gave some jocular stories of the Apprentices of his time, some, he admitted, against himself. But probably what gave him greater pleasure was an interesting event which took place the same evening in the Upper Composing Room, when the members met to say farewell to him on his retirement. Each and every man and boy in the room, together with a few others now in other departments, had a share in presenting him with a silver cigarette-case inscribed to 'Our Ned', in this manner showing the esteem in which they held him.

Mr Ned, or 'Gramp', as he was affectionately called by some of the younger members, was described by one of those present as being a counterpart of 'Brother Ned' of Cheeryble fame, and as this character he will be remembered by us; always striving to do that which he knew was right, with his admonition 'be fair'.

A few remarks from Mr Ned were very feelingly given. In particular did he mention the trust that was placed on those in command of boys, saying the Press had always been fortunate in having good men to take charge of the young, and he believed such would still be found. After shaking hands with each one present, Mr Ned wished us all good-bye and went away.

1939   Walter Walker r. Messenger and liftman; J. Beesley r. from the Bindery after 55 years' service; E. (NED) HARRIS r. j. June 1884 and apprenticed as a compositor. Secretary of the Stute Council, member of the Dramatic Society, and took part in the Oxford Historical Pageant of June 1907. d. 17

January 1952; **A. W. McGregor** d. j. 1911 to work in the Machine Room; **R. N. Johnson** r. j. 5 September 1887 as a compositor; **A. E. George** r. j. 16 January 1888 aged 14 years. d. 12 December 1959. Member of the Press Orchestra as a violinist; **H. W. Parslow** r. from the Bindery after 39 years' service. Member of the PFB. d. 16 November 1950 aged 76 years; **E. C. Reid** r. from the Bindery; **R. L. Surman** r. from the Machine Room. Served his apprenticeship with Parker & Son, Crown Yard. j. February 1897. Secretary of the Ministrels and the Musical Society. Member of the Piscatorial Society and the Bowls Club; **John Stewart** r. from the Reading Department. j. 15 April 1912. First President of Stute Slate Club and member of the Dramatic Society. d. 27 April 1950 aged 90 years; **W. T. Walker** r. j. 8 February 1888. General Secretary of the AAC for 37 years. Compositor who later became a proofreader on 7 January 1907. d. 20 November 1943; **A. C. Wicks** r. from the Stereo Foundry. j. 28 November 1887 but for a time worked elsewhere. d. 23 August 1965 aged 90 years; **W. J. Casemore** r. Hand compositor. j. 29 October 1888 aged 14 years. d. 20 April 1956

1940  **W. G. E. Pratley** r. after 32 years' service as a proofreader. j. March 1908. d. 1946; **E. J. Goddard** r. aged 56 years due to ill health. j. 26 September 1898. Member of the PFB; **Miss C. M. Winterbottom** r. j. 2 March 1889. d. 25 December 1971; **T. Bruce MA** r. Was classical proofreader at the Press for 28 years except for 3 years spent on Government service in the First World War. He read the whole of the then new edition of Liddell & Scott, *Greek Lexicon*; **W. R. Crook** d. j. as a boy and stayed for about 5 years. After some years elsewhere he rj. in 1914 as a machine feeder; **A. E. Higginson** r. d. 16 February 1953; **Miss L. J. Bolton** r. j. 25 May 1895. d. 26 January 1957 aged 76 years; **A. A. Adnams** drowned whilst serving in the RAF. Last seen diving from the deck of the *Lancastria* as she was sinking from enemy action whilst evacuating troops from France; **A. H. Case** r. j. prior to 1908. Played cricket for the Press; **G. J. R. Boswell** d.; **H. B. Gardner** r. from the Machine Room

1941  **L. M. Clark** d. Worked in the Bindery; **W. Hope** r. j. 4 February 1891. d. 25 November 1961 aged 85 years; **W. J. C. Collier** d. Worked in the Counting House; **J. H. Backhouse** r. from the Bindery

1942  **H. Stone** killed whilst serving in the Royal Navy; **C. F. Garrard** r. j. 26 March 1906. d. 30 November 1951; **Kenneth Sisam** succeeded R. W. Chapman as Secretary to the Delegates; **H. C. Fulker** r. j. 6 January 1890 aged 13 years. d. 2 March 1957; **F. Schule** r. j. as a bookbinder 28 November 1921. d. 26 May 1951

1943  **E. B. Eldridge** r. In May 1904 he was brought to the Press by Mr Horace Hart to become manager of the Photographic Department. d. 5 September 1951; **J. P. Hine** r. j. 3 October 1892 as a compositor apprentice aged 14 years. d. 13 February 1956; **A. Tomkins** r. from the Warehouse. j. 29 February 1900. d. as a result of an accident, 13 August 1960 aged 83 years; **H. Horseman** r. j. 10 October 1892 at 14 years of age. d. 13 September 1952; **F. W. Hart** r. j. Press on 14 September 1921. d. 30 June 1954 aged 77 years; **William Henry Bruce** r. j. Monotype Keyboard Department March 1936, already having had 49 years' service in the trade. d. 17 December 1949; **F. Bayliss** r. j. 23 February 1891. d. 9 December 1959 aged 81; **G. J. Estherby** r. Served in CJV in the South African War and gave 29 years service to the Press. d. 3 December 1948 aged 73 years

1944 **H. S. Miller** r. j. 1907 as a proofreader specializing in African languages and dialects. Member of the SJAB for 30 years. d. 2 March 1952 aged 76 years; **C. E. Barham** r. from the Warehouse. b. 25 April 1878. j. 10 March 1902. d. 25 March 1954; **Miss L. Day** r. j. 30 January 1893. d. 20 September 1957; **J. J. Edmonds** r. j. 18 September 1899 as a machine minder. d. 24 July 1962 aged 84 years; **E. Tratt** r. j. 2 December 1907? as a compositor. d. 1 February 1961 aged 81 years; **A. W. Foster** r. j. August 1892 after 52 years' service in the Bindery. Committee member of the AAC and played cricket and football for the Press. Also played football for Oxford City and took part in the Amateur Cup Final of 1903 against Stockton. d. 8 September 1948; **A. Vallender** r. j. 20 January 1908. d. 24 April 1961 aged 82 years; **A. F. Lusty** r. j. 29 July 1901 and worked as machine minder. d. 21 February 1962 aged 85 years; **Sidney G. Squires** r. j. October 1883 in the Type Foundry and remained there for his whole service. About 1895 he was entrusted with the care of the old printing materials, some 7,500 matrices and 2,000 steel punches that had been unused for 200–250 years and were all rusted, mixed, and tied in confused bundles. Later these were cleaned, sorted, identified, and put in proper order. d. 24 December 1954; **A. Trinder** r. j. 16 April 1894. d. 27 February 1960 aged 80 years; **W. Tomlinson** r. j. 18 December 1911. d. 22 January 1948

1945 **F. W. Heath** r. j. 22 January 1900 aged 22 years. d. 21 May 1957; **J. L. S. Surman** r. aged 70 years of age. j. as a compositor on 26 February. d. 24 July 1949; **P. G. Tomkins** r. j. 8 May 1893 as a machine feeder. d. 22 June 1959 aged 79 years; **E. Morse** r. j. 17 June 1911. d. 29 November 1948 aged 68 years; **W. F. Faulkner** r. j. 2 February 1916 and worked in the Warehouse. d. 10 February 1962 aged 83 years; **F. C. White** d. j. 1933 as a proofreader; **F. Winterbourne** r. j. 1892 as a compositor. l. and rj. February 1936. d. 12 February 1959

1946 **P. G. Hine** d. r. after 52 years' service in the Bindery; **W. W. Shirley** r. after 51 years' service in the Reading Department. j. 16 September 1895 as a compositor. d. 27 March 1977 aged 96 years; **E. J. Hallett** r. j. 1893 to be later apprenticed as a machine minder. d. 2 January 1952; **J. Roby** r. as Head

Porter after 23 years' service; **F. W. Frost** r. after 51 years' service; **S. Dixon** d. after 32 years' service as a proofreader; **A. E. Durham** r. Served on the Delegates Staff for 49 years, 42 of which he was Delegates' Accountant; **F. C. Binder** r. from the Bindery. j. September 1904. d. 16 January 1951; **William Rennie** r. j. 22 February 1892 aged 14 years. d. 17 March 1957; **A. C. E. Cox** r. j. aged 14 years as hand compositor. d. 28 December 1954; **P. P. Bennett** r. j. 25 January 1892. After a few months transferred to Entry Office. In 1901 appointed Secretary to Horace Hart, and served in that office under three Printers. Played football for the Press. Secretary to PFB for 31 years. d. 14 August 1967 aged 89 years; **E. H. Taylor** r. j. September 1889 as a feeder in the Machine Room. Worked in the Controller's garden for 20 years and later on Maintenance Staff. d. 23 March 1963 aged 87 years; **W. E. Green** r. from the Reading Department after 36 years' service. Father j. 1887 but started his own business in 1889. W.E. j. March 1910 after serving his apprenticeship under his father and then in Abingdon and Reading. Completed the booklet 'Uncommon Words and Phrases' which was widely acclaimed in the trade press. rj. 26 January 1953. d. 5 June 1974 aged 92 years

1947 **P. J. Papel** d.; **F. J. Master** d.; **F. W. Reaves** d. aged 44 after 20 years' service as a machine minder; **M. J. Howes** r. j. as a. boy. l. and rj. as a collotype machine minder. Was a member of the Choral Society, the Press Minstrels, and the Dramatic Society. d. 26 November 1955; **P. H. King** r. aged almost 80 years after 56 years' service. j. 1891 as a compositor, was transferred to the Counting House, and in 1905 took charge of the new Monotype Department from its formation in 1908 until 1910 when he returned to Counting House. Responsible in his early years for a Companionship of apprentices whose work under his direction included the *Dialect Dictionary*, and Index *Kewensis* d. 10 March 1956; **G. E. Kilbee** r. prematurely due to ill-health. j. 1912. At one time travelled between the Press warehouses in various parts of the city in a covered horse-drawn van delivering printed stock. d. 26 November 1951; **J. A. Roby** r. as Head Porter. j. 31 May 1923. d. 14 February 1956; **H. R. Court** r. Played cricket for the Press; **W. Wythe** r. after 20 years' service in the Monotype Department. j. 1927 and in 1929 took over the management of the entire department. Said to have had a wider knowledge of Casters and Keyboards than any man outside the Monotype Corporation. d. 25 January 1962; **E. Boore** r. from Jobbing Department after 40 years' service. j. 25 February 1907. d. 3 July 1961 aged 79 years; **A. J. Peakman** r. j. as manager of all the Composing Rooms; **Alfred Charles Cleaver** r. j. 1896 and worked as a type-founder for 51½ years. Played football and bowls for the Press and was a member of the Stute Council. d. 11 December 1949

1948 **G. A. Peach** d. aged 42 years. j. in the Machine Room aged 14 years; **G. W. Woodruff** d. aged 37 years. j. on 3 January 1926 as a machine feeder. Member of the PFB during the Second World War; **G. Rose** r. after 51 years' service in the Bindery. First Secretary of the Minstrels after it had been re-formed in 1920. Played cricket and football for Press; **J. Plested** r. j. August 1913. Employed as a gilder in the Bindery. Member of the Minstrels and the Orchestra. d. 23 August aged 79 years; **A. W. Simmons** r. j. 1896 in the Machine Room. l. 1900. rj. 1903 in the Warehouse and in 1921 was transferred to the Folders. d. 2 September 1968 aged 85 years; **W. P. Janaway** r. from the Jobbing Department. j. February 1897 aged 13 years. d. 25 November 1958; **S. Dearlove** r. j. 1897 and became overseer of the Bindery. In 1941 the degree of Hon. MA was conferred upon him. He was keenly interested in all aspects of the social and recreational life of the Press. d. 22 September 1951; **G. A. Wicks** d. aged 61 years. j. 1 October 1900 as a compositor; **R. G. Lewis** r. j. the Bindery April 1907. d. 6 April 1968 aged 84 years; **H. E. Eggleton** d. j. December 1899 aged 13 years. Worked in Counting House for whole of his service. Secretary of Provident Society. Treasurer of AAC; **W. Slaymaker** d. aged 46 years. j. straight from school as a machine feeder 10 May 1915

1949 **W. H. Bricknell** d. b. 13 October 1880. j. Bindery November 1901; **R. H. New** r. Sucessively a compositor and a proofreader he was later transferred to the General Office and later the Secretary's office. He compiled first *OU Alphabetical List*. Member of the PFB. d. 1956; **A. Corbey** r. Appointed overseer of Stereo and Electro Department March 1934. d. 21 December 1954; **H. Barson** r. from the Machine Room as a machine minder. j. aged 13 years on 30 December 1895. d. 1 May 1953; **H. E. Sparkes** r. j. as a machine minder February 1915. Appointed assistant foreman in the Letterpress Machine Department in November 1939. Member of the Piscatorial Society; **A. B. GOODING** r. j. 1907. l. but rj. 28 June 1913. Took part in the Oxford Pageant in 1907. Member of the Stute Council, the Dramatic Society, and the Minstrels. d. 17 April 1967 aged 83 years; **Bill (Marshall) Taylor** d. j. 12 June 1899 as an apprentice compositor. Became the expert on the Bodleian and Taylorian Catalogues; Walter Burgess **d.** b. 1863. j. aged 14 years as apprentice compositor; **Walter Mazdon** l. the Letterpress Machine Room to take up an appointment as a full-time teacher at the Oxford School of Arts and Crafts. He was still teaching Letterpress Printing at the College of Technology in 1962

*In 1949 compositors were still hand-setting and dissing on piecework. This meant that before they could handset a page of type they had to take another page that had already been printed and distribute it back into the typecase. They were paid for every page that they set but they had to diss for nothing! The pages of 'diss' were kept in the Type Store and had to be collected by the compositors and taken back to their frames for the dissing operation to begin. When Bernard Gooding retired from the Oriental Ship on 3 June 1949 he decided to put pen to paper in the form of this charming poem and then send it to his former workmates (just to cheer them up you understand?).*

## WHEN I AM IN MY GARDEN
### *To my old colleagues*

When I am in my garden
Here resting in my chair,
I dream of you all busy
With the 'copy' you compare!
'Cases' may be many      5
You need to do the job
While the 'mixture' may be awful
Which almost makes you sob!
You seek now the 'material',
To 'Store' you go for 'Dis.',      10
Where 'rubbish' may be given—
Tho' your language here will miss!
Then up the stairs you clamber—
Quite oft are red in face,
And cursing all and sundry      15
'Cause the 'dis.' is a disgrace!
On 'balk' you open packet,
You know what you have got,
As well as all the others
When your 'copy book' may blot!      20
And now you start to 'dis.' it,
To find 'tis not with ease—
It may stick something awful,
While you find no 'e's' or 't's'!
To level now your 'cases'      25
You go again to Store
To find the 'fount' is empty,
When you curse still more and more!
Now go you to the 'clicker'—
Hoping help from him to gain—      30
Then probably to store-man
He goes and 'raises Cain'!
When I am in my garden,
And 'dreaming' in my chair—
Regret I cannot help you,      35
'Tis not now my affair!

4 copy] The typescript.    5 cases may be many] the compositor may have needed anything up to six typecases at any one time to handset the job (three typesizes in both upper and lower case). 7 mixture] The typescript probably contained footnotes, extracts, and text that had many accents and/or foreign languages.    9 the material] the type that is fast running out    10 Store you go for Dis.] The Type Store on the first floor where the type was kept in pages waiting for the compositor to diss. (distribute) the type back into the typecases. The 'dis.' was handed out by the Type-Storeman who would log every page that was taken out of the Store.    11 rubbish] Very old pages of type that were stuck together with dried ink.    13 up the stairs you clamber] To the Top Comps on the second floor    16 the dis. is a disgrace] dirty type or rubbish    17 On balk you open packet] The 'balk' was the stone or nearby bench where the compositor would open the packet which contained a page of previously printed type. The page was wrapped in an old sheet of waste paper and the page was tied up with 'page-cord' (a thin strong piece of brown string). The compositor had to be very careful as he opened the packet in case it spilled out over the balk. Distributing the type back into the cases had to be done exactly in reverse of typesetting    18–20 You know what you have got, As well as all the others When your 'copy book' may blot] As soon as the compositor opened his page of dis. on the balk his colleagues would gather round to see how bad it was because they were all on piecework as part of a companionship. It only needed a few pages of 'rubbish' for it to affect everyone's earnings.    23 Stick something awful] If the ink had not been cleaned off properly by the printer the type would stick together and make dissing a slow, expensive, and laborious task.    24 you find no e's or t's!] The letter 'e' is the most used letter in the alphabet and the letter 't' was kept in a compartment half the size of an 'e' and was therefore always running out. If the page that was being dissed did not have enough of those letters to 'level' (fill) the typecase the compositor would have to return to the Store and diss another page. He could not begin typesetting again until his typecase was full.    27 the fount is empty] When this happened it was a real disaster because if the Store could not provide more pages that contained the typeface and sizes that the compositor required (or there were no supplies of freshly cast type) he would have to either wait until some was available or 'borrow' some from one of his colleagues.    29 clicker] The foreman of the companionship    30 hoping help from him] The clicker could help the compositor by, for example, moving on to another job that required a different typeface or he could go to the Store on the compositor's behalf and raise merry hell. (Storemen would often hold back diss for their favourites.) 32 'raises Cain'] Able's brother, Cain, was sent to Hell

*Bernard Gooding joined the Press in 1907 and died on 17 April 1967 aged 83 so he had 18 years to 'sit in his garden'.*

1950    **A. V. J. Walker** r. j. Delegates' Finance Department November 1903. d. 16 December 1955 aged 67 years; **C. Forty** r. j. as a bookbinder aged 70 years 12 August 1940. d. 12 April 1952; **Harold O. Quest** r. aged 65 years after 42 years' service. j. 1 June 1908 as a compositor from Parker & Son. Parkers was situated in Crown Yard, which is so-called from the inn of that name. The inn was a favourite rendezvous for printers and it was here that 'Q' was commissioned to fetch the beer for the morning lunch.; **H. Simms** r. j. in the Composing Rooms 3 July 1897. l. 29 September 1946. rj. January 1949. d. 24 August 1960 aged 75 years; **H. T. Kettle** r. b. 30 January 1885. j. 8 August 1898. Served continuously in the Stereo Department apart from short period spent away from the Press in London and at CUP. d. 23 March 1958; **Frank Brown** d. Served the Press all of his working life. j. as a boy feeder in Machine Room but left to become a shoe repairer. rj. as a porter in 1938 and became Head Porter 1946

1951    **William H. Goddard** r. from the Machine Room. j. January 1900 aged 14 years. Served in the SJAB for 21 years. Awarded the Meritorious Service

TO BE POSTED IN                                    Form 46,
THE WORKROOM.                                     July, 1938.

*Hard Composing Room.*

## FACTORIES ACT, 1937 — SECTION 2.

Notice specifying the
## NUMBER OF PERSONS who may be
employed in the WORKROOM.

I hereby give notice that having
regard to the provisions of
Section 2 of the Factories Act,
1937, the number of persons who
may be employed in this room
is          80

Signature of Occupier.

Date   *July 1950*

LONDON
PUBLISHED BY HIS MAJESTY'S STATIONERY OFFICE
To be purchased directly from H.M. STATIONERY OFFICE at the following addresses;
Adastral House, Kingsway, London, W.C.2; 120 George Street, Edinburgh 2;
26 York Street, Manchester 1; 1 St. Andrew's Crescent, Cardiff;
80 Chichester Street, Belfast
or through any bookseller
Price 1d. net or 2s 1s. 9d. net.
Printed under the authority of His Majesty's Stationery Office by Croydon Times Ltd., Croydon

(S.O.5846) Wt.1009/304 50,000 (4) 8/38 C.T. Gp 584                      S.O. Code No. 35-9990

*There were strict rules as to how many people could work in each department*

Medal in the First World War; **Herbert King** d. Balliol College groundsman 1894–1937. Superintended the laying out of the Jordan Hill sports
ground but the laying of the cricket square, bowling green, and tennis courts
was undertaken by Mr C. Hickman, then Lincoln College groundsman formerly Mr King's chief assistant on Balliol ground [*Deserves mention in this
list because of their close association with Press sport.*]; **C. Hawley** r. d. 1960;
**H. T. Richmond** d. j. May 1914. Member of PFB; **F. C. Ford** r. j. 25 June
1934. d. 11 August 1962 aged 78 years; **Frank J. Isaac** r. j. 28 June 1909 from
the Monotype Department where he worked as an assistant. b. 18 February
1886. d. 14 January 1956. His father, daughter, and grandson all worked at
the Press; **H. Belcher** r. j. June 1899. d. 26 February 1965 aged 78 years; **J. A.
Deeley** r. from the Machine Room. j. aged 14½ years 27 August 1900 as a
machine feeder. His five children all worked at the Press at some time. d. 28
September 1969; **H. Hookham** r after 52 years' service. Played football for
the Press. d. 17 June 1964 aged 78 years; **A. Beesley** d. aged 64 years. j. 28 December 1910. Joined Warehouse office after service in the First World War
where his records of printed stocks and his knowledge of Bible and Prayer

Book corrections were renowned for the completion in detail; **E. G. Pegler** r. j. 10 September 1923 in the Bindery. d. 27 August 1960 aged 76 years; **P. Green** d. j. 30 December 1901 aged 64 years. After short service in Bindery was apprenticed as an engineer where he joined his father Joseph Green. Joined the PFB in 1904 and served until his death; **E. W. Lindley** d. j. 24 February 1941 aged 57 years; **P. A. Benwell** d. aged 49 years. j. 6 January 1941; **F. Mankelow** r. j. 26 June 1909. d. 24 January 1964 aged 77 years; **J. F. Martin** r. j. 3 November 1909. d. 10 July 1957 aged 71 years

1952 **P. S. Mills** d. j. 1910. Member of the SJAB. Treasurer of the Provident and the Benevolent Fund; **G. R. Rogers** r. j. the Bindery 31 July 1945. d. 17 September 1961 aged 76 years; **T. E. Nurser** d. when chief clerk in the Bindery. j. 1909. Assistant Secretary of the AAC for many years. Chairman of the Provident Society and Treasurer of the Stute Slate Club. Played cricket for the Press with considerable success; **Mrs Faulkner** (formerly **Miss Alice Bolton**) d. Worked in the Bindery for 33 years, much of that time on the sewing machines; **J. W. Culverwell** r as a machine minder. j. 11 March 1940. d. 15 July 1960 aged 67; **F. H. A. Robinson** r. j. 4 June 1905 aged 19 years. Appointed Foreman of the Warehouse Department in 1945, President of the Stute Slate Club for 17 years, the Benevolent Fund for 16 years, and the Hospitals Fund for 10 years. d. February 1963; **E. J. Walter** r. j. 10 November 1942. Later years spent as a messenger. d. 24 July 1955; **T. H. Isles** d. j. Reading Department 20 April 1942 aged 48 years; **A. J. (Ting) Harrison** r. after 41 years' service. j. Reading Department 1911. *Oxford University Gazette* reader for many years. Appointed Head Reader 1933. Played cricket for the Press. d. 26 February 1976; **T. A. Smith** d. aged 62 years. A compositor, he spent his entire working life at the Press; **E. R. Wright** r. as a machine minder. j. aged 14 years 20 February 1899. He stayed for almost 56 years and also played cricket and football for the Press; **A. W. Hookham** r. Formerly a machine feeder in 1916 he went on to be the plate storekeeper in the Machine Room. j. 23 September 1901. d. 20 April 1956; **Thomas H. Chandler** r. b. Beccles virtually on the site of William Clowes & Co. Ltd., 4 March 1888. Served his apprenticeship in the Machine Room of Whitefriars Press. j. March 1926 as Deputy Machine Room Overseer and was appointed to manage the department in August of the same year; **R. J. Mayo** r. j. 31 August 1903 as a proof puller. d. 7 July 1960 aged 72 years; **R. E. Best** r. as a compositor. j. 11 August 1902. d. 3 January 1964 aged 75 years; **F. J. Dunning** r. as a machine minder. b. 14 November 1885. j. 11 July 1927. d. 28 October 1967 aged 81 years

1953 **Miss L. D. Clements** r. j. 2 March 1925. d. 17 February 1976; **FREDERICK (FREDDIE) MANN** r. as a machine reviser. b. 25 January 1879. j. 30 May 1906

*Freddy Mann, who was born on 25 January 1879, started work at the Press on 30 May 1906. He was yet another compositor who ended up as a Machine Reviser. He retired on 23 January 1953 and his colleague Reg Allison had this to say.*

Just before leaving off on 23 January [1906] I had a visitor—my old friend 'Freddie' Mann. He had come to say farewell, and as I took him by the hand I saw that his heart was full and there were tears in his eyes. I confess that there was a lump in my throat as I said a few words of farewell.

Here was the going of a man with whom I had worked for nearly half a century; a man whose very presence created more fun and happiness than anyone I ever knew. It brought back to me the brightness and care-free atmosphere of the Top Composing Room where we worked together for many years, first with dear old Teddy Taylor and then with Jessie Foster. Freddie was always a plodder, and although never very fast, could always be relied upon for accuracy.

He came to the Press in 1906 and started on the Bible Side under Mr. W. Goodger, and later under Mr H. Denton. He did a good deal of Bible work when conditions were not so good as they are today; working by an open gas-jet on very small type (and there was plenty of 'cutting the line' at that time!). After that he was transferred to Teddy Taylor's 'ship, of which I was a member. There he spent most of his time with 'the bonny boys', always creating that atmosphere of cheerfulness which means so much to men who had to work hard, often with very little profit to themselves. We were a happy band until April Fools' Day, 1937, when piecework was abolished!

He was just before this time, sent to the Reading Room, and from then on I saw very little of Freddie until I joined him about a year later. He had settled down quite contentedly to his job, and I am quite sure that he gave of his best. After a while he was moved to the Machine Room as a reviser, and was able by his ability and knowledge, to prevent many bloomers from getting through.

1954   **G. Beesley** r. from the Machine Room. j. 28 May 1946. d. 6 October aged 85 years; **G. S. Taylor** r. as a stereotyper. j. 7 October 1901. d. 16 March 1960; **Miss R. M. Winchester** r. j. 3 November 1891. d. 23 February 1964 aged 88 years; **G. Weinburger** r. j. 12 January 1948. d. 25 April 1975; **G. D. N. Walker** d. Lithographic Department. b. 13 September 1887. j. 6 August 1901 as a collotype printer; **A. E. Slatter** r. from the Machine Room after 52 years' service. d. 29 November 1967 aged 78 years; **A. R. Wilkins** r. j. November 1941 as a compositor and later as a proofreader. d. 9 October 1956; **Miss Mabel D. Ostler** r. from the Counting House. j. 22 January 1934. d. 8 June 1976; **Gordon T. Reeves** r. from the Stereotype Department. j. January 1938 from the *Oxford Mail*. d. 27 October 1977; **A. V. Corbey** r. j. July 1904 as a boy feeder on the old Scotch Platens. Later served his apprenticeship as a machine minder; **A. H. Howkins** r. j. June 1903 and after 5 years in other departments appointed to supervise the issue of paper to the machines. About 1924 appointed to take charge of White Paper Department. Appointed Father of the Chapel aged 18 years. Founder member of the SJAB in which he served for 38 years, 15 of them as Superintendent. Played football for the Press. d. 14 June 1962 aged 73 years; **E. Muncaster** r. Formerly a teacher and a journalist, j. as a proofreader after 4 years' service on similar work at Jarrolds. Editor of *The Clarendonian* from 1947 to 1951. d. 1974; **H. D. Smith** r. j. April 1904 in the Warehouse. Transferred to the Bindery in October 1926

1955 **E. F. Cleaver** r. j. September 1901. After apprenticeship as a compositor in both the Bible Side and the Learned Side, transferred to the keyboards in 1908. A fine athlete he also played football and cricket for the Press. He, with his father and two brothers, served the Press for 206 years; **H. R. Darnes** d. 2 months before his 65th birthday. j. 29 April 1912 and spent many years on forme trucking duties and then as a cleaner in the Machine Room; **N. C. Chapman** l. j. 1924. At the time of leaving was employed in the Editorial Department. His father was formerly a compositor in the Top Composing Room and two brothers, both compositors, were killed in the First World War; **A. J. Bishop** r. j. October 1907 in the Warehouse before being transferred to the Bindery in 1920. d. 1 November 1971; **A. R. Sparrow** r. j. 1943, after service at Eyre & Spottiswode who he joined in 1898 and Harrison & Sons, as a caster attendant. During his service at the Press he was responsible for the casting of the whole of the Ruby and Beryl bibles, also the Coronation Bible. In all he devoted over 57 years of his life to the service of printing; **A. Trait** r. j. for a short time in 1906. rj. 16 November 1937 after spending some time as a ship's printer. d. 27 April 1959; **David C. Faulkner** r. j. 1903. In 1924 succeeded Mr Frimbley in charge of apprentices and during the Second World War was appointed to take charge of the Top Composing Rooms, a post he held until retirement. Played football for the Press. d. 27 December 1969; **Miss L. H. Denton** d. aged 94 years. She was the third daughter of Lamech Denton (Engineer) and was the last survivor of her family, which had included her brothers, George Denton (Chief Forwarder under Horace Hart and Frederick Hall), Henry (who was for many years the overseer of the Bible Side Composing Room) and her niece Bessie (who had some 22 years' service in the Correspondence Department); **C. H. Foster** r. from Letterpress Machine Room. j. January 1900. Played football for the Press. Father and three brothers also served the Press as engineer, machine minder, compositor, and bookbinder. d. 5 May 1970; **W. H. Wheeler** r. after 63 years' service. d. 27 March 1958; **Miss G. L. Cann** r. j. 22 June 1942 d. 5 July 1975 aged 79 years; **H. C. Harris** r. after 52 years' service. Awarded MM during the First World War and spent 30 years in the Jobbing Department; **W. J. Ward** r. j. 16 January 1911. d. 11 March 1957;

**L. Green** r. from the Engineers Department. j. 13 January 1922 after many years served in the Regular Army. d. 24 November 1968. His grandfather served 60 years, father 25 years, 24 years, 6 uncles, 2 brothers, and other relatives added another 300 years of Press service; **W. T. Hine** r. j. 10 February 1902 aged 14 years in the Letterpress Machine Room. Member of the Rowing Club and the first captain of the Swimming Club. Also a cyclist of repute. Awarded BEM in 1955 for outstanding service as a craftsman. Acted as a guide to visitors after retirement from November 1956 to 8 June 1973. d. 20 September 1978 aged 90 years

1956  **A. Sims** r. after 51 years' service, j. 1905 at 14 years of age. Worked in many departments, ultimately taking charge of the graining of collotype and lithographic plates. d. 4 July 1969; **R. M. Clifford** r. Worked as Monotype Composing Room proof puller, j. 23 November 1903. Member of the PFB and the SJAB; **Albert E. Tooby** r. worked as compositor. j. October 1904.. Member of Piscatorial Society; **Arnold Prosser** r. after 52 years' service j. 1904. Succeeded his father in charge of the Examinations Paper Department, transferred to the Reading Department November 1919 and appointed Press Reader for the *Oxford University Gazette* in 1931. d. 21 April 1979 aged 90 years; **B. T. Bull** r. j. 1906. Ill health caused him to leave. rj. 1914 to serve almost 45 years in all. For 26 years he was a member of SJAB and was also a member of the Stute Council; **Joseph R. Borthwick** r. j. November 1927 as assistant manager in the Letterpress Machine Room. d. 15 January 1974 aged 82 years; **Frederick Joseph D. Ayres** r. at almost 70 years' of age. j. in 1900 Became deputy and later overseer of the Keyboard Department. In 1948 became manager of all the Composing Rooms. d. 6 April 1978 aged 92 years. He had two sons that worked at the Press: Stanley who was a Keyboard Operator and Raymond who worked in the Stereotype Department; **W. Legge** d. j. 15 September 1904 aged 13 years. Letterpress Machine Department; **B. H. Cook** r. Served in Top Composing Room from May 1900 until retirement. d. 3 August 1958; **F. M. Gilder** r. j. 9 August 1943 aged 59 years. Worked in the Monotype Casters operating the proof press. d. 17 July 1968; **E. A. Bowen MA.** d. Worked in the Secretary's Office. j. 1925 at the invitation of Mr John Johnson, a former schoolmaster. His death ended 100 years of 'Bowen' tradition as his grandfather, father, and three uncles preceded him in Press service; **William Kislingbury** r. from Monotype Casters after over 50 years' service. j. 16 November 1905. Helped produce first Bible set in Monotype at Oxford. Notable Press cricketer. d. 6 January 1965; **G. W. Ayres** r. after almost 47 years' service in the Monotype Department. j. as a keyboard operator 19 July 1909. d. 2 April 1960 aged 71 years; **R. J. Pellis** r. after working 60 years as a compositor and a proofreader. Member of original Clarendon Press Minstrels. d.

16 May 1960 aged 77 years; **C. D. Hoy** r. Served apprenticeship as a machine minder. l. 1917 after service in the First World War. rj. 1930. Member of the Piscatorial Society. d. 1 February 1968 aged 75 years; **C. G. (Gordon) Remington** r. j. service August 1907 as compositor and then transferred to the Reading Department 1932; **W. Judge** d. b. 1864. j. January 1878. Exact length of service not recorded but believed to have been about 64 years; **G. M. Adams** r. j. 4 September 1939 as clerk to the Engineers' Department. Transferred to the Lithographic Department January 1943 and on 3 March 1947 took charge of the Maintenance Stores. d. 25 May 1962 aged 71 years; **A. E. Cripps** r. j. May 1900 as a compositor. Played football for the Press. d. 9 November 1959 aged 74 years; **F. P. Frost** r. j. November 1898. d. 13 July 1959 aged 74 years

1957 **J. F. Moulder** d. after 17 years' service at the Jordan Hill Warehouse; **A. F. Willoughby** r. j. February 1906. Appointed foreman of Composing Rooms in 1928 before being transferred to the Counting House in 1944; **V. A. D. (Vic) Saint** d. j. 17 October 1940. Wife and son worked at the Press; **S. H. Mills** d. j. Litho Department February 1908. l. 1948; **P. G. H. Halfacree** r. j. 29 July 1940; **F. H. Clifford** r. j. February 1905 from the Bindery. Appointed foreman in 1918. Member of the SJAB. Played bowls for Oxfordshire. d. 11 December 1962; **H. Slatter** r. after 53 years' service. j. at the age of 13 years for 4s. 6d. per week of 56½ hours; **B. J. Kitchen** r. j. the Machine Room 14 June 1897. Presented with a TV set on 14 June 1957 on completion of 60 years' service. d. 22 September 1958; **E. Bevan** r. after 26 years service, j. in the Boiler House 1931, d. 7 December 1967 aged 80 years; **F. H. Dunford** r. from the Clearing Department. j. February 1907 on the Learned Side Composing Room. Joined the RFC in 1917 where he served until the end of the war. d. 27 February 1978; **W. T. Wright** d. aged 51 years. j. 1920 working in the Machine Room but transferred to the Delegates Drawing office in 1922. Became chief draughtsman in 1935. Played cricket, football, and tennis for the Press and was a member of the Stute Council; **W. H. Peyman** r. j. 28 November 1949 as letterpress printer. d. 24 April 1974 aged 82 years; **Sidney G. Cherrill** r. j. 28 June 1909. Worked as hand compositor (music composition) in the Top Composing Room. d. 21 October 1961; **C. H. Taylor** r. after 53 years' service j. Delegates Staff 1904 aged 14 years at a wage of 5s. per week. Appointed to take charge of production and head of Delegates Main Office 1926. d. 1969

1958 **W. Clifford** r. j. 2 February 1906. d. 20 April 1970. Member of the Stute Council for over 30 years and Secretary for 13 years; **I. F. Green** d. 62 years of age. j. 1940. Member of the PFB during the Second World War; **J. Washbrook** d. j. 2 September 1946; **B. H. Bough** r. j. 20 July 1921 after serving apprenticeship at Morley Bros. as a bookbinder. For many years responsible for binding presentation volumes and leather binding; **I. R. G. Smith** d. Almost 30 years' service, most of which was spent in the Monotype Keyboard Department. Formerly member of the Stute Council, and vice-captain of the Bowls Section; **C. W. Collins** d. j. January 1911. Served as cavalryman, being a member of the first unit to engage the German cavalry in the First World War, later was an infantryman in many of major battles. Member of the Home Guard in the Second World War being responsible for building gun replacements covering approaches to the Press in Walton Street 1940; **J. H. Williams** r. j. 15 July 1907 was transferred to the Counting House 1909. A great athlete in his younger days. In 1912 he won 100 yards, the ½ mile, and the 1 mile races at the Press sports in one afternoon. For 23 years Secretary to the Holiday Fund and Treasurer of the Stute Council from 1950 to 1957; **G. H. Lapworth** r. j. December 1905 and served whole time on blocking machines. Member of PFB for 38 years; **Miss I Fry** d. j. March 1913 on leaving school. Supervisor of the girls in the Bindery from about 1930; **F. P. Carter** r. j. 10 January 1907 as letterpress machine feeder. Played cricket, football, and bowls for Press and was also a member of the Rowing Section. His only son, Ken (a compositor in the Monotype Department) was killed in 1944 during the Battle of Caen. d. 9 June 1974; **C. V. Winstone** r. j. 1908 aged 15 years, coming from Hazell, Watson and Viney in London. Member of the Stute Council for some years and also of the Minstrels being member of the Quartette with L. Howes, R. Best, and T. Best. d. 16 May 1982 aged 89 years; **Miss C. Wilkins** r. after more than 50 years' service. Took an active interest in the Press Flower Shows. d. 21 April 1970; **F. W. Horwood** r. j. August 1907 in Composing Room Type Stores but soon moved to the Bindery where he served his apprenticeship. In younger days he was an athlete of note and played football for the Press. d. 16 July 1969; **Jack Snow** d. j. 2 July 1917 working as a compositor Member of the Piscatorial Society and the 1939–45 Ex-Servicemans' Association; **R. E. Johnston** r. j. as Bindery Manger. b. 21 October 1893. d. 13 June 1968; **Stanley A. W. Goddard** r. j. 19 May 1913. d. 12 January 1970; **Mrs M. F. Muncaster** r. j. Examination Paper Dispatch Department March 1941 before being promoted to supervise the department in 1953. Wife of E. Muncaster. d. 15 April 1976

1959   **L. P. Collier** r. j. 1911 and almost all his working life in the Warehouse. d. 7 October 1985 aged 96 years; **George W. Webb** r. from the Monotype Composing Room Office. j. 1904 and served his apprenticeship as a compositor. l. and rj. 1913. Member of the Stute Council and also rowed for the Press. Chief ARP warden during the Second World War. d. 10 February 1974 aged 83 years; **Mrs Lilian L. Webb** r. from the Warehouse. j. 1 January 1911 aged 13 years. l. 1924. rj. 9 June 1937. During both World Wars she worked in the Machine Room as a 'dilutee' feeder. d. 2 August 1975; **H. T. Weller** r. Played football for the Press and a cricketer of repute, who in his teens in 1910 when playing for the Press took seven wickets for no runs. d. 26 June 1974 aged 81 years; **W. A. Collier** d. j. as a compositor 29 November 1926; **W. D. Brooker** d. aged 60 years. j. 1930 as a compositor. During the Second World War he was employed on aircraft work. rj. 1949; **George W. Butcher** r. after 51 years' service. j. 9 March 1908. Appointed as collotype machine minder. Severely wounded in the First World War. rj. 1921. d. 18 November 1971; **F. Huckin** r. j. 31 January 1927. Worked as a maintenance builders. d. 19 March 1962 aged 71 years; **M. A. H. Tuffrey** r. j. 19 June 1911; **W. C. (Bill) Farthing** r. j. 11 February 1942. d. 10 June 1967

1960  **Harry Cramp** (the man with the lamp) r. aged 70 years. j. as compositor September 1940. d. 31 August 1968; **A. V. Bolton** r. due to ill-health. j. February 1915 and served his apprenticeship as a machine minder. d. 6 November 1975; **J. F. Phelps** r. after 51 years' service. j. 1909. Went to the Bodleian Library 1919 as Library Photographer. Member of Minstrels and Secretary for 10 years and also a member of the Dramatic Society. Revived Music Society 1936–7 and member of the SJAB for 28 years. d. 20 November 1974; **L. A. Littler** r. from the Reading Department. rj. 1 November 1948. d. 19 February 1977 aged 82 years; **William Fitzwalter** r. Previously a ships' printer. j. June 1939. l. 1940. rj. 1951. d. 23 April 1960; **W. H. P. Williams** r. as a compositor. j. 17 July 1909. d. 17 June 1982 aged 87 years; **H. E. Franklin** r. j. June 1913 in the Warehouse. Transferred to the Bindery Stores in 1931; **A. L. Holton** d. aged 69 years. j. August 1946 and worked in the White Paper Department until being transferred to messenger duties in 1952; **Mrs K. F. Buckle** d. 5 August 1960. l. 1 March 1940. rj. 7 November 1949; **E. S. Masters** d. Compositor. j. 15 June 1908. Played football and cricket for the Press. His father, brother, and son worked at the Press; **Stanley Copeman** d. j. 18 March 1907 as an apprentice compositor. Played football for the Press. Worked on Liddell & Scott, *Greek Lexicon* for 11 years; **Harold W. Saxton** r. from the Electro and Stereo Department. His son, Terry also worked in the same department; **Percy C. Taylor** r. as a compositor responsible for the plates imposition. Member of the Minstrels and Treasurer of the Stute Council. d. 14 May 1977 aged 83 years; **George E. Webley** r. j. as compositor 25 January 1943. d. 5 July 1980 aged 86 years. **Vernon V. Collett** d. j. June 1913 as a messenger boy in the Bible Side Composing Room. Member of the Bowls Section and became its Secretary in 1947; **F. G. Smith** r. j. 4 May 1907. Gave 54 years' continuous service most of which was spent in Monotype Keyboard Department. Played football and cricket for the Press. Secretary of the Stute Slate Club for 25 years and

*Three generations of Deacons: Henry, Les, and David*

Treasurer for 7 years. Founder member of the Mono Benevolent Fund being Hon. Secretary for many years. d. 1 April 1975; **W. H. Masters** r. after 56 years' service. Member of the Football and Cricket sections for 25 years; **V. R. C. (Vic) Turner** d. aged 35 years after a long illness. Keyboard operator. j. 30 December 1940; **H. F. Hill** d. aged 64 years. j. 5 September 1939 as a night watchman; **Albert J. (Snuffy) Hall** d. j. 4 November 1918. In charge of the Monotype accents and Type Store. Prominent member of the Boy Scout movement and member of the Piscatorial Society; **E. Green** r. j. 25 June 1941 and spent all but short period in White Paper Department. d. 30 April 1967 aged 77 years; **E. Stone** r. after almost 51 years' service. j. October 1910 when he used to walk to work from Wolvercote. d. 10 January 1976; **A. Childs** d. j. 18 October 1941 as a carpenter. Member of the PFB during the Second World War; **HENRY A. (COMP.) DEACON** r. j. 9 February 1903. Compositor in the Music Ship, later specialized in hieroglyphics. Played football and cricket for the Press. His son. Les, and a grandson, David also worked at the Press; **R. E. Stanley** r. from the Keyboard Department after 53 years' service. j. 1908 as an outside messenger often cycling up Headington Hill and Boars Hill. Served his apprenticeship in the Bible Side Composing Room. Member of the Minstrels being Secretary during its last years of existence. d. 1967 aged 73 years; **R. C. Hicks** r. j. 24 October 1949 in the Maintenance Department. Continued as Lodge Porter after retirement. d. 14 November 1962; **R. T. Beckett** r. j. Bindery October 1923; **Reginald H. Mott** d. j. as office boy on 13 April 1909, later apprenticed as a compositor; **E. H. (Ted) Harris** r. after 51 years' service j. 27 June 1910. Spent over 30 years in the Monotype Keyboards taking a special interest in the University's Hebdomadal Council papers.

*Harry Lapworth retires (his brother, Jasper, is second from the left)*

Member of the Football section and Food Production and Flower Show Society. He also took a special interest in the *Oxford University Gazette*. d. 7 December 1971; **HARRY LAPWORTH** r. j. September 1902 and spent his whole service, except for short time during his apprenticeship, in the Jobbing Department. His brother, Jasper, also worked in the same department; **Miss C. G. Goodger** r. j. September 1971. Closely connected with collotype work throughout her service; **R. C. Bellinger** r. j. 24 January 1910. Employed in the Machine Room but lost an arm on service in the First World War. On rejoining transferred to the Monotype Casters where he managed two casting machines. d. 27 September 1962 aged 67 years

1962 **T. G. (Gerry) Dawson** d. as a result of a road accident. j. after service in the Royal Navy in the Second World War during which he was awarded the Distinguished Service Medal in recognition of his services during the D-Day landings in Normandy. His wife, Sylvia Launchbury worked in the Monotype Composing Room Office; **E. J. Eeles** r. after over 50 years' service. His wife also worked in the Bindery and his son Ivor worked on the Engineering Staff. d. 13 May 1969; **G. E. Hine** r. j. November 1908. His father was employed in the Bindery and his grandfather had been a compositor. d. 31 December 1980 aged 86 years; **J. W. Leatherby** r. j. 1914. Worked in the Collotype Department moving to the Jordan Hill Warehouse after normal retirement date. d. 19 May 1967 aged 78 years; **G. Hine** r. j. 1909. Machine minder known as an expert in fine Bible printing. d. 21

March 1974 aged 79; **H. H. Howes** r. as the Chief Engineer. j. 1927. Supervised in his 32 years' service, the new Delegate's offices, the Printer's new library, the Counting House, and the extension of the Jordan Hill Warehouse. d. 9 January 1968 aged 70 years; **T. H. Allsworth** r. j. Letterpress Machine Room 1922. Member of the SJAB. d. 4 March 1965 aged 70 years; **Harry Kimber** r. j. 31 January 1910. d. 30 September 1963 aged 71 years; **E. G. (Ted) Kislingbury** r. j. 3 August 1909 in the Monotype Casters. Played cricket for the Press. d. 19 December 1962; **George H. Hope** r. after 51 years' service. In charge of the Platen Room for 24 years. Captain of Tennis Section. d. 24 June 1972; **A. J. Newton** r. j. March 1927. Awarded DCM in the First World War. d. 1 March 1968; **H. Wells** r. j. 31 August 1953. d. 4 March 1965 aged 71 years; **President F. R. (Ferris) Carr** r. b. in Wellington Street just 100 yards from the Press. Married for 60 years. j. 18 April 1910 as indoor messenger boy. Joined Jordan Hill Warehouse when it opened. Member SJAB for 19 years. Three sons worked at the Press in the Keyboard Department and in the Machine Rooms. d. 18 October 1978 aged 81 years; **William J. (Bill) Colmer** r. from the Monotype Casters. j. 22 November 1926. d. 5 February 1965 aged 67; **Frank (Much) Margetts** d. Compositor in the Monotype Composing Room. j. 13 September 1913; **Albert E. (Bert) Pontin** r. from the Engineering Department. j. 1929 and was the last blacksmith to work at the Press. Captain of Press Bowls Section. d. 2 October 1979 aged 82 years; **William G. (Bill) Clements** r. after 53 years' service. Awarded the Military Medal. d. 5 December 1979 aged 83 years; **Percy Williams** d. aged 59 years. j. Composing Rooms 3 April 1945; **Arthur E. (Arty) Saw** d. j. 17 January 1916 aged 17 years. Became assistant to A. E. Bowen and when he retired succeeded him as Chief Estimator. He served for many years as a Special Constable; **A. P. Janaway** r. after over 50 years' service in the Bindery. Formed OUP Ladies Physical Culture Club. After ceasing to play for Oxford City FC became the trainer to the Football Section

1963 **FRANK J. (SIRRAH) HARRIS** r. j. 19 May 1908 as a hand compositor. He claimed his biggest job was the *Shorter Oxford English Dictionary*. He had set by hand from letter F to the middle of T. Served on Stute Council and was a member of the Ministrels and the Music Society; **Fred W. Chamberlain** r. from the Reading Department. j. 1913. l. 1922 to work in Watford. A keen Labour Trade Unionist he was responsible for 'putting the union in' to the firm in Watford and was forced to leave the area. rj. 1948; **H. J. N. McF. Jacob** d. j. Reading Department *c.*1930; **Jack Biggs** d. Monotype Composing Room. j. 25 January 1943. His daughter worked at the Press; **Bertie H. Gray** r. j. 1 May 1905. d. 5 February 1970; **W. Kirkley** r. from Jordan Hill Warehouse after 35 years' service. For many years super-

*Sirrah (3rd from right) takes a retirement drink with his colleagues in the Oriental Ship*

visor at Jordan Hill. d. 22 July 1985 aged 87 years of age; **Len Bullen** r. from the Type Foundry. j. 1913 as an apprentice type founder. Served in the Armed Forces 1918–22 and worked in London until 1927 when he returned to the Press. In 1932 was discharged due to shortage of work. rj. Press in 1946; **Miss D. A. Grant** r. j. Canteen on 9 February 1942. d. 16 June 1972; **Charlie F. Foster** d. after being absent from work since January 1961. j. 1917 as a compositor and worked on the Clearing before retirement. Member of SJAB 1920–60; **Percy Stone** r. from the Reading Department. j. 14 October 1912. Played bowls for the Press. d. 1 July 1965; **Miss F. A. Lyon** r. j. Warehouse 1940; **H. W. (Ben) Boult** l. to work at Pergamon Press after 26 years' service. Umpired for the Press cricket team for many years; **J. W. Howkins** r. j. Bindery on 25 August 1913; **Esmond H. (Essy) Fathers** r. j. 2 June 1913. d. 7 April 1967 aged 68 years; **A. T. (Tarzan) Harvey** r. compositor in the Monotype Composing Room. j. 3 May 1909. d. 16 September 1977; **C. H. Watkinson** r. j. 13 April 1959. d. November 1969; **Frederick W. George** r. j. 28 October 1912 to become a machine minder. Wounds in the First World War prevented this and he became a proofreader on his return to Press; **G. Cruse** r. after 23 years' service. j. 1940 as a machine minder. d. 23 December 1975 aged 78 years; **Alfred J. W. Hine** r. as a compositor in the Monotype Composing Room. j. 10 July 1906. d. 15 March 1964; **L. B. G. Bellinger** r. j. 20 November 1906. d. 28 December 1964 aged 71. Father of the Chapel of NUPB & PW for 45 years. d. 28 December 1964

*No more bets for Donna Cleaver*

1964 **W. G. (Bill) Collett** r. after 51 years' service. For many years worked in the Entry Office. Rowed for the Press; **Fred Fitzgerald** r. after 22 years' service. j. 23 March 1942 as a trucker before moving to the Maintenance Department where he worked as a cleaner in the Monotype Department. d. 10 November 1977; **Dr J. P. Naish** d aged 81 years. j. Press in September 1932 and in 1934 was appointed Chief Oriental Reader; **Arthur W. Panting** r. j. 24 April 1912 as a compositor and became overseer of the Jobbing Department after the retirement of H. Lapworth. His son, Neville, also worked at the Press in the Lithographic Department. d. 18 October 1974; **Les Hookham** d. Spent his entire working life in the Bindery. His son, Peter, worked at the Press. Member of the PFB; **Frederick C. F. Jacob** r. from the Letterpress Machine Room after 51 years' service. d. 12 September 1965; **George P. Keep** r. j. 1912 in the Reading Department, became compositor, and was later transferred to the Bindery Warehouse office. Served in the First World War and returned to Press in 1919. In 1925 he was put in charge of the then new Forwarding office (with Bertie Gray and Bill Collett) where he remained until he retired. d. 26 February 1964; **Walter E. Gregory** r. j. 11 January 1926. Worked in the Warehouse and drove the van between the printing works and the Warehouse. d. 29 October 1976 aged 80 years; **REGINALD A. (Donna) CLEAVER** r. as a compositor in the Jobbing Department. j. 1910. Played football for the Press. d. 21 June 1965;

**R. E. Taylor** r. after 52 years' service. Played cricket for the Press. Church officer at St Barnabas Church for 40 years; **R. Grinyer** r. from the Bindery. j. 6 September 1923. d. 26 April 1982 aged 85 years

1965  **Miss Frances M. (Fanny) Williams** r. from the Reading Department where she was employed as a graduate proofreader. j. January 1927. l. for a while to become a teacher but then rj. She was editor of *The Clarendonian* 1929–30 and 1939–45. With wide interests she was also a member of the Dramatic Society; **William (Chip) Beal** r. j. 28 February 1910. Served with the 4th OBLI and was transfered to the 2/4th OBLI and landed in France in May 1916. Saw action on the Somme, Avras, Passchendael, and Cambrai. Returned to active service with the OBLI from 1939 to 1945; **Harry Jupp** r. j. 6 March 1911, and became a compositor apprentice. On return from service in the First World War he became a keyboard operator and was responsible for keyboard work on Bruce Rogers's *Lectern Bible* and Snaith's *Hebrew Bible*. The latter was the first setting of Hebrew by Monotype. Member of the Dramatic Society. When he retired he made his infamous speech where he said, 'I may not have been your cup of tea but I have to say that some of you were not exactly mine!' d. 19 January 1982 aged 85 years; **H. J. (Jasper) Lapworth** r. j. February 1911. Served in the 4th OBLI and 1st Bucks in France from 1914 to 1919. Gassed and taken prisoner in 1918. Member of PFB during the Second World War. Had four brothers who all completed 50 years service for the Press. d. 28 February 1982 aged 85 years; **W. G. McCoy** r. j. 16 September 1959; **A. Evans** r. j. 19 October 1959; **J. A. Fox** r. j. 5 February 1962. Served during the First World War in 'D' Squadron of the Oxfordshire Hussars and South Buckinghamshire Hussars in Egypt, Suvla Bay, Salonica, Macedonia, and Malta. Took part in the relief of Evquelinnes in Belgium in 1918. d. 5 June 1975 aged 79 years; **Charles Masters** r. j. 6 May 1946. Member of the PFB from 1925. In 1962 received a certificate in recognition of his 37 years' service with the Fire Brigade. d. 2 December 1979 aged 83 years; **Albert C. V. Saxton** r. j. June 1914. Served as a lance-corporal in the army of the Rhine until April 1920. He machined the whole of the *Coronation Bible* and the *Lectern Bible* commissioned for the Coronation. Was the scorer for the Cricket Section for over 30 years. d. 3 November 1980 aged 80; **R. T. Jenner** r. as the Lithographic Department's storekeeper. j. 1947 after service in the First World War and the Merchant Navy and as a London bus conductor. After short time in the Cleaning Department he took over the litho plate graining until it was superseded by new types of plates; **Oliver G. Brooks** r. from the Clearing Department. j. 4 December 1939 after coming to Oxford in 1928 and working at Kemp Hall Press as a compositor. d. 16 September 1970 aged 85 years; **Arthur H. R. (A–Z) Young** r. from the Reading Department.

j. 1901 as a proofreading apprentice. He had clocked up more than 60 years' service when he retired and was presented with an armchair

1966  **Harold Robinson** r. from the Reading Department. j. 10 June 1904. d. 30 July 1974; **Leonard (Len) Griffin** r. j. 1908. Awarded the Military Medal during service in the First World War. Officer of PFB. d. 27 May 1979 aged 85 years; **J. B. Cann** r. j. 10 December 1914. d. 25 April 1970; **S. W. (Bill) Clare** r. from the Composing Room. j. May 1939. d. 29 March 1968; **Jack Powell** r. j. as a compositor January 1950. d. 31 May 1982 aged 90 years

1967  **Tom Bennett Senior** r. after 52 years' service. d. 17 November 1971; **Alfred Bishop** r. due to ill health. Caretaker at Jordan Hill Pavilion, after helping to build it, and from 1947 groundsman. d. 22 May 1976 aged 77 years; **Miss L. Salt** r. j. Joined Education Department of OUP 1942 and went on to become Head of Department. General Editor of the *Oxford Junior Encyclopaedia*; **J. E. Harwood** r. j. 1926 in the Letterpress Machine Department. Played football and tennis for the Press. Clerk to the Machine Minders Chapel for 25 years. d. 20 December 1982 aged 80 years; **G. W. G. Laitt** r. j. 1915 at 13 years of age. Awarded Hon. MA 1966. Appointed Chief Accountant to the Delegates 1946; **Miss Betty Haycock** d. Machine Folding Department. j. 15 May 1933; **Harry Clifford** d. aged 59 years. Machine reviser. j. 11 September 1922; **C. H. (Chi) Youngman** r. after over 50 years' service most of which were spent in the Jobbing Department. Played football and tennis for the Press; **FRANK BOLTON** r. j. 1913 After serving his apprenticeship he became a hand-setting music compositor. He had chosen printing as a career although as a boy he had been trained as a church organist. Later he became a Press Reader specializing in music and University work. d. 18 June 1974 aged 75 years; **S. C. (SID) ALDERMAN** r. from the Monotype Casters. j. 17 January 1947. d. 24 October 1973; **FREDERICK W. COOKE** r. as a machine minder after 53 years' service. j. 8 August 1914. Member of the PFB and played cricket and football for the Press. Was a 'bouncer' at the Stute right up until the day he died. d. 16 July 1976 aged 76 years; **R. H. Stone** d. aged 59 years. A Monotype Keyboard operator, he spent his whole working life at the Press. Member of the Piscatorial Society; **H. J. Whitlock** d. j. August 1920 and spent almost all of his working life in the Folding Machine Department in the Bindery; **Miss O. Hunt** r. after 47 years' service from the Folding Machine Department in the Bindery; **Dr G. J. Harvey** r. as a graduate proofreader in the Reading Department. j. 13 May 1957. d. 26 January 1971; **Miss I. Wheeler** r.; **F. W. Jones** r. as supervisor of the Monotype Keyboard and Casters Department, a post he was appointed to in May 1953. j. 7 February 1916. Played football and tennis for the Press and was a member of the Stute Council; **Charles (Charlie) Coles**

*R. Jakeman with Frankie Bolton who retired in 1967*

r. as Head Lodge Porter after 27 years' service. j. September 1950. d. 23 February 1976 aged 81 years

1968 **W. E. Town** r. j. May 1916 in the Letterpress Machine Room. Transferred from the Litho Department September 1942. d. 29 October 1976 aged 74 years; **L. W. Cooper** d. aged 63 years. Litho Department. j. 13 March 1919; **W. C. (Bill) Hearne** r. aged 68 years. j. 1914 in the Letterpress Machine Room. l. 1920; rj. 1939 in the Litho Department later returning to Letterpress. Rescued, on separate occasions, three people from drowning. d. 6 March 1981 aged 80 years; **W. C. Buckingham** r. after 32 years' service in the Letterpress Machine Room. Noted athlete; **Miss D. Cooper** r. j. October 1921. l. March 1950. rj. April 1957; **Eric W. Scroggs** r. j. Reading Department 1 June 1926. Brother, Ken, worked in the Stereo Department; **Miss M. Cann** r. j. 14 May 1945 and spending 23 years in the Examination Dispatch Department; **Sam Snelson** r. For many years a reader; failing eyesight following a cycling accident, he worked in the Bindery. Member of the Stute Council and the SJAB; **A. R. G. (Robbie) Burn** r. j. March 1938 as a classical proofreader. A book lover, he accumulated over 10,000 books

*Farewell to the Bindery's Arthur Gray (wearing black apron) in 1968*

most of which he gave to the Dominican order in Edinburgh. A mountain climber he scaled Snowdon aged 80 years. d. 2 June 1972; **Frank Brown** r. 6 September 1968. Had earlier service but rj. 26 June 1939 in the Maintenance Department. Played football and tennis for Press. Member of the Stute Council and the PFB. d. 9 September 1985 aged 82 years; **H. G. (Bert) Innes** d. Keyboard Department. j. 5 January 1931; **Mrs D. Sones**. r. j. September 1941 as a letterpress machine feeder before being transferred to the Warehouse October 1945; **H. J. L. Walker** r. j. August 1955; **L. Lardner** r. from Clarendon Press; **Tom Bennett** r. j. December 1915 and spent his whole working life in the Letterpress Machine Department; **P. G. Wickens** r. j. 6 November 1916. Was the last Collotype printer to work at the Press

1969 **Albert E. (Hammer) Jaycock** r. from the Letterpress Machine Room as a Feeder after 51 years' service. j. 16 September 1918. d. 13 May 1978 aged 74 years. His daily routine never changed—rollers in, oil the machine, disappear for 10 minutes, a pinch of snuff, and them work solidly all day feeding the paper into the machine—and every sheet was perfect; **George T. Liley** r. from the Letterpress Machine Room. j. March 1940. d. 31 May 1974 aged 71 years; **Reg Huxtable** r. j. October 1938. Supervisor of the Post Packing Room from 1957. d. 8 April 1982 aged 77 years; **Harry Hewlett** r. after 52 years' service. Began his working life in the Type Store before being transferred to the Monotype Casters where he ran a supercaster producing display types, furniture, and leads. d. 1 December 1976; **Fred Matthews** r. as a

*A Monotype Casters send-off for Sid Alderman in 1967*

compositor. j. 30 October 1917. From *c.*1938 'Clicker' of the Exam Ship; **Mrs E. C. N. (Nan) Humphrey** r. after 14½ years' service in the Press Canteen; **Cyril A. Moss** r. from the Monotype Keyboard Department. j. 10 September 1917. Member of the Rifle Club. d. 6 September 1975; **W. J. Long** r. from the Letterpress Machine Room. d. 22 March 1982 aged 78 years

1970  **JIM F. ALLEN** r. as the compositor in the Letterpress Machine Room after 53 years' service. j. 28 June 1917 at the age of 13 years. Played football for the Press. d. 16 January 1976 aged 71 years; **Henry (Enner) Rawlings** r. from the Monotype Composing Room Office where he was employed as a 'looker-out'. j. 8 October 1914. d. 20 December 1981 aged 80 years; **B. F. (FRED) BOLTON** r. j. 27 May 1918. Apart from 8 years in the Reading Department he spent his working life in the Type Store becoming its overseer January 1953; **D. J. Davey** d. j. 29 December 1930 aged 14 years; **Jim Hedges** r. from the Pre-Make-Ready Department. j. 1918. Played water polo for the Swimming Section, was a keen horticulturist. and a member of PFB for 35 years. d. 6 December 1980 age 75 years; **A. J. Cross** r. from the Clarendon Press. j. February 1920; **G. E. Durham** r. from the Clarendon Press. j. June 1920; **M. H. Westell** r. from the Clarendon Press. j. August 1920; **Bernard G. Gosling** r. from the Clarendon Press Staff. j. October 1920; **Mrs D. Lucas** r. j. August 1924 in the Hand-folding Department of which, in January 1956, she became supervisor. l. September 1935 to get married. rj.

*Fred Cook bids farewell to his*
*'Father', Gerry Fulton*

October 1951; **ARTHUR GRAY** d. aged 63 years. j. 4 January 1921 as an apprentice in the Bindery. Was for a time a member of the SJAB; **A. C. Clements** r. after 52 years' service. j. 20 August 1918 aged 13 years. Formerly ran a Monotype Caster but for the last 32 years of service was responsible for the many thousands changes necessary to accommodate 'specials' that were required in the department. d. 15 August 1975; **W. (Bill) Morse** r. j. 19 January 1948 in the Monotype Composing Room; **MICHAEL J. HUGHES** r. j. 1948 as a graduate proofreader in classical languages. Formerly a missionary worker in the USA during gang warfare and on one occasion had to administer the last rites to a gunman who had been flung onto steps of a church where he was assisting at a service. d. 16 July 1974 age 72 years; **Miss V. N. Smith** d. after spending all her working years as a bench hand in the Bindery; **Percy Best** r. j. April 1919. Gave more than 15 years' service to the SJAB and was also a member of the PFB. A children's entertainer of great talent. d. 5 November 1979 aged 74 years; **W. H. D. (Bill) Hartwell** r. prematurely due to ill health. j. Maintenance Staff 5 July 1937; **W. Langston** r. j. 22 May 1934; **C. H. (Harry) Hamblin** r. from the Monotype Composing Room. j. 5 May 1919; **Fred Allen** d. aged 62 years. Member of the PFB for 40 years; **J. Simmons** l. as Printer's Librarian after 16 years. j. August 1954. Had earlier been involved with John Johnson (1938) and seventeenth-century Cyrillic types and Charles Batey helping Stanley Morison with the 'Fell Book'. Mr Paul Morgan was then appointed as Printer's Librarian in his place; **Cyril D. Piper** r. j. 1908. Enlisted in 1914 for the First World War was wounded. For several weeks was in Somerville College, which was used

*Jim Allen laughed all the way to retirement in 1970*

as a wartime hospital within the sound of the Press clock. As a proofreader he was responsible for many bibles, particularly the *Jubilee* and *Coronation* editions. He was also responsible for proofreading the 'Fell Book'. d. 28 November 1971; **J. Sutton** r. Was for a while a keen member of the Rifle Club; **George W. Richardson** r. at the age of 70 years. b. 29 January 1900. j. 5 September 1927. l. December 1945. rj. 10 November 1947. Responsible for the maintenance of the Keyboards, Casters, Linotypes, and the Monotype filmsetters; **A. F. (Bert) Greenman** r. after 25 years' service as a compositor in the Jobbing Department. d. 25 October 1978 aged 72 years; **R. T. (Clarence) Humphrey** r. after over 40 years service in Monotype Department. Worked for many years on the Clearing Department. His wife, Nan, was for many years one of the Press tea ladies; **C. G. Remington** r. for the third time aged 85 years. j. August 1907. Served in the Forces in the First World War from 1917 until the end of the war. rj. and retired for the first time in June 1950. rj. September 1965 and retired for the second time February 1957. l. and then rj. and then stayed until his final retirement

1971 **M. (Micky) Hall** r. after 57 years' service. d. 23 July 1977; **W. Holloway** r. j. 9 February 1920. d. 25 July 1980; **Leslie W. Taylor** r. j. 1924. Moved to Oxford with Education Department in 1943 and later appointed Education Publicity Manager. Hon. MA for his services to education; **C. A. Carlton** r. from the Bindery Office. j. June 1962 after long career in the armed

*Fred Bolton leaves the Type Store in 1970*

forces; **L. Bridgewater** r. j. 1920 as a machine feeder. Became night watchman at the Press on 25 August 1964. Wife and two daughters all worked at the Press; **Kenneth Scroggs** r. j. 1921 and completed his apprenticeship in the Foundry in 1928. l. 1929 and after 11 years in Plymouth moved to Lever Brothers, Port Sunlight. Served in the Army from 1944 to 1946 and then worked in Liverpool for *Liverpool Echo* and Eric Bemrose. rj. February 1949 and was appointed Manager of the Foundry December 1951. His brother, Eric, worked in the Reading Department; **J. T. Baker** r. from the Inspection and Dispatch Department after 14 years' service. d. 30 November 1972 aged 68 years; **Reginald Beal** r. from the Bindery. j. December 1912. l. March 1914 to serve his apprenticeship elsewhere. rj. 1920. Served in the First World War, the ARP, and the Second World War. Secretary to Bindery Chapel, member of the PFB, member of the Bowls Section, and Secretary to both the Hospital Fund and the Benevolent Fund; **A. J. (Jack) Cox** r. as a boilerman in the Maintenance Section. j. September 1939 to work on the boilers; **JESSE COX** r. as a trucker in the Composing Room after almost 51 years' service. Was the last apprenticed ink-maker at the Press. Member of the Rifle Club from 1931 until retirement. Member of the Tennis, Swimming, and Piscatorial Sections and served on the Stute Council. Served in India and Burma with the RASC in the Second World War; **J. L. Leach** r. after 22 years' service; **Miss W. M. Mobley** r. j. December 1922. Completed 49 years' service; **A. W. Simmons** d. j. Bindery 31 January 1921. In 1941 joined SJAB. He had suffered ill health and had not

*Graduate proofreader*
*Michael Hughes retired in 1970*

worked since 1966; **E. N. (Ern) Harvey** r. after 53 years' service. j. 13 July 1918. d. 16 November 1976 age 71 years; **J. Joyce** r. from the Cleaning Staff. j. 25 May 1959. d. 30 January 1980; **Roy Morley** d. Machine Room. j. April 1929. Boxer, footballer, and swimmer. Served in the 14th Army in Burma in the Second World War; **Frederick J. R. Clifford** r. from the Paper Office. j. December 1920. Following tragic industrial accident transferred from the platens to the Machine Room Office and during the Second World War to the Paper Office. His brother, Harry Clifford, worked 'next door' in the Machine Revise Office; **E. J. (Ted) Spalding** r. from the Jobbing Department. j. May 1951. Last 10 years of service was as the compositor in charge of the *Oxford University Gazette*; **W. (Bill) Fitzgerald** r. as the labourer in the Jobbing Department after more than 52 years' service; **Jack P. Clifford** r. as a compositor in the Maths Ship where he was the Clicker. d. 6 March 1982 aged 78

1972 **J. W. Howkins** d. after 50 years' service; **F. J. Herbert** d.; **A. E. Foster** r. as the engineer responsible for the Machine Room. j. November 1915. d. 13 March 1982 aged 79 years; **W. J. Simmons**. d.; **Ron J. B. Buckingham** d. j. January 1933. Commenced apprenticeship on 18 October 1934 as a stereotyper and electrotyper. Served in the Royal Navy from October 1939 to December 1945 during which he was torpedoed. Played football and cricket for the Press; **Arthur (Joe Sling) Josling** r. from the monotype casters. j. August 1920. First caster operative to set up and run Hebrew and Arabic type; **T. E. (Pat) Wright** r. from the Clearing Department. j. December 1945. Founder member of OUP Ex-Servicemen's Association and its first

*Jesse Cox—Trucker and the last apprenticed
ink-maker at the Press retired in 1971*

President. Played bowls for the Press. d. 16 October 1979; **Horace G. Sawyer** r. from the Lodge. j. 1920 as a machine feeder. Following service in the Second World War rj. 1946 as an electrical assistant. In 1968, due to medical reasons, he transferred to lodge; **Jason James** d. Worked in the Counting House; **Arthur R. Bolton** r. from the Monotype Keyboard Department. j. February 1922. Athlete and tennis player and was a founder member of the Rifle Club; **STEVE EDDLES** r. from the Machine Office, a post he had held since 1932. j. 1921 and after a period in the Jobbing Department became one of the first Monotype Keyboard operators. Member of the SJAB from 1928 until his retirement. d. 6 September 1977

1973     **Gilbert Tyrell** r. as Assistant Manager in the Letterpress Machine Room since 1951. He followed his father into the Machine Room after starting his apprenticeship in 1922. Member of PFB for 47½ years and won the championship cup in 1929 and 1930, a trophy his father had won in 1917–18. Chairman of Swimming and Football Section; **F. Smith** r. having spent his whole working life at the Press. j. 8 November 1920. Employed in the Letterpress Machine Room for many years, he was transferred to the Bindery in 1947 to take charge of the first Sheridan Gathering Machine to be installed. d. 16 September 1978; **Dennis Murphy** r. from the Letterpress Machine Room. Captain of the Press football team for 10 years and also played cricket for the Press; **G. B. D. Morley** r. from the Estimating Dept.

*Steve Eddles, machine revise reader, with the author in 1972*

j. 1926 and worked in Machine Room until 1936 when he joined Counting House staff. Much associated with Press and City sport. Both his sons worked at the Press as compositors. d. 20 July 1986; **W. A. Bull** r. j. 1 January 1925 in Dispatch Department. Transferred to the Litho Department during the Second World War and then to the Folding Department in 1944; **R. Jakeman** r. j. 1963 as a graduate proofreader after a distinguished career in the Colonial Service; **Arnold Reason** d. j. 1 February 1954. Member of Christ Church Cathedral choir from the mid-1930s to 1973; **Reginald J. Ricketts** r. j. 3 April 1923, in the Composing Rooms as apprentice and transferred to the Monotype Keyboards 5 June 1931; **Percy G. Boswell** r. after 52 years' service. j. 9 January 1922 and appointed manager of the Paper Department in 1954. Member of the Rowing Club and the PFB for 25 years during which he was Secretary for 5 years. Secretary to the Provident Society for 10 years and Treasurer of the Stute Council for 7 years. Continued as a Press guide after retirement. d. 5 November 1975; **Len Bush** r. Worked in the Monotype Department from 1930 to 1936. l. then rj. 1950. Member of SJAB and member of Oxford and District Trades Council for 17 years; **Cyril Foster** r. j. as an apprenticed letterpress machine minder 1922. Member of the Swimming Section, and the Ministrels between the wars. Chairman of Piscatorial Society for over 20 years. Member of the Stute Council and served as its chairman for a long period. Brother, Charlie Foster, worked in the Clearing Department. d. 9 December 1978 aged 70 years; service of the Press 14 July 1930; **JACK THOMAS** r. j. 1922 as a machine assistant, later apprenticed as a machine minder. Appointed supervisor in the Letterpress Machine Room 1953. Played cricket for Press and was a member of the Rifle Section. Vice-President of the Ex-Servicemen's Association. His retirement ended 160 years, service to Press by his grandfather and father. d. 11 November 1978 at the Annual Dinner of the

*Jack Thomas says goodbye to his Machine Room colleagues in 1973*

1939-45 Ex-Servicemen's Association aged 70 years; **A. Deverson** r. after 36 years service at Amen House and the Oxford Depot (the Press Bookshop) where he had served since 1946; **Percy E. E. Busby** r. after 51 years' service. j. December 1922. d. 14 December 1975 aged 67 years; **E. (Ted) Marlow** d. aged 57 years. j. September 1956; **F. C. Cox** r. Manager of the Oxford Depot (the Press Bookshop) since 1950, following service at Amen House since 1923; **H. Higgins** d. j. 2 September 1963; **W. A. Glasspole** r. from the metal pot on the Clearing; **A. G. (Alf) Walker** r. as proof-puller in the Monotype Annexe working mainly on examination papers. j. 28 March 1938; **Miss Una Carter** r. j. the Bindery November 1928. Appointed senior fore-lady 1958

1974 **Sid Pratley** r. as a compositor in the Monotype Composing Room. j. 14 July 1930; **P. G. (George) Pearce** d. aged 56 years. j. February 1946 as a machine assistant and took charge of Plate Store (the Strong Room) 1956; **Peter B. Charlett** d. Stonehand in the Monotype Composing Room. j. 12 August 1929; **Fred Allington** d. aged 65 years. Played football for the Press and was a member of the SJAB; **R. Heard** r. j. 2 October 1939; **F. C. (Cyril) Collins** r. from the Bindery where he operated a Dexter Folding Machine. j. 5 June 1923. Played football and cricket for the Press. d. 29 July 1975; **Alfred J. Wharton** r. from the Letterpress Machine Room. j. 3 September 1923; **Miss L. Lowe** r. from the Bindery. j. 3 November 1947; **P.Wyatt** d. Bookbinder apprentice. j. October 1970; **Gerry Fulton** d. Work Study Department. j. 6 December 1954 as a letterpress machine minder. Was for many years Father of the Chapel and later Imperial Father of the House Chapel. Was responsible for countless improvements in working conditions at the Press during hard (often acrimonious) nego-

*Chris Woodward—*
*Mentioned in Dispatches*

tiations with the management. His wife, Kath, was a supervisor in the Bindery and had been Mother of the Bindery Chapel; **Harold J. Hinton** d. aged 62 years. Machine Room. d. 6 January 1937; **C. H. Roberts** r. Secretary to the Delegates; **Albert H. (Bert) Eaglestone** r. from the Counting House j. 9 April 1923 as a proof folder and dispatcher. It was also his responsibility to arrive early to light all the gas jets in the composing rooms. He was then apprenticed to be a proofreader. When the incentive bonus scheme was introduced he became the Head of the Office that ran it. Librarian at the Stute for 10 years. Member of the Minstrels and the Bowls Section; **John H. G. Hall** d. Personnel Manager; **CHRISTOPHER F. WOODWARD** r. as a compositor. j. before the Second World War as a compositor apprentice. l. to join the RAF to work on Wellington bombers where he was Mentioned in Dispatches and awarded the Oak Leaf. After the war he took up farming. rj. 1960s working under Fred Matthews in the Exam Ship. Daughter, Rosamund, worked in the Bonus Office and son, Richard, was a compositor. d. January 1993 aged 83 years; **Sid E. Wickens** r. j. as a boy. l. then rj. 29 February 1960; **L. J. (Les) White** r. as a compositor in the Monotype Composing Room. j. 28 March 1940. After a spell in the Jobbing Department he was transferred to the Mono Annexe where he was involved in the composition of secret codes and cypher material during the Second World War. Played cricket for Press and was a member of the PFB; **Revd Aubrey William Argyle** r. as a graduate proofreader. j. 1964 after 13 years' service as a Baptist minister in Hertfordshire and 13 years' service at Regents Park College, Oxford. d. 6 June

1981 aged 71 years; **Stanley J. (Stan) Kitchen** r. from the White Paper Department after almost 51 years' service. j. 21 April 1924. His father, Bertie completed over 60 years' service and his grandfather, John could only muster 52 years; **W. (Bill) Wilkins** r. from the Reading Department 16 May 10 aged 73 years. j. 19 June 1916. For many years associated with the AAC and played tennis and bowls for the Press; **Mrs G. E. Smith** d. Bindery Office. j. 17 September 1928. Her husband, William, had for some time worked in the Letterpress Machine Room; **Mrs W. Lamble** r. One of the first members of the 'Wantage contingent'. (Workers transported from the Wantage area by a special bus service paid for by the Press to fill serious staff shortages in the Bindery.) j. May 1959; **Mrs H. B. Masters** r. j. 1927. l. 1937. rj. 1969 and worked in various sections in the Bindery. Her husband, Les, worked in the Machine Room; **E. T. Hazell** r. j. 10 August 1959; **Mrs F. E. C. Harvey** r. as canteen manageress. j. 1 September 1959. Husband worked as a proof-puller in the Monotype Composing Room; **H. A. (Lal) Harvey** r. as a proof-puller in the Monotype Composing Room. Previously worked as a proof-puller in the Top and Middle Composing Rooms serving the compositors that were working on piece-work. Wife worked in the Canteen. j. 30 June 1924. d. 22 December 1979 aged 69 years; **Stanley S. C. Webb** r. as chief carpenter j. 1947. Became a member of the SJAB in 1948 and ultimately became its Superintendent; **Mrs Doris Saint** r. 5 September 1975. j. Canteen 1957 and later transferred to the Bindery Inspection Dispatch Department. Husband and son both worked at the Press as compositors; **Miss Winifred (Win) Surrage** r. 26 September 1975. j. the Bindery Inspection and Dispatch Department 5 March 1947; **Arthur H. Washbrook** d. in service 9 October 1975 aged 64 years. j. as a compositor April 1975 aged 14 years. A fine musician (particularly the banjo, the guitar, and the ukelele) he was a member of the Minstrels. He served as a radio operator in an RAF unit that was engaged on the interception of coded messages from the enemy; **M. L. Mayo** r. from the Bindery Folders. j. 29 December 1924; **Aubrey S. Beesley** r. j. 25 May 1920 as an apprentice bookbinder. Served for 30 years as Chief Officer of the PFB. d. 24 May 1981; **Ron C. Fidler** r. as foreman of the Folding Department after almost 51 years' service. When the Incentive Bonus Scheme was introduced in the Bindery in 1951–2 it was the Folding Department to which it was first applied. j. 5 January 1925. Served with Oxford & Bucks Light Infantry from September 1939 to November 1945. Appointed supervisor of the Folding Machine Room March 1952; **Ron G. Gardner** r. j. February 1925 as a compositor apprentice and later served for a period in the Reading Department before transferring to the Counting House in 1937. Became Chief Estimator in 1963. Chairman of the Stute Council for many years. His wife Gladys King worked at the Press in the Monotype Composing Room Office; **Charles R. (Charlie) Chambers** r. from the Jordan Hill Warehouse where he worked in the bound-stock section. j. 2 May 1955. Member of the 1939–45 Ex-Servicemen's Association and a keen Trade Unionist. d. 9 June 1978 aged 68 years; **Arthur Holliday** r. after 10 years' service in the Cartographic Department; **F. N. L. Smith** d. from the Clarendon Press Production Staff but had started work in the Printer's Entry Office

1975   **Helen Palmer** r. as Assistant Editor of the *Dictionary of National Biography*; **Miss A. Dewe** r. from the Bindery Inspection and Dispatch Department. j. 2 February 1970. Member of the Abingdon Salvation Army; **G. Milburn** d. aged 66 years after 4 years' service; **A. Bricknell** d. r. 20 February 1970

1976   **S. G. (Sid) England** r. j. 20 April 1925 as a machine feeder. l. to emigrate to Australia in November 1946. rj. 2 July 1951. H returned to Australia on retirement; **G. R. (Jock) Dennett** r. from Jordan Hill where he worked as an assistant in the Warehouse. j. 18 February 1957; **Norman (Gang) Davies** r. as a compositor from the Monotype Composing Room with particular skills as a make-up hand; **Fred Rand** d. a member of the Cleaning Department. j. 11 June 1951; **H. G. (George) Muton** r. from the Jobbing Department after 20 years' service. j. 1932. l. twice and rj. 1934–6. rj. again April 1956. d. 24 April 1979; **George Ball** r. from the Estimating Department. j. October 1925 as a compositor apprentice and remained in the Oriental Ship from the end of his apprenticeship until joining the RAF in August 1940. rj. January 1955 in the Counting House. He was a notable gardener and a member of the committee of the OUP Horticultural Society for many years. He was also a member of the Rifle Club and the Bowls Club and played cricket for the Press in his younger days; **W. T. (Rocky) Knight** r. from the Monotype Composing Room where he worked as a proof-puller on such presses as the Vandercock and the Soldan. j. June 1925 and worked as a proof puller for the whole of his working life; **E. C. (Ted) Rogers** r. from the Jobbing Department after 20 years' service; **Maurice T. R. Howkins** d. Letterpress Machine Room. Joined Press as a machine feeder on 25 November 1946; **G. E. Rawlings** r. from the Bindery where he worked in the Case-Making Section. j. 9 December 1925; **Percy R. F. Cox MBE** r. from the Keyboards. j. 18 March 1914. Long military connection with Oxford & Bucks Light Infantry which commenced in 1918; for these services he was awarded Territorial Efficiency Medal and the MBE; **Harold B. Dotterill** r. from the Monotype Casters after 36 years' service. j. 17 October 1940. Originally a compositor specializing in mathematical work he spent most of his working life in

Casters where he was eventually promoted to Caster Room Supervisor. He had been a teacher and an examiner at the Technical College in Oxford; **Ron Evans** r. from the Reading Department. j. 7 June 1920. l. 4 October 1946. rj. 9 March 1953; **Miss B. Gunning** r. from the Bindery. j. 25 January 1960; **Miss Mildred Pether** r. from the Bindery after over 53 years' service. j. 9 April 1923 and worked almost all her working life in the Inspection and Dispatch Department. She was for some time the assistant supervisor. During the war years she operated many machines to cover for the Bindery men that were away on service; **Miss M. Scarsbrook** r. from the Bindery. j. as assistant in the Examination Paper Dispatch Department 3 February 1958 and continued there until retirement; **Mrs E. A. Macdonald** r. after 17 years' service. j. May 1959 when the Wantage bus first ran; **C. Moyses** r. as Head Porter. j. 28 April 1969. Formerly a chef, he had served the Royal Household and on the Royal Yacht; **H. C. (Tam) Edens** r. as a letterpress machine minder where he worked on Miehle Perfectors. j. 1926. l. 1940. rj. December 1945. l. again 1947. rj. again June 1956; **Ron E. Foster** r. as a compositor in the Monotype Composing Room. j. 10 January 1938. He was a highly skilled make-up hand and was responsible for providing specimen pages; **A. R. (Reg) Plaister** r. from the Production Office. j. 28 August 1933 as a compositor. Transferred to the Reading Department in June 1936 and to Composing Rooms office after the Second World War to take charge of Progress Control. d. 24 December 1993 age 83; **Mrs Margery (Midge) Brindley** r. from the Accounts Department after completing 46 years' service. j. 12 January 1931. When she first joined the Press, Mrs Brindley was employed in the Bindery, moving later to the Bindery office and ultimately to the Accounts Section, where after working in the Costing Section she became Cashier in 1964; **Jack C. Rees** r. from the Cleaning Staff working in the Lithographic Department. j. 24 July 1967 after working many years as a coal-miner. d. 13 July 1980 aged 73 years; **George Huggins** r. from the Maintenance Department aged 68 years. j. 2 November 1970; **Henry (Jock) Whyte** d. j. the locker room 1 July 1974; **Miss Mabel D. Ostler** d. j. 22 January 1934. r. 1 October 1954 after 20 years' service; **Henry Stopps** d. j. 16 October 1972. r. from the Bindery Marshalling Department 21 February 1975; **Mrs Nina Ryman** r. j. 3 February 1969; **Mrs Myrtle Cobb** r. from the Letterpress Machine Room Office. j. 1970 in the Correspondence Department before transferring to the Machine Room; **A. G. Thorne** r. j. 4 April 1972 in the Jordan Hill Warehouse; **Cyril E. Neale** r. from the Letterpress Machine Room where he worked as a Work Checker and Counter. j. August 1938. His son, Colin, also worked at the Press; **Miss S. A. L. Stevens** d. aged 84 years; **B. Williams** d. r. 28 February 1969

*'Oxford' style and Fred Stewart*
*were synonymous*

*The death of Keyboard operator Charlie Morgan on the football field in 1977 was a major shock to everyone at the Press because he seemed to play a part in everyone's life.*

Charlie was a keen sportsman and represented his department and the Press at running, football, cricket, swimming, snooker, billiards, rifle shooting. He would help out his colleagues with clock-repairing, car maintenance, electronics, and photography. He was always willing to help anybody in difficulty and will be sadly missed by his workmates and the many people he came into contact with.

1977    **W. Horwood** r. from the Bindery. j. April 1926. Had been absent through ill-health from July 1971. d. 18 August 1978; **CHARLES MORGAN** d. aged 48 years. Keyboard Operator. j. as an apprentice 3 May 1943. A keen sportsman he played football for the Press and was a member of Swimming Section and Rifle Section. It was whilst playing football that he collapsed and died. He had been a keen photographer and introduced many Press employees to the hobby; **Leslie F. (Les) Brogden** r. as a compositor in the Monotype Composing Rooms after 55 years' service. Member of the Piscatorial Society. He was also a fine artist and many of his cartoons have been left behind as part of his legacy. j. 1 May 1922. Prominent member of the Piscatorial Society; **Norman Mansfield** r. as Letterpress Machine Room Manager. j. 1952. Commissioned in the Second World War and served with the Royal Artillery. City and Guilds examiner for 20 years and member of many other professional organizations; **Frank E. B. Wilkins** r. from the Keyboard. Deaprtment after 50 years' service. j. 8 August 1927. He was regarded as a Latin expert typesetting the *Oxford Latin Dictionary* and *Medieval Latin Dictionary*; **Philip Walker** r. from the Keyboard Depart-

*Ben Kerry receives a tankard from the Chief Engineer, Bert Ashby in 1977*

ment where he specialized in typesetting Russian. j. 14 March 1927. b. 28 September 1912. He was Father of the Chapel for 13 years and Imperial Father from 1971 to 1974; **Mrs Dorothy Jeffries** r. from the Sheridan Gathering Machine in the Bindery where she was responsible for checking that the books were correctly 'made up'. j. 12 February 1968; **FRED STEWART** r. as manager of the Editorial Department after 49 years' service. j. as proofreading apprentice 20 August 1928. Member of the Rifle Section and the Horticultural Society. Played football and cricket for the Press; **Andrew (Andy) Chalmers** after 54 years' service. r. from the Engineers Department. j. 4 June 1923 in the Letterpress Machine Department and 2 years later transferred to the Engineers to serve 7 years' apprenticeship. Active member of the PFB, SJAB, and Horticultural Society. Brother was the Manager of the Bindery; **George Oliver** d. Worked in the Publishing Division but formerly was a machine minder in the Letterpress Machine Room d. in tragic circumstances; **W. W. (BEN) KERRY** r. from the Engineers Department. j. 1 April 1973 from Knowles and Son to take control of the Boiler House; **Eric Haydon** d. aged 70 years. j. 30 October 1967. r. as Senior Lodge Porter; **Arthur (Martin) Harvey** d. j. 3 May 1909 aged 82 years. r. as a Stonehand in the Monotype Composing Department 4 October 1963. Famous for his corned-beef sandwiches!; **Margery Eady** r. j. the *Oxford University Gazette* 1958. Her first few weeks were hectic. One particularly difficult day she received the fifteenth telephone call of the morn-

*Plumber Les Strange gets the retirement treatment in the Carpenters' Shop in 1978*

ing, 'This is the Wilde Lecturer in Chinese History.' 'This is the wild editor of the *Oxford University Gazette*' she replied, her knuckles whitening over the receiver; **Ray (Tackley Joe) Bryant** r. from the Maintenance Department. Tackley was a larger-than-life character and was always up to scams. His last idea to get rich quick before taking retirement was to export ferrets to Canada; **Mrs D. E. Hunt** d. j. June 1973 in the Bindery when the Mini-Bus service started bringing workers into the Press from the Witney and Carterton area; **A. Ball** d. r. 26 February 1971 after 51 years' service

1978  **Frank Isaac** r. j. July 1956 and worked in Composing Rooms operating the Metal Pot until 1977 when he moved to Cleaning Staff due to ill-health. Member of the Bowls Section, Entertainments Secretary of the Stute; **Mrs Kath Hoyle** r. from the Bindery Packing Room j. 30 September 1968 from Eastern Press in Reading. During the Second World War she was a passenger guard on the railways; **LES STRANGE** r. from the Engineers Department where he was employed as the Press plumber. j. 14 October 1946 from Hutchins & Green. d. 10 January 2000; **William F. (Bill) Cooper** r. from

*Press van driver Bob Belcher with Bindery Manager, Reg Chalmers*

the Bindery Department after 51 years' service. j. 8 August 1927. d. 19 August 1981 aged 68 years; **W. R. BELCHER** r. j. 25 April 1960. d. 19 May 1993; **W. J. (Bill) Pearce** r. from the Monotype Composing Room j. 30 May 1939. d. 12 April 1996; **Norman G. Reeves** d. aged 49 years. Engineering Department. j. as engineering apprentice 17 August 1942. Was the author of many Press pantomimes that he wrote with his brother, Garvin, who also worked at the Press as a compositor and then type storeman; **Aubrey G. Beasley** r. from the Bindery Department. j. 8 February 1960. d. 4 August 2002; **Harry Brown** r. from the Reading Department. j. 30 November 1931; **W. S. (Bill) Morgan** r. from the Reading Department. j. 2 October 1961 as an apprentice compositor 17 August 1942; **W. (Wally) Butt** r. j. August 1927. Member of the Piscatorial Society and many other sporting clubs. His son, Bill, worked at the Press as a compositor before emigrating to Australia. d. 15 August 2001; **Miss Stella Brewster** r. as a graduate proofreader in the Reading Department. j. 17 February 1969; **W. A. (Wally) Connor** r. from the Composing Room. j. 22 November 1937, l. full- time employment April 1976; **Mervin R. Bull** r. from the Maths Ship in the Monotype Composing Room. j. 13 November 1939. Member of the Stute Council and a member of the Oxford City Military Band; **Peter B. Davey** r. from the Lithographic Machine Room after almost 52 years' service which included time in the Collotype Department. j. 2 January 1928; **Mrs Winifred (Winnie) Mason** r. from the Assessor's Office. j. 1960. l. 1970. rj. August 1971. r. for the second time 31 March 1981; **Robert B. White**

*Gilbert Woodley says farewell to his beloved Kelly (the machine!)*

r. from the Bindery Department aged 64. j. 19 August 1928. d. 14 July 1989; **F. (George) Morris** d. in service whilst a member of the Cleaning Staff. j. as Jordan Hill Groundsman 4 April 1978; **William G. Savage** d. in service aged 65 years. j. Jordan Hill Warehouse October 1972; **Cyril Cudd** d. in service. j. 1974. Worked in the Wages Department and was also the Caretaker of the Press Hostel; **Hugh C. Ewen** r. from the Front Lodge. j. 17 March 1975. d. 17 March 1980

1979    **H. Cowan** r. from the Jordan Hill Warehouse. j. 20 December 1976; **Stanley J. Floyd** d. 2 February 1979 aged 62 years. j. 9 February 1976 to work on the Cleaning Staff; **Gladys Joan Rudge** r. from the Exam Dispatch Department. j. 1933. l. 1939 to work at Mansfield College and then the Foreign Office. rj. 1946; **Nathaniel (David) Nevins** r. from the Cleaning Department. j. September 1974. d. 21 August aged 67 years; **GILBERT WOODLEY** r. from the Colour Room. j. 6 September 1926. For many years his name was linked to his beloved Kelly platen. It was thought that the machine would not function for anyone but Gilbert. d. 2003; **Stanley (Dick) Eastman** r. from the Monotype Composing Room. j. 31 October 1950. d. 15 March 1981 aged 71 years; **Frederick Morgan** r. from the Mono Composing Room. j. 11 August 1930. Chemistry and Maths expert. d. 22 October 1979 aged 63 years; **Kenneth Osborne** r. from the Mono Composing Room. 'Clicker' of the Exam Ship. j. 29 November 1937; **DORIS CROFT** r. from the Bindery Department. j. October 1933. l. 1940. rj. January 1942. l. again October 1942. rj. again January 1951. l. again December 1962. rj. again March 1963. Was for many years Mother of the Chapel in the Bindery. d. 13 April 1982: **Charles Beecham** r. from the Bindery Packing Room aged 66 years. j. 9 January 1950 after working for 23 years at the Cannon and Clapperton Paper Mill. He also had the responsibility of starting

*Doris Croft: sometime
Mother of the Chapel*

work at 6 a.m. every morning to switch on the power to all the machines and light the gas jets to heat the glue so that his colleagues could start work at 7.30 a.m.; **LESLIE A. G. MASTERS** r. from the Letterpress Machine Room. j. as an apprentice 20 May 1928. l. 26 July 1946. rj. 28 January 1952; **Gilbert D. Williams** r. from the Jobbing Department Readers aged 70 years. j. 28 April 1943 and on his first day at the Press he had the unique experience of being given bed and breakfast by the then Printer, John Johnson. 'Johnny' even brought Gilbert his shaving water the following morning; **Aubrey Freeman Baker** r. early from the Monotype Composing Room aged 64 years. j. December 1929 and worked for many years in the Exam Ship. l. November 1931. rj May 1932; **Barbara Watson** d. aged 55 years. j. Exam Department of the Bindery; **Ken Walker** r. aged 64 years. j. as a compositor 11 August 1930. Member of the Stute Council and Entertainments Secretary for many years. d. 22 August 1998; **A. E. (Bert) Cox** r. from the Bindery due to ill health aged 67 years. j. January 1926. r. October 1976. His nephew, Cyril Cox also worked at the Press in the Reading Department; **Gordon B. Taylor** r. as Production Manager after 50 years' service. j. 10 September 1928. d. 2003; **RALPH DRESCHLER** r. aged 66 years from the Lodge. j. October 1973; **Rowland A. Pavier** d. j. 23 November 1936. r. 23 December 1965. Was for some years a chauffeur and was then transferred to the Dispatch Department as a van driver; **FREDERICK THOMAS** r. from Jordan Hill warehouse. j. the Bindery December 1930. d. 15 June 1982 aged 66 in a road accident in Scotland; **Gordon L. (Chalky) White** r. from the Stones in the Monotype Composing Rooms, j. April 1946; **Leonard Collins** r. from the Litho Inspection Department aged 71 years. Worked previously with IPC as a Ludlow operator. j. June 1975; **GODFREY O. (GEOFF) ELAM** r. from the Monotype Keyboard

*Les Masters retires from the Machine Room in 1979*

*Geoff Elam for many years considered the 'official' Press photographer*

*Fred Thomas receives a radio from Stan Thompson on transfering from Jordan Hill Warehouse to Walton Street*

Department due to ill health aged 57 years. Considered to be the 'official' Press photographer for many years. He was a keen student of the arts and also a knowledgeable presenter of big band music (especially Glenn Miller) on BBC Radio Oxford. d. 1 October 1981; **H. (Bert) Pollard** r. 26 April 1979 as part of the new early retirement scheme that had been introduced. j. January 1946 after being apprenticed at the *Bicester Advertiser*, working as a compositor in Jersey, and then serving in the RAF

1980   **Ronald (Bomber) Harris** r. as Composing Room Manager. j. 12 August 1929. Son, John worked as a compositor at the Press before moving to Oxuniprint following the closure of the Printing House; **George Wilfred Bradley.** r. as Deputy Manager of the Lithographic Department. j. April 1946; **Frank Young** r. j. November 1936. Worked for many years in the Pre-Make Ready. d. 27 August 1981 aged 66 years; **W. McPherson** r. j. May 1976 to work in the Lodge; **Jack D. Maskell** d. aged 70 years. j. 3 January 1972 as a storeman; **Kenneth E. Butler.** r. aged 64 from the Forwarding Department; **Ronald P. Castle.** r. from the Machine Room. j. August 1929 and worked in Hand-press Companionship from 1932. He and Ron Veal were the last two to be apprenticed as hand-pressmen; **Mrs Mary Brown** r. from the Bindery. j. September 1964; **Muriel Morris** r. from the Exam Dispatch Department. j. February 1946. d. 30 September 1992; **Ronald Hall** r. from the Lodge. j. March 1975; **Harry Carter** r. aged 79 years as Press archivist. j. April 1954. d. 10 March 1982; **John M. (Jack) Webster** r. from the Top Composing Room. j. 1925. Member of the Stute

*Ralph Dreschler retires in 1979*

Council and its Librarian for many years; **Roy Smith**. r. from Monotype Composing Room. j. February 1971 after service at Nuffield Press. d. 26 June 2001; **Doreen Howes**. r. from the Bindery. j. October 1972; **Arthur C. Axford** r. from Letterpress Machine Room/Colour Room as Supervisor. A student of the arts with a passion for travel. j. 8 September 1930. d. 28 April 1999; **Leslie Dunning** r. from Letterpress Machine Room where he was mainly engaged on running a proofing press for reproduction. j. November 1955. His wife, Anne worked in the Work Study Department. d. 19 January 1995; **Anne Dunning** r. Work Study Department. j. August 1962. Her husband, Les, worked in the Letterpress Machine Room; **Arthur Cross** r. from the Lodge. j. January 1973 having been a plasterer for 44 years. d. 29 October 1990; **Robert W. (Bob) Deeley** d. aged 63 years. j. as an apprentice compositor 18 August 1931. Worked in the Clearing Department for many years; **Leslie Arthur Deacon** r. from the Monotype Department. j. 4 January 1932. d. 16 January 1997; **Leonard C. Ryman**. r. from Keyboards. j. 2 December 1940; **Mary Chalmers** d. j. the Folding Department when she left school 1941. l. under the voluntary redundancy scheme 19 September 1980. Her husband Andy worked in the Engineers Department. **Olgierd Czarlinski**. r. as a graduate proofreader. j. 12 March 1962 to read Slavonic Languages. d. 30 September 1994 aged 87 years; **Harold Brown** r. aged 68. j. 6 May 1940 working in the Dispatch Department. His son, David, worked in the Bindery; **Mrs L. Church** r. from the Accounts Department. j. 24 April 1962; **Percy Barrett** r. from the Reading

Department. j. as mathematics specialist 24 April 1930. Author of *The Printing of Mathematics: Aids for Authors and Editors and Rules for Compositors and Readers at the University Press, Oxford*, with T. W. Chaundy, the University Reader in Mathematics, and Charles Batey, the then Printer to the University (Oxford: Oxford University Press, 1954); **William (Bill) Lewis** r. from the Machine Room where he worked as a machine feeder. j. 2 January 1950. d. 10 August 1985; **Archibald H. Buck** r. from the Reading Department as a graduate proofreader specializing in classics aged 80 years. j. 21 January 1957. d. 20 April 1987 aged 87 years

1981 **J. Bricknell** r. from the Jordan Hill Warehouse. j. as an assistant 26 October 1970. d. 24 June 2002; **Gwen Souch** r. from the John Hall Room Kitchen. j. 19 May 1969; **Harry C. Stevens** r. from Letterpress Machine Room. j. as Machine Room Assistant 5 May 1930; **Mrs B. Lane**. r. from the Engineers Office. j. 2 February 1970; **Sam Titus** r. from the Cleaning Staff. j. 22 November 1976; **W. H. Tombs** r. from the Bindery. j. 11 December 1972. d. 27 November 1991; **Mrs S. M. Wickson** r. from Bindery as an assistant. j. 31 July 1967. d. 1 May 1991; **Dennis Rudd** r. from the Boilerhouse. j. 4 June 1962. d. 5 December 1992; **Harold E. Boyce** r. as Head of Reading and Copy Editing. j. 22 August 1932. A prominent member of the local Salvation Army, was for many years their Bandmaster. His son, Keith, worked in the Letterpress Machine Room and his daughter-in-law, Betty worked as the office assistant in the Reading Department; **Mrs I. O'Leary** r. from the Assessors' Office. j. 28 July 1979; **Mrs Nora Smith** r. from the Assessors' Office. j. 9 May 1960; **Miss Elsie Franklin** r. from the Bindery as Dispatch Supervisor. j. 29 May 1940. d. 15 December 1988; **Gordon S. Sutton** r. as a machine feeder in the Letterpress Machine Room. j. 22 August 1949; **Anthony Chadwick** d. j. Machine Room as a machine feeder January 1950; **Edwin (Ted) Millard** r. from the Monotype Office. A member of the Jobbing Department for many years working under Arthur Pantin. j. 20 January 1941 d. 2003; **Mrs G. Grimshaw r.** from Bindery where she was employed as an assistant. j. 17 February 1969

1982 **Donald (Don) Gibbons** r. as a compositor from the Monotype Composing Room. j. 8 August 1937; **C. H. (Basil) Fifield** r. as a compositor from the Monotype Annexe under the voluntary redundancy scheme. j. 25 May 1936. Son, David, worked as a compositor at the Press; **Len Turner** r. as a compositor from the Monotype Composing Room under the voluntary redundancy scheme. j. 4 December 1939; **Malcolm W. Poulter** r. as a compositor from Monotype Composing Room under the voluntary redundancy scheme. j. 22 September 1947; **Alfred C. H. Messenger** r. from the Editorial Department under the voluntary redundancy scheme. j. 8 August 1933. d. 3 September 2002; **Patrick Elsom** r. as a compositor from the

*Printer Eric Buckley says farewell to Ken Stewart of the Layout Department in 1984*

Monotype Composing Room under voluntary retirement scheme. j. 6 February 1928. A keen and knowledgeable radio ham. d. 2 August 1985; **KENNETH F. STEWART** r. from the Layout Department. j. 23 August 1926. His brother Fred was in charge of the Editorial Department; **F. C. (Jack) Guy** r. from the Post Packing Room where he was the chargehand. d. 6 April 1996

1985    **Stan G. Nash** r. from Lithographic Machine Room where he worked as a feeder. He had previously worked in the ink store in the Letterpress Machine Room. j. 3 February 1947. d. 20 October 1999; **H. (Barry) Barron** r. from the Paper Store where he was employed at a Warehouseman. j. 15 November 1948. His son Martin also worked at the Press before transferring to the Publishing Division. d. 12 April 2001; **Mrs V. Cooper** r. from the Bindery where she worked as an assistant. j. 19 November 1979; **H. (Bert) Ashby** r. as Chief Engineer. j. 12 September 1960. d. 20 June 1996

## GOODBYE

As sunset's glow is dying from our gaze,
　Another world is waking at its smile:
As life fades from us, in a dark'ning maze
　　We lose each other—'tis but for a while—
　　　　Good-bye! farewell!
Beyond, thy loved ones will be always nigh:
　　　　Farewell! goodbye!
The sunset's blush is but a crimson morn,
　The day that dies is but a day new-born:
And so, in truth, as with the setting sun,
　　Death is not death, but only light begun—
　　　　Farewell! good-bye!
And gladness only there with thee may dwell:
　　　　Good-bye! farewell!

W. King, 1924

# CHAPTER NINE

# The Press at War

OXFORD UNIVERSITY PRESS employees have more than played their part and given much distinguished service during the two world wars. In the aftermath of the First World War Frederick J. Hall wrote of the OUP warriors:

From the firing of the first gun in the great fight for freedom and the safety of the community, to the signing of the Armistice, the men of the Oxford University Press answered ungrudgingly to the nation's call, whether for service abroad, for army service at home, or for special work in Walton Street. A number of trained men, moved by patriotism and lofty ideals, went into the ranks immediately on the declaration of war, and were followed by other men from time to time, as calls were made, until 356 had gone. At the same time many who were too old or were otherwise unfit for active service were requisitioned for war printing, the resources of the Press being at times taxed to the utmost to print the reports and documents which played no mean part in securing the final victory.

There are many First World War stories involving Press employees. While the grim reality of war was all around him, a Press man still had time to think of his mates and the pint of stout waiting for him at the Stute. From the Western Front he wrote:

Not so many mornings ago, long before you gentlemen at home thought of rising (to be precise, about 2.30 or 3 a.m.), Jerry took it into his head to counter-attack us. Well, he started off all right—but never finished, as we advanced a bit farther and captured two of his tanks (he had the audacity to attack us with four of them, you see); and prisoners rolled in to the number of five or six hundred. Not a bad morning's work before breakfast, was it? And although the bacon had a lump of mud on it and the tea tasted of petrol, yet it went down like some of that Institute stout used to. It is surprising what an appetite it gives one, to go crawling about on hands and knees in a turnip-field in the dark, never knowing but what the next minute might be your last. . . . Still, we have great hopes of finishing this game very shortly, once and for all.

The war memorial in the Quadrangle erected in memory of the forty-five Press employees that were killed during the First World War was completed at a formal unveiling ceremony on 5 October 1920. The ceremony had been preceded by a 'most moving' Memorial Service held in the Quadrangle in July 1919. The money to pay for the memorial was raised by the workers at the Press under the aegis of the War Memorial Committee. The Memorial was originally placed on the grass immediately opposite the archway to the Quadrangle so that it was the first thing that employees saw as they entered the Press each morning and afternoon. It still saddens me that later it was moved round the corner to a place where it could not be easily seen. It should be always clearly visible as a perpetual reminder of the liberties that we all take for granted and that these were due in no small measure to the great price that the forty-five men had paid.

Admiral Sir Reginald Hall addressed the 1920 gathering as follows:

> When the call to arms resounded through the nation, nowhere was the response more immediate or unreserved than in our universities. How speedily Oxford's four thousand undergraduates dwindled to two or three hundred, and the ancient peace of the college quadrangles was broken by the sharp commands of drill sergeants and the tramp of men in khaki.
>
> It was wholly natural for the men of this Press to respond with equal alacrity to their country's call. You are as pledged as they to those high ideals. You are in daily contact with the great literature not merely of distant ages and lands but also with that of your own country. In the 'Bible Side' you are familiar with the divine philosophy of life; in the 'Learned Side' you are in constant communion with the human wisdom of the ages. We are here this afternoon to pay our tribute to the memory of those who died that 'the flood of British freedom should not perish in bogs and sands'. Have they not richly earned the eulogy of Pericles: 'They gave their lives for the common weal, and in so doing won for themselves the praise which grows not old and the most distinguished of all sepulchres—not that in which they lie buried, but that in which their glory survives in everlasting remembrance.'
>
> While, however, we recall with affectionate gratitude the war-services of those men of the Press who made the supreme sacrifice, I seize on this opportunity to express the nation's indebtedness to those other services of the Press which though less hazardous were of vital importance in winning the War. Some of those services were of a nature which depended on the skill, rapidity, and secrecy of execution. In, none of those did this great Press fail. The printed page never played so important a part in war, and that weapon you supplied in abundance. . . .
>
> During the War, and particularly in those dark days when the victory of the Allied cause seemed far off, it really appeared as though two thousand years of the teaching of the gospel of love was at last to bear its richest fruit; the capacity for brotherhood appeared to be realized by all; in the face of a common peril and amid the glowing light of sacrifice, we were so united in spirit and effort that we stood on the threshold of a new social order. Unhappily that light has since faded. The gospel of love has given place to a melancholy revival of class division and class hatred. Such memorials as this are a stern rebuke to any faithlessness to our ideals.

What we require today, if we are to honour our dead with more than stone memorials and lip-service, is that we strive to the utmost to awaken in peace time that heightened spirit which was evoked during the stress of the War. Perhaps we are too much inclined to place unreasoning faith in the mere machinery of reconstruction. We may, for example, be counting too much upon the far-off results of legislative measures, but 'if the world needs changing, we cannot leave the task simply to a better-educated posterity. We must expect more from ourselves.'

To order our lives in the spirit of the men whom we commemorate today will be the highest tribute we can pay to their memory. You have wisely chosen for the form of this memorial that altar-shaped model which is so eloquent of the purpose to which it is devoted. But there is sacrifice in life as well as in death. Let us resolve as we pass this stone from day to day to make of our daily task an offering in the service of the community and nation which have been preserved to us by the life-blood of our own comrades.

During the early stages of the First World War the government of the day turned to Oxford University Press where they found the staff fully equipped to take on the most intricate and special letterpress printing; no matter what the language. The Press employees also had the skill to prepare and print maps to help the war effort. During 1917 and 1918 there were more than 200 employees engaged in 'war printing'. The women and girls shared the work equally with the men and boys. There was an enormous amount of war work done during the hostilities and the Press never had a single security leak. Because of the high quality of the work the Admiralty and Whitehall demanded more and more printing from them and they often had to work all through the night. Even after the war many people would not discuss with others exactly what work they had been engaged on. This was not surprising because they often did not know the true nature of the work that they were producing. This may sound unkind but it is a fact that printers, compositors, and proofreaders often do not take in what they are working on because all of their concentration is spent in trying to produce a perfect product.

The OUP Ex-Servicemen's Association always ensured that there was a ceremony held every year to remember their brave comrades but the association folded following the closure of the Printing Division. The following was written by a Press man in 1921:

> Who knows the stress of rudely sudden parting,
> When Death disrupts the tender bonds of years;
> The reeling shock, the shattered hopes, the smarting,
> The sense of loss, the heartache, and the tears?
> 'Let not your heart be troubled.' Love Unsleeping,
> Our Royal Guide o'er this world's dim-lit way,
> Has all the worlds within His sovereign keeping:
> Naught severs us from Love's paternal sway.
> Who knows the hurt may surely know the healing.
> Death snaps no ties but Earth's. A little while

At most, and light of morn shall break, revealing
The Better Land, where angel faces smile.

The war effort did not stop at the Front Lodge. Many Press employees who had
not gone to war for multifarious reasons got themselves very much involved in
war work to help those who had. They worked with unflagging zeal united by a
common peril in many different ways. A notice was placed on the Press notice
board asking for 'twenty volunteers to dig 40 poles of potatoes for the hospital in
Headington'. They only had to do the digging because 'the Boy Scouts will pick
up'. The twenty volunteers were signed up in minutes and the job was duly completed. On another occasion the Chairman of the Cultivation Committee called
the Press and asked for 'a score of Press men' to level some land on Port Meadow.
Twenty men spent three evenings completing the task. They asked for no reward
nor did they get one except for the honour of knowing that they were doing their
bit!

Under the leadership of a Mr A. D. Godley a group of employees set up a Press
Volunteer Platoon (a home-grown Dad's Army) in the early stages of the war with
a view to providing the 'last ditch' in the event of the Press being attacked. When
carrying out their drill they were subjected to much good-natured 'chaff' from
their mates. The thought of this little group of 'last-liners' fighting hand-to-hand
with the enemy caused much amusement. They were never officially recognized
as a fighting force. When the Rifle Volunteer movement was formed as part of the
1st Battalion Oxfordshire Volunteer Training Corps (the VTC) the 'squad'
acquired a standing and they went on to form the nucleus of No. 8 Platoon, B
Company under the leadership of Platoon-Commander W. C. Burnet, who was
then the Secretary to the Oxford Local Examinations Delegacy. The VTC developed into the Oxfordshire Volunteer Regiment and the Press Platoon were kitted
up in new uniforms and allowed the privilege of wearing the cap badge of the
Oxford and Buckinghamshire Light Infantry. They supplied guards for the railway lines and for the wireless station and worked at the Ordnance Depot at Didcot where they were highly commended by the military authorities. When, in
1918, there came a call for volunteers to form an East Coast Defence Corps several
of the high-calibre members of the Press Platoon were selected and did duty on
the East Coast for 3 months. When the Armistice was signed and the war was over
the Platoon slipped silently out of existence. Someone said that the Platoon 'was
distinguished throughout by its keenness and good work, and no one who had
anything to do with it is likely to forget it'. Not bad for a bunch of 'chaff'.

The Press Division of the Oxford Corps of the St John Ambulance Brigade was
sanctioned in 1909. During the war part of the Oxford Corps was mobilized for
war service. The problem was that although there had been about twenty-six
members before the war many members had been enlisted to fight. This left just

thirteen members to tackle a mountain of work. They had to meet 134 convoys of Red Cross trains full of wounded soldiers at the station and accompany them to hospitals. They would distribute cigarettes and other comforts for those that could enjoy them. The only time that their tolerance was stretched was the day that they had to meet a train full of wounded German soldiers. It was said at the time that although 'a difficult task' the Press Corps completed the task with professional dignity. They also had to attend hospital duty and this often meant being away from their families day and night. Remember that they were all volunteers.

Members of the Press Fire Brigade carried on protecting the Press on the Home Front even though many of their members enlisted. The Fire Brigade members, like the Ambulance Division, met Red Cross trains carrying the wounded back to Oxford for treatment. They also took turns of night duty at military hospitals as well as assisting the Oxford City Fire Brigade right until the end of the war.

As the nation's food supply began to dwindle the University Press Gardening Association was formed in 1917. Like millions of people in Britain members of the Press started to rip up their flower beds, take on allotments, and start to grow their own food. Large parcels of land were earmarked for growing vegetables on Port Meadow and many of these were taken up by Press employees. The quantity and quality was so high that it was decided to hold a Food-Production Show in the Quad and that the proceeds should go to the Christmas Comforts Fund. The Comforts Fund was set up to send parcels of 'goodies' every year to the 150 Press men serving in the armed forces. The committee set themselves a target of £25 but said that they would be happy with £20. In fact they raised £62 for the fund and needless to say the Food-Production Show went from strength to strength and continued for many years until the closure of the Printing Division in 1989.

Another fund that was set up was the Mono Parcels Fund. This fund was organized by members of the Monotype Department to send parcels to colleagues who were away serving their country. It was a smaller-scale operation than the Comforts Fund but parcels were sent on a more frequent basis, mostly to members of the department. Money was raised by a weekly collection of pennies and this was supplemented by gifts and donations from many people around the Press. As money and gifts came from other departments several of the parcels were sent to men from those departments.

During the war the Clarendon Press Institute (the OUP's social club known as the 'Stute') and the various sports clubs all suffered terribly as most of the young men had been taken away. Membership of the Stute dwindled but the Entertainments Committee, the Press Dramatic Society, and the Press Orchestra struggled on and tried to maintain some semblance of normality for those left behind.

All of the outdoor games had lost their young men to service abroad. The football club ceased to operate but the cricket club and the bowls club managed to keep a limited fixture list. When men came home on leave they could nearly always 'get themselves a game'. In August 1915 a Press eleven played against an Oxford & Bucks Light Infantry eleven at Hebuterne. Although there was a serious risk of the bails being dislodged my enemy guns the match was played out. I never managed to get details of the result!

## CARRYING ON AT HOME

Of the Work undeniably dreary:
And sing we again, in a buoyant refrain
Ho! sing we a song of the Hours that are long,
Of the Workers untiring and cheery.
Ho! stick it, old boy,
At the job you enjoy,
'Mid the rumble of formes on the scooter
No harm in a song
As you 'carry along'
To the music of mallet and shooter.
Now, tune up once more, with reverberant roar,
To the lads who have flouted the thunder.
And yet once again, in a mellower strain,
To the Courage and Grit that went under.
Aye, murmur a stave
With a thought for the brave,
For the deathless who fell and are sleeping.
Then touch your top note
To the stalwarts afloat
And the 'grip' they are steadfastly keeping

Anon., 1919

After victory in the First World War things slowly started to get back to normal:

## IN TIME OF WAR AND AFTER

'Our Boys' are coming back—though slowly. Those who have returned to the Press have not yet manifested any decided inclination to write their reminiscences. However, there is no need for hurry. When Peace is declared, and becomes perceptible, their tongues may be loosed. Possibly it may also then be easier to persuade the quondam soldiers to handle the pen in the intervals of talk. At present they are coy. *They* have had no 'adventures'. What should they want with 'adventures'? And the inquisitor is tersely recommended to go to Jericho—or elsewhere.

One good fellow, more willing if not more able than others, really did appear to search the files of memory for 'incidents' in his military career; but all he could recall was a disastrous occasion, in Blighty, when he had travelled far only to reach his destination at an hour so late that 'all the pubs were closed'! And that harrowing recol-

# AIR WARDENS
## AND
# DECONTAMINATORS

Owing to the enlarged responsibilities of the Press in this area, further recruits are needed for these two services.

Recruits **MUST** be
1. Men of thirty or over.
2. Men living within 2 miles radius of the Press.

Names may be sent to Mr. Howes, Mr. George Webb, or to the Printer.

8 November 1938.

*The chilling notice posted at the Press prior to the Second World War*

lection put an end to the search: memory went out of action, and nothing further could be expected from him until that dire catastrophe had sunk back into the limbo of forgotten ills.

But if we must wait a little longer for testimony from the silent ones themselves, there is no need to be silent about them. Press men have seen much of the world; they have written home from three continents, and from the accumulation of letters a great deal that is of interest may be gleaned. There is, for example, the narrative of one whose battalion received orders to be in a certain town, some five and twenty miles distant, within twenty-four hours, and marched the whole way, over wild hills and under a tropic sky, tramping in just ahead of time, with blistered feet, and with husky voices trolling forth the regimental song.

There is a story, too, of a battalion finishing a three-days journey on an Indian railway at a small station and in the very early hours of the morning. It was decided to give the men breakfast there and then. Ammunition-cases and other baggage on the platform served for tables and chairs, bread and bully-beef for breakfast, and healthy appetite for much else that was lacking. Tommy made the best of things— as Tommy always does for Tommy *never* 'grouses'. Private Tapley in particular was even disposed to regard the affair as a picnic. Having done the best he could for his personal comfort, he took his bread firmly in his right hand—and a swooping raven took his bully-beef firmly in its thievish beak! And whilst the astounded Tommy was still trying to size up precisely what had happened, a second raven descended and snapped up the unguarded bread. *Then* Tommy found his tongue!

That, of course, was not the end of it and the war to end all wars turned out to be a lie. In the late 1930s you could almost smell the fear in the Press that another devastating world war was about to erupt. Immediately after the outbreak of the Second World War a Volunteer Platoon was formed in conjunction with the Press, mainly through the efforts of Mr G. Denton. Some thirty or forty commenced drilling in their spare time and this figure rose to sixty or seventy souls. A section of about fifteen boys was formed, every one of whom went into the Army. Although it was a strain on the older members of the platoon to keep up the required number of drills they were prepared to do them and help defend their country should it be required. W. J. C. Collier had been gazetted 2nd Lieutenant and took charge of the platoon. They were a pretty professional outfit and Lt Collier, Sgt Bryan, and Cpl Mapleston had attended a school of musketry and gained instructors' certificates. Mapleston had also attended courses of instruction at an Army Bombing School.

The Stute, like the Windmill Theatre, 'never closed' and war could not stop the Children's Party taking place on 30 December 1939. Although a cold and dismal day the children enjoyed a tea that was 'eaten with gusto'. The Printer John Johnson presented the prizes from a Christmas tree donated by Mr Dearlove. Christmas trees were very difficult to come by at this time. The children were entertained with jokes, and they sang, danced, and played games before going home each clutching an orange blissfully unaware of the horrors going on in the outside world.

The members of the Stute often met for an evening's entertainment of singing and dancing. These events were called 'The Members' Soirees'. In February 1940 there were fears that the next session would have to be abandoned but it went ahead anyway with some 300 people in attendance, including some of HM Forces who were home on leave. There were refreshments and dancing and it was reported as being 'an enjoyable and orderly soiree'.

With their usual generosity, Press employees began thinking of their fellow printers who had left the Press to take up more arduous duties in the ranks of HM armed forces. A Christmas Comforts Fund was suggested and an appeal to the House resulted in 628 subscribers volunteering their financial support of 1*d.* per week. With such a strong backing the Committee were able to send a present and greeting-card to all those serving. Four who were already overseas were sent 15*s.* each and sixty-one who were on home service, including one lady, were sent 10*s.* The gifts were dispatched in time for Christmas

By the end of 1940 the Press was well into the second winter of the war and it was proving much grimmer than the previous winter.

The *Clarendonian* editor at the time wrote:

Much has been lost since our last Editorial was written—the Finns were betrayed, Denmark stolen, Norway, Holland, and Belgium brutally overrun, while the collapse of France at midsummer brought us face to face with the end of western civi-

*The rifle section with the guns they were to lend the Press Home Guard*

lization as we knew it. It was a sad Commemoration this year; and the Bishop of Oxford's Commemoration Sermon, in the circumstances of its delivery, was as grave and tragic an utterance as the University can ever have heard. But we have not perished yet; and light from the East appears, with the successes of our new allies the Greeks. As Christmas draws on we may take renewed cheer from the lands which but a short while ago were most full of perplexity and discomfiture for us.

Although Oxford had escaped 'actual molestation' by the enemy the Press people's lives had by no means been unaffected. The working day was compressed into the hours of daylight, and the five-day week had been temporarily abandoned. A siren had been placed on the tower, sandbags were put into place, and the blackout rules were carried out to the letter.

The OUP Platoon of the Home Guard was formed in August 1940. At the invitation of the Printer, twenty-seven old soldiers signed the necessary forms and the Home Guard became established. The organization was made up of one section divided into four squads, each with a Squad Leader. They suffered from lack of equipment and because of this their efforts were badly affected. However, they were compensated, through the generosity of the OUP Rifle Section. The Section had generously handed over all it rifles and equipment to the Press Home Guard for the duration of the conflict. (This kindness, of course, effectively closed down the Rifle Section until after the hostilities had ceased.)

The Home Guard were then able to take their place alongside the ARP and the Fire Services of the OUP, and places of strategic importance were taken over when the alarm was sounded. The Press was protected by a guard posted every night and their Saturday mornings were devoted to squad drill and rifle exercises.

The fire-fighters at the Press were known then as the AFS and they not only protected the Press buildings from fire but also gave a hand to any area that needed their skills. This included the Radcliffe Infirmary and the Eye Hospital in which they considered 'we have a sacred duty to perform'. They even took turns to sleep at the Press. They would rise at 5.30 a.m., cycle home for breakfast, and then report for work punctually. The pond in the Quad was drained and replaced by 100,000 gallons of clean water lest the water mains burst.

By 1942, 209 men and women from the Press had joined HM Forces in various active and auxiliary services. Reports started to filter back to the Press about casualties and the Press became a very sad place. One report that shocked everyone to the core concerned Leading Aircraftman Alfred A. Adnams who was marked 'Missing, believed drowned'. He was last seen diving from the deck of the *Lancastria* as she was sinking, when evacuating troops from France, on 17 June 1940. He never returned.

The Press employees at home continued to raise money for the comforts of their fighting colleagues and they also took part in the 'Save for Victory' Fund by purchasing thousands of War Savings Certificates and even raised £70 towards the Mayor of Oxford's Fund for an Ambulance for Soviet Russia!

During the Second World War the Press was heavily involved in the typesetting, printing, binding, and packing of the secret codes used by HM Government. This secret coding work was carried out by carefully vetted personnel and there is no record of any lapse in the security arrangements. The codes copy came to the Press by special courier and tens of thousands of rows of figures (no words) were punched out by keyboard operators such as Jack Webster and a Mrs Head. After the galleys of type had been produced in the Monotype Casters they were made up into pages by the wives of Arthur Washbrook and Arthur Drage and another lady by the name of Mrs Rennie. The ladies had been drafted in because of the severe labour shortage at the time. The pages were all 39 ems wide (an unusual measure) and every line had to have a pica clump placed in between. (Interestingly, after the war, the Press cellars were filled to overflowing with 39 em leads and furniture and it took many years for the Clearing Department to 'Diss' them!) The page proofs were pulled by John Bowley and taken to Arthur Panting for proofreading. Arthur performed this job on a high chair in the middle of the Mono Annex (later to be used as the Exam Ship) surrounded by compositors waiting to carry out the corrections. The pages were them imposed by Mervyn Bull and the formes transported to the Letterpress Machine Room for printing. Everything had to be locked away each night in what was later to become the Pre-Make

Ready Department (the bars at the windows and the large metal sliding door remained for many years after the war) and was constantly guarded. The printed sheets were taken to the Bindery for folding and stitching under the watchful eye of Harold Brown. When the packets were ready for dispatch every one contained a heavy lead weight so that, in the event of attack, the packages would sink to the bottom of the sea as they were being shipped abroad.

Sport at the Press was badly affected and the Piscatorial Society could organize just one competition during the 1942 season. The Hockey Section continued playing on alternate Saturdays and the Swimming Section swam only on Sunday afternoons at Temple Cowley Baths because of blackout difficulties. Football lost most of its stalwarts to the Forces, but it managed to carry on by using very young players. Many enjoyable games of Bowls were played at Jordan Hill but owing to war work and overtime, the tennis courts were very little used. The cricketers too suffered a shortage of players but they still managed a few games against members of the Army.

> *Amongst all the doom and gloom the willow was weeping but with the help of the copper beech tree they were showing signs of hope.*
>
> Another friend, whose mere shadow is all that returning members will see, is the weeping willow in the Quadrangle. Over 100 years old, wind and weather had sadly shaken it, and now a stump and one branch are all that remain. But still there is that branch, which in spring will delight us with its tender green, against the more subtle tones of the copper beech.

There is very little documentation about life at the Press from 1942 to the end of hostilities because, owing to a paper shortage, the publication of the *Clarendonian* had been suspended. A News Sheet was published and Press employees were then able to catch up on the news after the long silence. They learned that K. Carter and H. Stone had been killed in action—making a total of eighteen Press men who had either died or been killed on service.

It was time to not only assess and praise those that had served their country and gave up their lives but also to give thanks to those at the Press who gave up every minute of their spare time to support their colleagues and make the Press safe. The Press Fire Brigade had adapted itself to the increased demands of war: from 1940 until September 1945 crews had been posted during the night (week-ends included) in the Press to keep the buildings under continual observation. They had been more than assisted by the cooperation of the Press ARP wardens and the Press Division of the St John Ambulance Brigade. The OUP Wardens and Ambulancemen's achievements included the evacuation of 170 cases from the Radcliffe Infirmary on 31 August 1939, and, next day, the reception there of 280 stretcher cases from London hospitals—each ambulance being got away within 2 minutes. From then onwards, during 169 Alerts, 40 Wardens, and 18 Ambulance-men manned the Infirmary. More stretcher work had been occasioned by the reception of the Dunkirk wounded in 1940. Then came D-day (June 1944), with air-flown casualties arriving day and night. To cope with these, mixed teams of six Wardens and six Ambulancemen slept at the Radcliffe Infirmary, each man doing one night in ten there, and one night in ten at the Service Station, for about 2 months.

Since its opening on 19 January 1942 the Press canteen served over 120,000 din-ners, on working days; and high teas on overtime days; and sent round the Press over 750 cups of tea daily during the mornings and afternoons. It was considered by Press personnel that the ten-penny dinner was 'the best value in the town'.

Victory had been achieved in this war. The craftsmen and women of Oxford University Press will never forget their colleagues who made the supreme sacrifice in two world wars. Let everyone spare them a thought each time they pass the war memorial as they circumnavigate the beautiful garden Quad.

### THE FALLEN

They slept that Liberty might wake—
Went to their graves that she might make
The world her throne—passed to the dark
That men might see her holy spark
In lands where tyrants' poisonous breath
Had bred but slavery and death.
To-day we gather round their pyre,
And from its consecrated fire
Lift high the light that shall not wane.
O patriots, heroes !—not in vain
Your glorious sacrifice, since we
And all the world, through you, are free !

J. W. EMBURY.

# CHAPTER TEN

# Beginning of the End with Sweet Memories

*Following an* Oxford Times *feature on this book in 2001 Isobel O'Leary wrote:*

I have many fond memories of the Press. It was my first job after leaving St Dennis' Convent School aged 14 years. Before I left I called in to the Press on my way home every day to see if I could get a job. I remember the porter saying to me, 'Keep pegging away and you'll get it.' He must have got fed up with me but I did get the job and I rushed home to tell my mum and my dad. I was a messenger girl for the Readers under Nina Judge. I thought she was beautiful. The Readers were all in little cubicles like telephone boxes reading all the long proofs. They were very kind to me and I remember them all going on an outing and bringing me a little bottle of Devonshire Violet scent with little violets painted on it. I had never had anything like it in my life and kept it for years. What a proud day it was to take my first wage-packet home to give to my lovely mother—eight shillings in old money—a fortune to me. My mother said that I could keep it all the first week and then I could give her half a crown for my keep. Sometimes the older girls would send us on wild goose chases to the Bindery or the Litho and ask for things like tins of elbow grease but I soon caught on. My fondest memory was the smell of the ink as I walked round the Quad. It was so peaceful and it was more like going into a church than going to work. I retired at 61 (I am now 81) and have lots of lovely happy memories of my time at the Press and am grateful to OUP. I now have a small pension which helps. God bless.

The truth as to why the Printing Division was closed down is known only by a small number of people owing to a 'thirty-year rule of security' imposed by the University authorities. I have much documentary and verbal evidence as to the whys and wherefores but do not see it as my brief to use this evidence to delve too deeply. The main reason is that nothing that I can write will bring back the glorious chapter of printing at Oxford and I do not want to end my little treatise on a bitter note. The people who worked in the Printing Division and experienced the phenomena at first hand will know what I mean.

The first indication that the Delegates of the University Press were looking critically at the Printing Division was a paragraph that appeared in the Franks Report

*The last frame in the Monotype Department*

published in 1966. This was the 'Commission of Inquiry into Oxford University'.

> We realize that there are serious problems here: the Press is manifestly not a normal university department—it is a big business . . . we recommend that Council should institute a full-scale inquiry into the status, functions, and workings of the University Press . . .

As a result, by 1967, the most comprehensive inquiry into the Press began under the chairmanship of Professor Sir Humphrey Waldock. The Committee produced their 184-page report in 1970. The Report itself makes interesting reading and Waldock's research (although the end result signalled the end for the printers) actually put things into perspective and will help the reader understand the fine tradition of the greatest university press in the world. I have snaffled a few key extracts from the report, which in my opinion, set the scene for what was to come, and print them without comment or alteration. The full report can be found at <http://www.btinternet.com/~akme/waldock.html>.

> 19. The Press in its own sphere is comparable in importance to the University itself, and the Secretary to the Delegates is the executive head of a publishing organization of national—indeed worldwide—importance. The real position of the Press, however, owing to the reticence which surrounds its affairs, is very imperfectly known to anyone in the University outside the Delegates. For this reason and for the proper understanding of our report, we think it essential to present at the outset a general

*Only a corner remains*

picture of the Press as it appears today from the evidence submitted to us. . . .

21. The first book printed in Oxford was a Commentary on the Apostles' Creed printed in 1478. Some of the seventeen books known to have been printed here between that date and 1486 bear the University arms. Printing was resumed between 1517 and 1519, and one of the books issued in this period had a privilege from the University, the earliest example of a form of book copyright in England.

22. After a gap of some sixty-five years the University lent £100 to a bookseller, Joseph Barnes, to set up a Press. Barnes's first book was issued in 1585 and printing has been carried on continuously at Oxford ever since that year. The Star Chamber decree of 1586 which forbade printing outside London expressly excepted the Press at Oxford (as also the one at Cambridge).

23. Archbishop Laud, when Chancellor of the University, played a notable part in promoting Oxford printing. In 1636 he secured a Royal Charter empowering the University to print books of all kinds. The work was given under licence to small printers in the town, but Laud provided that there should be a chief printer, whose duties were those of Editor and manager and who was required to be a Greek and Latin scholar.

25. No less notable was the contribution made later in the seventeenth century by Dr John Fell, Dean of Christ Church and Vice-Chancellor. He conducted the long struggle with the Stationers' Company and the King's Printers from which the Uni-

versity's privilege of printing Bibles and Prayer Books emerged. He promoted the setting up of a paper mill at Wolvercote, and was instrumental in providing the Press with the printing house installed in the Sheldonian Theatre in 1668. With three partners, Dr. Fell leased from the University its right to print, gaining an international reputation for his books and making the collection of type-punches and matrices from which types known by his name are still cast by the Press. In 1690 the University received from his executors the printing equipment and remaining stock of books left by him to the University, and from that year dates the continuous history of the learned Press administered directly by a delegacy of the University.

27. In 1780 the Delegates took partners into the Printing business in order to obtain outside capital and regained sole control of the Printing Works only a century later.

Outgrowing the Clarendon Building, the Press moved to its present building in Walton Street upon its completion in 1830, and thereafter it continued steadily to expand. The Bible business grew and was diversified by the introduction of Oxford India Paper and by the publication (jointly with the Cambridge Press) of the Revised Version. Many editions of classical and modern texts were published.

In 1868 the Delegates entered on the publication of school books, and in 1884 the publication of the *New English Dictionary* (now known as the *Oxford English Dictionary*) began. In 1872 they acquired the Wolvercote Paper Mill.

28. The first Secretary to the Delegates was appointed in 1866 and the first full-time Secretary two years later. In 1867 a permanent Finance Committee of the Delegates was also set up.

All the editorial work for Clarendon Press books is done by the editorial staff in Oxford. In principle, every individual book proposed for publication by the Clarendon Press is submitted separately to the Delegates for decision. Proposals of the Education Department for school books are, however, now considered individually by the Delegates only if they are of some academic interest, initiate a new series, or involve exceptional expense.

34. In addition, it is the Clarendon Press which undertakes, at a loss, [ . . .] all the official publications of the University, i.e. the *Gazette* and its numerous supplements, the *Calendar, Statutes, Almanack, Handbook, Examination Decrees, Residents' List, Pocket Diary*, sundry pamphlets and such special publications as the volumes of evidence of the Franks Commission of Inquiry.

51. How efficient is the Press as a business? Is its return on capital employed reasonably comparable with that of other publishing businesses? Does it publish the right books, and in the right places? Is it desirable that it should be an international publishing house, with all the problems of policy and administration which this implies, or should it be restricted in its activities to this country, or even to Oxford? Should the Press continue as a general publisher, or should it restrict itself to the publication of learned works only? *Should the Press continue to have as part of its organization a printing works and a paper mill? Should the steady tendency of the Press*

*The mono truck stands alone*

*to expand continue, or should its growth stabilize, and if so, at what level? What, in short, should be the future shape of the Press?* [my italics]

The growth of OUP had been considerable and Waldock advised that the Press should continue to expand and diversify to avoid stagnation. The Committee endorsed the Delegates' decision to expand and modernize the Printing Division. Considerable extensions were made to the printing works and there was a fair amount of investment following the Waldock Report. Much of the modernization took place in the Lithographic Department and in the Bindery. Every few months the printers had to suffer major moves with entire departments being moved. The workers were getting demoralized because every time the management made a change the printing works became smaller and more crowded. This 'shrinkage' enabled more space to be taken up by the Publisher and the printers saw the Publishing Division as the enemy within.

Morale was further lowered because of the slow reduction of the workforce throughout the 1970s. Although the printers had no concrete evidence it was 'common knowledge' that one day the publishers would oust them from their home. No one could have foreseen that it would happen so quickly and that it would be total eviction! The University needed more space and the publishers, being spread through the city, were using some of that valuable space. If the publishers were going to be evicted then they would have to find space back on the Walton Street site.

*The Bindery was still in the process of modernization with the introduction of the Wohlenberg paperback line*

In retrospect there were many clues that could have told the printers of what was to follow. The Bindery people had their own views. One clue was that the Clarendon Press Institute (or 'Stute' as it was affectionately known) had six full-size snooker tables and this was reduced to one. The television room was closed, the table tennis table was dismantled, and the jukebox and the bar-billiards table were taken away. The bar was closed because it was 'not being used'. This was hardly surprising because there was nothing to do there once all the facilities had been taken away!

Even though the Press had embarked on a 'modernization' programme at a cost of more than a million pounds the volume of work began to reduce. This caused bonus payments to fall and there were disputes and overtime bans.

There were other clues that the printing works was under threat. It was decided in 1979 to award the typesetting of the *Oxford English Dictionary* to one of the Printing Division's rivals and have it printed and bound in the United States of America. The book was hailed as a triumph of British scholarship and publishing but the OUP printers saw the work moving abroad as a bitter betrayal.

Flushed with this success the *Compact OED* was also sent to America to be printed and bound. Things did not go quite so smoothly with this book and it proved very expensive for the Press. The workmanship was very poor and every one of the thousands of sets had to be unpacked and separated from its slipcase before being stripped, re-glued, and re-covered.

David Stanford was appointed in 1983 to replace Eric Buckley as Printer to the University. Buckley was a rotund man with rosy cheeks and had been popular with the workers because of his friendly manner and the fact that he rarely left his office, preferring to stay in his ivory tower in the North House. The workers thought that the Printing Division Directors had Buckley in the palm of their hands because he appeared to giving them a free rein. It was generally thought that, following Vivian Ridler's retirement, Buckley had been brought in by the upper echelons either to close the place down or to keep it on hold until they could decide what to do. Everyone thought that Eric Buckley was just 'too nice' to do anything that would hurt his printers.

David Stanford's arrival was greeted with mixed feelings. There were some that said he was a young man with all the necessary skills and experience to run a modern international business and there were others that thought that he had been brought in to close the place down! At his address to the workforce he delivered to the workers a speech brimming with confidence and finished with the now infamous rallying call: 'Let us now go back to our workstations and make books'! The printers were still divided as to what was going on. On the one hand Stanford's call to arms was thought by some to be the start of something big but on the other the union bosses were saying that Stanford had a reputation for moving into 'ailing companies' and then introducing 'generous redundancy packages'! They said that he was a competent industrial relations expert and could possibly be a 'hatchet man'.

As Editor of the *Clarendonian* I went to see the new Printer to ask if the quarterly in-House magazine was safe from the cutbacks. He told me that the *Clarendonian* was a 'nice-to-have' and was delighted to hear that I had planned a stirring welcome-to-David-Stanford article for the next issue. The issue went ahead and was published with great success. The ink was hardly dry when he announced publicly that the magazine was to close with immediate effect. The *Clarendonian*

*Rich pickings as a proofreader tries to 'rescue' books from the skip*

had been published quarterly since 1919 (there was a break during the Second World War owing to a paper shortage) and this was another nail in the creaky coffin. Some criticisms levelled at Stanford may have been unfair because there is evidence that he did try to turn the business round and once confided to a colleague that he was going to 'show them all how to run a printing business'. Nobody (except him, I presume) knows the pressures that he was under from those on high. When the closure was announced he is recorded as saying that he had been 'bitterly disappointed' and that he 'couldn't see the sense of it. We were just starting to move . . . on the way to recovery . . . I am very angry.' Whether he really meant it we will never know but we will give him the benefit of the doubt until the 'real' story is written once the 30 years have elapsed!

Was the end of printing at Oxford brought about by management ineptitude or by a well-executed plan by the Publishing Division? I don't know and I don't really care. I just know that something very special and precious was lost at 2 p.m. on Wednesday, 1 February 1989 when I and all the other Clickers at the Press shepherded their charges into the Lithographic Department to be faced by a grimfaced Printer and the Secretary to the Delegates of Oxford University Press, Sir Roger Elliot. Standing on a pile of wooden pallets they simply announced the closure of the finest printing house in the world. The stunned silence could be smelt. David Stanford followed up his devastating death sentence with the words, 'You are probably all very shocked and you are free to go home now if you wish.' There were no tears or the wailing and gnashing of teeth. Everyone filed out quietly with dignity.

*Buffet parties in the Bindery on the last day*

I took the advice of the Printer and headed for home. Half way through the journey the penny dropped and it suddenly dawned on me that I was now 'unemployed'. I diverted immediately to the Didcot Job Centre. I had never entered such a place in my life and felt embarrassed and ashamed as I wandered around the partitions with the little white postcards pinned to them. There were plenty of jobs had I been a lorry driver, a chef, an engineer, or a brain surgeon but there was nothing for a depressed and redundant printer. From the other side of the room I spied a partition labelled 'General Vacancies'. There was only one card pinned to it. It read: 'PIGMAN REQUIRED. £100 PER WEEK. OVERALLS PROVIDED. NO EXPERIENCE NECESSARY. TRAINING WILL BE GIVEN'. Had I come down to this? It was the only job that I could do—but I would need to be trained!

Everyone was in a state of shock about the closure. The Bindery in particular had seen a massive investment in new machinery and the workers felt that they had not been given the chance to prove themselves before the axe fell. The Bindery once occupied the centre of the building and over the years the more cynical among the bookbinders thought that they were being moved closer to the back door and their fears were confirmed on that fateful day.

The next day, along with the 250 or so hapless souls, I made my way back to Walton Street to hear the sordid details of the redundancy money that was to be paid. We were told that to qualify for the full amount of redundancy money we had to stay to the bitter end and complete all the work in progress. Because of this the bitter end came on different dates for different people but it is generally accepted that the old lady was laid to rest on 28 April 1989 although there were still people employed until 5 May 1989.

The 'official' redundancy notices were issued on 10 February and the workers had 90 days to complete all outstanding work.

There was a glimmer of hope for some workers that printing would continue at the Press and the formation of Oxuniprint was a lifeline to some of those who were facing the axe. Tony Bennell recalls that with the emergence of the high street 'quick print' shops 'much of the work that had previously been done by the Jobbing Department was being filtered away to some of these shops (i.e. business cards, stationery, invitation cards, posters, leaflets, etc.)'. Bennell went on to say that, 'it was Works Director, James Campling who was largely responsible for establishing a "quick print" section within the Printing House in an effort to halt the flow of much of this work away from OUP. It was called the "Coldset" Department and comprised a small team of typesetters and printers headed up by Mike Lyne who had at one time had been a caster operative and Sam Goodlake, a keyboard operator. This new section was given the responsibility for the *Oxford University Gazette*, Examination Papers, Lecture Lists, and the jobbing work that had been waning.'

A few weeks after the Printing House closure was announced the 'powers-that-be' decided that a printing unit should be retained at OUP. By this time the Cold-set Department had already become known as 'Oxuniprint' with a team comprising Tony (Archie Andrews) Bennell (Production Controller/Supervisor, Barry (Diddy) Walford (Ryobi 500 Machine Operative), Keith (Forty) Fortescue (Ryobi 500 Machine Operative), Peter (Shook) Hookham (Ryobi 3200 Machine Operative), Terry (HAB) Alcock (Imposition/Platemaking), Michael (Rocket) Rawlings (Imposition/Platemaking), Norman (Sandy) Dean (Keyboard Operator), Brian England (Keyboard Operator), Ralph Coates (Packer), Lorna Brown (Secretary), Michael Carlisle (Paste-up Artist), Michael (Washer) Walsh (Proofreader), and Kenneth (Runner Bean) Hudson (Proofreader).

Following the closure of the Printing House the management of the Publishing Division were keen to recruit a dynamic team to run the new venture and all the posts were advertised within the Press. There were many candidates for the top jobs of Printing Director and Printing Manager. Martin Slade, who had worked for many years as Bindery Manager in the Printing House, landed the Director's job' and his Printing Manager, who would also act as his Deputy, was Tony Bennell. After completing his apprenticeship as a compositor Tony spent most of his working life at the Press as a keyboard operator before moving to the Production Control Department.

Rather cruelly, OUP did not pay redundancy money to the workers who had been working in the Printing House before moving to the new unit; they simply made a small *ex gratia* payment to each of them. Considering the millions that were paid out in redundancy money, these workers (and the two or three others that were re-employed in the Publishing Division) felt cheated. They had been made redundant and had to apply, and be interviewed, for the new jobs and were disappointed that they had not been rewarded for keeping the art of printing alive at OUP.

A few of the Oxuniprint workers decided that they would take the money and run, and Barry Walford, Keith Fortescue, Terry Alcock, Brian England, Ralph Coates, and Michael Walsh left to take the redundancy package that was offered and Lorna Brown left shortly afterwards. Following a recruitment drive Oxuniprint was expanded to consist of about twenty people. They were Gary Mort (Litho), Colin Edwards (Bindery), Graham Norton (Bindery), Michael Brown (Bindery), Ray Perry (Oxford Text Systems), Mary Townsend (Technical Graphics), and Gordon Turland (Commercial Office). The Oxford printing company, Hunt & Broadhurst, closed down soon after the Press closure and Derek Marlow, Michael Richards, and Roy Smith were quickly snapped up by Oxuniprint.

Tony Bennell said that, 'some additional equipment for binding and finishing was required and this was purchased from Robert Maxwell's BPCC group who had bought most of the machinery from the Printing House as a "job lot"'. He went on to report that the 'transitional period following the closure was not easy but the printing of the core University work did not cease. At first Oxuniprint experienced a period when we were recruiting new staff as people migrated to other job within and outside the printing industry. Oxuniprint began recruiting and became a fully self-contained printing company and they continue today servicing the printing needs of the Press, Oxford University, and commercial customers.'

The people that now work in Oxuniprint are 'craftsmen' and they are proud to continue to provide a service and uphold a tradition of high-quality printing as part of a great University Press.

I finish as I began with a pensioner's reminiscences. Written by Philip Bennet in 1950 he maps out the geography of the Press and the people that worked there through the eyes, not of a craftsman or a labourer, but of a lad who entered as an errand boy in the Entry office and rose to the rank of Secretary to Horace Hart. He continued to serve under three Printers before he retired in May 1946; he died in August 1967 aged 89.

The buildings that Philip Bennet describes have hardly changed and a visitor to Oxford University Press today could still, with a little imagination, follow his route.

> It is a long way back through 'the corridors of time' to January 1892, when it was my privilege as a small boy to enter the service of the Oxford University Press. It may therefore not be uninteresting to present-day employees of the Press if I try to give them some idea of the layout of the work-rooms in those days, and to mention some of the principal characters who played their parts either as overseers or in their everyday capacity as workers with the compositor's stick and bodkin; and who, as craftsmen of the first quality, helped in their own generation to consolidate and spread the renown of the printing of Oxford Bibles, Prayer Books, and other famous works.
>
> On passing through the gateway near the Porter's Lodge, an important client, such as the Vice-Chancellor, or a famous author like Lewis Carroll or Professor Frederick Max Müller, would take the corridor on the right leading to the Learned Side, climb the stairs to the first floor and enter the doorway which still stands (now the middle door). Opening this he would find himself inside a small kind of glass-house, and then, passing through the door of this glass-house, he would step directly into the room adjoining the then Controller's private sanctum. In the outer room the client would be received by the Controller's secretary, in those days the late Mr Fred Hall. Immediately beyond this outer room, but inside the door of the Middle Composing Room, and on the right, was the Controller's General Office, and it was this office which housed the Senior Entry Clerk, the Chief Forwarder, a junior clerk, and perhaps a couple of boys. Here most of the administration work was done.
>
> In the centre of the Middle Composing Room, against the right-hand wall, stood a large glass office which housed the overseer and his assistant of the Middle and

*The compositors prepare to leave the Mono toilets . . .*

*. . . just before OUP Maintenance staff move in to demolish them*

Top Composing rooms, and from which all work and instructions were issued to the Clickers of the Ships. Both the two upper composing rooms were crowded to capacity with piece compositors hard at work setting up such famous works as the *N.E.D.* (now the *O.E.D.),* Monier Williams's *Sanskrit Dictionary,* the *Sacred Books of the East,* confidential work for the University, or, as sometimes happened, important work for the Government, such as *The Laws of British Guiana,* or the Egyptian *Penal Code Regulations.*

In those days the hours of work were from 6.30 to 8.15, 9 to 1, 2 to 4.30, 6 to 7, and when work was in full swing it was a great sight to look down those rooms of restless activity and see the hundreds of gaslights over the compositors' cases and stones. At the end of a dark winter's day the atmosphere became, to say the least of it, somewhat 'thick', and the smell of 'print', made up as it was of gas, old boots, snuff, paper, and ink, was undeniably strong! No Bible work was ever done on the Learned Side.

On the north side of the Middle Composing Room across the landing was, on the right-hand side, the office of the Editor of the *University Gazette,* while in a room facing Walton Street were three or four readers' boxes, which housed the special classical or foreign readers. The room on the opposite corner to the *Gazette* Editor's room, now occupied by Mr Davin, Assistant Secretary to the Delegates, was occupied by Mr John Pembrey, oriental reader, who was in the service of the Press for over 70 years. The majority of the readers' boxes were at the end of the landing next to the Top Composing Room.

Beyond the office of the *Gazette* Editor one descended three or four stairs into the then Controller's Counting House. Going round the side of the Counting House one passed through a door on the right of which was a room occupied by Mr Charles Doble, Assistant Secretary to the Delegates. He was an extremely courteous, kind, and pleasant gentleman to deal with. Passing along this passage-way one came to another large room, which was used as a waiting-room for those who had business with the Secretary or Assistant Secretary to the Delegates. Proceeding a little farther one came to the steps which led up to the Tower, the large room which was occupied by the Secretary to the Delegates, and wherein the Delegates met from time to time in Term, while, just beyond, was what was usually called the Back Office, in which the Delegates' accountant and clerks worked. In those days there were only the Senior Accountant, two clerks, and a boy. What a contrast with the Secretarial staff of today!

The Jobbing Department occupied the ground floor of the Learned Side, and ran for half the length of the main block of buildings on the north side of the Quad; the other half of the ground floor of the Learned Side was the Delegates' Warehouse. The ground running down Great Clarendon Street to the north of the Delegates' Warehouse and Jobbing Department was occupied by two very large wooden structures known as the Delegates' paper shanty and the Learned Side paper shanty. Both these shanties were done away with when the Monotype Department was built (one becoming the Shirley Chapel at Headington, the other a temporary pavilion at Jordan Hill). So much for the Learned Side.

Now as to the Bible Side. The space south of the Tower (occupied as the Service Station during the War) was once the ancient Wetting Cellar. The process of wetting the paper always greatly intrigued me, because the chief wetter of paper was a very large man of rugged appearance with a large nose and, when dressed in his sou'wester, leather apron, and large hip boots (he had to stand in a miniature pond of water at his work), he looked a rather fearsome creature—something like a Long John Silver, except that he had no large brass ear-rings!

In the room adjoining the Wetting Cellar were housed a number of hydraulic presses which have now ceased to function. Both the Wetting Cellar and the Hydraulic Press Room were at the south end of the Walton Street front. Crossing the corridor from the Hydraulic Press Room, one entered the Large Machine Room—the long ground floor flanking the south side of the quadrangle. When I first entered the Press the whole of the printing machines in this long room consisted of double-platen machines, the machines which ran in and out at both ends, and whose speed rarely exceeded 500–600 copies per hour. On these machines were printed the *O.E.D.,* Monier Williams's *Sanskrit Dictionary* and other famous Oxford books, the University *Gazette,* and much confidential University work. The wing next to the long Machine Room was known as the Wharfedale Room, for in those days the 'Wharfe' was the fastest and most up-to-date single-revolution printing machine on the market. Since those distant days the Machine Room has been revolutionized by the throwing out of all the old platens (except one), and the installing of modern American single-siders and perfecting Miehle Machines, fitted with the specially designed Cross Paper-feeder attachment.

On the first floor of the Bible Side was housed the Bindery with its stitchers and cutting machines at the east end, while the western end housed the gathering, warehousing, and collating department. The whole of the top floor of the Bible Side was given over to the storage of Bible and Prayer Book quires in bulk and to the drying of printed sheets. It was an inspiring sight to look down the long top room and see the whole place hung from end to end with printed sheets flying from the ceiling on what one would describe as light wooden hurdles. The room across the landing at the north end was known as the Hot Drying Room. This was given up to the drying of special paintings, which had to be hung up and dried at the earliest possible moment for urgent orders. The hot air was driven round the room by a very large fan. After spending a few minutes in the intense heat, one felt that one had been taking a Turkish bath. The drying-room attendants always wore large paper hats as part of their workaday dress. The hot room in winter was an ideal place for boys in which to 'mike', and on many a cold winter morning did I 'thaw out' with other cheerful conspirators after running about the cold paper warehouses or across the quad in bitter wintry weather!

Coming down the main staircase again to the ground floor and passing out of the Wharfedale Machine Room, one crossed the yard (for remember the third wing of the Machine Room, adjoining the Litho. Department, had not been built or come into existence at that date), to the Old School House and Type Foundry. In the Old School House many of my predecessors of the older generation had gone to school in the evening under Mr Thomas Combe or Mr Rowland Wheeler, or to the Sunday School which was carried on by Mr Combe, his managers, and overseers. The old Type Foundry was a largish building in which worked the principal type-casters, the two Fitchetts, and Mr Sidney Squires as well as a number of boys who were occupied in 'dressing' and 'rubbing down' the roughly cast types. Type-casting in those days was a very interesting process to watch. These two buildings were subsequently pulled down to make way for the erection of the Photographic and Collotype Department. I forget who it was that inspired Mr Horace Hart to evolve this department which, as it grew in productivity, became famous for reproducing some of the most attractive work for the British Museum, and for many of the great Learned Societies, such as the Vasari Society, the N.P.S., and the Roxburghe Club, to mention only two or three. The work done by the craftsmen of the Collotype Department during both Mr Hart and Mr Hall's regime added greatly to the prestige of the Press.

Leaving the site of this department and crossing the Machine Room one came to the back staircase. At the top of this stairway one passed through a doorway on the right leading to the Electrotyping and Stereotyping Department. Some years ago this department was reorganized and much more up-to-date plant installed, otherwise it is much the same as it was many years ago. Leaving the Electro Department one entered through another door on the same landing a small room which was in 1892, and for some time after, the Bible Side Composing Room in which many original editions of our Bible and Prayer Books were first set up into type. Subsequently about the year 1894 and owing to the increase in Bible and Prayer Book work the Bible Side Composing Room was transferred upstairs to the top floor and occupied the annex running south from the main building. Here there was much more scope, with plenty of light for the increased number of compositor craftsmen who set up our famous Bibles and Prayer Books in founts ranging from Pica to Emerald and Brilliant.

Retracing our steps we come to the passage-way leading into the Quad in the south-west corner. In this passage you find an iron door passing through which you entered the Strong Room in which are housed against future need all the 'mother' sets of electro and stereo plates, of the hundreds of editions of our Bibles and Prayer Books, of the great *Oxford Dictionary* and its subsidiary editions. Leaving the Strong Room and turning right one came to the Engineers' Department and Carpenters' Shop. This part of the Press has been so much altered during the last thirty years that it is really difficult to give a lucid description of the old buildings as they existed till 1900. Beneath the Blacksmiths' and Carpenters' shop were the Chief Engineer's Office and the ink-grinding mills, for in 1892 and for many years onwards we made a great deal of the ink (both black and red) which was required for printing our Bibles and Prayer Books.

In regard to the two houses in the Quad, in those days the South House was the official residence of Mr Horace Hart, the Controller of the Press, and his family, while the North House was occupied by Mrs Thomas Combe, and subsequently by Dr Henry Bradley, co-editor of the great *Oxford English Dictionary,* and his family.

In the First World War the greater part of the North House was occupied for some time by the late Mr H. T. Gerrans and his staff of the Oxford Local Examination Delegacy.

The last book to be printed in the Printing House was Aylmer's *Views of Oxford*. The men and women of the Bindery assembled at 7.50 am on 27 April 1989 and, led by Bindery Manager, Martin Slade, followed the last book as it was loaded onto the cutter, through the rounder and backer, into the casing-in machine, before coming to rest in the pressing unit at 8.01 am precisely.

The book was signed by Martin Slade and presented to the Printer, David Stanford, thus bringing to an end this chapter of printing at Oxford University Press.

At the closure service held earlier on 20 April 1989 in St Barnabas Church in Jericho to mark the end of the Printing House the hymn 'Be thou my vision' was sung. It contains one line that summed up our lifetime of work at Oxford University Press—'Riches I heed not nor Man's empty praise'!

Ah sweet memories!

# Chronology

1713    The New Clarendon Building next to the Sheldonian began to be utilized for printing

1715    John Baskett appointed Printer

1717    10,112 copies of the Almanack printed

1742    Thomas Baskett appointed Printer

1754    William Jackson appointed Printer

1775    Joshua Cooke appointed Printer

1792    Samuel Collingwood appointed Printer

1805    Joseph Parker appointed Printer. Two Stanhope presses ordered, one for the Learned Side and one for the Bible Side. Printed 250 sheets per hour on one side of the paper.

1806    Press paid 4s. 0d. for 2 gallons of beer for workers who helped to carry the two iron presses up the stairs

1812    60-inch Fourdrinier machine installed at Wolvercote Paper Mill together with a coal-fired boiler and steam-engine

1814    The Thames was frozen over, the ice being sufficient thickness to bear the weight of ten printing presses. These presses produced keepsakes of the event. The Thames had previously frozen over in 1620 and 1684

1825    The Delegates of the Press purchased land in Walton Lane because space in the Clarendon Press (now The Clarendon Building in Broad Street) proved inadequate

1827    The Front and South Wing completed and work commenced on the North Wing

1830    The North Wing opened and the Classical Side moved in. The architects were Daniel Robertson and Edward Blore. The Delegates purchased a fire engine for use at the Press

1831    Gladstone visited the Press

1832    The North and South Houses built

1834    The first steam engine was installed in the Press followed by the new printing machines that could be run by one man and two boys. Seventy or eighty machine room men went on strike and paraded through the streets of Oxford to air their grievances wearing their traditional working clothes that comprised of tall hats and frock coats. The new machines could print 1,000 copies per hour compared with the hand press that required two men and produced 250 copies per hour. Their action was in vain and the new machines were installed in October

1835    The Delegates paid £1,500 towards the cost of building St Paul's Church (now a cafe/bar) opposite the Press in Walton Street on condition that two pews be reserved for 'The Superintendents of the Press'. The church was completed in 1836 at a cost of £2,574 13s. 8½d.

1836      The first cylinder press introduced. Lamech Denton (Engineer) came to the Press. He worked at the Press for 60 years. His sons, George and Henry, and his granddaughter, Bessie also worked at the Press

1837      The first double-platen printing machine installed. From 1837 to 1847 the Press produced 2,600,000 bibles, 2,500,000 prayer books, 2,000,000 Testaments, and 1,500,000 Psalms

1838      Thomas Combe appointed Superintendent of the Clarendon Press (the Learned Side). Fire in the South Wing that took over 4 hours to extinguish and much type and paper was destroyed. The Delegates ordered that from the day of the fire, managers should check their departments before leaving the Press and that the first night watchman should be appointed. Press Sunday School was formed. On 20 January the coldest day of the century with 43 °F of frost recorded. Thomas Combe appointed Superintendent of the Press 24 June

1839      Edward Pickard Hall appointed Printer. Taylor Institution built (completed 1845)

1840      The first school was built inside the Press and the Sunday School for boys who worked at the Press was started. It remained until around 1880 when it was demolished having been used as a type foundry

1841      Thomas Combe took control of the Bible Side as well as the Learned Side and was also admitted as a partner in the Press holding 2½ out of 48 shares. Twenty-four copies of Diamond 24mo Bibles printed on paper brought from the Far East. As much as £20 per copy was offered for sale but none were sold. Copies were presented to the Queen and other dignitaries. Martyr's Memorial erected and the County Hall in New Road was built

1842      Oxford India Paper used for the first time for a Diamond 24mo bible

1845      Thomas Combe established a circulating library. There were 138 employees at the Press

1847      John Thomas I entered Press service at the age of 10 years. He was one of four brothers employed in the printing industry (Richard was a proofreader, Francis worked in the Warehouse, and William was employed at Parker & Son). Jack Thomas II, his son and his grandson Jack Thomas III, also worked at the Press

1848      Outbreak of cholera in the City

1849      The Typographical Association was formed and attracted 481 union members

1850    There were 140 employees at the Press and they were producing more than a million bibles per year

1851    The year of the International Exhibition gave the opportunity for Press workers to celebrate by going on the first Wayzgoose to end up in a local pub. The London, North Eastern Railway line was extended to Oxford. Joseph Castle Senior joined the Press as Chief Engineer. Mr Combe's room was broken into and all the cash stolen. The incident was investigated by Sergeant Whicker of Scotland Yard but without result

1852    The Instrument Society formed using instruments purchased by Mr Combe. The first performance was given on 28 December 1853

1853    The Press reduced the hours to a 63-hour week! A Night School opened on 8 February with an attendance of 28 boys. The school continued to function until 1870. The crank on the steam engine broke and worked stopped in the machine room for three weeks. Thomas Combe increased his shareholding in the Press to 8 shares. The Earl of Derby visited the Press. J. F. Mansell joined the Press and stayed for 73½ years. He was still at work when he died

1855    About 150 men and boys employed. Thomas Combe bought Wolvercote Paper Mill from the Duke of Marlborough. The Mill was completely rebuilt and equipped for £15,000. J. H. Stacey was appointed Manager at an annual salary of £400 and use of the Foreman's Cottage. The Mill had been idle for about 9 years. Joseph Goodger (Lodge Porter) came to the Press. His son, John, worked in the Warehouse from 1861, his grandson, W. A. Goodger, was Bindery manager, and his great granddaughter, Miss C. Goodger, worked in the Litho Department. The Reading Room (for recreational reading!) opened on the Middle Floor at the west end of the Bible Side

1856    The first type-casting machines were introduced. William Green (Engineer) joined the Press. This started a family tradition in that his seven sons, four grandsons, two great grandsons, and one great-great-grandson all worked at the Press. A Fourdrinier Machine (72-inch deckle) was installed at Wolvercote Paper Mill. This continued in production until 1940. The Bible Press purchased paper to the value of £15,000 from Dickinsons' and £6,250 from other sources. Great Western line to Abingdon was opened. Harriet Beecher Stowe, the author of *Uncle Tom's Cabin* visited the Press

1857    Thomas Combe given the degree of Hon. MA. Press Fire Brigade attended fire at Grimbly Hughes and Dews' premises in Cornmarket. The buildings were destroyed. First Saturday holiday given to the workers. Press Fire Brigade attended fire at Castell's in Broad Street. The building was destroyed and another badly damaged

1858    The proposal for the *Oxford English Dictionary* was laid before the Philological Society. Indian Mutiny suppressed and Queen Victoria proclaimed Sovereign of India

1859    The South House was occupied by James Wright who was the manager of the Learned Side. The Press paid for the chapel to be built in the Radcliffe Infirmary at a cost of £6,492 7s. 8d.

1860    The Clarendon Press Dramatic Society was formed. The first performance was in 1861 (*The Merchant of Venice*). The Workhouse, sited on the grounds of Beaumont Palace (later to become the Clarendon Press Institute), was closed when the new one was built on the Cowley Road in Oxford. The first stereotyping by the paper process introduced. Joseph Castle (who later became Controller of Wolvercote Paper Mill) joined the Press as an apprentice engineer under his father

1861    Press Fire Brigade attended a fire in an upholsterers in Queen Street which also involved the Globe public house and three other premises

1862    First public performance at the Star Assembly Room by the Clarendon Press Dramatic Society. Work ceased at 4 p.m. on the second day of the Regatta. Four Machine Room boys absconded on the first day and were discharged. A half a day's holiday on 8 and 9 September given for St Giles' Fair

1863    Electrotyping process introduced. Alexander Macmillan published books for the Press. The management of the Press was entrusted to partners. Dodgson (Lewis Carrol) approached Thomas Combe with a view to having *Alice in Wonderland* printed at the Press

1864    Working hours further reduced to 61½-hour week (6 a.m. to 6 p.m. with 45 minutes for breakfast and 1 hour for lunch). Boys' wages increased to 2s. 6d. per week. The site of the Stute known as 'Rats and Mice Hill' was sold by the Oxford Guardians for £8,000. Specimen set for *Alice in Wonderland*

1865    The site of the Stute was sold to the Revd J. H. Newman who intended to establish a Roman Catholic College. It was resold to the University in March 1865. *Alice in Wonderland* was printed at the Press and published by Macmillan

1866    The Hospitals Fund (then called the Radcliffe Infirmary Fund) was inaugurated

1867    George Denton joined the Press as a layer-on (they were later called 'Feeders' or 'Machine Room Assistants') in the Machine Room. He was

10 years old! The New Wing of the Machine Room North Wing was built

1869    The Press purchased a bindery in London. Hitherto all Press 'books' were sold in sheets. St Barnabas Church was consecrated. It was built by the Press at a cost of £6,500 and painted by members of the Press maintenance staff. The manager of the Bible Side, Mr E. Pickard-Hall, announced to the members of the Press that he would give a lecture on 'The Dignity of Labour'. Not one person turned up! Electrotyping introduced

1870    King Edward Street was cut through Oriel College land to give better access to the college

1872    The Paper Mill at Wolvercote purchased by the Delegates of the Press. The Depot (now the OUP Bookshop) in High Street was acquired by the Delegates of the Press and wholesale bookselling commenced. A Stitchery (the forerunner of the Bindery) was formed by Miss Smith. The first recorded Press cricket match played against the printers from the *University Herald* and the *Chronicle*. The Delegates purchased Wolvercote Paper Mill from Thomas Combe. J. H. Stacey remained as Controller. A great lead tank was built into the roof of the Bible Side. In 1930 it was found to be inscribed as having been lined by Robert Taylor, William Jewel, Fred Hiles, Frank Higgin, and Charles Bolton. Thomas Combe died leaving £80,000

1873    The Provident Society formed. An annexe to house the steam engine in the Letterpress Machine Room was built. This is the office that protrudes into the Quadrangle on the side of the South Wing. The working hours were further reduced to a 57½-hour week. The Clarendon Arms was built to 'supply the Press with good wholesome beer'. A sign was erected stating that 'No beer is allowed to be brought into the Press'. Before 1873 the 'beer man' came to the Press twice a day at 11 a.m. and 4 p.m. Thomas Aldridge became Head Reader, formerly manager of the Stereotype Department

1874    The average age of the printers at death at the Press was 41.9 years

1875    Wolvercote experimented with India paper. Production was suspended in 1877 owing to pollution problems in the area and the process was moved to Brittains in Staffordshire

1877    St John Ambulance Association formed nationally. The Press Division was formed 31 years later

1878    Frederick Hall joined the Press as Junior Clerk in the Counting House under J. Mansell aged 13 years. He later became Controller of the Press

1879    Type Foundry (in the School Room) demolished to make way for the South Wing of the Letterpress Machine Room. The boys were now paid 4*s.* 6*d.* for a 54-hour week (less than the men). Dr James A. H. Murray appointed editor of the *New English Dictionary*. G. Hawkins (compositor), elected President of the Oxford Co-operative Society, an office he held for 20 years being succeeded by another Press compositor, E. King.

1880    The Delegates purchased Sandford Paper Mill at Sandford-on-Thames. The contract with Macmillan was ended and Henry Frowde was appointed as the first Publisher to the University

1881    St John's Gospel printed at the Press in 'dull gold letter on a dark olive background' in 'Franklin' type. It was printed for Major General Gibbes Rigaud. Three copies only were printed of which one has been lost. F. Madan considered this to be the rarest book printed at Oxford since the fifteenth century. Horace Hart was in charge at Clowes. Horse trams were introduced in Oxford Streets. The University decided to abolish the Partnerships of the Press. The *Revised New Testament* was published on 17 May; the *Old Testament* followed on 19 May 1885 and the *Apocrypha* later in 1885

1882    On 17 May there were 80 compositors, readers, etc. on the Learned Side. The *New English Dictionary* was begun on 3 June by compositors J. C. Gilbert, G. Omerod, and W. Shepherd. One compositor was to spend 30 years continuous work on this *Dictionary*. In 1931 it was estimated that when complete, the production would cost £50,000

1883    Horace Hart appointed the first salaried 'Controller of the Bible Side and the Learned Side'. Press employees were still wearing tall hats and frock coats to work. J. H. Stacey, Controller of Wolvercote Paper Mill, died. He was succeeded by J. Castle who had joined the Press in 1860

1884    First fascicle of *The New English Dictionary* was published. Sixteen girls were now working in the Stitchery. No proper binding was undertaken and the work was on a small scale. Miss Smith was the Forewoman. Water mains were laid in the Quad for fire hydrants. Vocal Society formed. E. Griffiths succeeded A. Soanes as printer of the *Oxford University Gazette*. P. Lyttelton Gell appointed Secretary to the Delegates. Information reached the Press that compositors at Aylesbury were being paid 6*d.* per 100 ens for English or foreign, solid or leaded, and they would have to work 15 hours overtime before they were paid and extra 2*d.* per 1,000 ens

1885    The Press Cricket Club was formed. The working week for the men was now 58½ hours. The Strong Room was built with the Stereotype Department above it. An upper room was also added on each side of the tower. The Printer's Library was originally a warehouse and later became the Entry Office/Counting House. OUP Fire Brigade formed. One Gills Hot Rolling Press, nine printing machines, and a 16 h.p. gas engine were installed

1886      The Vice-Chancellor formed a committee to investigate the allegations from within the academic community that standards of printing had deteriorated at the Press. As a result one Perfector and five Wharfedale letterpress-printing machines were purchased. Internal water mains and cocks installed at the Press. Funeral of M. Aldridge (founder of the Press Fire Brigade).

1887      Press gave the boys (labourers) 6*d*. and the apprentices 1*s*. 0*d*. as a fairing to spend at St Giles' Fair. 1,000 men of eighty Voluntary Fire Brigades from all over the country attended a National Demonstration at Headington Hill Hall on 30 May

1888      Athletics Club formed following a cross-country run. First meeting was held at the Oxford University Running Ground

1890      The Collotype Department was formed. A clock was added to St Barnabas Church in Jericho

1891      Folding and Stitching machines were installed but was still not called a 'Bindery'. The Clarendon Press Minstrel Troupe was formed. Two fours from the Bible Side Composing Rooms rowed from the barge above 'Black Jacks' to the Perch at Binsey. Rowland Wheeler retired. He had joined the Press in 1841 to become a compositor. He was Chief of the Staff of teachers at Night School from 1853 to 1862. He died 15 June 1898

1893      *Hart's Rules* published privately (24 pages). It was not sold until the 15th edition was published in 1904. Hart himself was a strict disciplinarian and his annotations on the proofs were sometimes threatening. He once wrote: 'The man who mixes Fell with Caslon will get the sack'! His aim was to ensure that his 'little book' would ensure uniformity in the style of all books printed at the University Press. The Clarendon Press Institute was built and opened on 16 September by Bishop Stubbs, Bishop of Oxford. The first Chairman of the Institute Council was G. Hawkins and the caretaker was one Sgt. Major Wilsdon who fought in the Battle of Balaclava. It was to be known affectionately as the 'Stute' by thousands of Press employees over the years. E. Fitchett, head of the Type Foundry, died. The funds collected for the Radcliffe Infirmary and the Eye Hospital were merged to form the Hospitals Fund

1894      The cricket, football, and athletic clubs merged to become the Amalgamated Athletic Clubs. The Eye Hospital was moved to Walton Street. The hourly scale for apprentices 'clearing' on time was based on the number of years 'at case'. Under 1 year 3*d.*, over 1 year and under 2 years 4d., and over 2 years and under 3 years 5½*d.* John Thomas II rescued W. Drury [from drowning?] and was awarded the Royal Humane Society's Testimonial

1895 The Revised Version of the Apocrypha was published. River Thames blocked by ice-floes 6–7 ft. thick. Professor Joseph Wright and his staff moved into the Press to prepare the *English Dialect Dictionary*. Brought in over a ton of existing material

1896 The New York branch of OUP was established. The first fascicle of the *English Dialect Dictionary* was published. Mutual Help Society formed to provide financial assistance during sickness and other adversity. Disbanded in May 1925. Carfax Church (St Martin's) demolished except for the Tower. G. Hawkins (compositor) became a Justice of the Peace for Oxford City. Lamech Denton (Chief Engineer) died and was replaced by I. Hunt

1897 Wolvercote Paper Mill started producing over 11 tons of paper per week costing 2½*d.* per pound to make. Cycling Club formed. Work in the Bindery started at 6.30 a.m. and ended at 6 p.m. except when, as frequently happened, 3½ hours overtime followed. Wages were 20*s.* per week for a bookbinder and the Forewoman received only 18*s* per week. The total weekly wage bill for the Bindery was £27 18*s.* Horace Hart was awarded the degree of MA Honoris Causa. J. Mansell resigned as Secretary of the Press Fire Brigade and was replaced by J. De La Mare. Press footballers won the County Shield for the 1897/8 season. P. P. Bennett was one of the players

1898 C. Cannan appointed Secretary to the Delegates. Harry Lapworth appointed Secretary of the Press Fire Brigade, a post he held until 1912

1899 A bullock broke away from a small herd of cattle being driven along Walton Street to the old slaughterhouse in Walton Crescent and chased a woman who took refuge in the Front Lodge. The bullock continued across the Quad lawn and fell into the pond. The maintenance staff rescued it. An 80-inch Fourdrinier machine installed at Wolvercote Paper Mill at a cost of £20,000. W. H. Wheeler became Secretary of the Cricket Club (until 1930) and the Bowls Club (until 1921)

1900 Humphrey Milford joined as assistant to G. Cannan. William White resigned as Hon. Secretary of the Oxford Branch of the Typographical Association and was succeeded by W. King JP. W. T. Walker was elected Hon. Secretary of the Amalgamated Athletic Clubs (until 1936). The Clubs had a membership of 99. The Oxford Classical Texts series was started. *Hart's Notes on a Century of Typography at the University Press, Oxford, 1693–1794* was issued in an edition of 150 copies.

1901    The first Miehle letterpress machine was purchased and installed. The machine minder was Jack Thomas II. Arthur Young started work at the Press and was given an armchair 60 years later when he retired from the Reading Department! Death of Queen Victoria and Accession of Edward VII on 22 January so cancels then required for nine prayer books were ordered to be ready for plating before work on the Bible Side ceased that evening. In order to complete the Prayer Book cancels, Machine Room had to work all night on alternate nights and to 10 p.m. on the intervening nights, thus sleeping every other night.

1902    Piscatorial Society formed

1903    The first Miehle Perfector was installed. The 'Monotype' Department was established with two keyboards at the west end of the first floor of the North Wing and two casters in the Type Foundry. The first keyboard operators were J. W. White and C. Hill

1904    *Hart's Rules* goes on sale at *6d.* The average life span of printers at the Press rose to 52 years of age. The working week reduced by an hour to 56½ hours. The workrooms were lit by gas jets. The Canadian branch was established in Toronto. C. H. Taylor joined the Delegates' Staff at a wage of *5s.* per week. The Staff then comprised C. Cannan (Secretary), H. Milford (Assistant Secretary), A. E. Durham (Accountant), and just four other men!

1905    1,500,000 examination papers printed. Female staff numbered over 100. The secretaries were involved in producing 15,000 letters per year. H. Lapworth succeeded J. De La Mare as Overseer of the Jobbing Department. Final part of the *English Dialect Dictionary* was published. Short-time working started on 16 April because of lack of general book work but full-time working resumed on 3 July from 8 a.m. to 6.30 p.m. Short time working started again on 6 September and resumed with a greatly reduced staff on 2 October

1906    Five more Miehle perfectors were installed. H. S. Milford was transferred to the London Office

1907    The Music Society formed. Last copy of Wilkins's *Coptic New Testament* (published in 1716) was drawn from the Quire Warehouse. The paper had 'hardly discoloured and the impression still black and brilliant'. The Oxford Historic Pageant took place on 20 June close to Christ Church Meadow. G. Haggard (Reading Department) and E. Harris (Composing Rooms) were amongst the performers. Dr Samuel Langhorne Clemens (Mark Twain) visited the Press

1908    The Clarendon Press Division of the St John Ambulance Brigade was formed with twenty-four members. Forty girls were taken on in the Bindery to work under Miss Hutchins. The overtime rates were: for those on 36*s.* per week = 11¼*d* per hour.; 38*s.* per week = 11¾*d.* per hour; 39*s.* per week = 1*s.* per hour; 40*s.* = 1*s.* 0¼*d.* per hour. After working 10 hours overtime the rate went up by 1*d.* per hour. One night's work counted as 12 hours. In March a proofreader was allowed to work at home. On his way to the Press to deliver his work he was caught in a storm and his hat, copy, and proofs were blown away, never to be retrieved. Henceforth, proofreaders were not allowed to take work home. In April Oxford suffered 17 inches of snow

1909    OUP division of the St John Ambulance Brigade sanctioned. The Monotype Department was enlarged to six keyboards and five casters and moved to the Bible side in space vacated by the Engineers and Carpenters

1910    Another six Miehle Perfectors were installed with a specially designed 'fly-delivery'. The Press start to use the Tower and Eagle Breweries as additional warehouse space. Halley's Comet seen over Oxford for the last time. W. E. Green joined the Press. After service in the First World War he returned as a Bible Reader. He compiled *The List of Uncommon Words and Phrases.* He died in June 1974

1911    The *Concise Oxford Dictionary* was published. Several galleys of type of the *Oxford English Dictionary* were deliberately pied during the night. The culprit was never discovered (Cocker was the chief suspect!). The first aeroplane seen over Oxford. It flew from Brooklands and landed on Port Meadow

1912    The Bombay Branch was established. Parker & Son's printing works closed down. Wolvercote Paper Mill was now producing 1,040 tons of paper per year. A boy's wages were 4*s.* 6*d.* for a 52½ hour week. Royal visit of George V, Queen Mary, and the Prince of Wales. E. D. Willett (while still employed at the Press) became landlord of the Gardeners Arms in Plantation Road where he remained until 1926. J. H. Williams won the 100 yards, the half mile, and the mile at the Press Sports. The first local aircraft fatality, at Wolvercote on the site of the Press Housing Estate. Two Press employees were on the scene within minutes. They were F. W. Matthews and H. E. Hewlett

1913    Production of paper at Wolvercote Paper Mill reached 1,040 tons per year. H. Frowd retired and Humphrey Milford became the second Publisher to the University. Oxford's first buses were operated by the Oxford Tram Comapny. The Madras Branch was opened. A branch was also opened in Shanghai but this closed down in 1936. The Officers of the Machine Minders' Chapel had their salaries increased. The FOC's was raised from 5*s*. to 10*s*. and the Clerk's from 10*s*. to £1. Eagle Brewery Yard in Park End Street was used as a warehouse. (There had been other warehouses in use between 1905 and 1910: Somerville's premises in Walton Street and Phillip's Brewery (later Coxeter's Garage) in Brewer Street.)

1914    Formal contract drawn up with a builder to place a roof over the Quad! Great Britain declared war on Germany. There were 575 male employees at the outbreak of hostilities of whom 356 served and 45 died. Six men were awarded the Military Medal. The Bible press produced 4,500,000 copies of the Bible for use in the field. Press Volunteer Platoon formed. HRH Queen Mary and HRH Princess Mary visited the Press. Staff of Oxford Local Examinations moved into one of the houses in the Quad at an hour's notice because their premises were to be used as a base hospital

1915    The South African branch was established. Horace Hart resigned and went to live in Boars Hill just outside Oxford. He was found drowned the following year aged 76 years. Frederick Hall appointed Printer. B. Denton became the first woman ever to be employed on the printing staff. The Mono parcels Fund started. A Press cricket match was played at the Front in France

1916    The Bible Side and the Learned Side merged. Women feeders introduced in the Letterpress Machine Room because of the lack of men who were on war service. E. Griffith succeeded P. Molyneaux as Editor of the *Oxford University Gazette*. Woen Feeders introduced in the Letterpress Machine Room

1917    America declared war on Germany. A boy's wages at Wolvercote Paper Mill were 5*s*. for a 68-hour week

1918    Meeting held on Port Meadow to make plans for the Food Production Exhibition. The first flower show was held in the Quad. Regular concert parties were started. J. C. Pembrey, proofreader specializing in oriental work, died. Had worked at the Press for 70 years! W. King and A. H. Frimbley appointed Justices of the Peace for Oxford City. Press Fire Brigade assisted at fires in Bason's Yard in St Aldates and a house in the Woodstock Road. The latter fire had been discovered by the then Controller of the Press

1919    The first issue of the *Clarendonian* was published priced at 3*d*. The £3 minimum wage introduced. Press Fire Brigade assisted at a fire in the Co-operative Society store in Walton Street. The 48-hour week started. Winter 7.45 a.m. to 12 noon and 1 p.m. to 5.30 p.m.; Summer 7.15 a.m. to noon (11.30 a.m. on Saturdays) and 1 p.m. to 5 p.m. Electricity installed in the Clarendon Press Institute Reading Room and main hall. One thousand people attended a service in the Quad to commemorate those killed in the First World War. The Book Club was formed. The official annual 'Wayzgoose' was abolished but they went on long after 1919. First Press Sports held and over 1,500 spectators attended the University Running Ground. Benevolent Fund inaugurated. Bindery issued the first Interdepartmental games challenge to other departments. Bowls Club formed. First Annual Children's party held at the Stute. Press War Savings contributions amounted to £1,847 0s. 10d. Geoffrey Cumberlege appointed Manager of the Bombay Branch. Instruction in gymnastics and physical culture restarted under A. P. Janaway. There had been instruction in 1894 under A. and C. Bowen. Dinner held at the Stute to honour those that had served in the First World War (250 attended). Musical Society re-formed. Press Fire Brigade attended a fire at Weeks in Cornmarket

1920    Bindery equipment included 3 hand-fed folders, 1 case-maker, 3 blockers, 1 three-wing casing-in machine, 3 cutters, 2 nippers, and 6 sewing machines. Work started on building a new bindery called the 'Nagel Building'. Keyboards and casters increased from 12 keys and 11 casters to 15 keys and 14 casters. The Casters were housed in a new room formed by covering the yard at the rear of the South House. The war memorial unveiled by Admiral Sir Reginald Pall and the £122 10s. to pay for it was raised by the employees of the Press. R. W. Chapman became Secretary to the Delegates following the death of C. Cannan. The staff of the Delegates now totalled 20 (it rose to 270 by 1970). The Calcutta Branch was opened. A Branch was also opened in Copenhagen but closed in 1929. The Annex in the Quad (formerly the Engine House) became the Machine Revisers Office. A revived Minstrels Section performed at the Children's Party. H. Wheeler elected Chairman of the Amalgamated Athletic Clubs. There were 428 players at the Whist Drive held at the Stute on 23 December

1921    The new Bindery was opened. Total quantity of types in the Press was estimated at over 1 million pounds of metal including 550 different founts in some 150 different characters. The warehouse contained 3,500,000 copies of 4,500 distinct books. The Press's coal supply almost ran out owing to the miner's strike. Short time working introduced in the Letterpress Machine Room owing to a shortage of work. Children's Dancing Classes started. *Memorials of C. H. O. Daniel* was printed at the Bodleian Library on a press that formerly belonged to Provost Daniel. This, the only book to be printed in the Library, was printed by T. H.

Price and A. C. V. Saxton of the Press. The Seybold three-knive cutter was introduced and one was installed in the Bindery. During the Proofreaders' Wayzgoose on 11 June an airship was seen flying overhead. Press Fire Brigade attended a fire at the premises of Woodridge and Simpsons in Frenchay Road on 18 June. There was a fire in the Boiler House that was discovered by the Night Watchman at 10 p.m. on the night of 30 August. The Press Fire Brigade attended and were soon joined by the City Brigade. The Press Fire Brigade also attended a fire at Halls Brewery Malthouse

1922    Press employees went on strike for a month because the management cut their wages. Holiday Fund started with 200 members (464 by 1917). Tennis Club formed and allowed to use Balliol College's tennis courts during the Long Vacation. Monotype Department Sickness Fund started to give immediate help during illness and to pay union dues. It went on to become the Mono Benevolent Fund. First sports meeting with Cambridge University Press. One of the six American Aloes in the Quad flowered. They had been there for 60 years and had not flowered since 1917. W. King retired as Secretary of the Typographical Association. He was replaced by A. H. Sharpe. Press received a letter from Cambridge University Press suggesting sports matches between the University Presses. The first match took place on 5 August and was played on Balliol College ground. The first joint outing of Bindery men and women—a total of 85 people attended. Members of the Press Fire Brigade assisted when the new Bindery was flooded caused by a burst radiator pipe. Two thousand volumes were completely ruined and an equal number were damaged (but repairable). The Football Club became the first winners of the Woodstock Charity Cup

1923    The Clarendon Press Institute Slate Club was formed with 113 members. Bindery Sick Fund for Women and Girls started because they were outside the scope of the Benevolent Fund. An Art and Crafts group started. A. L. P. Norrington joined the London Office in January. Wireless demonstration given at the Stute during the interval of a show by the Minstrels. Meeting held to discuss the formation of a Rowing Club on 4 April. Members of the Press Division of the St John Ambulance Brigade, while enjoying themselves as guests of the Press Fire Brigade outing, rendered assistance to a cyclist who had been knocked down in a road traffic incident. N. Massey, an apprentice in the Jobbing Department, rescued a lad from drowning in Medley Pool on 10 August. The Piscatorial Society made a presentation to H. E. Mapleston to mark his 21 years' service as Secretary. A. W. Foster was presented with a desk to mark his services to Press sport. He had held the post of Secretary of the AAC for 20 years and spent 3 years as Football Club Secretary

1924    The hands of the clock in the Quad were stolen on 7 February. First Sports match and return visit against Hazel, Watson, and Viney the Aylesbury printers. Folk dance Society formed

1925    The warehouse at Jordan Hill opened. John Johnson appointed Printer. Electric lighting installed at the Press. Monotype building erected in the North Yard attached to the North Wing. The old 'shanty' building that it replaced was taken to Jordan Hill to be used as a pavilion. Swimming Club and Tennis Club formed. Sports Club opened at Jordan Hill on Whit Monday. Edward King was appointed a Justice of the Peace for Oxford City. The Press Division of the St John Ambulance Brigade won the Freeborn Cup. Swimming Relay and Water Polo were included in the Annual OUP and CUP sports match. Tennis Club was affiliated to the AAC on 27 January. Sports ground at Jordan Hill opened on 1 June. An anonymous author gave £1,000 towards the cost. The Bowls Club had their own rink for the first time. About 300 supporters travelled to Cambridge in a special train to accompany the Press contingent to Cambridge. Oxford won the tennis, bowls, water polo, and rowing. CUP won the other swimming events

1926    The Monotype Department opened and the Maths Ship was formed within it. Collections for the Fresh Air Fund raised £15 7s. 9d. The Stute Council presented the Editor of the *Clarendonian* (Allpress Hinson) with a typewriter. The General Strike started on 4 May. Jordan Hill Pavilion opened formally during the visit of the teams from CUP. Second billiard table installed in the new games room at the Stute

1927    Collections for the Caxton Convalescent Home commenced. Collections for the Fresh Air Fund reached £22. Membership of the AAC reached 625. J. H. Mansell died aged 86 on 2 April. Joined the Press in 1853 and served for 73 years. He was Hon. Secretary of the Provident Society from 1874 to 1915, first Secretary of the Press Fire Brigade 1885, and a member of the Press Dramatic Society (playing a female role in their first public performance on 5 February 1862

1928    Charles Batey joined the Press as the manager of the Composing Rooms. First cycle racks erected in the Quad. The *Oxford English Dictionary* completed in ten volumes with 414,825,000 words and 1,827,306 quotations. The illustrations in McDowell: *Dolomites* were printed from linoleum cuts: possibly the first time that this had been done at the Press. Joseph Parker retired after 60 years' service. Oxford University awarded the Degree of Hon. D.Lit. to the Printer (John Johnson), Secretary to the

Delegates (F. W. Chapman), and the Publisher (Humphrey Milford). L. Stevens (Machine Room) rescued A. Farthing from drowning at Hinksey Pool. The Jordan Hill Pavilion was damaged in a gale on 16 November and the cycle sheds were blown 40 yards. E. J. Morey retired from the Machine Room and was known to have been working at the Press by 1865

1929    Neasden Warehouse built. The Rifle section formed. The Press's tortoise, named 'Dr Fell', died. He lived in the Quad for many years and was probably poisoned by eating dahlias. The Press Cricket Club won the Amos George Cup. Some 430 children attended the Stute Christmas Party on 29 January. A hundred workers were absent from work during the influenza epidemic in February. G. Ostler, compiler of the *Little Oxford Dictionary*, died on 21 April. C. Beesley retired after 65 years' service. He is recorded as having won the first prize at the Annual Flower Show for 13 consecutive years. The last Flower Show held in the Quad. J. Green retired after 60 years' service. Fire in the electrical switchboard in the Stereotype Department

1930    The Football Club won the County Junior League (City Section) in the 1930/1 season.

1931    The Radcliffe Maternity Home was built opposite the Press. It became the Ear, Nose, and Throat Department after maternity services were transferred to the John Radcliffe Hospital in 1973

1932    The large hall in the Stute was renovated at a cost of £312

1933    The Cycling Club was formed but lasted only until 1939. The Record Room or Treasury was informally opened in what was known as 'the Controller's Office on the Bible Side'. The Cricket Club won the Amos George Cup for the second successive season in 1933/4

1934    Jordan Hill pavilion officially opened by Mrs Chapman. Sunday games for the Mixed Hockey Club were banned at Jordan Hill because 'they disturbed people in the cemetery'! G. Cumberlege appointed Assistant Publisher

1936    A contributory pension scheme was introduced. Dispatches of books from Neasden amounted to 21 tons per day. W. T. Walker resigned as Secretary of the AAC after 37 years' service. He was succeeded by G. D. B. Morley. Humphrey Milford (publisher) was awarded a knighthood

1937    Piecework was abolished. The 45-hour five-day week was introduced. The Jobbing Department was moved from the Bible Side (South Wing) to the Learned Side on the first floor (North Wing). Vivian Ridler joined the Press. The frontage of the Press was floodlit for the Coronation.

1938    Vivian Ridler left the Press to return again in 1948. The Jobbing Department was moved to the Middle Floor on the Learned Side

1939    War declared. 256 Press members served and eighteen died

1940    Press platoon of the Home Guard formed. Butter, bacon, and sugar rationed in Great Britain

1941    C. E. Batey, A. D. Clapperton, and S. Dearlove awarded the degree of Hon. MA

1942    Canteen opened at the Press and over the next 4 years served over 120,000 dinners on working days and high teas on overtime days. They also served 750 cups of tea daily during mornings and afternoons. R. W. Chapman resigned 31 July and Kenneth Sisam became Secretary to the Delegates. A. L. P. Norrington was appointed Assistant Secretary

1943    Charles Batey, then Assistant Printer, awarded the OBE. A. D. Clapperton (Wolvercote Paper Mill) died and his nephew (J. F. Clapperton) was appointed to succeed him as Controller. He took up his appointment on release from war service in July 1945. The German battleship *Scharnhorst* was sunk. P. J. Spicer (Clarendon Press) was serving in HM Destroyer *Opportune* and fired some of the torpedoes that completed the ship's destruction

1944    PAYE Income Tax introduced

1945    Dr John Johnson awarded the CBE. Humphrey Milford retired and Geoffrey Cumberlege DSO, MG appointed Publisher. A. E. Durham, Accountant to the Delegates, awarded an Hon. MA

1946    The working week reduced to 43½ hours. John Johnson retired in September and Charles Batey was appointed Printer on 1 October

1947    Flower Show and Sports Day re-introduced, not in the Quad but at Jordan Hill. Sheridan gathering machine installed in the Bindery capable of gathering 2,000 books per hour. Wolvercote Paper Mill surrounded by water. Employees had to be taken to work by punt. Women admitted as members of the Clarendon Press Institute. First official visit to the Press by a Mayor of Oxford

1948    Bindery production was 1,500,000 books per year. Vivian Ridler rejoined the Press as Works manager on 1 April. John Hall appointed Personnel Manager 25 October. Weekly wages bill approximately £1,097. R. E. Johnson succeeded S. Dearlove as Manager of the Bindery. John Johnson prizes first awarded. Joint Works Council held its first meeting on 27 January. A. L. P. Norrington appointed Secretary to the Delegates as successor to K. Sisam. F. J. Ayres appointed Manager of the Composing Rooms. J. Clapperton died and was succeeded by J. Henderson as Controller of Wolvercote Paper Mill

1949    W. H. Wheeler was awarded the degree of Hon. MA on 4 June. Vivian Ridler appointed Assistant Printer on 21 June.

1950    The Incentive Bonus Scheme introduced. Charles Batey appointed as a Justice of the Peace. Two Linotype machines (£8,000), pneumatic conveyor for transporting proofs from the Reading Department (£5,000), internal telephones and loudspeaker system (tannoy) (£1,250), and additional fluorescent lighting (£12,000) were installed. The warehouse in Wellington Street was taken over by the Lithographic Department and adapted for lithographic plate preparation and plate graining. Four girls were appointed to act as guides for visitors. They were aged 16½, 17½, 18, and 19 years. Keasey's warehouse in Wellington Street was taken over by the Lithographic Department and adapted for Lithographic plate preparation and plate graining. Old members of the Rowing Club which became defunct in 1927, rowed an eight from Folly Bridge to Sandford Lock. Five members of the crew, the total ages amounted to 364 years, were P. Boswell, F. Carter, G. Durham, L. Lardner, and M. Westell. They had all rowed in the eight of 1926!

1951    1,805 visitors toured the Press to celebrate the University of Oxford Exhibition of 1478–1951. The first pensioners' party held with forty-eight taking up the offer. They amassed a total of 2,085 years of service between them previously pensioners' parties had been in operation since 1928 and had been paid for by the Typographical Association. New office suite built for the Printer and his personal staff together with a library and a reception room. *Oxford Atlas* published, followed later in the year by the *American Atlas* and the *Canadian Atlas.* First atlas to be both published and printed at the Press

1952    Counting House occupied new office near the Front Lodge. The former Counting House Office, after re-decoration, was occupied by the Forwarding Office and the Layout Department. Last coal-barge docked at Wolvercote Paper Mill Wharf on 7 May. The Swimming Section's Folly Bridge to Iffley Lock River Swim was revived after 20 years. *Concise Oxford Atlas* published and the Cartographic Department in St Giles' was established. The Book Club members purchased 1,253 books to the value of £736 2s. 3d. during the financial year 1952/3

1953    The Pre-make-Ready Department was formed in the Letterpress Machine Room with the introduction of plates being imposed on honeycomb bases. A. C. V. Saxton printed the bible used in the ceremony of Queen Elizabeth's coronation. The Non-Contributory

Sick Benefit Scheme started. In the first 3 months £189 2*s.* was paid out to 114 recipients. The Press Cricket Section won the Amos George Cup for the fourth time. The Press footballers became the first winners of the Oxford City FA's Six-a-side Cup

1954 Over 10 million books passed through the warehouse. In this year OUP published more books than any other publishing house. Harry Carter OBE joined the Press as Archivist and to take charge of the Type Foundry and the ancient Fell materials. A. L. P. Norrington left the Press to become President of Trinity College and C. H. Roberts became Secretary to the Delegates. The Press Book Club members purchased over 1,300 book at a total cost of £776 8*s.* 0*d.* In the New Year Honours List W. T. Hine and P. Cox were awarded the BEM and the MBE respectively. The former for service as a craftsman and the latter for service to the Territorial Army

1955 Four Mallard ducks appeared in the Quad. First time that anyone could remember such an event. The War Memorial in the Quad was re-dedicated. Professor A. L. Goodhart opened the Jordan Hill Housing Estate on 18 June. The Press football section retained the Oxford City FA Premier Division Cup for the 1955/6 season

1956 John Johnson died 15 September. The Press football section won the Oxford City FA Challenge Cup for the second time and the Premier Division of the League for the third time in the 1956/7 season

1957 Wolvercote Paper Mill rebuilt and a new machine installed, A George Mann Extra Quad Demy perfector was installed in the Lithographic Machine Room capable of 5,000 sheets per hour

1958 Charles Batey retired on 1 October. Vivian Ridler was appointed Printer and awarded the degree of MA by Decree. G. Cumberlege DSO MC retired

1959 The Press extended its catchment area for labour to Wantage and workers were bussed into Walton Street. The National Printing Strike started on 19 June (it lasted until 6 August). The 42-hour week was introduced

1960 Monophoto composition machines introduced. Three new fully automatic oil-fired boilers were installed. They were capable of producing 4,300 lbs of steam per hour. The installation was said to have saved £2,600 per year on fuel costs. The two Linotype machines were hoisted from the Monotype Annex to the Jobbing department on 2 July. In the previous decade 145 full-length books, 57 journals, 15 issues of the *Clarendonian*, 50 smaller books, lectures, college magazines, and over 1,000 examination papers had been set on these two machines. The machines were moved without dismantling and only one day's production was lost

1961    The first Letterpress rotary web-fed machine installed. Clarendon Arms
        ceased to be a public house. Smyth link installed in the Bindery, linking
        the Rounder and Backer, the Triple liner, the casing-in machine, and the
        pressing unit. *New English Bible New Testament* was published. Working
        week reduced to 41 hours. Planning began for new extensions to the
        Printing House

1962    Two sheet-fed rotary letterpress machines installed. Working week
        reduced to 40 hours

1963    The OUP Car and Motor Cycle Club formed. Don Turner took charge
        of the Type Foundry following the retirement of Len Bullen. A single
        unit web offset perfecting press was installed in the Lithographic
        Machine Room with a maximum web width of 28 inches and a fixed cut-
        off of 34 inches. capable of 18,000 revolutions an hour (printing 700 feet
        per minute). The Clarendon Arms was converted to house the Illustra-
        tions Department and the Senior Staff Club

1964    Krause guillotine with a 52-inch knife installed and was programmed to
        cut within 3-thousands of an inch. George Oliver (Machine Room) com-
        mended for his unsuccessful attempt to rescue a drowning boy. HM the
        Queen, on opening the World Book Fair, was presented with copies of
        *The Oxford Book of Wild Flowers* and *The Oxford Book of Garden Flowers*
        that had been hand-sewn and bound in the Bindery to a special design by
        Vivian Ridler

1965    Annual output of examination papers rose to more than 12 million.
        Vivian Ridler appointed Professorial Fellow of St Edmund Hall. D. M.
        Davin appointed Professorial Fellow of Balliol. J. S. G. Simmons (then
        Printer's Librarian) appointed Fellow of All Souls. Amen House demol-
        ished November and the London Office moved to Ely House. A 1500
        computer was installed at Neasden on 1 August

1966    Work began on the new extensions to the Press. G. Laitt, Chief Accoun-
        tant of the Clarendon Press, awarded a degree of Hon. MA

1967    Five volumes of Adelmann, *Marcello Malpighi* printed on special paper
        made at Wolvercote Paper Mill to last 500 years. W. C. Buckingham was
        the machine minder that printed the books. Stanley Morrison's, *John
        Fell: The University Press and the Fell Types* was completed and published.
        An ICT 1903 computer was installed at Neasden on 20 February. Work
        started on the Press's Wolvercote Housing Estate on 13 March

1968    Annual production in the Bindery exceeds 4 million books. Richard Rus-
        sell appointed Assistant Printer on 1 April. Vivian Ridler elected Presi-
        dent of the British Federation of Master Printers in May. The Constance
        Meade Memorial Collection that had been formed by John Johnson was

transferred to the Bodleian Library. John Hall was awarded the degree of MA by Decree on 18 June. Bindery commence move into their new building on 9 September. The move was completed by 5 October. The Collotype Department closed down in December.

1969    The Lithographic Department moved into the new building in February. The Bindery women walked out on 3 February alleging that the work rooms were too cold

1970    D. M. Davin was appointed Deputy Secretary to the Delegates and P. J. Parker was appointed Assistant Secretary on 1 January. There were 953 printers and 250 publishing staff working on the Walton Street premises. Monotype keyboards moved to the former Examination Ship on the ground floor of the North Wing. An Air-Dome was erected at Jordan Hill Sports Ground as a temporary addition to the Jordan Hill Warehouse facilities. The complete *New English Bible* was published throughout the world. Strike by Compositors and Readers commenced on 8 June because of the way one of their members was treated when he wanted to leave to start a course at Ruskin College. The strike was settled on 16 June. The new extension to the Pavilion at Jordan Hill was opened by the Secretary to the Delegates on 3 October

1971    Vivian Ridler appointed Knight Commander of the Order of the British Empire on 1 January. Nursing Section of the Press Division of the St John Ambulance Division revived. John Johnson Collection of Printed Ephemera moved to the Bodleian Library in June. The *Oxford English Dictionay Compact Edition* published 7 October. Chess Club formed in November.

1972    Sulby Compact Binder and Harris Macey Saddle Gatherer installed in the Bindery. The former was to cope with the increased amount of paperback work and the latter to supplement the Christensen Gang-Stitcher on quire stitched work. The Harris Macey Machine produced 7,500 copies per hour from folded sheets. Supplement to the *Oxford English Dictionary* was published on 12 October. For the first time the Printing Division had a 'Board'. James Campling joined the Press as Production Director, John Hall was made Personnel Director, Richard Russell became Commercial Director, and Gerard Frost appointed Finance Director.

1973    A second Web-Offset press (36-inch web) was installed capable of 18,000 impressions per hour with a web speed of 1,200 feet per minute. A Quad Crown Urania Nebiolo was installed in the Letterpress Machine Room that printed from APR photographic relief plates. A Monophoto 400 with four MK V keyboards were installed in the Filmset Department.

*John Bowley: last hot metal compositor*

The 400 produced 40,000 characters an hour. A Log E flow film processor was installed and a Roland VI two-colour Litho printing press was introduced to the Lithographic Machine Room. A 42-ft long Crawley bookback nipper/gluer/drier/renipper was installed in the Bindery. The last Collotype machine was removed from the Press. Value Added Tax was introduced on 1 April. C. Scott was appointed Manager of the Oxford Depot (Bookshop) in October

1974    The Staff Association was formed. Bindery Handwork was moved back to its original room. The London Publisher, John Brown, received a Knighthood on 1 January. Three-day week introduced owing to the electric power restrictions. People working on examination papers were later allowed to work 5 days. In June one union withdrew its labour for a while following an overtime ban. Work commenced on further phases of the extensions that had originally commenced in 1966. In June there was a major fire in the Examinations Ship where almost everything was destroyed. Shipments of examination papers during the year totalled 150 tonnes. C. H. Roberts, Secretary to the Delegates, retired. John Hall collapsed and died in the Front Lodge on 21 November and Ian O'Reilly (later Meyrick) was appointed Personnel Director in December. Sophie Huelin employed as the first female indentured apprentice. She worked in the Lithographic Department as a Photo-Litho Retoucher. Severe flooding in the Monotype Department, the Bindery, and the Bindery

*The last bale*

Marshalling Area on 12 September causing much damage to both printed sheets and bound stock

1975　The Photographic Studio administered by the Printer and located in the Bodleian Library was handed over to the Curators of the Library. The Ancient Order of Pantomimers folded after 15 years of producing annual shows at the Children's Christmas Party. Harry Carter's *History of the OUP*, volume 1 published

1977　Genevieve Hawkins, who had started work at the Press as a graduate proofreader, was appointed Editor of the *Oxford University Gazette* following the retirement of Margery Eady.

1978　The Quincentenary. Proofreaders Harvie Willshire and Mick Belson appointed at joint editors of the *Clarendonian*. Quincentenary Service held in Christ Church Cathedral on 11 May. Manager of the Letterpress Machine Room, Norman Mansfield retired. Bindery manager Andrew Chalmers retired. Typestoreman Stan Coates retired. Joe Ayres died having retired in 1956. Peter Sutcliffe's *The Oxford University Press: An Informal History* published. The Quincentenary Ball was held in the Quad on 23 June. Vivian Ridler retired and Eric Buckley was appointed Printer

1979　*The Clarendonian* celebrated 60 years as the magazine of the craftsmen of Oxford University Press. *The Periodical* ceased publication after 83 years

*Last Spectron keyboard operators—'Sandy' Dean and 'Stalky' Evans*

*Harry Thornton: last letterpress machine minder*

of abstracts, anecdotes, observations, and facts about Press books. Sophie Huelin in the Lithographic Department completed her 4-year apprenticeship as a Photo-Litho Retoucher on 2 September. Joanne Organ became the first female compositor apprentice at the Press

1983   Eric Buckley retired. David Stanford appointed Printer. Last *Clarendonian* produced.

1989   Sir Roger Elliot, Secretary to the Delegates announced the closure of the Printing House on 1 February. A service to mark the closure of the Printing House held at St Barnabus Church on 20 April. Printing House produced its last book, *Aylmer Views of Oxford*, it came off the binding line at 8.01 am on 27 April. David Stanford closed down the Printing House on Friday 28 April on behalf of the Delegates of Oxford University Press. Oxuniprint was born under the directorship of Martin Slade and the managership of Tony Bennell on 2 May and continues to keep up the proud tradition of more than 500 years of printing in Oxford.

*Cameras . . .*

*makeup and platemaking . . .*

*and the Litho Machine Room staff*

# Glossary of Terms used at the Press

**Accent:** a 'sort' with a diacritic (e.g. acute, grave, cedilla, diaeresis, etc.)

**'According to Cocker':** 'I have it on good authority' or 'The rumour is . . .'

**Agate (or Ruby):** A type-size used before the point system (*c.*5½ pt)

**The Annexe:** The ground floor of the North Wing known also as the Exam Ship or the Mono Annexe. Used during the Second World War for secret code work for HM Government

**Apron:** An apron (usually white) with a large pocket in the front. Worn by compositors not only to keep their clothes clean but also to store such things as tweezers, bodkins, special sorts, and snuff tins

**Artwork:** The final interpretation of the design; the material that is supplied to the printer for making film and plates

**Author's corrections:** Alterations made by the author after the proofs had been produced

**'Aye Aye':** 'Fancy seeing you here'

**Baby to bed, putting the:** Signal that the print run was about to commence

**Back Page:** The colleague working in the frame, machine. or bench behind you

**Backs:** In imposition, the space between a pair of pages

**Bad copy:** Manuscript (usually handwritten) that was almost unreadable

**'Bah-Bah'** (like a sheep): 'You have had a haircut'

**Banging-out:** A ceremony that took place every time an apprentice 'came out' of his apprenticeship. The apprentice would have to run the gauntlet of every member of the department in which he worked. They would be carrying anything that they could lay their hands on that would make a noise (usually mallets, metal side-sticks, and chases banged against stones and metal frames). As the apprentice made his way to the printer's office to collect his indentures the cacophony of noise would be deafening. In some printing offices the apprentice would be tarred and feathered before being paraded around the factory. The Press banging-outs never went that far

**Bastard title:** The first printed page of a book. Also known as the half-title

**Batey:** Charles Batey. Printer to the University from 1946 to 1958

**Batter, battered:** Damaged type

**Bed:** The flat area on a letterpress machine where the formes are secured before printing

*Martin Honey, Stuart Glennister, and Ken McMahon were the last apprentices to be 'banged out'*

**Bible Side:** The first floor of the South Wing

**Bleed:** To extend an illustration beyond the trimmed edge of a page

**Blocking:** Impressing a design or lettering on a book cover or spine

**Blocks:** Text-figures, maps, etc. mounted on wood or metal to type height

**Blood-stained proofs:** The red ink of an over-reader's pen whilst checking the quality of the work of another proofreader

**Blurb:** The description of a book for the dust-jacket or cover

**Boards:** The material used to stiffen the covers of a case-bound book

**Bodger/Spiker:** A compositor who would use his bodkin to spike the type to falsely expand it to ensure that the page would lift rather than do the job properly by making further time-consuming adjustments to the lines of type

**Book Club:** Scheme that enabled Press employees to purchase OUP books at a generous discount in return for regular weekly payments

**Bourgeois:** A type-size used before the point system (*c*.9 pt)

**Branch:** The local Trade Union Headquarters

**Brass:** A brass die for blocking used in binding

**Brevier:** A type-size used before the point system (*c*.8 pt)

**Brilliant:** A type-size used before the point system (*c*.3½ pt)

**Broadside page:** Landscape

**Bromide:** Light sensitive paper used in photographic reproduction. Also a positive photographic print

**Buckers:** Eric Buckley. The popular, rotund, and jovial Printer to the University from 1978 to 1983

**Bullet:** A large dot used for ornamentation

**Burst binding:** A method of unsewn adhesive binding in which the sections are 'burst' by being punched through the spine to allow the adhesive to link the paper in each section, and the sections to each other

**Calendared:** A method of using rollers to compress paper during its making, to impact a finish or smoothness

**Camera-ready copy (or CRC):** Material ready for photographing for reproduction by lithographic process

**Cancel:** When a signature or part of a signature has to be reprinted because of an error found in the flat printed sheets prior to binding

**Canon:** A type-size used before the point system (*c*.48 pt)

**Cap I:** A person who is always talking about himself

**Caster Comp:** A caster operative who had been so-called because he had not been employed solely as a compositor apprentice. There were strict quotas as to how many apprentices the Press could employ each year based on the number of craftsmen available to teach them. The caster comp scheme allowed the Press to employ more apprentices on the pretence that they would work in the Monotype casters when they had completed their apprenticeship. Compositor apprentices would tease caster comps claiming that they were second-class citizens

**Casters:** The Monotype Casters Department or the casting machine itself

**Cast-off:** An estimate of the number of pages that a book will make based on the size and content of the typescript. **A good cast-off** was a good guess and **a bad cast-off** was a misreading of a situation

**The Caxton:** A sickness scheme run by the Caxton Benevolent Home. Subscriptions were collected locally and weekly by a nationwide network of collectors

**Chapel:** A group of workers that worked either in the same department or on similar jobs. e.g. Compositors' Chapel, Readers' Chapel, Bindery Chapel, Bindery Women's Chapel, Machine Minder's Chapel, etc.

**'Chapel Up':** This would be the call of the Father or Mother of the Chapel or one of their deputies to let everyone know that they were to stop work and attend an impromptu union meeting. The phrase was also used sarcastically when one noticed a small gathering of people chattering when they should be working

**Character:** A piece of type: a letter, a figure, a symbol, or a punctuation mark

**Chase:** A metal frame that became a forme once it contained pages of type

**Clearing:** The act of breaking up old pages and formes of type and returning the materials for further use or recycling.

**The Clearing:** An area in the Fairway that joined the composing rooms to the Letterpress Machine Room where workers would break up the type in the formes that had been printed. The metal was melted down in the Metal Pot and recast into ingots so that they could be recycled into new type via the casters

**Cleans:** When the initial proofs had been read by the first-proof reader and corrected by the compositor or keyboard operator a 'clean' proof would be pulled and sent to the author for approval

**Clicker:** The working foreman of a department or a section as distinct from a salaried foreman or manager

**Clothbound:** Bound in hard covers. Also **Hardback**

**Clumps:** Leads used for interlinear spacing in or around pages of type (usually 6pts or 12 pts thick) and cut to the width of the page

**Cocker:** A fictional character who knew everything. See '**According to Cocker**'

**Cod, codding, coddums:** jokes, tricks, or making fun of others

**'Colder!':** A cry made by compositors for more steam when the temperature in the workrooms dropped below an acceptable level. When the steam was turned on the airlocks in the pipes created incredibly loud bangs that always resulted in loud cheers of derision

**Collating:** Putting all the sheets of paper into the correct order. Also combining the proofreader's corrections and the author's correction on to one master set of proofs

**Collotype:** A planographic method of printing high-quality pictorial subjects

**Colophon:** A printer's imprint or device on a title-page of a book

**Comp:** A compositor

**Composition:** The art of composing type either by hand or by machine

**Compositor:** The craftsman that could hand-set type into a composing stick or setting stick, correct it, impose it, and then send it to Press

**Composing rooms:** The rooms where the compositors worked

**Composing stick:** The setting stick that the compositor held and into which he assembled the type

**Copy:** Typescript or manuscript

**Copy-preparer:** A person employed to perform editorial work on a typescript

**Crease:** To mechanically press a rule into heavy paper or board to enable folding without cracking

**Croppers:** A department that housed all the small platen letterpress-printing machines used to produce jobbing work

**Cutter:** A device (guillotine) used for cutting and trimming lengths of lead in the composing rooms or paper and books in the machine rooms and the Bindery

**Cutting:** Trimming off waste material in the bindery, usually at the finishing stage

**Cutting the line:** Short time

**Dad:** The father of the Chapel

**'Debrarse':** The weekly wages. 'Here comes Debrarse' would be uttered when the clicker was spotted carrying the weekly wage packets on Friday afternoons

**Diamond:** A type-size used before the point system (*c.*4½ pt)

**Diddlum:** A departmental savings club (often a Christmas or Holiday Club)

**Display:** Hand-setting or mechanical setting of large typefaces

**Diss:** Pages of type waiting distribution back to the type-cases

**Dissed:** Finished, dropped, ditched, got-rid-of, disposed of, or no-longer-friends-with

**Dissing:** The practice of distribution of type back into the type cases

**Dog's cock:** An exclamation mark

**'Door!':** A cry made when a door was left open

**Double Pica:** A type-size used before the point system (*c.*21 pt)

**Dressing:** A process in the preparation of roughly cast type

**Drilling:** Drilling of holes in folded sections, trimmed or untrimmed, or in finished books, which will permit insertion over rings or posts in a binder

**DTS:** The Direct Transfer Scheme that allowed money for savings to be stopped from the wages and paid directly into the Trustee Savings Bank

**Duff gen:** False (or incorrect) information

**Dummy:** A mock-up of the final article made up of the correct number of pages and the paper to be used to show the thickness and the binding style

**'DV':** God willing (*Deo volente*). 'I'll see you tomorrow, DV'

**Editorial:** The copy-editing and cast-off department of the Printing Division

**Eight lead:** A 1½-pt interlinear lead

**Electrotyping:** A plate-making process where the surface to be duplicated is moulded in wax and a film of copper is grown on to this electrolytically. When the copper shell is of sufficient thickness it is separated from the mould and backed with a type-metal alloy for support. After mounting an electrotype can be used in letterpress printing

**Em:** A space the same thickness as a capital M

**En:** A space the same thickness as a capital N

**English:** A type-size used before the point system (*c.*14 pt)

**Extra thin:** A space one-seventh of an em of set

**Face:** The top of a piece of type

**'Fair Cop':** You have been caught out doing something illegal, mischievous, or immoral

**The Fairway:** The passage linking the Learned Side, the Bible Side, the Machine Room, and the Bindery

**Fat:** Good easy work that paid well on the bonus scheme (earlier on piecework)

**Father:** The Father of the Chapel

**Father of the Chapel:** The elected union spokesman who would handle all negotiations with the management on behalf of the members of his chapel

**Feeder:** The person who fed the sheets of paper through the machine and who was also responsible for washing-up the machine either at the end of the day or whenever a colour change of ink was required. They were also known as 'layers-on' and sometimes cruelly as 'oil rags'

**Fell:** A typeface designed by Dr John Fell and for many years only used at OUP

**Filmsetting:** Phototypesetting

**First-proof:** The proof that was pulled immediately after the compositor or keyboard operator had finished setting a galley or a page of type

**First-proof reader:** The proofreader who was responsible for checking the first proofs and the subsequent revises up to the 'clean' stage

**Fixed rate:** As against 'in-pocket', 'piece work', or 'stab rates' to avoid short-time working

**Flat wire stitching:** To stitch with wire through the side of gathered work at the binding edge

**Flong:** A papier-mâché mould used in stereotyping

**FOC:** Father of the Chapel

**Foil:** Sized metallic or pigment leaf used in blocking lettering or designs on the surface of the cover or the spine of the book

**Foil blocking:** Metallic finish or other embossed finishes applied by specialist equipment

**Follow-the-copy-out-of-the-window:** Instruction to a compositor or a proofreader to follow the copy '*exactly*' even if it appears to be incorrect

**Foot:** The bottom of a piece of type

**Footers:** In imposition: the space at the bottom of the page

**Foredge:** Space to the right of a page on a recto and the left of a page on a verso. In binding the outer edge of the book opposite the spine

**Foreigner:** A printing job that was done usually for friends and acquaintances 'on the side' using OUP's time and materials. They were rarely done for personal gain

**Forme:** A chase full of pages after it had been locked up with furniture, side sticks, and quoins using a mallet and a shooting stick

**Foul proof:** An obsolete or superseded corrected proof

**Fount** (pronounced and sometimes spelled font): One of a range of type-faces

**Four-colour printing:** Printing that utilizes the four process colours: yellow, magenta, cyan, and black. A photographic or electronic process first separates the colours of the original

**Frame:** A compositor's wooden or metal workstation where type cases were stored and laid out to facilitate typesetting or correcting by hand

**Frisby Dyke:** A spoof person or someone that did not really exist. Frisby Dyke had all-seeing eyes and would often be quoted as the one who started rumours, scandal, etc. to hide the identity of the real perpetrators

**'Frocked':** Tired or worn out

**Front Page:** The colleague working in the frame, machine, or bench in front of you

**Furniture:** The lumps of lead that were shaped like a girder and used to separate the pages of type in the forme in the heads, feet, gutters, etc. They were produced on the Press's super-caster in 2, 3, 4, and 6 ems thickness and were cut to length with a circular saw

**Galley:** A two- or three-sided metal or wooden tray used to hold, transport, and store galleys or pages of type

**Galley proofs:** Proofs taken on a long slip of paper from the type while it was still in the galley and before it had been made up into pages

**'Get out?':** 'Really?', *or* 'Is that true?'

**'GH':** 'Go Home'. Said when someone had brought old news that everyone already knows. Similar to 'Queen Anne's Dead!' Some said it stood for 'George Harris' a compositor who always came late with the news

**'Go Down!':** 'Please visit the toilet' following a particularly disgusting passing of wind

**'God Save the Queen!':** 'Thank goodness that that is all over!' The national Anthem was often whistled to celebrate the end of a long and noisy chattering session by a group of people that should have been working

**'Got rid':** Disposed of type, evidence, etc.

**Grain:** The way in which the cellulose fibres lie in machine-made papers

**Grammage (gsm):** Paper is measured in grams per square metre and is available in various weights to produce different thicknesses

**Grand Snuffer:** The current record holder for the amount of snuff taken in one sniff

**Gravure:** Photogravure printing process

**Great Primer:** A type-size used before the point system (*c*.18 pt)

**Greeking:** A series of nonsense or Latin words used to represent text in a visual

**Greeneye:** Jealousy

**Guillotine:** A machine used for cutting and trimming sheets of paper or bound books.

**Gutters:** In imposition: the space between two pairs of pages. In binding: the space between the hollow and the board in the spine of a biding case, the inner margins of a book between the text and the binding edge, and the blank area between boundaries of pages on a lay down sheet

**'Had a bit off?'**—'You have had a haircut'

**Halftone dot:** The basic unit of a halftone screen. Grey level in a black and white halftone is determined by the size of the halftone dot. A halftone dot generated by digital methods may consist of one to 500 or more pixels whose number is dependent on the resolution of the output device, and the screen ruling on the halftone

**Halftone screen:** A type of screen that is used to convert the original continuous tone image into a pattern of dots on film. This screen, which works like a fine grid, converts the continuous tones to dots whose sizes vary depending on the value of the original

**Halftones:** The printed reproduction of a photograph reproduced by the positioning of a halftone screen on the original

**Hand press:** A press (usually made of iron) that was used for printing just one sheet at a time. The Stanhope Press at the OUP was still in use at the time of the closure of the Printing House. Its use was confined mostly to printing keepsakes

**Hart:** The OUP's classic publication, *Hart's Rules for Compositors and Readers at the University Press, Oxford* (first published 1904 (39th edition published 1983). Written largely by Horace Hart, who was Printer to the University from 1883 to 1916 and still considered by craftsmen compositors and printers throughout the world to be the bible of style

**Headers:** In imposition: the space at the top of the page

**Hot melt:** A type of adhesive used in the bindery that becomes liquid at high temperatures, and immediately reverts to the solid state at normal temperature

**Hot Metal typesetting:** A form of typesetting in which type is cast from molten metal as distinguished from hand-set (and therefore cold) metal type or phototypesetting etc.

**House Father:** The elected union representative and spokesman for the Combined House Chapel. Sometimes 'Imperial Father'

**'If the devil were to cast his net!':** A statement made when passing a group of people chattering

**Imposition:** The arrangement of pages of type on to a stone in such an order so that when they were printed the sheet of paper would fold into a signature and be paginated in the correct order

**Impression:** A number of copies printed at any one time

**Imprint:** The printer's or publisher's imprint is their name and address

**In pocket:** Rates fixed by the Chapel for 'specialist' compositors

**The Incentive:** The Incentive Bonus Scheme

**Inferior:** Subscript letters or figures

**Inset:** A group of pages (usually half-tones) inserted into the middle of a signature

**Italic spaces:** A fools' errand for apprentices

**Jacket:** The printed paper outer cover that wraps round a case-bound book in order to protect it and to act as a point of sale display

**Jackpot:** Top limit on the Incentive Bonus Scheme

**Jerry:** Similar to 'banging out' (q.v.) but usually reserved for people walking to the Printer's office to collect their final wage-packet when retiring

**Jigger:** The length of heavy brass rule that was weighted with page cord and then hung over the typecase on to the manuscript to assist the compositor so that he would not lose his place whilst hand-setting

**The Jobbing, jobbing:** The Jobbing Department on the first floor of the North Wing. Jobbing was work such as book jackets, invitation cards, notices, etc.

**Jumbo:** James Campling, the rotund Production Director in the 1980s

**Justified:** Setting where the spaces between the words is varied from line to line so that the last letter or punctuation mark in each complete line reaches the right-hand margin

**'Keep out!':** 'Mind your own business'

**Keys:** The Monotype Keyboard Department

**Lamination:** A film coating that is applied to book jackets etc. to give a more glossy or matt appearance and also to protect against wear and tear

**Landscape:** The shape of an illustration or book is referred to as 'landscape' when its width is greater than its height

**Last night?:** An enquiry from one person to another regarding their sexual exploits the previous evening

**Layer-on:** A feeder or machine assistant

**Leaders:** A series of dots leading the eye from one column to another

**Leading:** The interlinear spacing of a page, so-called because strips of lead were added between lines of metal type

**Leads:** Interlinear spacing material in thicknesses 1 pt., 1½ pt., 2 pt., 3 pt., 6 pt., and 12 pt. The last two were also known as 'clumps'

**The Learned Side:** The North Wing

**Letterpress Machine Room:** The department on the ground floor of the South Wing that housed the letterpress printing machines

**Letterpress printing:** The oldest printing process in which the print surface is higher than the non-printing surface and the paper touches only the area to be printed

**Letterspacing:** The addition of small spaces, usually between capital letters or small caps

**Lift:** A test to ensure that pages once imposed would not fall out (or pie) when removed from the stone

**Line drawing:** A drawing that consists of black lines, shading, and solid areas but no greys

**Line feed:** The distance between the base lines of successive lines of text

**Lino:** A Linotype machine that produce a complete line of lead type rather than single letters produced on a Monotype caster

**The List:** The overtime list

**The Litho:** The department where the Lithographic printing machines were housed

**Lithographic printing:** A planographic process in which the areas to be printed receive and transfer ink to the paper (often via a blank which is known as 'offset litho'). The non-printing areas are treated with water to repel the ink.

**Long Primer:** A type-size used before the point system (*c.*10 pt)

**The Long Walk:** A journey to the Personnel Department where one would be either cautioned or sacked for any serious misdemeanour

**Long weight (wait):** A fools' errand for apprentices

**Machine Minder** (later **Manager**): The craftsman who operated the letterpress and lithographic machines together with his Feeder (q.v.)

**Machine revise:** The final running sheet proof that was pulled before the final printing could begin

**Machine reviser:** The proofreaders that checked the final running sheets before the printing could begin

**Machining:** Printing

**Make-ready:** The preparation of a forme of type prior to printing which included the making of adjustments to ensure that an even impression was obtained from every part of the printing surface

**Make-up:** The making-up into page of typeset material

**Marked proof:** The copy of the proof on which the proofreader marks his/her corrections or queries

**Medicated:** A medicinal (non-tobacco) white snuff with a menthol flavour used by workers who did not like the mess associated with normal snuff

**Mid:** A space (four units to a mutton)

**Mike, miking:** Wasting time or messing around

**Minikin:** A type-size used before the point system (*c.*3 pt)

**Minion:** A type-size used before the point system (*c.*7 pt)

**Mitre:** A small hand-operated rotary machine used by compositors to mitre rules around displayed material. Also used to shave the individual pieces of type to make accents

**MOC:** The Mother of the Chapel in the Bindery who represented the women and girls that worked in that department

**Mono:** The glass-roofed Monotype Composing Room on the ground floor behind the North Wing.

**Monotype Corporation:** The company that made and supplied all the Monotype keyboards, casters, matrices, and moulds used to produce type at the Press

**Mother:** The Mother of the Chapel in the Bindery

**'Move up a thick':** To ask someone to move over slightly (about a thick space or 3 pts.) so that they could reach the type in a case that was already being used by someone else, or, simply, 'get out of my way'.

**'Much in hand?':** An enquiry from one worker to another as to whether he was ahead of his target on the Incentive Bonus Scheme

**Mum:** The Mother of the Chapel in the Bindery

**Mutt and Jeff:** A game of chance played usually for money on the stone using quads

**Mutton:** One em space

**NATSOPA:** The National Society of Operative Printers and Assistants. A Trade Union for lithographic workers

**Natty:** A member of NATSOPA

**'NB':** No brarse. A cry when the foreman was late bringing the wages round. (Later 'no bra' when a female employee was thought not to be wearing a brassiere.)

**'NF':** 'You are not speaking to me', 'not friends' because someone did not reply when greeted, or 'New Face' said when a possible new employee was being shown round the department

**NGA:** The National Graphical Association. The national union of compositors and machine minders

**Nonpareil:** A type-size used before the point system (*c.*6 pt)

**The North House:** The building on the west side of the quadrangle nearest the North Wing

**'Nuff said':** Reading between the lines

**Nulla:** The figure 0

**Nut:** Quad, space, rule (2 units to a mutton)

**Octavo:** A page one-eighth of the size of the original sheet used to print the forme

**ODWE:** *The Oxford Dictionary for Writers and Editors.* Another 'bible' that has been used alongside *Hart's Rules* for many years by countless numbers of compositors and proofreaders throughout the world. (Now in a new large-format edition and edited by Robert Ritter (a former desk editor at OUP)

**Offset:** Lithography

**Oil rag:** A feeder or machine assistant

**Old friend:** Generic name used when one could not remember someone's name or said in an appealing tone to give the impression that one was innocent of some accusation of misdemeanour

**On the box:** Off work through sickness

**'On the fat':** A statement made when the work that one had been given to do was either easy or would pay very well on the Incentive Bonus Scheme (earlier piece-work)

**'ON THE PRESS!':** The universally known call to all within hearing distance that one had claimed the right to be next to pull up one's proofs on the hand-proofing press in the centre of the composing room.

**Orphan:** The first line of a paragraph at the foot of a page

**OT:** Overtime

**Over the way:** The Publishing Division

**Overlay:** A transparent flap covering the front of an illustration

**Overmatter:** Typeset material that exceeds the allotted space

**Overeading:** Double-checking the quality of a new proofreader's work

**Overunning:** The rearrangement of lines of type caused by extensive correction

**Overs:** The copies that are printed over and above the print run to allow for spoilage

**Oxuniprint:** The in-House printing unit formed after the closure of the Printing House

**Ozalid:** A method of making photographic copies, used for making paper proofs from film

**Page-cord:** The strong thin brown string used for tying up pages of type that were to be stored for some time

**Pagination:** Page numbering

**Paragon:** A type-size used before the point system (*c.*20 pt)

**Paren:** A parenthesis

**Paste-up:** A paged layout with proofs of the text pasted in position as a guide to the typesetter. Also Camera-Ready Copy

**Pearl:** A type-size used before the point system (*c.*5 pt)

**Pellet:** In imposition: a piece of type with letter that had to be inserted in the backs of the first and last pages of a signature so that when printed it would appear in the spine. They were signatured from the letter 'a' throughout the entire book so that when the running sheets were being checked the checker could ensure that the signatures were all in the right order

**Perfect binding:** A style of unsewn binding in which the leaves of the book are held together at the binding edge by adhesive

**Perfector:** A printing machine with two impression cylinders that was capable of printing both sides of the paper at the same time and would guarantee that the pages would register

**Photogravure:** A process of printing from a surface in which the ink is contained in recessed cells of various depths

**Phototypesetting:** Typesetting by photographic means

**'Piano':** 'Be quiet.' 'You are speaking too loud.' 'You are going on about something for long.' 'Piano' was also whistled. It came from the musical term '*pianissimo*'

**Pica:** A type-size used before the point system (*c.*12 pt)

**Pie:** Printer's pie (a smashed line, page, or forme of type, usually on the floor)

**Piece ships:** Companionships working on piece-work

**Pink Slip:** All messages that emanated from the Personnel Department were printed on pink paper. When a pink slip was sent directly to an employee it usually spelt trouble!

**Planer:** In imposition: the small smooth piece of wood that was placed on the forme while it was on the stone and then hit with a mallet to ensure that all the type was the same height and the page would be inked evenly

**Plate:** An illustration printed separately from the text on a separate sheet. Also Any one-piece printing surface, such as a lithographic plate that prints the whole of one side of a sheet

**Platen:** A small printing machine (known at the OUP as a 'cropper') where the impression is imported by means of a flat surface where the whole of the printing surface and the paper come into contact at the same time

**PMA:** Printers' Medical Aid Sick Scheme. The contributions were collected each week by apprentices and were part of a nationwide network. Its main aim was to provide its members with free spectacles

**Point:** A full stop. Also as a measurement of type (approximately 0.35 mm)

**Pointer:** A feeder or machine assistant who had special skills feeding paper through a perfector. A small pin protruded from the feeding board and this made a small hole. The feeder had to ensure that he hit this point every time to ensure that the printing sheets registered

**Prelims:** Preliminary pages of a book

**Press proof:** The proof that is proofread last before sending it to be printed

**Press reader:** A proofreader that was paid more than a first-proofreader because he was responsible for the final read-by-eye after the author had approved the 'clean' proofs. They were considered to be the best proofreaders and it was considered to be 'promotion' to be made a 'Press reader'

**Printers' devil:** An apprentice in the printing industry

**Proof:** A roughly printed copy for checking and pagination

**Proof-puller:** The operative (usually an ex-machine minder) who pulled the proofs prior to having them proofread

**Proofing press:** A hand-operated press that was used only for proof pulling and not for full production

**Provident:** A Sick Scheme with weekly collection made by apprentices

**Pukka-gen:** The truth

**Putting the baby to bed:** Sending a forme of type to the machine room for printing

**Quads:** Spaces usually 2, 3, or 4 ems long used by compositors for filling out the line in the setting stick so that he did not have to use so many 1 em spaces

**Quarter bound:** Bound with the spine of the case in one material, and the sides in another

**Quarto:** A page one-quarter of the size of the original sheet that was printed

**Quoin:** A wooden or (later) a mechanical device for holding the type in a forme or in a galley secure

**Ragged right:** Unjustified type

**Rah Rah:** Richard Russell, the Commercial Director and onetime Assistant Printer used just his initials on all internal correspondence. Said to find that 'RR' opened many doors while on his regular sales trips to Africa (we were of course the Rolls Royce of printers)

**Range:** To align type

**Readers:** The Reading Department

**Rebind:** The binding of a second or subsequent batch of printed sheets

**Recto:** The front of a page of type or the right-hand page of an open book

**Register:** Pages of type that lined up perfectly when they were printed on both sides of the paper. This could be checked by holding the sheet up to the light

**'RF':** A red face or embarrassment

**Riff:** Fed up or annoyed; 'I've got the riff'

**River:** Apparent 'river' of space running down a page due to poor justification

**Rotary press:** A printing press in which the printing image, as well as the impression surface, is cylindrical

**Rubbing down:** The preparation of roughly cast type prior to dressing

**Ruby (or Agate):** A type-size used before the point system ($c.5\frac{1}{2}$ pt)

**Run:** The number of copies to be printed

**Running heads:** The heading at the top of the printed page

**Running sheets:** Once the forme of type had been placed on the bed of the printing machine one proof was pulled and this 'running sheet' was folded into a machine revise. This had to be checked by a machine reviser before the printing could begin

**Sans serif:** Typeface with no serifs, such as Gill Sans, Univers, etc.

**Scatter proofs:** Proofs of illustrations, with the illustrations placed close together and in random order

**Section:** A signature

**The Scheme:** The Incentive Bonus Scheme

**Set:** The width of a sort (piece of type)

**Setoff:** Damage to printed sheets caused by stacking printed sheets while the ink is still wet

**Setting stick:** A composing stick used by the compositors to assemble type

**Sew:** To fasten the sections of a book together by passing thread through the centrefold of each section in such a way as to secure the pages within that section, and to join it to the next section

**Ship:** A companionship or group of people that worked together. The Press had a Bible Ship, an Apprentice Ship, an Oriental Ship, a Jobbing Ship, etc.

**Shipmate:** A friend working in the same department or companionship

**Shooter:** A wooden or metal shooting stick used to lock up the formes by using a side stick, quoins, and a mallet

**Side page:** The colleague working on the left or right of you

**Side stick:** A wedge-shaped metal or wooden 'stick' that was laid alongside the pages of type before being locked up with quoins

**Sig:** A signature

**Signature:** A folded sheet of printed pages called 4-, 8-, 16-, 32-, 64-, and 128-page signatures

**Silver shoes:** The name given to Monotype caster operatives because of the splashes from the molten metal that fell on their shoes before solidifying

**Slasher:** Bill Moore, the local barber who worked opposite the Press

**Slate Club:** A scheme run by the Clarendon Press Institute (Stute) to provide benefits during sickness for its members

**Slug:** A solid line of type produced by a Linotype machine

**Small Pica:** A type-size used before the point system (*c.*10½ pt)

**Smash:** Damage caused to the type following an incident on the bed of a letterpress printing machine. Usually caused by type lifting, but often as a result of the machine minder or the compositor who had carried out the last-minute corrections leaving items such as tweezers, bodkins, shooting sticks, or mallets on the bed of the machine

**Smooting:** Working for another printer on a part-time basis while still being employed by the Press: a common practice

**Snuff rag:** A piece of rag that was kept in the apron pockets solely for blowing one's nose into. Using one's handkerchief would have caused problems at home

**Snuffy:** A person who took excessive amounts of snuff

**SOGAT:** The Society of Graphical and Allied Trades. The trade union for Bindery craftsmen and labourers

**Solid matter:** A page of type without interlinear spacing

**Sort:** A piece of type

**South House:** The building on the west side of the quadrangle nearest the South Wing

**SP:** The most popular brand of snuff (Wilson's S.P.) sold in quarter-ounce packets in the little shop opposite the Clarendon Arms in Walton Street

**Space up:** This was when the space rose up to type height during printing and appeared in the printed sheet as a black blob between the words

**Special sort:** A 'sort' or character that requires an accent other than a standard European accent or one that cannot be achieved mechanically

**Spiker:** see Bodger

**Square back:** A binding that has been collated, trimmed, and sewn, but not rounded and backed

**Stab rate:** The piecework rate eSTABlished by the management

**Stabbing:** To stitch with wire through the side of gathered work at the binding edge

**Stabilizer:** A scheme that restricted workers from earning too much bonus. The management introduced the scheme for fear that workers trying to earn too much money would account for a lowering of the Press's high standards

**Standing-type corrections:** Corrections that are made to pages of type when a new corrected version is being prepared

**Stanford:** David Stanford. Printer to the University from 1983. Remembered for his part in the closure of the Printing House in 1989

**Steam:** The heating system in the Press that was called 'The Steam'. It was a hot-water system that was pumped around the Press by a massive boiler that was housed in the cellar.

**The Stereo:** The Electroplating and Stereotyping Department now occupied by the Royalties Department in the Publishing Division

**Stereotyping:** A cheaper form of plate-making than electrotyping (q.v.). The printing surface forms the pattern from which the mould is taken. The mould is made of papier-mâché and is known as a 'flong'. Molten metal is poured into the mould and after solidification the plate is freed and is then ready for printing

**Stet:** Leave well alone

**Stick:** A composing stick used by compositors to assemble type

**Stone:** A large heavy flat workstation where the pages of type were imposed before being locked up and taken away for printing

**'Straight from?':** Said to someone who came to work in anything other than his normal working clothes. They would assume that he had a date, or was going out on some special occasion, but that he was not going home first. Sometimes it meant that he would be going for an interview for another job

**Striped ink:** A fools' errand for an apprentice

**Stute:** The Clarendon Press Institute in Walton Street, the OUP social club

**The Sucker:** The cleaner whose job it was to suck up all the type that fell on the floor during the day. He would use incredibly long lengths of ribbed piping that was attached to metal tubes in the wall that led to a massive compressor in the cellar and this would suck up everything in The Sucker's path

**Superior:** A superscript character

**TA:** The Typographical Association trade union (later the NGA (National Graphical Association))

**Tea money:** Payment made to workers who were asked to work overtime on the same day without any notice. (It was 9$d$. from 1958 to 1964.) The cooks in the Press canteen would fry up everything left over from lunchtime into a massive crispy bubble-and squeak and serve portions with a fried egg at 5 p.m. This was then all washed down with a cup of tea for just 9*d*.!

**Ten ems:** A short person

**Thick:** A space or lead that was 3 units to a mutton

**Thickun:** The fat wage packet following a large amount of overtime or the wage packet containing three weeks' wages prior to taking the annual holiday

**Thin:** A space or lead that was 5 units to a mutton

**Three-line Pica:** A type-size used before the point system (*c.*36 pt)

**TL:** Top Limit on the Incentive Bonus Scheme (after it had been stabilized)

**Top Comps:** The Top Composing Room (or Oriental Ship) on the top floor of the North Wing

**The Tower:** The Publishing Division

**Trunky:** Nosey

**Tweezers:** Used by all compositors together with a bodkin to pick up type when carrying out corrections

**Two-line Brevier:** A type-size used before the point system (*c.*16 pt)

**Two-line English:** A type-size used before the point system (*c.*28 pt)

**Type lice:** A spoof insect. When pages of types had to be dissed they were sponged down with water to make the lines easier to separate. Unsuspecting apprentices would be asked to check the pages for 'type lice'. As they checked the type at close quarters the type would be pushed together quickly thus squirting the water into the face of the victim!

**Upper case:** Capitals. So-called because the capital letters were stored in the upper case and the small letters were kept in the lower case in a compositor's frame

**Verso:** The left-hand page when viewing an open book

**VR:** Vivian Ridler. Popular Printer to the University from 1958 to 1978

**Wayzgoose:** An outing for printers

**'Well in hand':** Ahead of one's target on the Incentive Bonus Scheme (earlier piecework)

**Widow:** The last line of a paragraph at the head of a page

**Work and tumble:** Printing one side of the sheet, then turning the paper on its long edge and gripping the opposite long edge to print the other side

**'You 'ad 'im':** Said to the victor of the vanquished following an argument

# Unofficial 'Census' of 1978

Alcock, Terry *Casters*
Alder, Betty *Gathering and Handwork*
Alexis, Maggi *Inspection and Dispatch*
Allen, Georgina *Folders*
Allen, Marion *Gathering and Handwork*
Allsworth, Janet *Accounting and Wages*
Allsworth, Roy *Lithographic Machine Room*
Andrews, S. *Lithographic Machine Room*
Anton, Robert *Lithographic Machine Room*
Appleton, Norman *Keyboards*
Appleton, Paul *Folders*
Archer, Ken *Maintenance*
Archer, M. *Inspection and Dispatch*
Archer, Tony *Mono Composing Room Supervisor*
Aries, David *Engineering*
Armstrong, George *Reading*
Arnold, Edward *Folders*
Ashby, Herbert *Chief Engineer*
Ashe, Anthony *Production Planning*
Ashraf, A. *Maintenance*
Aston, David *Lithographic Machine Room*
Aston, Walter *Letterpress Machine Room*
Atkinson, R. *Sewing*
Austin, Hazel *Personnel*
Axford, Arthur *Letterpress Machine Room Supervisor*
Ayres, Robert *Lithographic Machine Room*

Bailey, D. *Engineers*
Baker, Aubrey Freeman *Mono Composing Room*
Baker, S. *Gathering and Handwork*
Baldwin, Colin *Reading*
Baldwin, Gerald *Lithographic Machine Room*
Barber, David *Bindery Assistant*
Barron, Barry (Harold) *White Paper*
Barrett, Fred *Security Staff*
Barrett, Percy *Reading*
Barton, Eric *Mono Composing Room*
Battman, A. *Engineers*
Batts, Alan *Accounting and Wages*
Bayliss, Brian *Exam. Dispatch*
Beal, Eunise A. *Exam. Dispatch and Jobbing Bindery*
Beal, Roy *Lithographic Machine Room*
Beale, Den *Gathering and Handwork*
Beale, P. *Sewing*
Beard, John *Reading*
Beasley, Peter *Composing Apprentice*

Beckley, Ken *Filmset Supervisor*
Beecham, Charlie *Inspection and Dispatch*
Beesley, Aubrey *Bindery Forwarding*
Beesley, Ken *Engineers*
Beesley, Michael *Casemaking*
Belcher, Ray *Bindery Forwarding*
Bell, Keith *Keyboards*
Bell, Sue *Bindery Office*
Bell, Tony *Keyboards*
Belson, Michael *Reading*
Bennell, Tony *Keyboards*
Bennett, Jack *Mono Composing Room*
Bennett, Tom *Letterpress Machine Room*
Berry, Alan *Composing Apprentice*
Betteridge, John *Maintenance*
Bibani, Muhammad *Folders*
Birchall, Eric *Casters*
Bishop, Sue *Bindery Office*
Black, J. *Gathering and Handwork*
Blackmore, Brian *Filmset*
Blackmore, Charles *Filmset*
Bloomfield, Janet *Exam. Dispatch and Jobbing Bindery*
Bolam, Shirley *Gathering and Handwork*
Bond, P. *Engineers*
Bonner, R. *Letterpress Machine Room*
Booroff, S. *Work Study*
Bowley, John *Oriental Composing*
Boyce, Harold *Head Reader*
Boyce, Keith *Letterpress Machine Room*
Bradbury, Mark *Lithographic Machine Room*
Bradley, Iris *Jordan Hill Warehouse*
Bradley, Wilfred *Lithographic Machine Room*
Brain, Richard *Bindery Forwarding*
Breene, Kevin *Jobbing*
Brennan, Peter *Composing Apprentice*
Brewster, Stella *Reading*
Bricknell, Joe *Jordan Hill Warehouse*
Brightman, Robin *Keyboards and Casters*
Broadbent, D. *Lithographic Machine Room*
Brock, Michael *Letterpress Machine Room*
Brogden, John *Inspection, Packing, and Postal Dispatch*
Brooker, Peter *Keyboards and Casters Supervisor*
Brooks, J. *Sewing*
Brown, David *Marshalling and Transport*

Brown, Harold *Inspection, Packing, and Postal Dispatch*
Brown, Harry *Reading*
Brown, Mary *Inspection and Dispatch*
Brown, Michael *Bindery Forwarding*
Buck, Archibald *Reading*
Buckle, J. *Gathering and Handwork*
Buckley, Eric *PRINTER*
Budwell, Linda *Bindery Assistant*
Bull, Mervyn *Mono Composing Room*
Bull, Stephen *Marshalling and Transport*
Bunker, Peter *Production Planning*
Bunn, John *Jobbing*
Burden, Marion *Inspection and Dispatch*
Bushnell, Ron *Folders*
Butler, Ken *Forwarding*
Butt, Wally *Bindery Forwarding*
Bywaters, Elaine *Bindery Office*

Cable, June *Folders*
Cakebread, Robin *Jobbing*
Campling, James *Works Director*
Candlish, Win *Inspection and Dispatch*
Caple, Stewart *Gathering and Handwork*
Carlisle, Michael *Jobbing*
Carmichael, Morris *Filmset Reader*
Carr, Gordon *Lithographic Machine Room*
Carr, Tony *Keyboards*
Carratt, David *Bindery Forwarding*
Carter, Dwayn *Casemaking*
Carter, Howard *Estimating*
Carter, Stella *Staff*
Cartlidge, Sue *Bindery Office*
Castle, Ron *Letterpress Machine Room*
Cetnik, Ann *Inspection and Dispatch*
Chadwick, Richard *Accounting and Wages Manager*
Chadwick, Tony *Letterpress Machine Room*
Chalmers, Mary *Exam. Dispatch and Jobbing Bindery*
Chalmers, Reg *Bindery Manager*
Chamberlain, A. *Gathering and Handwork*
Chapman, D. *Accounting and Wages*
Chapman, M. *Lithographic Origination*
Chaulk, Terry *Inspection and Dispatch*
Childs, Glenn *Keyboards and Casters*
Chivers, John *Jordan Hill Warehouse*
Church, Lynne *Accounting and Wages*
Church, Paul *Lithographic Origination*
Church, Ray *Reading*
Church, Sid *Printer's Chauffeur*
Churchill, Bob *Jordan Hill Warehouse*
Clarke, Eric *Letterpress Machine Room*
Clarke, J. *Maintenance*
Clarke, J. *Security Staff*
Clarke, Nick *Layout*
Clent, Jim *Marshalling and Transport*
Clothier, Celia *Library*
Coates, G. *Bindery Forwarding*
Coates, Ralph *Letterpress Machine Room*
Coates, Stan *Type Store*
Coggins, Jim *Bindery Supervisor*

Coles, Jim *Litho Manager*
Coley, John *Keyboards*
Collett, L. *Sewing*
Collett, Roy *Jordan Hill Warehouse*
Collington, H. *Sewing*
Collins, Joyce *Inspection and Dispatch*
Collins, Diana *Exam. Dispatch and Jobbing Bindery*
Collins, L. *Lithographic Origination*
Collins, Roy *Lithographic Origination*
Comley, Alf *Bindery Forwarding*
Connor, Wally *Mono Composing Room*
Considine, Peter *Maintenance*
Cook, Ron *Filmset*
Cooke, Alan *Folders*
Coombes, Ivor *Lithographic Machine Room*
Coombes, Nigel *Letterpress Machine Room*
Cooper, David *Bindery Forwarding*
Cooper, Bill *Bindery Forwarding*
Coppock, Roger *Exam. Dispatch and Jobbing Bindery*
Corbett, J. *Lithographic Origination*
Cosic, L. *Accounting and Wages*
Cowan, H. *Jordan Hill Warehouse*
Coward, Eric *Estimating*
Cox, Albert *Bindery Office*
Cox, Cyril *Reading Supervisor*
Cox, Pat *Correspondence*
Cripps, Edward *Letterpress Machine Room*
Croft, Doris *Gathering and Handwork*
Crompton, R. *Estimating*
Cross, A. *Security Staff*
Croston, J. *Maintenance*
Cudd, C. *Accounting and Wages*
Cumpston, Richard *Keyboards*
Curley, Pat *Lithographic Machine Room*
Czarlinski, O. *Reading*

Dandridge, Ron *Mono Composing Room*
Darroux, D. *Casemaking*
Davey, J. *Exam. Dispatch and Jobbing Binding*
Davey, Peter *Lithographic Machine Room*
Davies, K. *Sewing*
Dawson, Alan *Marshalling and Transport*
Dawson, Paul *Bindery Forwarding*
Deacon, Frank *Mono Composing Room Supervisor*
Deacon, Les *Mono Composing Room*
Deacon, Trevor *Lithographic Machine Room*
Dean, Norman *Keyboards*
Deeley, Malcolm *Carpenter*
Deeley, Robert *Mono Composing Room*
Dent, George *Painter*
Dillon, Melanie *Production Planning*
Dixon, H. *Maintenance*
Dodshon, Alan *Mono Composing Room*
Dreschler, Ralph *Security Staff*
Drew, Olive *Staff*
Drewitt, John *Casters*
Driver, Manfred *Reading*
Duffy, Pat *Filmset Reader Supervisor*
Dunford, Fred *Lithographic Machine Room*
Dunning, Anne *Work Study*

Dunning, Les *Letterpress Machine Room*
Dunsmoir, Andrew *Gathering and Handwork*
Dutton, Paul *Production Planning*

Eagling, S. *Bindery Forwarding*
East, Helen *Sewers*
Eastman, S. *Mono Composing Room*
Edgington, J. *Mono Composing Room*
Edmunds, A. *Maintenance*
Edwards, Colin *Bindery Forwarding*
Edwards, Gill *Reading Office*
Edwards, John *Estimating and Personnel*
Eeles, Ivor *Electrician*
Eeles, J. *Accounting and Wages*
Elam, Godfrey (Geoff) *Keyboards*
Elsom, Pat *Mono Composing Room*
England, Jack *Bindery Forwarding*
England, John *Folders*
England, Michael *Jordan Hill Warehouse*
England, Vi *Jordan Hill Warehouse*
English, Kath *Exam. Dispatch and Jobbing Bindery*
Evans, David *Bindery Forwarding*
Evans, Keith *Keyboards*
Evans, R. *Casemaking*
Evans, Rupert *Letterpress Machine Room*
Ewen, H. *Security Staff*

Fathers, Ingrid *Binding Assistant*
Fernandes, M. *Accounting and Wages*
Fettes, James *Reading*
Fifield, C. *Mono Composing Room*
Fifield, David *Oriental Composing*
Fillingham, D. *Lithographic Machine Room*
Fissenden, Keith *White Paper*
Fitzgerald, Don *Letterpress Machine Room*
Fitzgerald, Fred *Letterpress Machine Room*
Floyd, David *Gathering and Handwork*
Floyd, S. *Maintenance*
Fogg, R. *Folders*
Ford, D. *Production Planning*
Fortescue, Alec *Bindery Supervisor*
Fortescue, Keith *Casters*
Foster, L. *Accounting and Wages*
Foster, Terry *Letterpress Machine Room*
Fowles, Anthony *Folders*
Franklin, Elsie *Inspection and Dispatch Supervisor*
Franklin, Margaret *Gathering and Handwork*
Frew, Graham *Lithographic Origination*
Frost, Gerard *Financial Director*
Fuller, Michael *Reading*
Fulton, Kath *Sewing Supervisor*

Gage, John *Marshalling and Transport*
Gallacher, Nigel *Letterpress Machine Room*
Garrington, Andrew *Marshalling and Transport*
Garrington, J. *Lithographic Origination*
Garrington, June *Maintenance*
Geen, O. *Inspection and Dispatch*
Geen, T. *Estimating and Personnel*
Gerspach, D. *Sewing*

Gibbings, M. *Estimating and Personnel*
Gibbons, Don *Mono Composing Room*
Gibbons, Herbie *Bindery Forwarding*
Gilbert, Ernest *Folders*
Gilbert, Peter *Lithographic Origination*
Giles, D. *Lithographic Machine Room*
Gillett, Andrew *Production Planning*
Goddard, Geoff *Letterpress Machine Room*
Godfrey, D. *Engineers*
Goldby, Phil *Bindery Forwarding*
Goodgame, Frank *Engineering and Allied Services*
Goodgame, Linda *Bindery Assistant*
Goodgame, Malcolm *Folders*
Goodlake, John *Keyboards*
Gordon, J. *Lithographic Machine Room*
Green, David *Casemaking*
Grimshaw, Gladys *Inspection and Dispatch*
Gulliver, Pete *Bindery Forwarding*
Gunn, Geoff *Work Study*
Guy, Jack *Inspection and Dispatch*

Hacker, Michael *Filmset Reader*
Hakl, J. *Binding Assistant*
Hale, Chris *Bindery Forwarding*
Halford, Chris *Jordan Hill*
Hall, K. *Sewing*
Hall, Ron *Security Staff*
Halsey, Graham *Forwarding Manager*
Hambidge, Ivy *Maintenance Supervisor*
Hamblin, C. *Sewing*
Hanna, J. *Mono Composing Room*
Harding, Philip *Folders*
Hardy, Julian *Reading*
Harper, Bryan *Mono Composing Room*
Harris, Bert *Inspection and Dispatch*
Harris, Gary *Forwarding*
Harris, John *Filmset*
Harris, Martin *Exam. Dispatch and Jobbing Bindery*
Harris, Ron *Composing Room Manager*
Harris, Tony *Bindery Forwarding*
Hartwell, Ron *Letterpress Machine Room*
Harvey, A. *Mono Composing Room*
Harvey, B. *Lithographic Machine Room*
Harvey, John *Reading*
Hawkes, Ernie *Copy Preparation*
Healy, Theresa *Exam. Dispatch and Jobbing Bindery*
Hebborn, D. *Accounting and Wages*
Helm, G. *Bindery Forwarding*
Henley, Steve *Oriental Composing*
Henton, Nicky *Staff*
Herd, Sam *Reading*
Hesford, Tony *Lithographic Machine Room*
Hewlett, Dennis *Electrician*
Hewlett, Norman *Gathering and Handwork*
Hill, I. *Bindery Forwarding*
Hoare, Keith *Marshalling and Transport*
Hodge, Tom *Lithographic Machine Room*
Hogg, Nick *Bindery Forwarding*
Holford-Strevens, Leofranc *Reading*
Holliday, L. *Accounting and Wages*

Holloway, Brian *Letterpress Machine Room Supervisor*
Holloway, Roger *Filmset*
Hook, Robert *Lithographic Machine Room*
Hookham, Peter *Mono Composing Room*
Hookham, Steve *Bindery Forwarding*
Hopcraft, Tony *Mono Composing Room*
Horan, William *Letterpress Machine Room*
Horsley, S. *Sewing*
Horwood, Terry *Jordan Hill Warehouse*
Hounham, Phil *Casemaking*
Howard, Ralph *Accounting and Wages*
Howes, Doreen *Gathering and Handwork*
Huckin, Norman *Lithographic Machine Room*
Huelin, Sophie *Lithographic Origination*
Hughes, David *Casemaking*
Hunt, Kim *Personnel*
Hunt, R. *Bindery Assistant*
Hutt, L. *Letterpress Machine Room*
Hyde, Vic *Forwarding*

Iszkula, Frank *Bindery Forwarding*

Jackson, Clive *Bindery Forwarding*
Jackson, Pauline *Sewing*
Jacob, Iris *Inspection and Dispatch*
James, M. *Exam. Dispatch and Jobbing Bindery*
Jeffery, Richard *Reading*
Jeffery, Ron *Letterpress Machine Room*
Jeffery, Steve *Letterpress Machine Room*
Jeffery, Tony *Engineers*
Johnston, D. *Lithographic Machine Room*
Jones, Glynis *Gathering and Handwork*
Jordan, Barry *Bindery Forwarding*
Joseph, E. *Bindery Forwarding*

Keely, C. *Bindery Assistant*
Kemp, Richard *Mono Composing Room*
Khan, Noor *Accounting and Wages*
Kibbey, D. *Lithographic Origination*
Kibbey, Max *Stereotype Supervisor*
Kidd, Steve *Engineering and Allied Services*
Kindergan, F. *Maintenance*
King, Alan *Jordan Hill Warehouse*
King, Bill *Mono Composing Room Supervisor*
King, Roger *Mono Composing Room*
Kitchen, Peter *Letterpress Machine Room*
Knibbs, Kath *Exam. Dispatch and Jobbing Bindery*
Kowalski, Ingrid *Exam. Dispatch and Jobbing Bindery*
Kwiatkowski, E. *Lithographic Machine Room*

Lambourne, Ron *Lithographic Machine Room*
Lane, Elizabeth. *Engineers*
Langford, David *Letterpress Machine Room*
Law, Colin *Inspection and Dispatch*
Lay, D. *Work Study*
Ledger, David *Exam Dispatch*
Ledger, Norman *Bindery Forwarding*
Legg, Jesse *White Paper*
Legg, Maurice *White Paper*
Lester, S. *Inspection and Dispatch*

Levens, Norman *Work Study*
Lewis, Ann *Sewing*
Lewis, Dave *Bindery Forwarding*
Lewis, Ken *Marshalling and Transport*
Lewis, N. *Composing Apprentice*
Lewis, William *Letterpress Machine Room*
Loader, Don *Mono Composing Room Supervisor*
Lowe, Peter *Bindery Forwarding*
Luke, Derek *Lithographic Machine Room*
Luke, Trevor *Letterpress Machine Room*
Lyne, Mike *Casters*
Lyster, Ian *Production Director*

MacKay, H. *Security Staff*
McKay, J. *Security Staff*
McKeown, J. *White Paper*
McLoughlin, J. *Sewing*
McPherson, W. *Security Staff*
Madden, Andrew *Gathering and Handwork*
Manger, Alan *White Paper*
Mansell, Shirley *Personnel*
Mansfield, Norman *Letterpress Machine Manager*
Martin, Diane *Exam. Dispatch and Jobbing Bindery*
Martin, Peter *Bindery Forwarding*
Martin, R. *Lithographic Machine Room*
Maskell, E. *Security Staff*
Maskell, Jack *Engineering and Allied Services*
Mason, Brian *Keyboards*
Mason, Winnie *Work Study*
Massey, Iris *Gathering and Handwork*
Massingham, Roy *Letterpress Machine Room*
Masters, Les *Letterpress Machine Room*
Masters, Rodney *Lithographic Origination*
Masterson, A. *Bindery Forwarding*
May, J. *Gathering and Handwork*
Mayo, Dennis *Letterpress Machine Room*
Meade, P. *Sewing*
Meads, Richard *Jobbing and Oriental Composing*
Messenger, Alf *Copy Preparation*
Meyrick, Ian *Personnel Director*
Middleton, Alan *Casemaking*
Middleton, Chris *Bindery Forwarding*
Milland, Dot *Inspection and Dispatch*
Millard, Ted *Jobbing Supervisor*
Mills, Robert *Production Planning*
Mobley, C. *Sewing*
Mobley, Keith *Engineering*
Mobley, Ron *Stereotype*
Moona, B. *Casemaking*
Morgan, Bill *Copy Preparation*
Morgan, Fred *Mono Composing Room*
Morgan, Peter *White Paper*
Morley, S. *Sewing*
Morris, Muriel *Exam. Dispatch and Jobbing Bindery Supervisor*
Morris, Nigel *Estimating*
Morris, Robert *Casters*
Mort, Gary *Composing Apprentice*
Morton, Ron *Mono Composing Room*
Murphy, Terry *Work Study*

Nash, Stan *Lithographic Machine Room*
Nassib, M. *Lithographic Machine Room*
Neal, Clive *Reading*
Neal, Karen *Sewing*
Neal, Lisa *Sewing*
Needham, Geoff *Folders*
Nevins, D. *Maintenance*
Newell, Ray *Casemaking*
Newport, Carol *Gathering and Handwork*
Noel, Roger *Composing Apprentice*
Norris, Heather *Sewing*
North, Jeremy *Folders*
Norton, L. *Gathering and Handwork*

O'Connor, Maurice *Marshalling and Transport*
Ogden, M. *Sewing*
Ogg, Alisdair *Reading*
O'Leary, I. *Work Study*
O'Mahoney, G. *Composing Apprentice*
O'Neill, P. *Lithographic Machine Room*
Osborne, Ken *Mono Composing Room*
Osman, John *Reading*
Ousley, Chris *Mono Composing Room*
Owen, Sheila *Production Planning*

Palmer, A. *Accounting and Wages*
Palmer, Frank *Marshalling and Transport*
Paramore, A. *Exam. Dispatch and Jobbing Bindery*
Parker, Alan *Work Study*
Parker, Dennis *Filmset*
Parker, Stanley *Forwarding*
Parsons, Alan *Folders*
Pavier, Ron *Folders*
Payne, Michael *Forwarding*
Pearce, William *Mono Composing Room*
Peck, Vincent *Electrician*
Pepler, Geoff *Bindery Forwarding*
Pepler, Kay *Folders*
Perks, Michael *Engineering*
Perry, George *Forwarding*
Phillips, Nigel *Marshalling and Transport*
Phipps, David *Lithographic Origination Supervisor*
Phipps, Ron *Bindery Forwarding*
Phipps, S. *Lithographic Machine Room*
Pitman, Hugh *Personnel*
Plater, Brian *Accounting and Wages*
Plato, K. *Maintenance*
Plowman, Doris *Exam. Dispatch and Jobbing Bindery*
Plowman, Ernest *Lithographic Origination*
Pollard, Bert *Filmset Reader*
Porter, Phil *Mono Composing Room*
Poulter, Malcolm *Mono Composing Room*
Powis, Don *Jobbing*
Preedy, Ian *Engineering*
Price, Alf *Fine Binding*
Pritchett, Steve *Marshalling and Transport*
Pudwell, Linda *Sewing*
Pulley, David *Composing Apprentice*
Pullin, Sue *Binding Office*
Purvey, Alan *Casemaking*

Quick, Mervyn *Bindery Forwarding*

Radmore, Phil *Bindery Forwarding*
Rawlings, Doreen *Exam. Dispatch and Jobbing Bindery*
Rawlings, Mervyn *Forwarding*
Rawlings, Michael *Filmset*
Rayson, Bill *Casters*
Redding-Lang, David *Lithographic Machine Room*
Reeves, Fred *Casters*
Reeves, Garvin *Work Study*
Ridler, Vivian *PRINTER*
Roberts, Dave *Engineering*
Robinson, M. *Maintenance*
Robinson, Rose *Bindery Forwarding*
Rogers, Peter *Bindery Forwarding*
Rolfe, C. *Maintenance*
Rose, Charlie *Casters*
Ross, Ian *Bindery Supervisor*
Ross, W. *Bindery Forwarding*
Rothery, Pat *Gathering and Handwork*
Rozdeba, Anthony *Maintenance*
Rudd, Dennis *Engineering and Allied Services*
Rudge, J. *Exam. Dispatch and Jobbing Bindery*
Rugg, Brian *Work Study*
Russell, L. *Inspection and Dispatch*
Russell, Richard *Sales Director*
Ryman, Len *Filmset*

St. Jean, M. *Staff*
St. Pier, Marion *Folders*
Savage, Antony *Lithographic Origination*
Savage, W. *Jordan Hill Warehouse*
Savins, Peter *Accounting and Wages*
Sawyer, J. *Inspection and Dispatch*
Sawyer, John *Type Store*
Saywell, Linda *Bindery Assistant*
Scoins, S. *Letterpress Machine Room*
Scrivener, P. *Sewing*
Scroggins, E. *Inspection and Dispatch*
Sears, A. *Composing Apprentice*
Sharpey, Brian *Letterpress Machine Room*
Shevlin, C. *Work Study*
Shipton, M. *Lithographic Machine Room*
Simmonds, A. *Inspection and Dispatch*
Simpson, S. *Gathering and Handwork*
Sinclair, Jack *Lithographic Machine Room Supervisor*
Skelly, John *Forwarding*
Slade, Martin *Bindery Supervisor*
Smart, Nina *Copy Preparation Office*
Smith, Colin *Jordan Hill Warehouse*
Smith, E. *Work Study*
Smith, Ken *Lithographic Machine Room*
Smith, Linda *Estimating*
Smith, Nina *Work Study*
Smith, R. *Sewing*
Soden, Keith *Lithographic Machine Room*
Soden, Michael *White Paper*
Souch, Gwen *Maintenance*
Souch, Keith *Keyboards*

Spackman, Alan *Lithographic Machine Room*
Sparling, Maureen *Staff*
Spiers, Ernest *Casemaking*
Squiers, Shirley *Binding Assistant*
Stammers, Wendy *Production Planning*
Stansfield, Irene *Bindery Forwarding*
Steed, R. *Gathering and Handwork*
Steer, Maureen *Exam. Dispatch and Jobbing Bindery*
Stevens, G. *Letterpress Machine Room*
Stevens, Harry *Letterpress Machine Room*
Stevens, M. *Accounting and Wages*
Stewart, Ken *Layout*
Stone, Peter *Casemaking*
Strange, Les *Plumber*
Sugden, Vic *Exams*
Sutton, Gordon *Letterpress Machine Room*
Swain, Kevin *Lithographic Machine Room*
Swift, Alan *Marshalling and Transport*

Talboys, David *Folders*
Talmage, Brian *Forwarding*
Tandy, C. *Gathering and Handwork*
Tandy, J. *Gathering and Handwork*
Tarns, M. *Casemaking*
Tarry, E. *Work Study*
Taylor, Gordon *Production Manager*
Taylor, J. *Bindery Forwarding*
Taylor, June *Sewing*
Taylor, O. *Gathering and Handwork*
Templer, J. *Inspection and Dispatch*
Thomas, Fred *Jordan Hill Warehouse*
Thomas, M. *Bindery Forwarding*
Thomas, M. *Gathering and Handwork*
Thomas, R. *Staff*
Thompson, Dorothy *Jordan Hill Warehouse*
Thompson, Paul *Folders*
Thompson, Stan *Jordan Hill Warehouse*
Thorley, Ray *Layout*
Thorne, C. *Sewing*
Thornton, Harry *Letterpress Machine Room*
Tibble, Fred *Security Staff*
Tilling, Peter *Forwarding*
Tippett, Bob *Folders*
Titus, Sam *Maintenance*
Tombs, Bill *Bindery Forwarding*
Topp, Stan *Marshalling and Transport*
Townley, David *Lithographic Machine Room*
Townley, Dick *Engineering and Allied Services*
Townsend, Kath *Gathering and Handwork*
Trafford, Carol *Sewing*
Trafford, Ivor *Carpenter*
Tree, Theresa *Lithographic Machine Room Office*
Tuffley, John *Casemaking*
Turland, Gordon *Jobbing*
Turner, Don *Type Foundry*
Turner, Len *Mono Composing Room*

Turner, Richard *Forwarding*

Underwood, Ken *Maintenance*

Varndell, Malcolm *Letterpress Machine Room*
Veal, Ron *Letterpress Machine Room*

Wakefield, Irene *Inspection and Dispatch*
Walford, Barry *Letterpress Machine Room*
Walker, Ken *Mono Composing Room*
Walton, Don *Bindery Forwarding*
Wardrop, L. *Staff*
Waterlow, Caroline *Lithographic Origination*
Watson, Ann *Inspection and Dispatch*
Watson, B. *Exam. Dispatch and Jobbing Bindery*
Watts, Veronica *Exam. Dispatch and Jobbing Bindery*
Webb, Colin *Lithographic Machine Room*
Webber, Ann *Forwarding*
Webster, Jack *Oriental Composing*
Webster, A. *Bindery Assistant*
Wells, J. *Gathering and Handwork*
Wells, Peter *Bindery Forwarding*
Wells, Terry *Letterpress Machine Room*
Westell, Rodney *Bindery Forwarding*
Weston, Colin *Oriental Composing*
Whareham, Doreen *Exam. Dispatch and Jobbing Bindery*
Whareham, Jeff *Filmset*
Wharton, Tony *Mono Composing Room*
White, Gordon *Mono Composing Room*
White, Ron *Exam. Dispatch and Jobbing Bindery*
Whitehouse, E. *Exam. Dispatch and Jobbing Bindery*
Whitelaw, Alan *Estimating*
Whiting, Glad *Folders*
Wickson, Jack *Letterpress Machine Room*
Wickson, Peter *Letterpress Machine Room*
Wickson, S. *Inspection and Dispatch*
Wilkins, Wilf *Casemaking*
Willet, Rod *Layout*
Williams, Ada *Exam. Dispatch and Jobbing Bindery*
Williams, Gilbert *Jobbing Reading*
Willoughby, Mavis *Inspection and Dispatch*
Willshire, Harvie *Reading*
Winkworth, Keith *Carpenter*
Wonnacott, Ian *Bindery Forwarding*
Woods, Keith *Reading*
Woodward, Richard *Mono Composing Room*
Wootton, Iris *Work Study*
Worvill, Colin *Jordan Hill Warehouse*
Wright, J. *Accounting and Wages*
Wyatt, Derek *Composing Apprentice*
Wyatt, N. *Engineering and Allied Services*
Wyles, Pam *Gathering and Handwork*

Young, Frank *Letterpress Machine Room*

Zivkovic, M. *Jordan Hill Warehouse*

# INDEX OF NAMES